£5-∞

DEATH

THE TRIP
OF A
LIFETIME

•

DEATH

THE TRIP
OF A
LIFETIME

GREG PALMER

HarperSanFrancisco
A Division of HarperCollins*Publishers*

FIRST EDITION

TEXT DESIGN BY IRENE IMFELD

Library of Congress Cataloging-in-Publication Data
Palmer, Greg.
    Death : the trip of a lifetime / Greg Palmer. — 1st ed.
      p. cm.
    ISBN 0–06–250802–4 (cloth : alk. paper). — ISBN 0–06–250803–2 (pbk. : alk. paper) — ISBN 0–06–250954–3 (Int'l pbk. : alk. paper)
    1. Death—Psychological aspects. 2. Death—Social aspects. 3. Fear of Death. 4. Bereavement—Psychological aspects.
I. Title.
BF789.D4P35   1993
306.9—dc20   92–56122
                                                                           CIP

93 94 95 96 97 ❖ HAD 10 9 8 7 6 5 4 3 2 1

This edition is printed on acid-free paper that meets the American National Standards Institute Z39.48 Standard.

•

In memory of
Linden Alfred Mander,
ancestor

•

In honor of
Ira and Nathaniel Palmer,
descendants

•

CONTENTS

DEATH

THE TRIP
OF A
LIFETIME

•

INTRODUCTION

I was a member of the Liberal Religious Unitarian Youth from the age of five through high school. In the first five years of that period I went because my parents took me, and in the last five years I went because it was an opportunity to get away from my parents on a weeknight. But there was a middle period there when I actually had religion, or as much as any Unitarian can have religion. And yet looking back on the hundreds of LRUY meetings I went to, I can only remember one gathering with any real clarity.

I was nine, and it was a special meeting because instead of once again reading from and discussing *Jesus, the Carpenter's Son* by Sophia L. Fahs (back then the sole religious text for Unitarian youths, or so it seemed) the Reverend Chadbourne Spring himself was coming to speak to our class. With his wavy white hair and rich bass-baritone voice, Chadbourne Spring looked and sounded like a traveling evangelist, the kind of religious personage who saves souls, seems intimately familiar with hellfire and damnation, and plays trumpet in the Good News! Evangelical Brass Quintet.

In reality he was the chief man at the Eastshore Unitarian Church of Bellevue, Washington, and was truly loved by all even if he had never saved a single soul, or ever really tried. My mother loved him because he talked fast, had a droll sense of humor and didn't take himself too seriously, distinct pluses in a minister as far as my mother was concerned. My father liked him because Chadbourne Spring knew there were sometimes much more interesting things to do on Sunday morning than sit in a church and listen to Chadbourne Spring. Still, we liberal religious youth were a bit in awe of the Reverend Spring, and felt honored that he had come to our humble assembly. Mr. Squeak Schneider, our Sunday school teacher, certainly told us we should feel honored.

"I think you all know who I am," Reverend Spring began in his friendliest voice, "but I don't know much about you. So let's just start by telling a little about ourselves, and especially what we think the Unitarian Church is all about."

The answers came slowly at first, but soon we were practically fighting to tell our pal Chad what Unitarianism meant to us.

"We don't believe Jesus was the son of God."

"We don't believe in the Trinity."

"We don't believe Mary was a version."

"We don't believe the Bible is anything but a book."

"We don't believe in Easter except for the eggs."

"We don't believe most of the Christmas carols."

"We don't believe in hell and probably not in heaven either."

So it went. And I began to notice that each answer was like a dagger in the heart of Reverend Chadbourne Spring.

"What's the matter with us?" he finally boomed. "Can't anybody here tell me something we Unitarians *do* believe in?"

There was a long pause. We desperately tried to think of some answer that would please our pal. Finally Louise Wannemaker raised her hand.

"Yes, young lady," Chadbourne beamed, "what do Unitarians believe in?"

"Adlai Stevenson," Louise Wannemaker said proudly, and the rest of us nodded.

Chadbourne Spring left that day, if not a broken man then at least a bent man. We had given him a painful awakening, as well as sermon topics for a month of 1956 Sundays. And Squeak Schneider turned us to *Jesus, the Carpenter's Son* with a vengeance.

I now understand something of Reverend Spring's frustration. It's a lot easier for me to say what this book is not than what it is. For instance, although some strange rituals are described, this is not *Indigenous Peoples Do the Darndest Things!* Although religious persons state their beliefs about the life everlasting, this is not *A Day in the Life of Heaven and Hell.* Although some of the methods human beings use to prepare for death are discussed, this is not *So! You're Going to Die!* Although much factual information slips in here and there, this is not *A Cross-Cultural Analysis of Contemporary Death Attitudes, Belief Systems, Funeral Rituals, and Totemic Manifestations in Pre- and Postindustrial, Urban, and Agrarian Societies.* And finally, although this book is certainly associated with the PBS television series of the same name, this is not *A Companion to the TV Shows with the Same Stuff Just All Written Out.*

What this book is, I guess, is an attempt to take a closer look at death at a time in my life when death seems to be taking a closer look at me. I have no particular reason to believe I won't live for another thirty years. But I also have no particular reason to believe I won't die tomorrow. With that realization comes fear, but also curiosity. Death is one of only a very few things all living creatures have in common. And of eating, sleeping, breathing, and eliminating, death is by far the most fearsome and the most permanent. We only get one shot at it, without benefit of instruction manual or coach. So even though I often feel alone in my contemplation of personal mortality, I am not.

What do others do facing death, and how do their beliefs and customs help them? My culture views death as the opposite of life, the "wages of sin." But for millions of people, death is a *part* of life. Do they get comfort from that understanding, even if it seems to me it's rather like saying the fangs are just part of the snake? And do people who deal with death every day, voluntarily or not, find contemplation of their own end any easier? Are any of us comforted by the death rituals we've developed, or do they in fact hurt more than help us in facing the deaths of those we love, including ourselves?

This book is about some of the answers to some of the questions we have about death. Unfortunately, the questions we *all* have are unanswerable. Nobody told me from their personal experience what it's like to die and what happens after that. We'll all just have to wait and see.

I've been around the world now, asking people questions, listening to their answers and looking at the things they do to deal with grief, dying, and death. And one of the encouraging things that happened was that the journey was far from sorrowful. It was joyful, and funny, too. We laugh and cry at death in equal measure, especially at our own reactions to it. And I hope this book reflects that paradox.

The most frequent question I've been asked about this Trip of a Lifetime is how it has affected me personally. I guess there are two answers. The first answer is I don't know yet. Ask me again in thirty years. Or tomorrow.

And here is the second answer. On the night of June 5, 1944, the men of the 89th Airborne Division, stationed in England, were getting ready to leave for France. They would be the first troops to land in the biggest invasion in military history. D day. The job of the 89th Airborne was to make a night parachute drop in Normandy behind the German lines, landing in forests and swamps Field Marshal Erwin Rommel had booby-trapped specifically to make such an assault deadly.

As they were packing their gear, saying their good-byes and getting ready to board the planes that would take them across the channel, they looked up and General Eisenhower was there among them. The Supreme Allied Commander was paying a call. He had estimates back in his office that eight out of ten of the men he was visiting would not survive the night, but he put his hands in his pockets, slapped a big smile on his face, and shot the bull with the 89th for as much time as they had before leaving.

I should think it was agonizing for Eisenhower, but there was joy in it, too. He and those men laughed together, about army life, the weather, what they were going to do when it was all over and they went home. And then the paratroopers of the 89th went off to their fates, and Eisenhower went back to his headquarters. To wait.

On this Trip of a Lifetime I've often felt a little like Ike was that night, walking around with my hands in my pockets, trying to smile, looking death in the face and seeing sadness and joy there. And then going back to the office to wait. There have been times when I've felt like the men of the 89th too. If not tonight, then someday.

Many of those who did not make it through that night or the murderous weeks to follow are buried in the American Military Cemetery above Omaha Beach. There's a small chapel there, surrounded by more than nine thousand gravestones. And on the wall of that chapel this is written: Think Not Only Upon Their Passing, But Remember the Glory of Their Spirit.

Yes.

Greg Palmer
Seattle
Summer, 1993

CHAPTER ONE

FACE TO FACE

A t this moment there are thirty-seven different images of death in my two sons' bedrooms. I don't think either boy is abnormally morbid. So far they wouldn't know the Grateful Dead, DOA, Megadeth, and the Dead Kennedys from Les Brown and His Band of Renown. No death-head punk rock T-shirt has yet found its way into the Palmer Collection. But we do have pirate apparel, typically horrific video games and Halloween effluvia around, and my kids are almost lifelong collectors of what the toy trade calls the Male Action Line: He-Man, Transformers, GI Joe, Teenage Mutant Ninja Turtles, X-Men, and so on. Most of these small plastic figures wear very little besides fur jockstraps, so it's fortunate for them that their bodies are of the same general bulk and configuration as Arnold Schwarzenegger's. Just as Clive James once described the real Arnie, their arms and legs look like condoms stuffed with walnuts, only smaller. Male Action Line faces, however, apparently have been inspired by the grimmer fantasies of Hieronymus Bosch. It's as if they all patronize a little plastic gym where you can build your thighs into tree trunks while simultaneously getting rid of unsightly face flesh. It's a very odd combination—cadaver heads on meatball bodies.

Ira, my fourteen-year-old, also collects comic books. In the thirty-seven death images figure I haven't even counted the grisly drawings within their pages. I've only included the covers that were visible on the floor next to his clothes. If I had actually thumbed through his "comic" collection, the number of death images surrounding my family and infesting my home would rise into the hundreds and possibly even thousands. But my kids have nothing—nothing—out of the ordinary for young American gentlemen of the 1980s and 1990s. Still, little Ned goes to sleep each night clutching a creature called Dr. Doom. When I was his age I was a Howdy Doody man.

Perhaps America wasn't as death-filled for us baby boomers back in the 1950s because our parents had seen so much of the real thing in the previous decade. Maybe Mom and Dad were trying to shelter us tots. Or maybe my kid generation just fancied its death presented in other ways. Recently a local television station ran one of my favorite Bugs Bunny cartoons, the one where Bugs and Daffy try to convince Elmer Fudd that it's either rabbit or duck hunting season depending on whether you're a rabbit or a duck. And each time Bugs tricks Daffy into saying it's duck season, Elmer shoots Daffy in the head at point-blank range with the Fudd gun. Real classic comedy stuff, or so I told Ned when it started. But the television station (or more likely the cartoon distributor) had dutifully edited out all the violence for modern audiences not used to such ruination. In six jerky, incomprehensible minutes, Elmer never fires, and the Bugs/Daffy colloquy of "Rabbit season!" "Duck season!" "Rabbit season!" "Rabbit season!" "Duck season!" (no BLAM! here) just goes on and on without any payoff. Long before the end Ned gave me The Look, picked up his Dr. Doom, and left. I stayed to watch the next cartoon and was treated to an equally butchered Wile E. Coyote continuously falling off cliffs and mesas but never actually hitting the ground. The whole Road Runner saga looked like a particularly uninteresting commercial for the Acme Company. Older, wiser television executives had saved my child from exposure to all that meaningless violence I once found so enthralling, and by so doing created meaningless cartoons. Personally, I don't remember ever wanting to load up Dad's twelve-gauge over-and-under and blow my brother's beak off forty years ago. (Well, actually, I do, but I didn't get the idea from Elmer Fudd. He was an older brother and he deserved it.)

I guess each generation picks the death images it wants and doesn't want. But one thing is true for all generations, at least in my culture. No matter what representations of death our children choose (or are chosen for them), they still don't know anything about death itself.

As the product of a relatively normal American childhood, death was certainly a stranger to me for a long time. I knew it existed, as I knew Africa existed. I just didn't think I'd ever go there. According to experts who like to ask kids such questions, children are aware of the basic existence of death very early, even as young as age three. In those early years, however, death seems to have more to do with fear of abandonment than fear of personal involvement. If one morning the family goldfish is doing an extremely slow backstroke on the surface of the tank, does that mean the next morning we'll find Mommy stuck belly up to the ceiling of her bedroom, just because we fed her too much the night before? And if so, who's going to take me to get my new sneakers?

For kids, real beings don't die anyway. Pets are "put down" or "put to sleep," elderly neighbors disappear in the night, Uncle Bud "has found eternal rest" and Grandma's "in Heaven now," which as described to most kids sounds a lot like the place in Florida where she went two years ago with her friend Rose. Even if you hang out in places where the dead congregate, like cemeteries, you often see written on the tombstones a blatant lie: "Not Dead, Only Sleeping." My grandma's last stop before going to heaven was a cemetery called Lakeview. Lakeview? I doubt very much that Grandma or any of the other "sleepers" there spend a lot of time viewing the lake. And Grandma's not alone spending eternity in a place that sounds like a mediocre boys' school. America is full of cemeteries called Lakeview, as well as four hundred Fairviews, and dozens of Lakesides, Greenwoods, Evergreens, and Pleasant Hills. The generic town cemetery is a thing of the past. Even when it existed it wasn't semantically forthright about the activities of the residents. "Cemetery" comes from the ancient Greek, but it doesn't mean "to molder endlessly." It means "to put to sleep."

This linguistic effort to ignore or obscure death is therefore far from new. The *Dictionary of Historic Slang* lists more than five hundred expressions for the state of deadness or the various ways to die, euphemisms that for centuries have kept English-speaking people of all ages one verbal step removed from the truth. Historically, to be dead is to

- Become a landowner;
- Stick your spoon in the wall;
- Chuck up a bunch of fives;
- Be put to bed with a mattock, tucked up with a spade;
- Go to the Diet of Worms;
- Keep an ironmonger's shop by the side of the common;
- Ride backwards up Holborn Hill;
- Go to grass with your teeth up.

So, given the historic alternatives available to them, it was exceedingly honest of my parents to tell me in 1954 that our elderly dog Stocky had to be killed because he kept losing it at both ends on the living room rug. But I certainly wasn't encouraged to associate Stocky's demise with my own mortality. Nor did I. For one thing, I was damned careful around that rug.

Unreal beings don't die for kids either, especially not in the movies or on television. At least nobody dies who's worth caring about, nobody who doesn't really deserve it. On television they just don't. Howdy Doody, Huckleberry Hound, Wile E. Coyote, Lassie, Skeletor, and Wolverine are all Immortals, like the Greek gods. Only Mr. Hooper on "Sesame Stree" was allowed to die, and his death was significant as much for how it was allowed to happen as the fact that it happened at all.

Just as those high lamas who attend the Dalai Lama must ask his permission to die, so the Children's Television Workshop, Mr. Hooper's parents, also had to ask a higher authority for permission to shoot the Hoop. The authority they consulted was Research. CTW conducted extensive testing to determine how preschoolers would respond. They wanted to know whether a Hooper Croak could be a "learning experience" or just something that scared the hell out of America's youth. Suitably bolstered by statistics and other data that confirmed mass tot trauma would not ensue, Hooper breathed his last, long after actor Will Lee had done it for real. The actual episode was handled splendidly, with Big Bird once again assuming the role of Everytad.

In theatrical films principally for children—which of course these days are also the films that are watched endlessly on home video—major heroic characters are allowed to die but they rarely stay dead. It can't be coincidence that so many classic children's and family films that do have deaths also have real or symbolic resurrections. Consider, first in the kids' live action/classic horror category:

Dead Character	Resurrectional Mode
ET, the Extraterrestrial	alien powers from home
Dread Pirate Roberts (*The Princess Bride*)	sorcery
Obi Wan Kenobe, Yoda, Darth Vader	Force, the
Han Solo	defrosted
Frankenstein's Monster	electricity
Dracula	blood, human
The Mummy	curse

And in the animation category:

Dead Character	Resurrectional Mode
Snow White	kissed and made well
Sleeping Beauty	kissed and made well
Tinkerbelle (friend to Pan)	clap
Pinocchio	Blue Fairy magic
Beast	Beauty's love

And the dead beat goes on. Given his oeuvre, it's not surprising that so many people incorrectly believe Walt Disney is cryonically frozen, awaiting that time when medical science reaches such a level of sophistication that he can be defrosted and cured successfully. Walt was obviously a big resurrection fan, but he was far too romantic for the freezer. I suspect he's really in a glass coffin hidden in a cavern beneath Space Mountain. And there he waits, not for science, but for a kiss.

Within the general dead/not dead milieu of cartoon land, the demise of Bambi's mother is properly shocking. The first time I saw the breathy doe get it I waited through the rest of the film for that big buck to step up and give his lady love's carcass the "nuzzle of life." When he didn't, I was one angry kid.

I think the best live action kid's classic ever is the 1939 *Wizard of Oz*, with Garland, Bolger, Lahr, and Haley. And though without a resurrection, *Wizard* has more to do with death than any of the films mentioned above. In L. Frank Baum's original novel there really is an Oz, visited by a real kid. But Noel Langley's screen adaptation for MGM makes Dorothy's journey a dream—a special dream, not just a little nightmare brought on by too many pork fritters. Dorothy sustains a potentially lethal blow to the cranium, passes out cold, and immediately starts seeing herself floating above the earth. Sound familiar?

Yes! Dorothy isn't just having a dream! She's having the world's first cinematically recorded near-death experience!

> **UNCLE HENRY:** She got quite a bump on the head, we kinda thought there for a minute she was gonna leave us.
> **DOROTHY:** But I did leave you, Uncle Henry, that's just the trouble!
>
> —Noel Langley, *The Wizard of Oz* film script, 1938

True, Dorothy does not have the traditional near-death romp. She doesn't float up a hallway toward a blinding white light while the faces of deceased friends and relatives loom up around her smiling those benign, irritating smiles that make them look like Glinda the Good Witch. But therein lies a clue that Dorothy's near-death experience (NDE) may be more classic than it first appears. Although her parents are never mentioned, we assume they are dead. Therefore, they would be the most likely spirits to appear before her on the way to heaven. And that all makes sense if Glinda is in fact Dorothy's late mother, the Wizard her father and Oz The Great Beyond, attained immediately after Dorothy dies again in the poppy field. ("You're out of the woods, you're out of the dark, you're out of the night, step into the sun, step into the Light . . . ")

Even if you don't buy Glinda as the late Mother Gale, for a nontraditional near-death experience Dot still sees a lot of people she knows. Also, true to NDE form, she returns from her brush near death a much better person, one who finally realizes that the best place on earth is a sepia-toned, lackluster hardscrabble Kansas farm, where her prospects are nil and Miss Gulch *still* has the paper to "put down" Toto. (My personal belief is that MGM's *Oz* is not Dorothy's near-death experience, but Toto's. Munchkinland, with its fire hydrant–size residents, is just the kind of heaven a nasty yapping little dog would envision.)

So we have a long history of not only trying to avoid death but of avoiding any discussion of death. And on those occasions when we do actually ponder the possibilities, we have a tendency to put death in the best possible light, as something easily overcome. At the same time we accept the premise that we are obsessed with death, even attracted to it. And as the comedian says, when you buy the premise, you buy the bit.

•

Once, while working in the advertising racket, I was dragged by a colleague to a lecture. The lecturer was a short, drab man with combed-over hair and mousy eyes who looked like he had spent many years carrying a slide projector from town to town, which he had. There was just one lecture in him, and he'd been living on it for decades, like the guy in Las Vegas who knows only one trick, but it's quite a trick.

Standing on the foul line in a bowling alley, this Vegas legend can flip an ordinary playing card down the lane and knock down the head pin. Two or three tries, tops, and down goes the lumber. I'm not making this up; I heard it from an eyewitness who bet the trick man a hundred dollars that it couldn't be done, and when it was done, didn't mind losing the C note at all. There are some things—not many, but some—that are worth a hundred dollars to see.

The lecturer was not one of those things, which is why he worked bigger groups for a smaller take per person. He rented a room, usually a church social hall because of the religious nature of his target audience, and for ten dollars a rube told anybody who showed up all about the subliminal messages that godless and/or downright satanic advertising agencies were sneaking into magazine ads and television commercials.

The two high points of the little man's lecture, the bits that never failed to put the "awe" back in audience, featured Ritz crackers and ice cubes. He contended that the word *sex* was written on the back of many Ritz crackers—not *all* Ritz crackers, but a lot of them. He showed a slide of one of these pornographic Ritz, and darned if it didn't look like he was right. The letters *s e x* were crudely but obviously burned into the darker brown ridges on the back of the cracker. I'm a Ritz cracker consumer myself and have never since found one of the special ones, which leads me to believe that he went through thousands of Ritz crackers before he found the one he wanted. For all I know he still had stacks of Ritz in his basement back home in Keokuk with other

words he found first: *nex, hex, mex, sux, sax, six, dix, bix lives.* Or perhaps he was secretly in the employ of the National Biscuit Company,
because I guarantee you that all who ever heard him soon purchased
their own box of Ritz, looking for *sex* in their own homes. I still see
people who have heard this guy or Wilson Bryan Key, who originated
the theory, and are now incapable of eating a Ritz without looking at
the back first. Me, too.

The lecturer's other principal claim was that in magazine ads for
liquor that feature photographs of the beverage in frosty glasses with
ice cubes, death images are invariably hidden in the ice. The slide on
this one was less successful with me. While the little man was busy
pointing out skulls, snakes, and body parts, I was seeing kitty cats,
sheep, and Volkswagens. But mostly I was seeing ice cubes.

It was when he ventured into the area of the ad agencies' motiva-
tions that I finally got interested. The lecturer's interpretation of the
blurry images in the ice was questioned by even that audience of the
easily gulled, but everyone immediately accepted the premise that
liquor company advertising agencies sell more booze by associating
death with their products. We are attracted to death, the little man said
simply, and there was a collective nod from the audience. His interpretation of this cubist attraction phenomenon was that because the wages
of sin is death and we are attracted to sin (Eve's fault), we are therefore
also attracted to death. And not just the pagans among us who drink alcoholic beverages. *Those* people obviously have a death wish. There are
death images in Coca-Cola and other nonalcoholic advertising ice
cubes too, and even some advertising that doesn't feature any ice cubes
at all but just nebulous shapes, like Ed McMahon.

However, we are ashamed of our lust for sin and death. We imagine
ourselves not only above death, but above any obsession with death
too. So these images must be hidden from our conscious minds to be
effective. Slapping a portrait of a putrefying skull on the side of a milk
carton, even if it's the skull of a cow, will not sell more milk. In fact, it
may repel your average dairy consumer.

The lecturer is obviously crackers, but he raises a valid question. Are
we secretly attracted to death without knowing it? One could easily
make a superficial case that we are. Certainly death has been represented as an attractive creature in various artistic media, like the movies.
Bob Fosse chose the lovely Jessica Lange to play the Angel of Death in
All That Jazz, and I don't think Ms. Lange got the part because there
was just something about her that said "myocardial infarction."

•

Back in the Dark Ages, the recently dead that Rumanian villagers
thought had become vampires were short, fat men with florid expres-

sions and no fangs, according to Paul Barber's *Vampires, Burial, and Death: Folklore and Reality*. But now the Undead are usually played on stage and screen by the oddly attractive (Bela Lugosi, Christopher Lee, Frank Langella, Gary Oldman) rather than the completely repulsive (Klaus Kinski). And when these handsome creatures strike, it is always at someone beauteous of the opposite sex, and always with the "kiss of death," never the "handshake of death" or the "phone call of death."

The tobacco industry claims that cigarette sales went *up* rather than down when advertising for cigarettes was first required to include a health warning. And just ask the reptile keeper at the zoo which snakes are the biggest audience draw. It's the ones that can bring death with just the slightest nip. A reptile house without poisonous reptiles is a lonely place indeed, as lonely as Sea World without the *killer* whales.

Death attraction isn't always so subtle. In Hollywood, where hardly anything is subtle, a man named Mike Shellel used to stand with all the people hawking Maps to the Movie Stars' Homes and sell his own product, Maps to the Movie Stars' Graves. He did good business, too. Now there's a Hollywood tour that goes Shellel one better. Instead of being able to visit the resting places of the stars, you get to see the *dying* places of the stars.

It's called Grave Line Tours, and I called it. The pleasant female Grave Line person on the phone told me to wait around the corner from the Chinese Theatre on Hollywood Boulevard, and the "vehicle" would pick me up at the appointed hour. A lot of less bizarre Los Angeles tours start from that spot too, so huge air-conditioned buses arrive and depart every few minutes. But none of them seemed to be mine. And then a long gray hearse pulled into the "Tour Buses Only" slot; a liveried gentleman jumped out and began wiping the chrome with a chamois. If this wasn't Grave Line Tours, I didn't want to know what it was.

It was. Inside the hearse had been modified to be a nine-seater. I took my place about where the deceased's head rested in earlier times, a few other aficionados boarded and sat back in the lower extremities area, and we were off.

Narration on the tour was provided by the driver with the chamois and his partner, who came to us via tape on the hearse's cassette player and was therefore able to jazz up his spiel with a lot of sepulchral organ music and cheesy sound effects. We saw the apartment building where Jack "Dragnet" Webb died on the twenty-first floor ("Sorry, folks, but it's a private building and they won't let us go up there to see the actual spot"); the motel where massive female impersonator Divine hit the industrial carpet ("The only celebrity on the tour who actually took the tour when he was alive"); and the bungalow where Marilyn Monroe once lived but a long way from where she eventually died ("But she did die right here in Hollywood, folks.")

The tour had three highlights. We cruised by the Chateau Marmont Hotel where John Belushi committed his final stupidity. We drove to the hillside where Charles Manson's followers killed Sharon Tate and others but we didn't actually go up the hill because, darn the luck, it is also private property. And we drove past Nancy Reagan's place in Bel Air, now numbered 668 even though it should be numbered 666. Nancy felt numerologically 666 was ill-advised and she had the juice to get it changed. That particular stop didn't have much to do with death, but nobody complained. Given what led up to it, even a moment with Nancy was a relief.

Taking the Grave Line Tour is the kind of activity you pray nobody will see you doing. The English driver contended that it wasn't the dying places that attracted his customers as much as it was just another chance to get a glimpse of the private lives of the famous. But that doesn't quite explain why he had to tell us all who Jack Webb and Divine were. It seems to me that if you have to identify your celebrities then they aren't all that celebrated. Despite what the driver claimed, death fascination is what keeps Grave Line rolling. Even so, given death avoidance, I assumed my fellow Grave Liners had already taken all the other bus trips available and still had a day to, uh, kill. Not exactly.

"I saw about it in England where I live and I just had to try it. I go home tomorrow."

"The whole concept excites me, far more exciting than an ordinary tour of just homes."

"I think seeing where John Belushi died was the highlight so far for me."

"I was in the graveyard where Marilyn—Monroe?—where she's buried, and then somebody took a flower off Natalie Wood's grave, which I thought was tacky. This is much classier."

They were all swell folks, but I decided to jump hearse in midtour, so I missed the Old Actors' Home.

Dead tours are not just a wacko Southern California phenomenon, of course. One of the best and most economical ways to see London is by strolling through it with a company called London Walks. And one of their most popular offerings is a guided jaunt called Ghost Walk of London. Passing through the deadlier parts of the city, the stroll includes Smithfield, London's principal place of execution centuries ago, and now, ironically, an immense meat processing facility.

If you want to see death-memorable places from the comfort of a big bus, not on foot or in hearse, one English tour company offers a nightly romp through "Jack The Ripper's London." The trip includes stops at the actual places where he (or she) disemboweled his (or her) victims, and concludes with the tour guide's personal theory about who Jack really was. (He or she was the kind of person who would have taken the tour.)

•

I'll accept the premise that we are fascinated by death, or at least that the reaction we have to death and death images is easily mistaken for fascination. It's similar to the way most children are fascinated by dinosaurs and why so many youths go through a dinosaur phase. Death is huge, ominous, and powerful, but impossible to know completely. We have just the skeletons to look at, plus an occasional (cloven) footprint in rock. But what death really looks, smells, and feels like is unknown to us, and will remain so until it's too late to do anything about it. You can convince your children that all the dinosaurs are gone, that a *Tyrannosaurus* won't ever come lumbering down the street looking for lunch. But convincing ourselves that death won't call is impossible. Freud contended that man was incapable of contemplating his own death because he always saw himself as the contemplator, present and alive. But in most Western cultures, no contemplation is better than flawed contemplation. We'd rather not think about it, thank you very much. But we still do, because we can't help it. If there were a real *Tyrannosaurus* knocking on your door, he'd be damned hard to ignore.

The ice cube lecturer may be right about something else, too. We *do* hide our interest in mortality, as much I think for mental and emotional self-preservation as for any other reason. Freud's pal Carl Jung said, "When I live in a house I know will fall about my head in two weeks' time, all my vital functions are impaired by this thought. But if I feel myself to be safe, I can dwell there in a normal, comfortable way." Most human beings want to be nothing more than normal and comfortable, so it makes perfect sense that as time goes on we choose to ignore the obvious fact that our roofs are leaking and our foundations are beginning to settle. And we ignore what's causing the deterioration. We certainly try to ignore the inevitable collapse of the structure. But every time the walls creak, we can't help but find that interesting.

Given this curious cultural milieu, constantly bouncing between death avoidance and death attraction, it's no wonder we burst from childhood believing that the only way to die is to be melted by a Kansas virgin or dropped off a cliff by vengeance-crazed dwarves. Such toddler confusion is replaced during adolescence and early adulthood by an egocentricity so overpowering that death, like incontinence, is something that happens to others. Especially old others. If it's true we males reach our sexual peak at eighteen, it is also true we reach our immortal peak about then as well. And then we coast for a decade or two. That's where I was some years ago, early adulthood having degenerated into middle adulthood without my even realizing it.

It was during lunch hour that I realized I was going to die. I wasn't eating lunch at the time. This was not some blinding revelation over a tuna salad sandwich and potato chips. It wasn't even that much of a revelation, actually, just a small zigzag from childhood intellectual acceptance to adult emotional certainty, rather like the perceptual shift that happens after suspecting that you've stepped in something unpleasant to actually looking at the bottom of your shoe and seeing it. On this particular day I was forced to look at the bottom of my mortal sole, and there I was.

At the time I was working as the arts reporter for a local television station. I didn't cover the fire and fury stuff. No bridge jumpers, incinerated families, or grisly traffic accidents for this boy. My assignment was just the opposite. I was hired to create features that left 'em smiling at the end of the newscast after all the bloody stuff had already aired. So I certainly never expected to be on the clock when I came face-to-face with my own mortality. What happened to me was a work-related injury, a psychological injury to be sure, but still a lot more lasting than a bad back. Most bad backs go away eventually, but the damage done to me—if damage it was—will last for the rest of my life. Once you know you are going to die, you never forget. It's like falling off a bike.

A Japanese dance troupe called Sankai Juku had come to Seattle for a series of performances. As was their artistic and promotional custom, the company's first presentation was outdoors and free. The piece was called "The Dance of Birth and Death" and featured four nearly naked men descending down the facade of a six-story building on ropes. Sankai Juku had done this work hundreds of times all over the world, on buildings, in stadiums, and even on rock formations. It was their most famous piece and never failed to please.

The selected Seattle building was in Pioneer Square, our city's monument to urban renewal, historic preservation, and recycled red bricks. A lot of artists work in the theaters and galleries in the area, and it seemed like all of them were out that sunny Friday to see the show. I was there with two videographers to cover the event. It was the perfect arts feature for the tag of that night's 5:00 P.M. newscast: visual, local, entertaining, and free.

By the time the performance began shortly after lunch hour, there were more than a thousand people peering up the building into the sun. The mood was festive. The artists were festive. Even the gray-suited lawyers were festive. Mothers dangled babies on their arms, secretaries ate their sack lunches and tried to get a little sun. Kids ran in and out of the crowd. None of us considered for a moment that what we were about to see was dangerous. This wasn't dangerous. This was Art.

Somewhere somebody cranked up a recording of humpbacked whales singing, and four white faces appeared on the rooftop. Then they came slowly over the edge, curled in fetal positions around ropes ten feet apart that dangled down to the sidewalk. Covered in white body paint, the dancers looked like ghosts, not babies, as very slowly they lowered themselves toward the ground.

The ground was still fifty feet away when the second rope from the left broke, and Yoshiuki Takada fell like a stone to the sidewalk in front of us. He did not make a sound all the way down, and landed on the back of his neck. For a brief moment I thought it was a mannequin, that somehow they had tied a particularly animated dummy onto one of the ropes. I even remember a flash of disapproval. Dropping a phony was in bad taste, I thought for a split second, what if the kids in the crowd thought it was real?

It was real, and we all watched as Yoshiuki Takada died very quietly ten feet away from us. We weren't the only ones who hadn't considered the danger. There were no police officers around, no ambulance standing by. It seemed to take hours for them to arrive, those municipal employees whose job is to remove death from our communal sight as quickly and efficiently as possible.

I was luckier than a lot of the people in the crowd. I had something to do besides just stand there. My simple arts feature had turned into the lead news story of the day, especially since we were the only crew there who actually had video of Takada's rope breaking. We had exclusive pictures of a man falling to his death, not just some Hollywood stunt person hitting an inflated mattress off camera. Looking back now it seems crass and unfeeling even to have considered such a meaningless advantage over our competitors in the face of tragedy. But that's how it was. I rationalized my tasteless pleasure at knowing we alone had the shot by convincing myself that if we had also gotten a shot of Takada hitting the sidewalk we would not have used it. But then and now I thought it was important to show what happened, to show an artist before an audience of artists giving his life for his work. That's the way I wrote it for the news that night, and that's the way it played on newscasts around the world throughout the following week. It seemed like everyone suddenly developed an intense interest in watching Yoshiuki Takada die. NBC even called to "congratulate" me.

He was the first dead person I had ever seen. That's not surprising in contemporary society. Modern medicine, improved diet, and sporadic outbreaks of peace have made death the province of the elderly, especially in postindustrial nations. Because more and more of us are dying of old age in hospitals and care centers, removed from family, friends, and the community, fewer people under the age of forty have even seen a corpse, much less had any real association with the dead. In Britain more than 70 percent of the population now dies in a hospital. A hundred years ago that figure was 5 percent. A hundred years ago in America and Western Europe—and to this day in some other countries— death and the dead were daily facts of life, as common as horses in the city. Children didn't need action figures for death images. They had Grandpa dying in his own bed in the next room, or baby brother dying of pneumonia in Momma's arms. I did not, and so this bizarre accidental death was my first.

Immediately after the event, however, it was easy for me to dissociate myself from Yoshiuki Takada and what happened to him, and certainly from any connection it might have to my own mortality. I had no plans to strip, paint myself white, and come down the front of a building on a rope. That act was as unlikely as being forced over a cliff by dwarves. Death still could not touch me.

That same night I took my son Ira to the circus, which ironically was also in town; ironic because Sankai Juku was trying to make a dangerous performance look safe—and failing—while Ringling Brothers Barnum & Bailey was trying to make a safe performance look dangerous—and failing too. (Why is it that the circus these days, even in person, looks like a television show?)

Ira and I were seated down front in the free media seats. I was working again, preparing a review of that year's edition of the Greatest Show on Earth. Midway through the first half it was time for the wire walkers, two men doing a standard tightwire act fifty feet up. Suddenly I had to leave the arena, unable to watch them or even be in the same room while they worked.

Out in the hallway, alone except for bored popcorn and souvenir vendors, I broke down, crying for a Japanese dancer I never knew, never even met. All I had in common with Yoshiuki Takada was that we were both present when he died. Without realizing it, I was going through the five stages of emotionally dealing with death formulated by Elizabeth Kübler-Ross. And I wasn't even terminal—yet. Stage one, Denial, had taken place in a few seconds at the scene, my assumption that the fallen object was a mannequin. Now I had arrived at Anger. I was furious that Takada's death was so stupid, so meaningless. And it was. For aesthetic reasons, the Sankai Juku dancers insisted on using hemp rope in "The Dance of Birth and Death," rather than synthetic rope. Their manager inspected the ropes before the performance and insisted they looked sound, but that's the thing about hemp. It can rot from the inside out and you don't know until it breaks. For sailors it's an inconvenience, and experienced mountain climbers wouldn't consider using hemp. But they don't consider aesthetics either. Just survival.

Meaningless death. I suppose it was there in the hallway, with the circus band blaring on in the background and my son wondering what had happened to me, that I first realized what *was* going to happen to me. I was going to die. Any day now I would never see my sons and my wife again and they would never see me. More anger. That I was going to die without so much as a hearing seemed completely unfair. I didn't deserve it and I could think of a lot of people who did. I had slipped very easily into Kübler-Ross's third stage, Bargaining, and my particular bargaining was so lame—first take the guys who never signal for left turns, then I'll go quietly—that the fourth stage followed immediately. Depression. Unless you're lucky enough to throw yourself on a hand grenade, save your buddies, and win a tubful of posthumous medals, isn't *all* death meaningless? Yoshiuki Takada had it good. Instead of being run into by a beer truck, he was allowed to die for his art, *meaningfully*, before an audience that will never forget his sacrifice. He had caring witnesses, not just some lone beer truck driver sitting in the back of a patrol car telling the investigating officers that "the dumb son of a bitch wasn't signaling for a left turn, that's how come I ran into him."

About this time, the popcorn and souvenir vendors who had been watching me curiously were beginning to look around for the nearest investigating officer themselves. Generally speaking, the Greatest Show on Earth is not supposed to drive grown men to tears, unless it's the season they do their all-chimpanzee tribute to *La Dame aux Camélias*. So I went back to the circus a doomed man—doomed not only to die, but to the terrifying knowledge that I must die and will probably have no control over when, where, or how.

Elizabeth Kübler-Ross's five stages usually apply to the terminally ill. But at the risk of quoting a bumper sticker, Life is a Terminal Disease. Even without the overpowering immediacy felt by the cancer patient, the stages still apply to all of us who have reached that moment when our intellectual understanding of the existence of death is enhanced by the emotional realization of our pending personal involvement. And the fifth stage is Acceptance.

In the two years this Trip of a Lifetime has taken, most of the people I've met, regardless of their culture, background, or social status, have been trying in various ways to accept the fact that they will die some-day. Some have actually succeeded, or at least I think they have. Death acceptance is like sexual prowess, especially among men. It lends itself to exaggeration. One of the most successful acceptors I met was a dying man, another a Zen Buddhist monk, still another a man who has probably killed people and almost been killed many times himself.

A lucky few others I've met seem to have been able to ignore death completely, which is significantly different from accepting it. I don't know what scares them at three in the morning, what thoughts they have when a sore throat just won't go away, how they feel when another birthday passes or they learn of the death of a friend. Per-haps, like me, such events are just as disturbing, but for their sake I hope not.

Most of the other people I've talked to have developed ways to deal with their mortality. They haven't found Acceptance, but they haven't mired themselves in Anger or Depression either. And more often than not one of the ways they handle death is to give it a recognizable face. Death is terrifying because it is omnipotent, omnipresent, and brutally impartial. At the same time death is unknown and completely mysteri-ous to us, a monstrous invisible presence threatening to take away every-thing we care about in an instant. We look at the stars and say they are the universe, but they really comprise only an infinitesimally small part of an unimaginably gigantic entity. We look at death, and we don't even have the stars.

So we create our own stars, our own comprehensible death surro-gates. Just as death for my sons is a four-inch-tall piece of Male Action plastic that can be tossed in a drawer or flushed partway down the toi-let, so death for many of us is a self- (or society-) created entity that can be defeated just as easily. Or at least understood. I don't know what it is to die, but I can imagine sticking my spoon in the wall, kicking the bucket, or sleeping in Lakeview.

The death entities we create have an effect on the way we live our lives. They influence our priorities, our art, certainly our religious and secular beliefs. So they say something about us, as individuals and indi-vidual cultures. The difficult part is forcing ourselves to think about death in any form. And once we do, it is equally difficult to resist mak-ing value judgments based on cultural biases or inbred fears and super-stitions. At least that was the difficult part for me. The purpose of this Trip was to find out how different people and different cultures deal with death, not give a critical review of the death choices other people make. Therefore I've tried to avoid value judgments. Instead, I'll just tell what I saw, what it seemed to mean to the individuals and their society, and what questions raised by the people and rituals I encountered might be answered differently elsewhere. "Man, those Greeks, they really know how to do death!" is as unlikely a sentence in this book as "Hey, look at what these Chinese wackos do!"

However, coming from a white American background, not being an anthropologist, sociologist, or anything else appropriately diplomaed, and not having traveled much before except to similar industrialized nations such as England, I can't possibly claim objectivity. (Although I don't consider that a handicap. When I hear anybody say he or she is objective about death, I assume I'm talking to a fool or a liar.) I went into a lot of the situations that follow with preconceived notions, and I can now honestly say that one of the most enjoyable things about the journey is how often I was wrong.

•

Consider, for instance, Mr. Nana Kofi Adu, who lives in a small village in central Ghana. Mr. Adu is a professional man; specifically, he's a witch doctor. Or at least, that's what you would call him if you were ignorant. The more accurate title, the one he prefers, is fetish priest. And that means he is not someone who has just created surrogate death images. For a lot of people he *is* a surrogate death image. Some residents of his and the surrounding villages believe Mr. Adu both can and has put lethal curses on people, and that he can and has protected people from the lethal curses placed on them by other fetish priests. And that's just part of his practice.

My expectations before meeting Mr. Adu were strictly *National Geographic,* circa 1938: an old charlatan squatting in the mud in front of a semicircle of huts straight out of *Tarzan,* scaring the bejesus out of ignorant natives with dime store magic tricks. I was just sophisticated enough not to expect a bone in his nose. What I found was a gracious, pleasant young man with small shells in his dreadlocks who takes his work as seriously as any other kind of priest. It wouldn't surprise me at all if Mr. Adu has a large stack of *National Geographics* piled up in his house from which he gets a great deal of amusement.

To get to that house, Thomas, the driver, and I traveled two hours from Kumasi up into the hills, over roads that are roads only because someone has designated them as "roads." Though he didn't say it, Thomas thought I was crazy to be messing about with a fetish priest. Such people, such powers, are to be avoided until you need them. But then Thomas is the kind of driver who likes sitting at the hotel not driving. Given the way people drive in Ghana, that's a perfectly understandable reaction. As a friend of mine says, it's a place they drive "romantically."

We finally reached Mensase, the village where Nana Kofi Adu works and lives, and drove down the main street. I didn't see a single hut, just adobe-like houses with corrugated metal roofs and walls that are as red as the earth from which they were made. By American standards Mensase is a bit primitive, but compared to what I expected it looked like Grosse Pointe, Michigan.

Soon Nana Kofi Adu and I were sitting across from each other in the open courtyard of his home. Filling out the circle of folding chairs were fifteen village elders. What seemed like hundreds of other villagers stood against the interior walls of the house watching us intently. There were also children everywhere, and just like elsewhere in Ghana, they all seemed to be ten-year-old boys.

Ghanaians are very formal people, or at least the Ashanti are. You don't just walk into their homes, tip your hat and commence talking, especially not when meeting a fetish priest, a man who knows something about rituals. First you shake hands with everyone present, then you all have a shot of palm wine from an ancient white plastic jug, then you present the bottle of schnapps you've brought for the occasion and everyone in the circle has a bit of that, and then there is drum-and-bell music and sedate dancing. During the musical interlude, Mr. Adu went into his back room, removed his civilian clothes, and slipped into his more formal priestly garb, a brown coat and hat decorated with dozens of small leather purses. Underneath he wore long white pants that looked like they came off the rack at Sears. When the dancing was done, he returned and reclaimed his seat next to his mother. I thought we were about to start.

I was wrong. Suddenly another fetish priest burst into the house and then the circle. His face was blackened with charcoal dust, he wore a bright orange robe, and he looked like he'd been up for three weeks drinking more coffee than any living creature should have. He danced and sang around the circle of chairs, staring wildly at a spot about a foot to the left of my nose and occasionally sticking a knife so far into his mouth that his cheek jutted out. The assembled crowd was delighted by his surprise entrance and subsequent dance, but their reaction was more than just pleasure at a good performance. The actions of a fetish priest always mean something. Though I didn't know what this man was saying, I could tell the villagers had gotten some kind of message from him. This junior priest—a trainee, I suspect—finished his presentation and then quietly sat down next to Mr. Adu, who gave him a nod of praise. Instantly he was just another person in the group, and his wild-eyed character was gone.

Finally there were formal greetings, with an exchange of speeches. I told who I was and what my mission was, and then Mr. Adu officially welcomed me to his village and his home as only he could.

"I thank you for coming," he said, "and I will show my thanks by praying for you. Believe it, believe me, from now on every endeavor of yours will be successful. Everything!"

We talked then, talked as if we were not being watched by the entire population of Mensase. Unlike other people of the cloth, Mr. Adu did not get the Call, the Call got him, right in the hand. "My father, some of my uncles were fetish priests before me. I am one of twelve children; some of them are priests as well. But it is not just automatically passed from father to son. It is a gift from God. The very day I was born, I was born with something in my hand. And that thing I brought from the universe is now here, doing miracles."

He was born clutching a talisman, or fetish, from the Portuguese word *feticio,* or "charm." The elders were called and confirmed that the baby Kofi was possessed and would undoubtedly have special powers. The talisman was placed on a shrine, and from that moment on Mr. Adu, as he said, "was able to perform wonders."

Most of his current wonders are directed toward helping people, rather like a doctor and a priest combined. "I take care of sick people. I look after the health of the children. Those who are deaf, I can help them to hear. Those who are impotent, I can help them to have children. If you come here with your problems, I will go to the bush and collect some herbs that will cure your disease. I will find the proper corrective action to take."

Often the proper corrective action depends on the cause of the problem. Although he believes that simple accidents do happen, more often than not he ascribes calamities to the work of evil spirits.

"Evil spirits exist. God did not create man to be miserable, but an evil spirit may cross you somewhere while traveling and cause a calamity. We have witches who are always around hunting people, trying to destroy people. If you are being hunted by evil spirits, I take you to my shrine and I pray. The witch will be apprehended and he will be destroyed, because I am more powerful than evil."

There's another way to avoid evil spirits besides a visit to the neighborhood fetish priest. You can live a good and righteous life. Mr. Adu tells his followers that no evil fetish priest can kill you if you have not committed evils yourself.

"But if you do wrong, if you go for somebody's wife, for instance, you definitely are bound to have repercussions of evil spirits. They will follow you by all means.

"The same applies to death. I can prevent death, but eventually death is inevitable. We are always about to die. If anybody comes to me afraid of death, I educate him. I tell him to do good, be righteous, so that the number of years given to him by God will last. If you do bad things your life will be shortened. So we priests are like reverend ministers. We preach for good doing, right will, not bad will. If you go bad, then of course you have your own self to blame." In other words, the wages of sin is death.

Mr. Adu told me he could prevent death, but could he also cause it? He said that if I brought a live goat to him, he has the power to kill it instantly without touching it. But if I was looking for help in killing someone, I would have to go elsewhere. He was very polite about it. It is other fetish priests, he said, who use their powers to kill people. Priests have a choice whether they will do evil things or not. But those who choose evil get a handicap, because the force for good is always stronger than the force for evil, and therefore, as a good fetish priest, he can always defeat and destroy a bad fetish priest.

"You're Obi Wan Kenobe!" I said. "The Force is with you. And the bad priests are Darth Vader."

There was a long pause. "Let us go to the shrine," Mr. Adu said.

Mr. Adu's shrine, a block away, is where his power comes from, the source of his Force. We got there by parading up the main street; first Mr. Adu, then the drummers and bell players, then two other fetish priests: the trainee with the knife and a visiting priest from a neighboring village who helps Mr. Adu on special occasions.

I was especially intrigued by him. Fetish priests seem to have performance characters. Mr. Adu is the calm, professional actor/manager, a heroic leading man who pays attention to details. He even stopped in midparade to correct the tempo of the drummers. His knife-wielding apprentice is a classic hero's crazy best friend, like Gabby Hayes was to Roy Rogers. For the visit to the shrine, he had covered himself with a white powder, the wild look had returned to his eyes, and the knife was back in his cheek.

But the third priest had created a unique persona, especially for someone in his business. His priestly character was that of an intensely indifferent observer. Intense indifference may sound like an oxymoron but this guy played it wonderfully. He was a remarkable-looking man anyway, with a vaguely comic expression accentuated by perpetually half-closed eyes and puckered lips. He always had a cigarette in his hand or dangling from his pucker, and for the visit to the shrine, he didn't dance up the street like the others, but walked flat-footed, gazing at the rest of us with utter apathy. If you can imagine the late George Sanders as a thin, twenty-five-year-old black Ghanaian wearing a grass skirt, you've got him.

The shrine was a twelve-by-eight-foot wooden building with a dirt floor, set against a hillside behind a circle of statues and short plinths. Mr. Adu sat in the middle of the statues, either praying, addressing the crowd, or wishing me well.

"God has been welcomed, and will see that everything you do here is successful, and then He will lead you back to the United States successfully."

With the two other priests and a few male townspeople, we went inside the shrine, where there were more statues, more prayers, and another ceremony. George Sanders took a blackened stick out of a gourd hanging from the ceiling and scraped charcoal off it. Mr. Adu put some of the charcoal in his hand and then licked it off. Then they gave me some charcoal and I did the same, I who had been drinking bottled water exclusively in Ghana for a week because that's what the travel medicine types back in Seattle told me to do. We followed the charcoal with a schnapps chaser and then went back outside, back to Mr. Adu's house for final dancing, farewells, and his personal assurance of a successful journey back to Seattle.

A week later my plane home lost two out of four engines just after takeoff from London. We dumped fuel over the Atlantic and headed back to Heathrow, a brief but tense journey. I wouldn't admit that possessing Mr. Adu's travel blessing made me completely calm during that flight, but at the same time I know that if he had cursed me I would have been a lot more . . . restive.

He may have the power to perform wonders. Certainly he thinks he does, and the people of Mensase think he does, and that, I should imagine, is half the battle in the fetish priest business. Here's all I know for sure. After having been warned about local food and water, I drank homemade palm wine from a communal cup and lapped up ritual charcoal and did not spend the rest of the month knocking back Immodium and contemplating plumbing fixtures. And there was something else.

I thought I would send Mr. Adu a letter, just to say hello and thanks. I knew I'd have to send it early because it takes a minimum of a month to get mail to or from Ghana. But I put it off, and finally mailed it from home just a few days before Christmas.

When I got to my office that same day, there was a letter from Nana Kofi Adu waiting for me. It began "Dear friend, Thank you also for your humble letter written to me recently . . . "

CHAPTER TWO

DEATHSTYLES OF THE RICH AND FAMOUS

Precious Gold Mountain and Happy Peace Garden are about an hour by car from downtown Taipei. Driving along with the flat sea on one side and green hills rolling off under a hazy sky on the other, it's hard to believe I'm still so close to that fervid city. Taipei is full of energy, Male Action Line factories, and motorbikes. But here in the country, out of motorbike range, you don't even feel the city's overwhelming desire to be mistaken for Tokyo. Here life seems much more like a Chinese watercolor than a Chinese comic book.

Then you get to the nuclear power plant. It squats a mile up from the beach in a pretty little river valley next to a gurgling stream that's probably 104 degrees Fahrenheit and full of giant three-headed golden carp. For some reason seeing the nuke plant makes the reality of modern, industrial, business-is-business Taiwan rush back in. "Yes, ladies and gentlemen, the power from this one plant enables 1,000 factories to turn out 3 million X-Men, 150,000 plastiform fly swatters and 6,000 neon-esque portraits of Jesus with the eyes that follow you wherever you go, each and every day!"

Since Chernobyl and Three Mile Island, nuclear power plants have become images of death, and not just for me. This is a small facility, very low-key. It looks more like a sewage treatment plant with one hell of a smokestack. But it's a very ominous sewage treatment plant nevertheless, as much for what's not there as what is. As I go by I can see not a single human being anywhere near it.

I pity those people who have to do public relations for nuclear power plants, but I still don't think they do it very well. If I got the contract for this Taiwan terror the first thing I'd do is slap some amenities around the base of the cooling tower. Tennis courts, a swimming pool, an open-air cafe, and gondolas bobbing gently on the stream would be about right. Workers on a twenty-four-hour rotation would be assigned to slip out of their bright orange radiation protective wear and into their Speedos and baby blue sweat suits. Then they'd have to get out there in front and recreate so nobody like me would ever drive by and spend the next thirty miles wondering where everybody is, and why they left in such a hurry. (Once the reality of death enters your life, fantasies of death find it a lot easier to get in too. "AMERICAN MOTORIST FOUND DEAD AND GLOWING IN TAIWAN" the headlines would say, with the subhead, "National Assembly to Consider Multilingual Meltdown Notification Signs.")

Just beyond the nuclear power plant I take a right turn onto a narrow road that heads up into the hills away from the sea and the radiation. Next stop, Precious Gold Mountain, and waiting for me there is the King of Happiness himself.

Mr. Tsao purchased the hillside seventeen years ago, intending to build high-quality housing. He soon discovered that the Taipei businesspeople who could afford the homes he wanted to build didn't want to live so far out of town. Mr. Tsao thought the problem over and then proceeded to build specialty housing for businesspeople who couldn't go anywhere even if they wanted to. He turned his hillside into a cemetery, and called it Precious Gold Mountain.

A lot of people moved permanently to Precious Gold Mountain over the next dozen years, including one industrialist whose $800,000 monument would be considered spacious living quarters for a family of four in most cities. But Mr. Tsao was not satisfied.

"Eight years ago I realized that I would never make money in the cemetery business," Mr. Tsao says with the smile of a man who already has a lot of money from picking his parents well. "So if I couldn't be rich, I decided to be famous." Mr. Tsao proclaimed himself the King of Happiness and began extensive alterations to his kingdom, including the addition of Happy Peace Garden. He wanted to turn his hillside into a place where the living could learn about death, not just a place to leave the dead. Precious Gold Mountain and Happy Peace Garden are now the closest thing to a death theme park you're likely to find, and Mr. Tsao is the Deadland Disney. He's a tall, muscular man with a severe crew cut, in his late fifties but trying (and sometimes succeeding) to look like he's in his early forties. And from the way he moves, the way he laughs, the way he is in complete control of all he surveys, it's clear Mr. Tsao has always known freedom from want and freedom from fear.

Sometimes it's difficult to make the connection between Mr. Tsao's various attractions and his goal of death education. Practically the first thing I see after passing through the entry gate is a quarter-life-size statue of copulating elephants. A little farther into Happy Peace Garden I stare for some time at another artwork, trying to figure out what it is, until Mr. Tsao finally says, "Turtles." Indeed, a ten-times-life-size statue of two turtles in flagrante delicto. Mr. Tsao puts sex and death together with the ease of a Hollywood producer.

Besides hundreds of graves tightly packed together in rows going up the mountainside, among the other attractions is a lavish hundred-foot-tall bone tower where relatives deposit their ancestors' remains after exhumation. In the lobby of the bone tower is the world's largest Chinese block, with a hitting stick so big and unwieldy Mr. Tsao has a standing offer of a thousand dollars to anyone strong enough to pick it up and belt the block with it. There's also a statue of what he calls the Death Buddha, the Hall of the Eighteen Giant Wax Arhats—famed Buddhists, like the Apostles, who achieved Nirvana—and out front, a full-size bronze tree and assorted religious statuary. The bone tower forecourt is the crest of the Hill of a Thousand Buddhas, although currently it's the Hill of Approximately Seven Hundred Fifty Buddhas, as workers feverishly carve more Buddhas daily. Just as Walt Disney used to say that Disneyland would never be finished but always searching for ways to improve, so Mr. Tsao says Precious Gold Mountain and Happy Peace Garden will never be finished either, but will always have room for new graves, new bones, new turtles and elephants. And there are a lot more mountains out here to conquer.

The final PGM & HPG attraction is clearly Mr. Tsao's favorite, his equivalent of the Disneyland E ticket experience. It's called The Trip of a Lifetime (good name!) and is a moody tunnel that arches through part of the hillside under the 750 Buddhas. Like any good theme park ride, the one-hundred-yard-long Trip takes its visitors through a story—in this case, *the* story. Mr. Tsao and I enter at Birth, walking slowly past statues on the path and frescoes on the wall representing those early mewling and puking days. Paintings and crude statues are the principal artistic media of the tunnel, every aspect of which Mr. Tsao personally supervised.

"The Trip of a Lifetime," he says, "is meant to show that life is a cycle and that death is just a natural part of that cycle. If you do good work, show respect to your ancestors, and live an honorable life you have nothing to be afraid of when that life ends. If my efforts are in some way also entertaining, so be it, but I think my life's work is to enlighten, not to amuse."

At the top of the arch the paintings suddenly turn quite graphic sexually, and I am enlightened and amused simultaneously. Eager heterosexual couples are depicted enjoying each other in a variety of positions: the elephant position, the turtle position, and so on. I ask Mr. Tsao if this is meant to be life's peak, the pinnacle of life's inevitable arch. He looks confused by the question, and finally says, "Top of the arch is not life's peak. It is just the top of the arch." But figuratively and literally it's all downhill from here, and in rapid succession the next three paintings are of sickness, old age, and death. The big finish is a statue of a putrefying body, which makes Mr. Tsao laugh his very biggest laugh.

"See?" He chuckles. "Now this is no longer something to be afraid of. It's just part of the Trip."

The King and I emerge into the bright sun of the afterlife and are blinded for a moment. He wonders if I have been enlightened, and I wonder where he thinks he is on the arch.

The first thing His Highness did when he decided to become famous was build himself a bachelor apartment right at the heart of Precious Gold Mountain. It's a spectacular place, carved into the rock of the hill below all the graves. Large goldfish burble around in deep pools, water cascades down rock faces. (I do have a passing thought about where the source for his drinking water is. Let's see now, the graves are up there . . .) We finish our visit with tea and cookies at the apartment, gazing out at his beautiful view of other, nonprecious, nongold mountains to the west.

He proudly shows me his bedroom, the huge bed, adjoining sauna, and the movie screen that lowers from the ceiling at the push of a bedside button. And then we go to his office down the hall. It's a regular office, with one exception. Right behind Mr. Tsao's desk is a kind of closet, but very fancy for a closet. It's almost a shrine.

"It will be a shrine someday," Mr. Tsao says, "because when I die, that's where my bones are going." So he spends his working day sitting practically on top of his own grave. That would bother some people, but not Mr. Tsao. He is surrounded by death twenty-four hours a day and enjoys it. He certainly enjoys life, but why shouldn't he? Life treats him well, with good food, good wines, spacious living quarters and an adoring staff that runs heavily to pretty young women. Mr. Tsao has got it made. Precious Gold Mountain and Happy Peace Garden are his personifications of Death, and he has complete control over them. He's at the top of the arch, and he's staying there.

•

Like Mr. Tsao, Bob Wilkins lives in a recognizable death world too, but not one of his own making. When he was eleven his parents enrolled him in a school near London. One night early in the term a group of upperclassmen appeared in his room to conduct the school's unique initiation ceremony. Two events were planned: sticking little Wilkins's head in a toilet, and then throwing him over the wall of the town cemetery—a right of flush-age, followed by a rite of passage. By midnight Bob was lying in the pitch black on top of a cold, mossy grave. With wet hair.

As most any eleven-year-old would be, I suspect he was terrified. But that was forty years ago, and all Bob will say these days is that the cemetery was "rather more interesting" than the toilet. However, there's no question that the experience changed the direction of his life. Dr. Robert Wilkins is now a psychiatrist, not a plumber. And he specializes in the fears of adolescents. From his research, the number-one fear in the eleven to sixteen age group is examinations. Number two is death.

Wilkins is also one of England's foremost death hobbyists. He's both a living compendium of death facts and fun, as well as someone with the professional expertise to tell us what it all *means*, psychiatrically speaking. A psychiatrist obsessed with death sounds like an instant comic stereotype. You expect a cross between Boris Karloff and your Uncle Max, who's been dead for three years, someone who should be lurking in the background of a Charles Addams cartoon. In fact, Bob Wilkins is a rounded, pleasant, not the least bit sepulchral fellow, the loving husband of one and the father of two. True, his colleagues do call him Dr. Death, but he seems much more like the Dr. Dolittle of Death, jolly in his eccentricity and fully conversant with death's more intriguing oddities and embellishments. I've got it. He's Dr. Watson to the Grim Reaper's Sherlock Holmes.

"For most of us and for most of the time, we're able to batten down the hatches and push uncomfortable thoughts of death and dying into our unconscious," Dr. Wilkins tells me. "But every now and again fears come to the consciousness and we start getting worried about what lies beyond the grave. If we weren't able to repress those fears we wouldn't be able to lead productive lives."

He says this as we're perched on a tombstone in the cemetery of St. Mary Magdalene, located in London's Mortlake district. A few yards away is the grave of Sir Richard Burton, the nineteenth-century Africa explorer who also first translated the Kama Sutra and other erotic classics into English. Burton lived a fantastic life, and he's spending eternity in a place to match. When he died in 1890, his wife, the Lady Isabel, applied to have her world-famous husband interred in either Westminster Abbey or St. Paul's, with all the kings, queens, and other empire heroes. The Crown's response to her request was succinct: "No." Prior to her application—in fact, the moment she heard Sir Richard was dead—Lady Isabel committed one of the best-known literary crimes in history by burning his irreplaceable collection of erotica as well as all of his notes and diaries. But apparently her little fire was not enough to remove the sexual taint from Sir Richard's reputation for the minions of Queen Victoria, a monarch and minions I assume eschewed the Kama Sutra for inspirational reading of a different nature.

Undaunted, Lady Isabel applied to plant Sir Dick in the cemetery out back of St. Mary Magdalene. She was accepted, and to make sure everyone would remember her husband and visit his remains even in the suburbs, she had constructed as his grave a full-size, all stone explorer's field tent. (It could be argued that Lady Isabel cared not a bit whether *he* was remembered, as long as *she* was. They reportedly hated each other with a rare passion.)

Into the tent went Sir Richard, eventually to be joined by Lady Isabel herself, but first she spent her years of widowhood regularly holding séances inside the tomb, covering the floor and Sir Richard's casket with various Christian and pagan religious articles. There the tent sits to this day, looking as if at any moment a pith-helmeted Bwana Burton will step out through the tent flaps to scan the horizon for wildebeest and/or erotica whilst Lady Isabel snarls from within. Indeed, the stone tent flaps used to open, but they were sealed some time back to deter vandals. You can still see Sir Richard and Lady Isabel, though. For the benefit of the curious she thoughtfully had the stone masons install a picture window around the back.

Sir Richard's tomb is part of Bob Wilkins's self-created therapy. He's visited many times, and the tent tomb is a highlight in Wilkins's splendid 1991 tomb tome, *The Bedside Book of Death*. The book also includes sections on "The Fear of Premature Burial," "The Fear of Posthumous Indignity," and "The Fear of Bodily Disintegration."

"What I've done is make a conscious decision to confront my death anxieties, the thesis being that the more you address issues about death, the less fearful they become. It hasn't worked, of course, as therapy anyway. I'm just as frightened as I ever was."

Yet in the best English tradition he stiffens his upper lip and presses on with his inquiries. In a sense confronting his anxieties *has* worked for Bob Wilkins. He may be just as frightened of death itself, but by learning everything he can about selected death effluvia he has been able to reconstitute death as an understandable collection of effects, events, and phobias. Bob Wilkins's World of Death is a world Bob Wilkins knows. That makes sense. A person who is afraid of lions is not afraid of a stuffed lion, and will poke about its sharp incisors and vicious claws without the slightest qualms. He still may be ignorant of what a real lion is like, but if he does chance upon the real thing he should be more prepared for the experience than that person who has never even heard of lions. "Ah! A lion! I've got to watch out for the teeth," is a lot more reassuring thing to say to oneself when a lion bursts unexpectedly from the underbrush than "What the hell is that?" (Even if it doesn't make any difference to the lion.) Like all of us, Bob Wilkins doesn't know death, and won't until it bursts upon him. But he sure knows death's equivalent of a stuffed lion.

In Wilkins's case a *mummified* lion is probably the more accurate analogy. After the Burton tent tomb we went into the square-mile City of London, to the Church of St. James Garlickhythe. As London churches go, it's not even on the B list as a tourist attraction, but it does have one unique feature that makes it a very special place in Bob's world. The church's only permanent resident is a fellow known as Jimmy Garlick. He's estimated to be about three hundred years old, and looks rather like Pablo Picasso's brother, the anorexic. Jimmy Garlick is Britain's only indigenous mummy.

"They were doing some restoration work on the church in 1839, quite close to the altar, when Jimmy surfaced," Bob says, talking as if the late Mr. Garlick is an old army buddy. "A naturally mummified body, with no signs of being embalmed at all. And no identification either. To this day we really don't know who Jimmy is. There are theories, but I prefer to ignore them. He's much more affecting as an unknown entity. I think he's quite beautiful."

Jimmy Garlick is more than just a historical/morbid curiosity for his fans. He offers a rare opportunity to look death in the face. At least he does for Dr. Bob. "You want to tap him on the shoulder and say 'Wake up, tell me what it's like on the other side. What is it? What is death?' Whereas if you're strewn in ash form after a cremation or you're buried out of sight under the ground, that opportunity is lost."

Wilkins is not arguing for mummification to replace burial or cremation. His personal postmortem plans do not include being stuffed and propped up in his parish church. But he would contend that those millions of schoolchildren who are trotted through Westminster Abbey every year, not to see the remains of English royalty but merely their tombs and monuments, could learn just as much about a subject far more relevant to their personal concerns by dropping by St. James Garlickhythe and having a sack lunch with Jimmy.

Dr. Bob doesn't have anything against tombs and monuments, though, and to prove it our final stop on his abbreviated World of Death Tour is Bunhill (formerly Bone Hill) Fields, the only cemetery left within the City. The relatively small Bunhill was closed to new "residents" in 1852, but by then at least 120,000 people had been buried there. That's a population figure large enough to indicate there are places within Bunhill Fields where the bodies underground are probably stacked six or seven deep. These days the cemetery has been sanitized and nicely landscaped. But to be safe, visitors aren't allowed to walk among the graves for fear some poor sap with a Nikon will suddenly drop down to plague times through seven layers of ancient cadavers.

"Imagine this place in Dickens's time," Bob says. "The smell, the odor, the bodies literally stacked up everywhere. It must have been quite glorious!" We pass a young couple on a bench sharing their lunch hour, completely unaware of the glorious experience they've missed by a century and a half.

Love blooms in Bunhill not just on the benches but also on the graves. Bob Wilkins leads me to a large chunk of rectangular stone. Commemorated on one long side is the Reverend Theopolos Lindsey, "who lived a blameless and exemplary life" until he died in 1808 at the age of eighty-six. On the opposite side his wife, Hannah, is similarly praised. And in the middle, on the short side of the rectangle, appears the Mystery Woman, Mrs. Elizabeth Rainier. "Obviously a blue blood," Wilkins says, "because she was a member of the house of Percy. But she put that aside to be buried with her 'great friends and fellow worshipers, the Reverend and Mrs. Lindsey.' The question one must ask is where is *Mr.* Rainier? The fourth side is blank. A ménage à trois, perhaps? Did the man of the cloth—the 'blameless and exemplary Reverend Lindsey'—steal away first the soul, then the heart, and then the rest of Mrs. Rainier? Oh, Theopolos!" Novels in stone, that's what Bob Wilkins calls his favorite tombstones. He is still afraid of death, but how can you be afraid of the Reverend Theopolos Lindsey?

•

"The British have never been overtly emotional. We are cold-blooded, and not hot-blooded. It would be wrong to say that we have a stiff upper lip. We have a reserve."

Julian Litten sits in his quiet, well-appointed drawing room in Walthamstow, immaculately attired in a pinstripe suit. He is the very model of a modern English gentleman with reserve. To look at him you would never guess that he has an eccentric obsession. Or rather, you might suspect he has one, but never guess what it is. Like his friend Bob Wilkins, Julian Litten is fascinated by death. Where the former is a death generalist, however, Litten is a specialist in one particular field. And if he doesn't know that field better than any other person on the planet, he'll do for now. Julian Litten is the Source about English funerals; not Welsh funerals, Irish funerals, or Scottish funerals, but *English* funerals. It may seem to be an area of scholarship that's both outré and of limited commercial and/or historical value, but Julian argues that like the death rituals of many cultures, the way the English have buried their dead over the centuries says a lot about what they value in life and how those values have changed as times, priorities, and tastes have changed.

As you might suspect, English funeral traditions are rooted in the English class structure and the effect historical events have had on the classes and their values. The British *Cassell's Family Directory* of 1894 listed funerals according to an individual's status. The proper rites are described for the upper middle class, middle class, and lower middle class, right down to the color of the horses leading the cortege. Suitable funerals for the upper class and nobility aren't mentioned, presumably because the peerage could just send a boy round to fetch Mr. Cassell himself when the time came. And the lower-class funeral needs aren't detailed either, possibly because the lower classes didn't need and wouldn't buy *Cassell's Family Directory* to see how they should bury old Mum.

For the social elite, the English funeral of past centuries was usually modeled on the most recent royal funeral. It was an elaborate and very precise affair, where the wrong plume on the wrong horse could be an unconscionable social gaffe.

"But that began to change towards the end of the nineteenth century," Julian says. "For two reasons. It was impossible to repatriate the remains of a large number of young soldiers killed in the Boer War. To put on an ostentatious show for a person who had died, next door to a family who had lost a son serving abroad who was not to return, was thought to be in very bad taste.

"But what really changed, indeed purified the English funeral, was the introduction of the motor-driven hearse. You couldn't put plumes on the roof of a motor hearse, nor could you hang velvets along the side." You could, of course, but it would look foolish, and since 1066 the English have tried diligently not to look foolish, which may be why the rest of the world enjoys it so much when they do anyway.

The fancy English funeral did not entirely disappear at the end of the last century, however. It was adopted by the middle and lower classes twenty-five years later when they were at last able to afford it, long after the upper classes were regularly choosing more modest, sedate rituals. This twenty-five year lag in middle-class aping of upper-class rituals is not limited to funerals, but pervades all English social history, or so says Julian.

He has spent much of his life learning English funerals from under the ground up. And though we didn't talk specifically about that moment of mortal realization that led to his avocational joy, two events clearly influenced his career choice. The first was the 1952 funeral of Queen Elizabeth's father, George VI. Little Julian was six then, and it was the first thing he remembers ever watching on television.

"I was impressed by the profound solemnity and dignity, which I thought was more meticulous than that witnessed at the Coronation of Elizabeth some months later. So I think that over the years I have, as a social historian, realized that far more has been known about royal weddings and coronations, but nothing affects and embraces our society more than a funeral. Alas, it is something we haven't necessarily wished to discuss."

The second event in his life was considerably more personal, although Julian speaks of it now with nonchalance, as if it too were a television show he just happened to catch in passing.

"My sister and I had to identify our parents' remains when they were killed in a rather ghastly car accident. The people in the other car were also killed. We were shown into one of the rooms at the police station, and there on two large billiard tables were the effects taken out of the car. And the policeman said in a very somber voice, 'Can you tell me, are these items associated with your parents?' My sister pointed to a rather ghastly shoe which must have come from the female occupant of the other car, and said, 'Indeed not. My mother would not be seen dead wearing shoes like that.' "

Litten collects not only funeral facts, figures, and attitudes, but also death objects and art. His treasures include the death masks of John Keats and William Blake, a splendid seventeenth-century skull, photographs and paintings of crypts and tombs, and coffin models that undertakers used to place in their shop windows to attract the drop-in, dropped-dead trade. In 1992, when the Victoria and Albert Museum put together an extremely popular exhibition of death artifacts, many of the objects on display were from the personal collection of Julian Litten.

These days Litten works as a curator at the Victoria and Albert, an author (*The English Way of Death*, 1991) and an advisor on decorous funerals. In that capacity there are indications he even advises the Royal Family, but like a proper English gentleman Julian is discreet about his relationship with the Windsors. All he will say is that he admires them greatly, especially the Queen Mother, now in her nineties.

"When that grand and noble woman dies, her funeral will cost the Crown more than twenty-five million pounds. But I assure you it will be done right, and draw the English people together as nothing has since the war."

More than anything else, Julian seems to be a quiet crusader for funerals that are a proper tribute to the deceased as well as a comfort to the mourners. He calls for a return to funerals that are elegant and tasteful but without undue extravagance or ostentation.

"The funeral itself should be the knot on the bow of life. Now we see memorial services being held six or seven weeks after the funeral itself, it being thought that the disposal of the dead is necessarily private, done by the intimate family alone. I find that odd. Death does not conform to the social calendar. When it does take place, I can see nothing wrong in everyone down tools and going to attend that particular disposal. To have a memorial service that is convenient to everybody's diaries seems to me to be turning away a little bit from the direct effect."

Litten's other crusade is for personal funeral preparation and involvement. Recently it's been reported that grief counselors in Britain are swamped with work because the British, following their national tradition, are so repressing their feelings that they are doing themselves a psychological injury that requires professional attention. Julian believes the reason British grief counselors are so busy is because people haven't given themselves anything to do in the death ritual process. They feel uninvolved in the funerals of others because they have neglected to become involved in their own pending rites.

"The best way to cope with bereavement is to get involved in organizing the funeral itself. Choose the coffin, look at the shrouds, the grave clothes. Select the lining and the handles you're going to have on the box itself. Just enjoy it. You would never rush into a bridal shop and say 'Do me a wedding for next Saturday.' You'd want to plan it as much as you can. And a funeral should be just as memorable, just as carefully planned."

Though only in his forties, Julian has already planned his own funeral down to the smallest detail—except when it will be, of course—and strongly suggests that we all do the same upon reaching what we hope are our middle years. "After that, for the remaining forty or fifty years, you can get on with enjoying your life because you know at the last you've taken care of everything. And then everyone can say 'What a generous person he was!' and you will never hear those words uttered timorously by the person most closely associated with your death, 'I *think* we did what he wanted.' "

But would you have heard such remarks anyway? This is more than just a spiritual question, I think. It goes to Julian Litten's success in dealing with any fears he might have about his own death. As Bob Wilkins has reduced death to an amusing, benign collection of oddities, Julian Litten has reduced it to the quest for a perfect funeral. He seems to have no apprehensions at all about his own demise other than finding himself the centerpiece at a tacky, tasteless burial. While the rest of us have nightmares about dying and going to hell, Julian has nightmares about going to Las Vegas and dying. Indeed, I suspect his only regret is that he probably can't observe how his careful planning has paid off. But he still imagines himself there and aware of all that's happening, even to the point of listening in on his relatives as they comment on his generosity. Julian Litten doesn't know what death will be like any more than the rest of us, but he's quite sure his last moments aboveground will be tasteful, elegant, and not the least bit foolish. And in that he takes pride and gets comfort.

•

Lloyd Kaufman is a tasteless, uncomfortable man, and proud of it. In his career he has killed thousands of people in bizarre and gruesome ways: brains skewered by milkshake machine agitators; faces thrust into deep fat fryers; bodies punctured by heat-seeking chopsticks; throats severed by exercise equipment; elderly ladies ground up by motorboat propellers. Lloyd's homicidal specialty is hogsheads of green, glowing toxic waste sloshed over bikinied teenagers. But of all the deaths he's organized the only complaints he received were when he terminated a Seeing Eye dog by blowing it across a restaurant, propelled by the force of a shotgun blast.

Lloyd Kaufman is the president and creative force behind New York-based Troma Films, one of America's oldest independent film production companies. Troma movies are so cheap, so tacky, they weren't even thought worthy of home video release until quite recently. Even now, to see Troma classics like *Surf Nazis Must Die, Bloodsucking Freaks, Chopper Chicks in Zombie Town, A Nymphoid Barbarian in Dinosaur Hell,* and *Demented Death Farm Massacre* you probably have to go into a movie theater. Usually the eighteenth theater in an eighteen-theater multiplex. For it was the advent of the multiscreen shopping mall "cinema center" in the 1970s that was the impetus for Troma. Mr.

Kaufman was then a bright young Yale grad with production experience on a few Hollywood films, including *Rocky*. He realized that the owners of new multiplex theaters would be needing a lot more product; no longer just one movie to fill one big screen, but a dozen movies to fill a dozen little screens. These way-down-the-hall movies would have to be of a very special type, with lighthearted sex to avoid offending the shopping mall moms, but enough raunchy action to attract the teen date audience. Above all, no theater owner would want to spend very much for something he slaps up to entertain fifty yabboos in theater number 18. For the exhibitor these movies would have one purpose only, to provide ready-made customers for the extremely profitable snack bar. And a movie with the sole purpose of providing Jujube and Milk Dud customers would have to be *cheap*.

Troma was born. The company's slogan is either "World Peace Through Celluloid" or "Excellence on Celluloid"—it depends on whom you ask. The company's aesthetic philosophy isn't as succinctly stated, but after watching the first ten minutes of any Troma film the corporate artistic guidelines become obvious:

1. Spend as little money as you can.
2. Eschew such frills as "plot" and "character development." People who want such things are home reading novels anyway.
3. For actors, seek out the rising stars, the undiscovered talents, the bright young hopefuls. But if they want a penny more than union scale, anyone who can walk and talk at the same time is acceptable, especially if they look like sleazy Barbies (particularly the girls).
4. Include a lot of pointless and not the least bit sensual or erotic nudity.
5. Kill many, many people.

These priorities are not necessarily in order of importance, although number one is always number one. And has it worked? As Lloyd Kaufman says with simple, semantically shoddy pride, "Troma is very unique because the studio is twenty years old and we have never had a hit. Not one." But when the average Hollywood film costs fifteen million dollars or more, a film made for less than three million doesn't have to sell a lot of tickets to make money. Lloyd makes money. And nobody who ever attended a Troma show had any fear about going to the snack bar in midfilm because they'd "miss something." Quite the contrary.

The closest Troma has come to hits are the *Toxic Avenger* series and the *Class of Nuke 'Em High* films. The Toxic Avenger, or "Toxie", is a chronic underachieving dweeb who falls into a vat of toxic waste and emerges a very ugly, very strong, very stupid, obsessed-with-killing dweeb with a blind girlfriend. (It was her dog.) Portions of America have found these character traits so winsome that Toxie and his doxy are the first Troma creations to spawn a cartoon television series *and* a set of Male Action Line figures, none of which (I'm proud to say) my children possess.

Toxie lives in Tromaville, New Jersey, which is also where Nuke 'Em High is located, right next to a nuclear power plant with more leaks than a beer hall during Oktoberfest. The student body at Nuke 'Em, all of whom appear to be in their late twenties chronologically and in the low eighties intellectually, is so casual it is the rare young scholar who attends class fully clothed. If there were any classes. These kids just party all the time, which, as any aficionado of teen slasher horror movies knows, means they're asking for it. Writer/producer/co-director Lloyd continuously lets them have it, with both nuclear waste and waste-created mutations such as a thirty-foot tall squirrel with an attitude. *Nuke 'Em High III* is subtitled *The Good, the Bad, and the Subhumanoid,* which is probably all you need to know. And just remember, ladies and gentlemen, that the *Toxic Avenger*s and *Nuke 'Em*s are considered Troma's *good* movies, not throwaway trash like *Stuff Stephanie in the Incinerator* and *Rabid Grannies.*

The secret of Troma's nonsuccess, according to Kaufman, is Death. "It's the star, Death is the star. We don't have Kevin Costner, we don't have stars. Death is bigger than the stars. You go to a Hollywood film, you see Paul Newman, then maybe you see Death. You go to a Troma movie, you see Death first, then the actors."

But just as you don't really see actors in Troma movies, you don't really see death either. And that's not because the "actors" don't actually die, however much one might hope. Death in Tromaville doesn't even resemble death in more mainstream movies like the *Godfather*s or even the *Halloween*s. Kaufman, with co-director Michael Herz, has succeeded in making death utterly inconsequential, rather like the sex in a Russ Meyer soft-core porn film. In neither filmmaker's work do you associate what's happening on screen with anything that could possibly happen to you, anyone you know, or in fact any other human being on the face of the earth. And in both cases the technique is to reduce the body function in question—sex and/or death—to slapstick parody. Not a parody of the real thing, either, but a parody of sex and/or death as presented in other, better movies.

"Toxie *is* rather Chaplinesque," Kaufman says shyly, a statement that would be grounds for a libel suit if the plaintiff weren't dead. But in one sense Lloyd is right. In classic comedies people are hit by pies, slip on banana peels, fall down, and get up. In classic Tromedies, people are hit by pies and their heads fall off and blood spurts out of their necks and then their guts explode so they fall down and land in their own intestines and get their bikinis dirty and don't get up before they get stepped on by the big squirrel. That's the principal difference between the two kinds of films. Toxie isn't Chaplinesque, he's Elmer Fudd-esque, but more graphic and for keeps. He looks like a mutated Elmer Fudd, too.

Lloyd Kaufman shouldn't be surprised that the only complaints he's ever gotten about violence and death in Troma movies were in response to the Seeing Eye dog's demise in *Toxic Avenger*. Bowzer's is the only death in a hundred Troma films you believe could actually happen. And maybe that's just as well. Lloyd claims, "The guys who barricade themselves in their apartments with all the machine guns, they don't have cassettes of the *Toxic Avenger* movies stacked up in the corner. They got cassettes of these Hollywood movies."

Kaufman deals with death by diminishing it to slapstick, which even in comedy is one of the more nonthreatening forms. It's hard to say whether that works for his audience, especially since his audience is primarily eighteen- to twenty-four-year-old males who think they're immortal anyway. But there's no question it works for forty-six-year-old Lloyd.

"I think about death every day. Every day. And I've thought about it since I was a little kid. I always thought I was gonna die early. I'm amazed I'm still alive, quite honestly. Very surprised. Having read a lot of Nathaniel Hawthorne and things of that nature, the Bible of course is pretty good on this, you think about it quite a bit. In a certain way, it's amusing, it's rather amusing. There are certain aspects of it that make you want to laugh in death's face."

And so he does. And a small percentage of the world laughs with him, at seven dollars a head. In Troma films, that works out to about a dime a death.

During six years as a television arts reporter my principal job was to review movies. I saw hundreds of them in that time, and therefore thousands of cinema deaths. Somewhere about 1981 I finally did the generic *Halloween/Friday the Thirteenth/Nightmare on Elm Street* review I kept threatening to do. My remarks were, in toto, "I hate these crazed unstoppable teen-killer films, and I refuse to see or review them anymore. Thank you." And I haven't been to one since. But that didn't mean I escaped death on screen. I still had to watch Arnold, Sylvester, Chuck, Bruce, Jaws, and various Alien creatures collectively wipe out a city the size of Oshkosh, all in the name of art and entertainment. I

once read that Robert Altman's only direction to the screenwriters of
Nashville was, "I don't care what happens, as long as somebody dies in
the end." That could be the motto for more than half the Hollywood
movies today. Except now they die before the opening titles, and are
still dying when the credit rolls by telling you the first assistant key
grip's name. Why?

Lloyd Kaufman contends that it is these Hollywood action-adventure
movies with their believable deaths, rather than his death-as-frisky-
romp cheapies, that inspire less stable Americans to stock up on ordi-
nance and barricade themselves in sixth-floor apartments commanding
a view of the dormitories. He may be right, but the percentage of us
looking for towers to climb and innocent bystanders to waste is so small
as to be inconsequential. I'm more interested in whether ubiquitous
death on screen has any kind of positive, therapeutic effect on audiences.

Mr. Tsao, Bob Wilkins, Julian Litten, and Lloyd Kaufman all lessen
their fears of death by creating recognizable and/or conquerable death
worlds; death worlds that are as different as the men themselves. Julian
Litten would find Lloyd Kaufman's films appalling and Mr. Tsao
bizarre. Bob Wilkins would be unable to stroll through Mr. Tsao's Trip
of a Lifetime without collapsing in laughter, and he'd probably offer
Lloyd Kaufman a few free sessions on his office couch as a hands-
across-the-sea gesture for mental health. If the King of Happiness were
in charge of St. James Garlickhythe, he would immediately prop Jimmy
Garlick up at the Trip of a Lifetime exit. And Lloyd Kaufman would
certainly wonder why a guy like Julian Litten, who knows everything
there is to know about the funeral business, has never been a funeral director so he can make a few bucks on the deal. Nevertheless, the death
world each man has created for himself serves its purpose for the man
who created it.

The rest of us borrow our death worlds from others. We let others
give death an understandability. We read Julian's and Bob's books, we
stroll through the King's tunnel, we buy Male Action figures and
Stephen King novels and other kinds of art on death themes—and we
see a lot of movies in which death, if not the star, is certainly a key character. The movies, television, and horror fact and fiction have become
the principal death world of the rich and famous for a lot of us. But do
they help to lessen our death phobias, as Jimmy Garlick helps Bob
Wilkins lessen his?

Erich Salzgaber, self-described "gore hound," international action
film distributor, and horror writer, thinks vicarious deaths do help people deal with their own fears.

"Most people are pretty scared of the 'Big D,' " he says. "They want
to have some type of cathartic death experience. If the books and films

are done well, you have an opportunity to explore areas you can't explore naturally. You can't go out in the street and cut somebody's head off with a chain saw, but by God you can sure simulate it on screen. You can take a look at it and, if that's your bent, that's kind of a cool thing to look at. Then you can say, 'Okay, I've had my little death kick here, now I can go back to being a good model citizen.' And it's not just American films or American audiences I'm talking about. There are some Asian movies, they'll have a guy with a gun blasting away, just obliterating this human being off the planet. Nobody feels remorse, you know? Nah, they're darn happy they cut the guy up."

•

Dick Warlock has cut heads off with a chain saw, and killed scores of people in other cinematically interesting ways, as well as died himself on screen more than two thousand times. Once, in the film *Delta Force Two*, he even killed Dick Warlock, playing both the victim and the bad guy with the big gun. One of Hollywood's premiere stuntmen, Warlock has done everything from survive the shark in *Jaws* (doubling Richard Dreyfuss) to slaughter teenagers as the immortal crazed killer in the *Halloween* films. Warlock thinks Salzgaber may be right—that movie death offers the closet murderer in us all a chance to commit our crimes vicariously—but he thinks it's more likely people enjoy watching death in movies not to see the bad guy get it, but to see the good guy *not* get it.

"Your audience, they're not in the death part. They're in the survival part. They're the hero. People watch our stuff not to see me die, but to see Clint Eastwood live."

Personally, I prefer Dick Warlock's explanation to Erich Salzgaber's. Movies become entertaining moral lessons, teaching us that if we live the iconoclastic but honorable life of Clint, John Wayne, Bruce Willis, and so on, we shall not die, no matter who tries to kill us or how they try to do it. Death is not only given a comprehensible face (Dick Warlock's face, actually) but shown to be escapable through intelligence and integrity, and not just because you have a bigger gun. The big gun is helpful, but it's not *essential,* and that's an important point in contemporary society, where so many people seem to have much bigger guns than us good guys. It doesn't matter, say the death books, movies, comics, and television shows. And then they give us a hero who proves it by surviving. That hero has to be recognizably human, however, with at least some mortal frailty.

•

Consider the Superman dilemma. Back in the late 1930s, with millions of Americans out of work and incredible bad guys rising to power in Europe, Jerry Siegel and Joe Shuster created an incredible good guy to appeal to a generation that felt increasingly like powerless pawns in somebody else's chess match. Superman was omnipotent, immortal, able to leap tall buildings in a single bound, and the rest of it.

Though his invincibility may have been initially appealing to power-less audiences, Supe's creators and their successors soon introduced kryptonite to make the Man of Steel a bit more vincible. Eventually it seemed as if there were thirty-six different kinds of kryptonite, each of which had a different debilitating effect on Our Hero. A kid practically had to have a periodic table of kryptonites just to figure out what the hell was going on. At the same time, other people were introducing new superheroes who weren't so super. Usually they had just one or two of Supe's powers, like the Flash, who moved very fast, or Aqua-man, who was one terrific swimmer. And ultimately there was Batman, who had no super powers at all, just brains, money, athletic ability, and a really fast car.

Superman doesn't even own a car. He doesn't have to worry about traffic accidents/bullets/knives/bombs/numchuks or anything else. He doesn't even think about *dying*. Superman's only personal concern is whether someone will discover his secret identity, as if that would create a real big problem for him. If the bad guys find out, will they ransack Clark Kent's apartment and steal all his credit cards? Or maybe they'll put the snatch on Clark's only friends, Lois and Jimmy. But they're al-ways doing that anyway! The big mistake Superman's creators made is that the character has so many weapons he doesn't share a single fear with his mortal audience. He never has to use his intelligence, charm, or integrity to survive, like the rest of us. And we hate him for it.

(As this is being written, Superman has recently died at the hands of somebody named Doomsday, who himself expired in the effort. Be-lieve it or not, kryptonite was not involved in the Man of Steel's demise. So after more than a half century of hokey kryptonic devices, when Supe's number was finally up they just did him in, and the hell with plot and character consistency. It should therefore come as no sur-prise that he is already back from the dead. Four different creatures now claim to be Superman, including a cyborg and a robot. I'm not sure what the other two are, and neither is my comics consultant, a so-phisticated fourteen-year-old who now finds all Supermen passé. Even-tually we are promised that one of these new Supes will take over the job permanently. If Superman's owners are smart, the victor will be more the Man of Particle Board than the Man of Steel, minus half a dozen powers and thus a bit closer to the ground we all trod. And then I hope a trend develops, and Disney brings back Bambi's mother. I've been waiting a long, long time, Mr. Eisner.)

Nobody feels like Superman in the face of life, much less death. Money, power, friendship, love—weapons that are so important to earthly existence—mean nothing when death calls. You not only can't take it with you, it won't help you when it's time to go. So movies and popular fiction reinforce our futile hope not only that death will be merciful, but merciful to *all* the "good guys" among us, regardless of our material success in life. Death will take the time to recognize that even if we are small-time detectives, high-plains drifters, or Jimmy Olson (and thus, by association, CPAs and homemakers and high school dropouts), our intentions are good. We get passed over and that SOB next door with the dog who barks all night gets it first.

Supposedly the reward for a good life comes after death, amongst the fluffy white clouds and daily harp concerts. But as long as we're healthy, isn't what we really want and expect divine consideration for our good deeds on *both* sides of the Last Breath? The movies imply such consideration is possible. They help us forget, at least for a few hours, that death is brutally impartial and treats all biological units equally. The first question the great majority of people ask when told they are going to die is "Why me?" The answer, if we are willing to face the reality of death, is "Why not?"

CHAPTER THREE

DEATH FESTS OF THE MYSTERIOUS EAST

When an individual is obviously obsessed with death and its effluvia, society thinks that person is at best eccentric—Wilkins, Litten, Kaufman, King of Happiness—or at worst a morbid appalling necrophiliac serial-killing monster—Stalin, Ripper, Hitler. However, there are occasions in practically every culture when whole societies play with or celebrate death together; death festivals, if you will, and they are most certainly among the oldest communal observances we have.

In the Smithsonian Museum in Washington, DC, I paid a visit to the seventy-thousand-year old Neanderthals—Mom, Dad, and Junior—as they were burying one of their friends. This fetching diorama, based on a discovery in France, is a theoretical recreation with mannequins posed as they must have been in life. What makes the scene sociologically interesting is that the Neanderthals are burying the deceased at all. Perhaps it's unfair to their memories, but one tends to think of our early *Homo sapiens* ancestors as being mighty close to the beasts of the forest in some of their personal habits. And you don't catch weasels, grizzly bears, or even gorillas burying their dead. They may haul the carcass away into the dingle so it won't foul the nest or attract predators, but that's about it, ritually speaking. But these Neanderthals obviously were burying this dead guy, *in* their living space, *with* food in the grave. Dr. Elizabeth Brooks of the Smithsonian also points out that the body was tightly bound in leather thongs. Why?

"The theory," says Dr. Brooks, "is that Neanderthals believed the dead had a spirit that continued. The food was to keep the spirit happy, and the thongs were to keep the spirit contained so it couldn't escape and harm the family." And from believing that the spirits of the dead were hungry, could cause trouble for the living, and needed to be appeased, it's not difficult to see how death festivals came into being.

What defines a death festival? It is when the events are in some way meant to accommodate the spirits of the departed rather than celebrate and recall their good works while they were still alive. Therefore, Presidents' Day in the United States is not a death festival even though the principal honorees, G. Washington and A. Lincoln, are dead. Nobody expects Lincoln's ghost to return to his monument in Washington, DC, on February 12 to see how sales are going on the Emancipation Proclamation printed on simulated parchment. We honor George and Abe for their accomplishments, just as we honor Dr. Martin Luther King, Jr., and war veterans, living and dead, on their respective days. To be true death festivals we would have to believe that physical manifestations of George and Abe still existed and were still able to affect our actions and be affected by our actions. In a true death festival, in other words, the dead are active participants.

Some regional observances are not so easily categorized. Harry Houdini Day, in honor of the late magician, escape artist, and séance buster, is celebrated October 31, the day of his death, or March 24, the day of his birth, depending on whether you're in Michigan or Hungary, respectively. Houdini's remarkable career and abilities are recalled, but some celebrants try to recall Houdini too, because he indicated before he died that if it was possible to communicate from beyond the pale he was just the boyo to pull it off. Houdini Day is what you (and Harry) wish to make of it, death fest–wise.

So is Pennsylvania's Edgar Allan Poe Festival. Nobody in Lancaster County tries to get in touch with Poe's spirit during these late October Poe Days (at least, nobody you'd want to be around) but the honoree was so personally and professionally obsessed with death that you can't just pass this one off as yet another nine-day tribute to a short story writer and poet. Dead had a lot to do with Poe, and therefore it has a lot to do with his Days.

Then there is Halloween, based principally on an ancient Celt festival. We don't know who had the original idea for a Celtic celebration of the dead in late October, but it's not hard to imagine how it came about. There were the Celts, wandering around the rocky tors and boggy fens of Britain in 750 B.C., wondering why they hadn't stayed back in sunny France like the smart Celts. They couldn't help noticing that about the same time each year the world around them started decaying and dying. Leaves on trees that looked fine just a few weeks ago were suddenly turning red and falling to the ground. Even with their lack of medical sophistication, the Celts knew from experience that when you turned red and fell to the ground, you were dead.

But there was more. Forest creatures no longer gamboled in the glens or skulked through the mighty oaks. Most of them had disappeared underground or into caves, as if they knew something was coming and they didn't want to be around when it arrived. Rigor mortis seemed to have struck the water in the streams, turning it hard, slimy, and cold. The Celts' bodies were cold too, as cold as Uncle GwyynUrr got and stayed after he fell off that rocky tor into that boggy fen.

This inexplicable onslaught of death in nature, coupled with the disappearance of the lesser beasts, must have given the Celts pause for thought, especially the Druids, a Celtic religious group that paused for thought a lot more than your average barbarian. Druids could put up with a few fallen leaves and frozen rivers, but the sun had gone into hiding too, and in its place was a deathlike, partly cloudy, chance of showers through the weekend. The Druids weren't drizzle worshipers or overcast worshipers, they were sun worshipers, and the disappearance of the sun each October must have disturbed them no little. The effect was probably similar to what would happen today if the Japanese suddenly announced they were getting out of the electronics business for six months, but they were not at liberty to say why. There would be a lot of speculation.

One night in the midst of all this natural death, a group of Celts were squatting around a fire trying to keep warm. Then Llryybyrrdd, the mightiest Celt of them all (until a shoulder injury forced him to stay home with the women) took the Speaker's Turnip in his gnarled hands, and spoke. "This is our fault somehow," he mused. "We have offended the sun, or the Great God Lug, or our ancestors. Somebody's pissed off, that's for sure."

There was a murmur of assent among the others, until the ancient wizard Howrrbokk rose slowly to his feet, shaking his huge bald head back and forth like a melon, if there were such things as melons. "We Celts haven't done anything wrong, Llryybyrrdd! Au contraire! Look at what we've accomplished! We discovered how to make iron before a lot of other cultures, we're alone amongst Indo-European peoples in using prose in epic narratives and just using verse for lyric poetry, we dig nice, big burial mounds, and our language has done more to popularize the consonant than any other language! True, compared to the Chinese we're bog-sucking root eaters, but still we Celts are Number

One, and we're going to stay that way until the Romans get here. Stop this negative thinking and get with the pre-times, Llryybyrrdd! Do you want to be a barbarian all your life?"

"Well, it has to be somebody's fault," Llryybyrrdd grumbled. "Everything is somebody's fault. Who can we blame? You, Howrrbokk? You're the big wizard, make the clouds go away, bring back the sun and the stoats and the newts!" And with that the rest of the firewatchers began to sharpen their swords and look at Howrrbokk without fondness.

"Wait!" exclaimed the object of their disaffections. "If the world around us is dying, then the spirits of the dead are responsible! Whose fault is it when ten people die suddenly in the village? It's the fault of the person who dies first, because his spirit calls the others to him. Everybody knows that!" (And in a sense he was right, because the first man brought the disease that killed the rest. Similar reasoning was used to explain death by plague in the Greater Transylvania area some years later. Igor dies, and soon many others are dying. Igor has obviously become Undead and is sneaking out of his grave at night to kill everybody else. So they dug up Igor and then reburied him facedown, staked through the heart, without his head, and so on.)

Meanwhile, back at the campfire, the boys decided to agree with their ancient wizard, although they kept their swords handy. They concluded that for some reason in late October the natural barrier was down between the Real World and the Other World of the Dead and Nasty, or at least the barrier had become easy to cross. As a result, evil spirits were abroad in the land, probably the ghosts of those who had been mistreated in life or inadequately acclaimed in death (poorly mounded burial mounds, possibly.) It was these unhappy ghosts who were doing evil to the trees and the streams and especially the sun. And once you accept the premise that the spirits of the dead have such power on earth it becomes fairly easy to blame those spirits for all the bad things that happen to you. Suddenly all misfortune, from Uncle GwyynUrr's header into the fen to Llryybyrrdd's bum shoulder, was the work of these October spirits. The furry little creatures of the forest knew. That's why they hid for months. But the mighty Celts were not about to hide like hedgehogs from the spirits of their ancestors. They would do something.

Fortunately for the parents of the future, the Celts passed on the option of digging up their late loved ones and doing disgusting things to their corpses, or Halloween would be a whole lot messier today. The Celts were trying to get rid of the dead, not air them out. So instead they decided that a party was called for, a yearly night of remembrance for the dead, with a witch's sabbath to follow. The less sophisticated spirits would mistakenly assume the party was in their honor and be appeased. But the real purpose of the party was not to celebrate the evil spirits. Appeasement was not the Celtic tradition—or anybody else's tradition back then. The various party events were meant to drive the witches and evil spirits away through trickery and treatery.

The Druids were put in charge of the festivities because it was generally agreed that the Druids gave the best parties. And besides, they were already hosting the biggest festival of the year on November first, an annual New Year's dinner dance and sacrifice called Samhain. Tacking on a Festival of the Dead the evening before was as easy as adding a line to a few posters.

The first thing the Druids did was call for huge bonfires to be built on the hills around the villages. They said it was to combat the powers of darkness, confuse the evil spirits, and show the Druidic affinity with the biggest fire of them all, the sun. But it's also true that throughout history, when you get a bunch of guys together thinking up things to do, nobody ever says "no" to the suggestion of a huge bonfire.

Fire was also their execution of choice for witches. They assumed that a witch flying by on the way to the big Witch's Sabbath would look down and see a large fire and hear Druids carefully chosen for their loud voices shouting, "Throw another witch on the fire!" and this would send them scurrying back to wherever it is witches come from. (Why is it witches always seem to be in transit?)

In much later years, boys would go door-to-door in Celt Country saying "Gie's us a peat to burn the witches," or more simply, "Trick or peat!" Burn the Witch, in fact, became one of the most popular and long-lived Samhain eve events. According to F. Marion McNeill's *Hallowe'en: Its Origins, Rites and Ceremonies in the Scottish Tradition,* one of the high points of Queen Victoria's year was the annual witch burning in the courtyard of Balmoral Castle, where she was seen to giggle like a schoolgirl before the big fire. She even tossed a faggot or two in the direction of the blaze herself. They did not use a real witch at Balmoral, although I should imagine Lady Isabel Burton was nervous as a cat every October.

Besides "orgiastic rites"—another suggestion guys the world over have always had a hard time turning down—the one other significant event of Samhain eve was dress-up. Various citizens would disguise themselves in the most horrible ways as the spirits of the dead. These faux phantasms would then wander around playing tricks on the populace, tricks that were unpleasant but not quite lethal. The theory was that real spirits passing by would see their colleagues working a particular neighborhood and move on to less competitive territory.

A thousand years later the early Christians pulled one of their most successful tricks, that of sticking in a Christian festival at the same time as a pagan one. In this way the ancient Nordic festival of Yule, celebrating the winter solstice, just coincidentally turned out to occur at exactly the same time as Christ's birthday. And Samhain became All Hallows' Day, with the night before All Hallows' Eve, or Halloween.

That's why every year American parents find themselves in variety stores spending $49.95 for light-reflective/fire-retardant/all-plastic/ size 4 Ninja Turtle costumes, complete with E-Z-See masks; why on Halloween night I stumble around my neighborhood carrying a flashlight (instead of lighting a nice big bonfire) and my children feel perfectly justified extorting sweets from the neighbors; why I hang a cardboard cadaver on my front door, the sheet of a dead person in my living room window, and a flying rodent from my oak tree while the guy across the street puts five flaming orange vegetables on his front porch because he doesn't know that to be historically accurate they should be turnips and not pumpkins.

There seem to be only two groups in America who have retained any sense of what Halloween is really all about. First are those religious extremists (at least I think they're extreme) who insist that the event is dripping with devil worship and should be abolished. And though they apparently know their Halloween history, I think they misread it completely. The Halloween origins described before are fanciful. For all I know Samhain was conceived late one night in the back room of the Celtic Convention and Visitors' Bureau as a way to attract tourists, just as the big operators in Atlantic City thought the world needed Miss America, and they needed an extra week of business. But the basic facts (spirits coming, scared to death) are accurate, and would seem to indicate that the Celts were trying to drive the devils away, not worship them.

The second group of Americans who still take Halloween seriously is far less organized than the "Let's Get the Hell Out of Helloween" bunch. According to a *Wall Street Journal* article of a few years ago, Halloween night is psychologically terrifying for some people, maybe even millions of people. Dr. Donald Dossey, a psychologist and owner/ operator of the Phobia Institute/Stress Management Centers in (here's a surprise) southern California, has named this previously unnamed dread. He calls it Samhainophobia. The most common fear among Samhainophobes is the fear of witches—wicaphobia—because witches subconsciously remind us of Mom.

Stay with me here. As infants, when Mom brings us the bottle or changes our Huggies, she is the Good Mother, but when we cry and she doesn't show up, she is the Bad Mother, or witch. We wee babes eventually figure out that Good Mom and Bad Witch are the same person, which is even more frightening because it means Glinda can turn into the Wicked Witch of the West at any time and we're up the creek without a bucket. And though eventually most of us realize that the bad witch isn't that bad (and the Good Mom isn't that good? Sorry, Mom) somewhere deep in their psyches wicophobic Samhainophobes never quite believe it. And that's why the expression "A wicophobic Samhainophobe's best friend is his mother" never really caught on.

It may sound like Dr. Dossey is trying to drum up a little business for the old Phobia Institute/Stress Management Center, but some organizations take him seriously. Universal Studios, the people who brought us *Frankenstein, Dracula, Psycho,* and *Jaws* and therefore know something about scaring people, now operates America's third most popular tourist attraction, Universal Studios Hollywood, the famed backlot tour. Each Halloween, Universal hosts a giant graveyard party featuring chain saw wielding maniacs doing roadside surgery and people being eaten alive by real rats. But to accommodate those Samhainophobes who might suddenly get in touch with their true feelings and start beating up the rented monsters, Universal hires a team of psychologists to stand by when the Halloween show is playing. (Only in America, and maybe only in southern California, would you ever see an actor come out on stage and say, "Is there a psychologist in the house?") Down the road at the theme park competition, Knott's Berry Farm, roving packs of psychologists have not been summoned, but the Knotts' "Halloween Haunt" manager is quoted in the *Journal* article reassuring potential guests that Berry Farm werewolves and goblins have received sensitivity training.

Despite a few fools and phobics, however, there's no question we've purposely drained all the death out of our only nationwide death festival. I'm not pushing for the return of witch burning, bonfire lighting, or even orgiastic rites. Nor do I think we should try to convince our children or ourselves that there are real spirits floating above us on All Hallows' Eve, just waiting to swoop down and transform the population into warty toads and small pools of grease. But I would suggest that by turning Halloween into a sales opportunity for costume and candy drummers, and not much else, we have lost something valuable; the opportunity to confront death, our fear of it, and some of the possible ways to lessen that fear in a relatively painless way. Or in the words of some of the great thinkers of the 1970s, "Halloween could be a big help in finding our oneness with the spirit world, but we've blown it."

This especially applies to our kids. I don't know what Mom and Dad Celt told their little barbarians about death. Given that much of what we know about the Celts comes from excavating their elaborate burial mounds, chances are good that Celt tots were well acquainted with the subject from an early age. "Where's Dad?" "Out digging another burial mound, eat your gruel" was probably a fairly common exchange around the Celtic midden. Also, with the high mortality rate and frequent hostilities, your average barbarian-on-the-moor saw and buried a lot of bodies in the course of his or her short lifetime. So they didn't need Samhain Eve as a conversational starter. But we do.

What real chance do I have to acquaint my children with the notion that all things must end, including them, before that reality hits them like a two-by-four between the eyes? As the late goldfish goes in the toilet? Standing around Grandma's open casket, gazing down on a face caked with Max Factor #2, a face over which someone has labored hard to make her look *not dead, only sleeping?*

Perhaps I can work it into the conversation around the television, which (let's face it) is where most kids are at any given moment. Just slip in the cassette of *Halloween Part Three,* wait thirty seconds for the first teenager to get nailed, and then hit the pause button. As we all sit watching the frozen image of a marlin spike piercing a teen sternum, I can remark in an offhand way, "You know kids, someday this is going to happen to you. . . . "

Then there is the question of ancestors, and the roles they play in society after they become ancestors. Regardless of a particular family's belief in the life everlasting, in my culture most children and adults rarely have a sense that they are part of a continuing chronicle of experience; not just another stop on the genetic line but an advancement of the metaphysical line as well. Not long ago my son Ned and I were talking about his great grandfather, a political scientist and anthropologist named Linden Mander, who died in 1967. Ned has always been curious about him, partly because he's named Nathaniel Linden Palmer in that splendid man's honor, and partly because he realizes that Grandpa Linden is the only ancestor his father still truly mourns.

I was rambling on about how his great grandfather had come to the United States from Australia to teach, how he was a man who believed so profoundly in the elimination of world hunger that one year he announced that all the money he was going to spend on Christmas gifts for his relatives he would instead donate to UNICEF. Even though I was ten at the time and *very* fond of gifts, I bought the concept, because Linden Mander was the kind of man who could sell it, and also the kind of man who actually did it every year thereafter until he died.

"Yes," Ned said, "you told me all that already. But what did you learn from him?"

Ned is a Down's syndrome eleven-year-old. Like many developmentally disabled people I've known, he has the ability to cut through crap in the simplest, sweetest ways, possibly because he doesn't realize that's what he's doing and therefore doesn't push for it. I tried to answer his question that day, and I will be trying to answer it for both of us as long as we live. I would like him to think that the spirit of his great grandfather is still alive in our hearts and minds, if not hovering above our heads. I want Ned to understand that this man who died fifteen years before he was born will still have an effect on his life, through me. But the task would be a lot easier if we were Japanese.

•

When the Buddhists came to Japan in the sixth century, they brought with them a rite for the dead called Ullambana, which eventually became Obon, the Japanese Festival of the Spirits, or the Oshorai-san. The festival originated in an ancient legend concerning a follower of Buddha who had a near-Mom experience. In a vision he saw his deceased mother suffering from starvation in the Land of the Dead. The follower went to Buddha and asked what he could do for his mom, and Buddha told him to hold a memorial service in her honor. He did, and Mom was saved. Or, because she was already dead, it's probably more accurate to say Mom was served.

Nowadays Obon is celebrated in different ways in different places and even at different times, but the emphasis is always the same. Traditional Japanese believe their ancestors are watching over all that happens in the world, apparently even those ancestors in eternal agony because their descendants have failed to hold the proper memorial services. Obon is the time to welcome the ancestors back, honor them, and then send them away again.

At least that's the way it should be. Some Japanese have lamented recently that the traditional Obon Festival is dying, especially in the big cities. It has become a time for just the living members of families to gather together, rather like the American Thanksgiving. And like Thanksgiving, although ancestors are discussed and remembered, they aren't particularly honored and they certainly aren't presumed to be present, in spirit or any other way. It's more of a "how about the time Uncle Kunio dropped that huge bowl of cranberry sauce on Aunt Reiko?" kind of remembrance.

There are still thousands of believers, however, and a good place to find them is Kyoto. This is a city that continues to take its Obon Festival seriously, including holding the event when tradition says it should be held, in August, the seventh month of the lunar calendar. (Tokyo has chosen the seventh month of the solar calendar, and therefore celebrates the Obon Festival in July. So a spirit with descendants in both Tokyo and Kyoto can pretty much plan to spend the whole summer on the road. Or above it.)

Kyoto, the capital and focal point for Japanese Buddhism for a millennium, is a pork chop–shaped metropolis of more than 2.5 million people, most famous as the site of hundreds of temples. There are huge, breathtaking religious palaces where clusters of monks, tourists, and monk-tourists walk around whispering, and tiny temples on very narrow side streets, tucked in behind fish markets and camera stores. In such places you can step out of a brand-new Toyota taxi right into the twelfth century.

One of the slightly larger pocket temples is the Rokudo Chinko-Ji, overseen by a charming eighty-year-old Zen priest named Sakaida Koshu. He has lived at Rokudo Chinko-Ji since he was eleven and, like Bob Wilkins in London, literally knows where the bodies are buried around the place. Obon is his busy season, because of the bell.

"There are things you must do for Obon," he tells me over tea. "You must clean your ancestors' graves on the eighth day of the month so they see that you care for them. At the same time, and for the same reason, you must also build an altar in your home in their honor. And then you must let your ancestors know you are ready for their arrival. You must come here and ring the bell."

He volunteers to ring the bell for me, even though we're a few days past bell-ringing season. Out we go to the temple's interior courtyard; the little old monk, the little old monk's little old attendant holding an umbrella over his master, and me, feeling like two tons of big Caucasian.

Before us is the bell. It's a very old, medium-sized bell in a ten-foot-tall bell tower, with a rope attached to a log sticking out the side of the tower so you can hit the bell. From what I can see of it, it doesn't look any different than a lot of other temple bells. But long ago Rokudo Chinko-Ji was at the entrance to a famous burial ground called Toribeno. The crossroads between temple and cemetery was considered the border between this world and the next. Kyotoites believe that this strategically placed temple bell's tones are so sonorous "they reach to the deepest hells." This is, in other words, the only bell on earth that can be heard on the Other Side. As a result, for three days at the start of Obon, from 6:00 A.M. to midnight, Kyotoites line up around the block to take a whack at Sakaida Koshu's bell and call their ancestors home.

"Have the neighbors ever complained?"

"They wouldn't dare."

He gives the bell rope a solid pull, producing a full, fuzzy note. Then back he goes inside to wait for next year's bell season, and eventually the day when he dies and the bell tolls for he.

I went to two other Obon events in Kyoto. The cemetery of Higashi Otani-san rises up steep hills behind yet another temple. The gravestones are very close together, so it looks like four million people are buried here, and there may be. Every year for Obon, volunteers string thousands of candle-laden paper lanterns along the graves and narrow paths. As night falls this mountain of death turns into a glittering, magical place. Families stand and chat beside the freshly cleaned graves of their ancestors. But whether they're chatting with each other, their neighbors at the next grave, or the spirits of their ancestors, I don't know. Though I know what I'd like to believe.

The bell, grave cleaning, and home altar building encourage the ancestral spirits to return for Obon. However, they are not invited to stay, so Obon's end is meant to gently but firmly say farewell. This invitation to depart is accomplished in Kyoto principally through big bonfires on hillsides that light the way back to the spirit world. The Celts would understand.

On August 16, the last night of Obon, I was standing with about a thousand other people on a bridge over a river on the east side of town. It is here, according to legend, that the spirits of the dead embark for "the pure lands of the bodhisattvas and buddhas." It is also here, according to the August issue of the *Kyoto Visitor's Guide,* that we Kyoto visitors can get the best view of the best bonfire.

There are actually five fires, collectively called the Gozan Okuribi— "the five mountain send-off fires." They are built high on the surrounding hillsides by special fire preservation groups composed of families that live at the base of each hill, usually people who have been building these fires for generations. The fires are now officially designated by the government as "Intangible Folk Properties," so the preservation groups get financial assistance from the city to build them. And they probably need the money for wood and labor. I'm talking very big fires here.

Each fire is in the shape of a Chinese character, so each has a name and a meaning—no generic big fires for these folks. The fires are Torii, or "Shinto Gate"; Myo and Ho, which stand for "The Supreme Law of Buddha"; Funa-Gata, or "Ship"; Dai, meaning "Great" or "Big"; and Hidari Daimonji, which is just like Dai but on the hillside to the left and smaller, so the name means approximately "Great or Big to the Left and Not Quite So Great or Big." You used to be able to see all the fires from downtown Kyoto, but as the urban core grew in space and height that became impossible. Now Obon fire fans have to pick their conflagration. The undisputed favorite is Dai on Mt. Daimonji, the first fire to be lit and at 80 by 160 meters, the biggest of them all.

(One year Dai got a little too big. The figure is supposed to look like this 大 but a small forest fire started and Dai acquired an extra stroke, so it looked like this 犬 which is the character Inu and means "dog."

But given the animals Dai could have turned into, the departing ancestors had no cause to complain, and they didn't.)

Precisely at 8:00 P.M. a murmur went up from the crowd on the bridge as a small speck of light appeared on the mountainside. In just a few minutes Dai was full and fiery, and around me cameras started clicking. If this had been a crowd of Americans a lot of the cameras would have been using a flash to photograph a subject more than a mile away, the way Americans use their flash in football stadiums. But not these people. They knew their cameras.

The *Kyoto Visitor's Guide* warned me not to expect "the kind of merry-making that characterizes some of the country's other fire festivals." Kyotoites are bidding farewell to the spirits of their loved ones for another year, and therefore the bonfire ceremony is "tinged with sadness." True, I didn't see any merry-making, but I didn't see a bit of sadness, either. Most of the crowd on the bridge seemed to be young couples who were there because the alternative was another evening playing Pachinko or hanging around the karaoke bars singing "Rockin' Robin." They were quiet and respectful, but then compared to the teens I'm used to, Japanese adolescents always seem to be quiet and respectful. They may not believe it anymore, but they certainly act as if their ancestors are watching over them all the time, ready to swoop down at the slightest uncivilized behavior and rattle a few cups.

•

If the ancestors who visit during Taiwan's Ghost Festival rattled the cups, nobody would notice. Like Obon, the Ghost Festival (Chung Yuen) is the time of year when ancestors come back for tricks and treats. Graves are cleaned, home altars built, and a lot of food is put out for the spirits, who are apparently always hungry. But the Ghost Festival is a much noisier, more rambunctious event than Obon, at least where I was. The Taiwanese don't use a bell to summon their dead. They prefer explosions.

Keelung, a port city of a half million people on the north end of Taiwan, has become a principal center for national Ghost Festival activities due to the area's death history. Many Chinese escaped to Keelung when Mao took over their homeland, but the refugees' luck didn't change when they reached the city. Keelung is called "rainy harbor" because of the damp climate, a climate that encourages malaria-carrying mosquitoes that look as big as your thumb. In the past, tropical diseases were common in the area and many thousands of people died from them.

This was especially tragic for the immigrants, many without families to honor their memories. Lacking descendants, and also dying from disease, meant their ghosts became neither gods nor ancestors but instead turned into wandering spirits with no place in the social structure of the world of the dead. (This socially marginal afterlife status also applies to those who die by violence, accident, or suicide; people who die before they have children; and particularly people who have rotten kids who don't worship them.) It is these poor outcast ghosts who are especially celebrated during the Ghost Festival. Not because the living fear them, even though they are capable of mischief, but because they deserve compassion and pity. And the skies above Keelung are supposedly crawling with them.

My Keelung Ghost Festival events began with a parade through the center of town, a parade that looked like all the community festival parades I've ever seen, from the Rose in Pasadena to the Chitlin Strut in Salley, South Carolina. The only difference was that everyone in the 3,653d Annual (I made that up) Keelung Ghost Festival Parade was Chinese and did Chinese stuff. About all that was missing was the presentation from Chinatown. I kept waiting for the Americatown float to go by, with Yankees in native dress playing harmonicas and singing a march tempo version of "Ghost Riders In the Sky." Never happened.

The Ghost Festival parade had an American feel but a Chinese face, rather like the McDonalds you now see all over Asia. Instead of the local high school band there were clusters of guys playing horns that intentionally sound like ducks. Instead of the Queen and Her Court riding along in new Buicks and waving there were acrobats leaping about. And instead of floats there were small trucks crammed full of members of important local families sitting around three-foot-tall, ornately decorated paper houses. I was to see those houses again.

The next event was in an area called Sea Watching Lane, and when I finally got there I found hundreds of people sea watching . . . nothing. But something was up. Next to the parking lot was a small beach, and on the cliff above the beach an Imax film crew had set up a camera the size of a bank vault. They walked around up there talking to each other on two-way radios, adjusting light standards up and down, handing film cans back and forth—all those things a camera crew does to look busy and important when there's nothing to do but wait.

And so we waited. Set up down the center of the parking lot was a long line of empty tables. Occasionally a car full of locals would arrive and plop one of those big paper houses on a table, along with food, fireworks, and stacks of play paper money. I'd seen the money before in Taipei. When burned it's a traditional gift for the ghosts.

And then all of a sudden the parking lot was chaos. The two dozen trucks from the parade all arrived at the same time, fluorescent lights flashing, car-mounted loudspeakers blaring music so overamplified the heaviest of heavy metal fans would have covered their ears, if they could find them. Soon there were thirty paper houses set up on the tables and thousands of milling paper house viewers in the parking lot. It then occurred to someone that what this event needed was more noise. So from the backs of the trucks came long rolled-up strings of firecrackers, five thousand firecrackers to a string and each firecracker the size of a ten-dollar roll of quarters. I know kids in America who would lick green slugs to get their hands on just a few of those babies around the Fourth of July—I used to be one of them—and here the Keelungians were going to set off whole strings at once. Which they did. In the middle of the parking lot. In the middle of the crowd. Around huge piles of burning play money that were consequently blown into the air, to drift slowly down and ignite the heads of the assembled. Small hair fires broke out and were quickly extinguished. It looked, smelled, sounded, and felt like hell, and it wasn't over yet. But one thing was already clear. This was not Fire Prevention Awareness Month in the greater Keelung area.

After every cracker had fired, the more athletic men from the trucks picked up their paper houses and ran down the rocky path to the beach, one family at a time. At water's edge they stuffed more funny money in the paper walls and rafters, carried the houses into the bay, set them afire, and then swam them out to sea until the houses were consumed by fire and sank, usually on top of the men swimming with them. All this was accomplished with such seriousness that you would have thought they were launching the admiral's barge of the Taiwanese Navy.

"Many of the ghosts are people who drowned," a young man in the crowd told me afterwards, eager to explain this interesting cultural event to the visiting foreigner. "The burning houses are for them, to show them we are thinking about them, to give them places to live in the spirit world."

"No, that's not right exactly," his girlfriend said. "The burning houses are gifts for the ghosts, but they are to encourage them to go away and not bother us anymore. And the farther out to sea a house goes before it sinks, the more luck the family who sent that one will have, because their bad ghosts will be farther away."

"No, please," the boy said, "they are houses for the drowned mostly. The smoke goes up for the ancestors, the house goes down for the drowned ones. A gift of farewell."

"Then they should just burn the money and not burn the houses. Why would the drowned want houses on fire?" asked the girl. "We are asking our ancestors to come stay in burning houses? We want them to go away."

"The ghosts are not ancestors, that's why they are ghosts. You must pay closer attention."

And then she said something in Chinese that I gathered was not entirely complimentary, and he responded in kind, and I slipped away before they started throwing firecrackers at each other.

The next evening I went to the last Ghost Festival event of the year in Keelung. I know this may be hard to believe, but it was a big bonfire. But where the Kyotoites (and presumably the Celts) liked their fires on hillsides some distance from the living but close to the dead, Keelungians are proximity people. I already knew that from the firecrackers, but it took a really big fire in the middle of a small downtown courtyard with hundreds of visitors five feet away to bring it home to me.

Monks chanted for an hour or so before the scheduled conflagration. A great deal of food was displayed but not eaten, including a whole pig that had been butchered and laid out to look like Superman when he's flying. Meanwhile, off in a corner of the courtyard across from the Chin An temple front steps, an actor was making up in garish black and white for the role of Zhong Kui, the ghost-wrangling exorcist whose work is the festival's symbolic big finish.

At the appointed hour the food was cleared. Then, without so much as a "Fire in the hole!" the Bic squad stepped up to ground zero and began flicking. This fire was also made up of paper houses, eight of them gathered in a tight semicircle, stuffed with about ninety kazillion dollars in funny money. Fire fans moved back quickly, especially those on the downwind side, as flames shot up twenty feet and still burning paper money floated over the assembled. It was brief but spectacular, terrifying for those of us who began learning "Fire Safety Tips" in the second grade, and an impossible act to follow. Off in the corner Zhong Kui went into his bit, but the fire and the audience were going out.

I would not presume to judge the effectiveness or sincerity of Obon and the Ghost Festival as death galas based on such short and superficial visits to both places. The events I saw looked like typical community creations meant solely to entertain the locals and attract the tourists, but that may be because I saw them as a tourist. While I watched paper houses burn, in the real houses nearby people who had too much sense to get anywhere near an exploding parking lot could have been using the occasion to talk of their dead, and of death itself. Believers don't always show up at rituals, especially if the rituals no longer have anything to do with belief. And besides, a meeting with one's ancestors should be private.

Before I left for Japan and Taiwan I heard the term "ancestor worship" a lot, but I never heard it from Asians themselves once I got there. It's an easy way to describe—and dismiss—a complex body of beliefs that seems alien and unsettling to Westerners. "Oh, a Ghost Festival," some people back home would say. "How quaint. But then those people are really into ancestor worship, you know." Yes, I guess "those people" are, but they may be right to make a special point of remembering their ancestors and celebrating their spirits. They may even be right to think that those ancestors have some kind of real presence and watch over them. And I'm not sure how alien that belief really is to my culture.

When the Public Broadcasting Service aired Ken Burns's documentary series "The Civil War" some years ago, one of the highlights of the programs was a letter written by Sullivan Ballou, a major in the Second Rhode Island Volunteers. It was the eve of the Battle of Bull Run, the first real engagement of the war. His letter was to his wife, and in it Major Ballou talked about the validity of the Union cause, and the chance he might not survive. Then he spoke to her directly, in a way no one who has read the letter will ever forget.

"Oh Sarah, if the dead can come back to this earth, and flit unseen around those they love, I shall always be with you, in the brightest day and the darkest night, always, always. And when the soft breeze fans your cheek, it shall be my breath, or the cool air your throbbing temple, it shall be my spirit passing by."

Sullivan Ballou died a week later. And did Sarah Ballou feel his spirit? We'll never know for sure, of course. But consider this. The day after that episode of "The Civil War" was broadcast, I called the Rhode Island Historical Society to find out more about the Ballous. When her husband died, Sarah Ballou was a young, handsome woman with two sons. She raised their boys to be honorable men, as her husband hoped she would. And though she lived for fifty-seven years after his death, she did not remarry.

CHAPTER FOUR

THE NIGHT OF THE DEAD

During the Vietnam War many Americans were convinced or convinced themselves that the Vietnamese didn't care about dying as much as we did. That was the explanation for Buddhist monks immolating themselves in the streets of Saigon, and eventually for Hanoi continuing to pursue this "hopeless" war against the all-powerful United States. Such a ludicrous propaganda contention had its historical precedents, most immediately in some Americans' beliefs about the Japanese attitude toward death in the Second World War, and death and the Koreans during the Korean conflict. And the "death as nothing" bit has had its historic successors as well. During the Gulf War I heard more than one commentator trying to explain the nature of personal sacrifice in a "holy war" to Western audiences, and the subtext of the remarks was always "them Arabs don't care about dying as much as we do."

Like all successful propaganda, there is just enough truth in the lie to make it something fools believe and nonfools will accept, at least for the duration of the conflict. Of course other cultures care about dying as much as Americans do, but they care in different ways. And as I've learned many times over on this Trip, the death rites, rituals, and relationships of any culture almost always looks weird to any other culture.

Like exhumation and reburial. It seems like half the people on earth practice it, and the other half think it's about as peculiar as you can get while still standing up. Rather like what Churchill said about sodomy in

Britain: half the people think it can't be done, and half the people are doing it.

The most common accusation about other cultures' views of death comes in two contradictory parts. First, Group A says that the people of Group B don't care whether they die or not, and are willing to sacrifice everything for the slightest reasons. And second, Group A says that Group B is obsessed with death. Group B responds that Group A thinks they are obsessed with death because Group A *is* obsessed with death and in psychological self-defense accuses everybody else of their own problem. "Wow," says Group C, "look at those As and Bs go at it. Those people are obsessed!"

As far as death is concerned, I don't think anyone can define what's obsessive and what isn't, especially on a national or cultural level. But there is at least one place I visited that admits to an obsession with death, and once a year even revels in it. That yearly event may just be *the* Death festival of the planet, the one to which you have to compare all the others.

In the early afternoon of the day of The Night, Maria Guillen goes to the cemetery in Tzintzuntzan, Mexico. Even though the graves are just fifty yards up the highway from her small room, the journey takes a long time. Maria is very old, and she has nothing else to do.

Once she reaches the cemetery wall, I watch her stand outside for a long time, looking over at the grave of her husband, José. It's a simple mound of earth covered with a year's growth of weeds, surrounded by a dilapidated picket fence. Finally she goes in to do what she must. Visitors are coming, but only a few will notice the final resting place of José Guillen. It's not one of the famous graves, not one you see on the postcards. But once a year Maria does what she can to make it presentable. Tradition demands it, and her husband's spirit expects it.

As she claws at the weeds, she peers at me suspiciously out of the corner of her eye. I am another stranger in a world that has become nothing but strangers to her. Just one of the difficulties of growing very old. I ask Maria what the Night of the Dead means to her, and she shoots me a look that clearly says "I've seen far too much to answer questions about what anything *means* to me from the likes of you." Maria is not in the mood to get in touch with her feelings.

"I'm the last of my family," she says finally. "I'm waiting to die and go to heaven."

And who will clean her grave for the Night of the Dead when she is gone?

"What do I care, if I'm in heaven? There's no one here to care for me now, so there will be no one here after I am dead. I will get to heaven and stay there."

With the edge of her shoe she scrapes bits of newspaper and broken bottles off the flat, unmarked ground outside the fence. Her two sons are buried here, next to José. All her life, all her history are in this one small place.

"That will do for now," she says, not to me but to José. She starts walking slowly back down the road toward home. Maria will come back later to put marigolds and the few candles she can afford on her family's grave, but not until dusk. Another woman tells me that flowers and candles left too early in the day disappear onto other family's graves by the Night.

"Spirits?"

"No. Thieves. Not people from Tzintzuntzan. From everywhere else."

Before 1971 Tzintzuntzan's fame was all in the past. For centuries it was a capital city, where as many as forty thousand Tarascans (more properly called Purepechans) managed a vast empire. For a place named for the sound of hummingbird wings, it was a real power center. But the sixteenth-century Spanish conquest of Mexico changed forever the status of the town and its inhabitants. Ten miles away an insignificant village called Patzcuaro became the dominant colonial city in the region, and Tzintzuntzan went into a decline that continues.

Now, 364 days a year, Tzintzuntzan looks like little more than a minor diversion on Highway 35. Other than the big American-style arts and crafts center, there are only a few shops open, and they are dark and forbidding. The single-story adobe homes all have their backs to the streets. Beyond the walls are inner courtyards, filled with chickens, fruit trees, and kids. But you can't see the courtyards unless the doors are left open, and that doesn't happen often here. Tzintzuntzenos keep to themselves. It is only their ancestors they wish visitors to consider, and then only one night a year. On that night, Tzintzuntzan is once again the capital—the capital of death.

The Days of the Dead have been celebrated in Mexico for a long time, although exactly how long is open to debate. Some scholars believe that various features of the festival, like death effigies in Oaxaca, have survived from pre-Columbian rituals. But the more cynical contend that the "ancient" origins of the Days are strictly a concoction of Mexican tourist officials trying to make the whole package a little more attractive to tourists. ("A Little Bit o' History, a Little Bit o' Death! It's Waiting for You in Sunny Central Mexico!"—something like that.) For the disbelievers, Los Dias de Todos Muertos are principally the combination of the Roman Catholic All Saints' and All Souls' days and what Octavio Paz called in *The Labyrinth of Solitude* his countrymen's enduring fascination with death, "one of his favorite toys and his most steadfast love."

In the old days in the state of Michoacan, which includes Tzint-zuntzan and Patzcuaro, visitors usually watched Mexican death-love manifested on the island of Janitzio, rising appropriately like a burial mound in huge Lake Patzcuaro. But in 1971 the Michoacan govern-ment agencies overseeing tourism, culture, and the arts joined forces to make the Days a statewide attraction. And with a sense of the promo-tionally dramatic Lloyd "Toxie" Kaufman himself might admire, they renamed Michoacan's festivities La Noche de Muertos—the *Night* of the Dead. Tzintzuntzan was a natural for their promotional efforts. It was historically important, cemetery-accessible, and gorged with local color. (Involuntarily, Maria Guillen was spending her twilight years as local color. If she realized it, she would not be amused.) Tzintzuntzan even had an ancient Purepechan pyramid, called a *yacatas*, that you could actually see from the cemetery! True, the cemetery didn't have a convenient nearby parking lot, and Tzintzuntzan was lacking the kinds of hotels and resorts a truly first-class death destination should have, but when you give the people what they want, they'll park and sleep anywhere. Then all you need is more cops.

What effect these governmental doings had on the Tzintzuntzenos is hard to tell. Chances are none of it meant a damn to the Maria Guillen, but possibly the younger folks spent a bit more time sprucing up, what with additional company coming—additional living company. I watched families work for hours in the Tzintzuntzan graveyard, comb-ing the mounds of earth and then scrubbing the white marble slabs until you could eat off them, which they actually did at dusk. The im-mediate area around each tomb was weeded and raked, but only the very immediate area. A family would work all day on a grave, but ig-nore a pile of trash an inch over their burial plot boundary line.

Most Tzintzuntzenos find it neither hard nor somber labor. For the Lucases—grandpa, his son- and daughter-in-law, and their five chil-dren—trying to get corn out of ten rocky acres of family farm is hard, so once a year caring for a twelve-by-twelve-foot burial plot that they don't want anything to come out of is child's play. They bring a bucket of water for scrubbing, a rake for mound maintenance, and a boom box for entertainment. Grandpa goes right to work on the earthen mound covering his late wife, raking the brown soil over and over again with the care of a Tibetan monk creating a sand mandala. His son props the boom box on the back of an adjacent headstone, tunes in something sprightly, and then he and his wife begin scrubbing the mar-ble tomb of his brother. After a few minutes watching their elders work and pretending to help, this child's play actually becomes child's play. The little Lucases start a game of tag, laughing and shouting to each other as they run up, down, and around the small dirt and marble hills. As it gets darker, the game changes to hide-and-seek. Graveyards at dusk are excellent places to play hide-and-seek, something these kids know and most American kids probably will never know.

"The Night of the Dead is good for families," Mrs. Lucas says. "It gives us a reason to talk about death with our children, so they are used to it before it happens to one of us. They are not afraid of it. And they get a feeling for the family, too. That it's not just the living, it's still my mother and my husband's brother and the baby they did not know."

Grandpa Lucas says La Noche de Muertos is also good for both the spirits who will be coming back, and the town. When the spirits see their clean, beautifully decorated graves, they will know their descendants still care about them and they will be happy. "The tourists will be happy too, to see what we have done," he says. "Nobody wants a cemetery full of angry spirits and disappointed tourists on the Night of the Dead."

The Tzintzuntzan Night will be something special this year because one of the major players is in his rookie season. Town priest Efren Cervantes, a dark, intense, hardworking young man, has recently been reassigned from Guaunajuato up north. He's never seen the Night of the Dead vigil in Tzintzuntzan or anywhere else. He's certainly never seen thousands of tourists tromping through a graveyard, but then neither have I. (It's about the only thing we have in common, other than a fondness for Ford pickup trucks. Father Cervantes' is blue, with a sticker on the rear bumper that says "¡Yo ♥ Tzintzuntzan!" He uses the truck constantly to visit the dozen other towns and villages in the area that are also his spiritual responsibility.)

Back in 1971, it was Father Cervantes' predecessor who first asked the government to include Tzintzuntzan in official Night of the Dead promotions, a request he came to regret as the succeeding years' visiting horde grew bigger and bigger. But Father Cervantes doesn't hear the thunder of tourist hooves . . . yet. His only concern is that the real purpose of the Night not get lost amidst the merry-making.

Sitting in the church atrium, under the first olive trees planted in the Americas, he discreetly inquires as to my religious affiliation. And when I answer "lapsed Unitarian" he says "Ah!" and becomes a shade more intense. "Soon I must leave for Patzcuaro," he says.

I get his drift, and begin.

"Does the competitive aspect of the Night of the Dead bother you at all?"

"Competitive aspect?" Father Cervantes looks confused. "What competitive aspect?"

"Between villages. Even between families. I'm told that families com-
pete to see who can decorate their ancestors' graves in the most spectacular ways. And nobody in Tzintzuntzan will say anything good
about what they do tonight in Janitzio, and vice versa. They agree,
though, that the Days of the Dead in Oaxaca are no good, just a show
for the tourists."

Father Cervantes begins shaking his head halfway through the translation. "This has nothing to do with competition, or tourists," he says
with conviction. "The Night of the Dead is the people's affirmation of
the glorious life after death." He speaks carefully, so even Unitarians
can understand, and then rises to leave.

Well, we didn't learn much in the Liberal Religious Unitarian Youth,
but we did learn not to be intimidated by priests. Psychotherapists, yes;
priests, no. So I try again.

"But Father, what about the humor in this—the funny artwork and
the Old Man's Dance and all that? Aren't your people trying to show
that death doesn't frighten them, that in fact they can laugh at it?"

Father Cervantes turns and sighs a very long, priestly sigh. "There is
no fun. There is no humor. We are not afraid of death because we know
a better life awaits us with the Lord. That's what you will see tonight.
Nothing more, nothing less." And he's off at a trot for the blue Ford.

An hour later, ten miles away, I walked into the Patzcuaro town
square for the first time. Patzcuaro actually has three downtown plazas,
but for the week preceding the Night of the Dead, Plaza Don Vasco de
Quiroga is the only one that matters as far as visitors are concerned.
Artists from all over Michoacan fill the two-block-long rectangle with
their death work. It's what Main Street in Disneyland would look like if
Walt had been a necrophiliac.

Along one side of the plaza are dozens of marigold peddlers, selling
the bright orange flowers as fast as they can get them off the trucks.
The narrow streets nearby are clogged with tough old women carrying
gigantic loads of flowers to and fro on their backs. They look like huge,
walking nosegays. The flowers have a meaning besides decoration. Cut
flowers, the old women say, are the perfect decoration for the events to
come. The marigolds look fresh and alive, but they are dead, decapitated in their prime. And combined with the proper incense, marigolds
smell like old bones. The old women find this idea extremely amusing.

On the wide porch of the government offices that make up the east
side of the plaza, children are selling the most famous Michoacan
Night of the Dead offering, small human skulls made of sugar and
glue. Some skulls are unadorned, white and ghostly, while others have
a few features outlined in bright paint; red for the teeth, blue around

the eye sockets. Tables and benches are covered with hundreds of these nearly identical little heads, interspersed with candy angels and the occasional edible crucifix.

The most spectacular death art is down in the plaza itself. Pottery skeletons are everywhere, playing baseball, sunbathing, watching television, having babies. Candelabras three feet high look like femurs sticking up through the tops of skulls. Large round plates are decorated with skull-head tarantulas picking amongst scattered human remains, and a charming portrait of a smiling, fleshless bride. At least I thought she was charming enough to buy. My wife has never allowed me to display my purchase in any place in our home where even the dog might see it. (I have discovered in my researches that the fun-loving spirit of the Night of the Dead art is very difficult to pass on to those who weren't there.)

The artists in papier-mâché seem to favor cadaverous groups, like twenty skeletons riding in a bone yacht, and a jury deliberating in a coffin. Patzcuaro's plaza may be the only place on earth where the discerning shopper can choose from ten different versions of an all-skeleton papier-mâché Last Supper. For children there are marionette skulls with jaws that flap and little wooden coffins with strings sticking out one end. When you pull the string a clay cadaver pops out of the coffin.

During sales week the artists sleep at night on the plaza benches, in their cars parked nearby, or with local relatives. Whole villages come to Patzcuaro together for this annual chance to sell their wares. Prices range from a few pennies for the candy skulls to five-hundred dollars for a papier-mâché skeleton obstetrician slapping a skeleton newborn. But you can always dicker, no matter how foolish you feel doing it.

"How much for the little skeleton sitting on the toilet?" a large American wearing a Chicago Bulls sweatshirt inquires of a ceramicist. When told twenty dollars, he goes into his astounded act, offers fifteen and settles for seventeen. Away goes the defecating cadaver, to sit on the back of a real toilet in Evanston. Nearby I listen to a woman argue for half an hour about the price of a large wooden crucifix featuring a papier-mâché Jesus. Only this artist is not so accommodating, and the woman and her friend stomp off empty-handed.

"C'mon Angela," says the friend just loud enough for the artist to hear, "there are plenty more crucifixes around the other side."

I have already paid my respects to the Michoacan Deputy Minister of Tourism, and now he walks up accompanied by a short, leathery man in his sixties. They both admire my bridal death plate, nodding and smiling. (These guys know what people should be allowed to put on their coffee table if they want to.) Then the short man makes a little speech, not in Spanish but in his native Tarascan language. He is from Uranden, an island in Lake Patzcuaro, but not a famous island like Janitzio. "He is inviting you to come visit," says the Deputy Minister.

"He says his ceremony is very traditional, very sacred, not for the tourists, as in Tzintzuntzan or Janitzio." The Minister translates this with a pained smile. He doesn't want to talk about intervillage rivalries any more than Father Cervantes does. "He would like you to come, to see their altars and their ceremony. He would like you to be the first-ever outsider to see these things on Uranden."

Having just said no to ten thousand different kinds of skeletal remains, it is a pleasure to say yes to this courtly, *living* human being.

•

From the mainland shore, Uranden island looks more like a peninsula with drainage problems. Here the lake is full of long grasses, lily pads, and medicinal leeches. Local entrepreneurs collect the leeches by hiring young boys from Uranden to wade up to their hips in the water, occasionally coming out to be de-leeched and then sent back in. The leeches are shipped all over the world, although I doubt the bottle labels include the interesting story of the leech harvest.

Now it is dusk and there are no young boys around. (Perhaps leech harvesting is seasonal work.) There doesn't seem to be anybody around, in fact, on shore or apparently on Uranden, a steep hillside a hundred yards away. I can see a dozen small houses over there, wedged between the ridges of the cliff or squatting on the lowlands below. The houses look modern, with electric lights visible, but everything else about the place says pre-Columbian, dugout canoe, native spearfishing country.

Finally a dugout canoe appears around the corner of the marsh, only as it gets closer I see that it's made out of fiberglass, powered not by colorful indigenous peoples with long poles but an elderly outboard motor. The man from the town square is alone at the helm, gently and easily maneuvering the bow into a soft spot on the lake bank. Five minutes later I'm walking up the path to the home of the Castillos.

Dimas Camilo Castillo has his own land for farming, nets for fishing, a fiberglass dugout canoe to fish from, a good wife named Gumezinda, good children and grandchildren whose names I didn't catch, two houses, and a cow. Among the four hundred Purepechans who live on Uranden, he is not El Hefe—that was the man in the square—but when decisions are made on the island, Dimas is in the room. He is a satisfied, proud man.

As assorted offspring look on, he shows me his immediate world, the three buildings that are his home. I peek into the low, dark structure that is entirely kitchen. Four women are inside, squatting in the dirt and intense heat while they make tamales as fast as they can. The women are surrounded by more children, who stare at this process as if they, like me, have never seen it before.

Outside another building Dimas's catch for the day is drying, hundreds of fish so small they'd fit easily into two paper lunch sacks. And inside that building is the reason he has invited me to his home. It is the Castillo family altar for La Noche de Muertos, filling the wall and covering the floor of most of the room.

Besides marigolds, the altar is principally about food—various kinds of fruit, bread loaves shaped like angels and crosses (called *pan de los muertos*), sugar skulls, and four full Coca-Cola bottles.

"The Coca-Cola is for the *angelitos*," Dimas explains, "the spirits of my dead children. They like Coca-Cola very much, so this is for them when they come back tonight. Also the candy. And the fruit is for my parents—my mother who likes bananas, my wife's father who likes oranges. If we didn't include these things every year, then the spirits would be angry. One year they pounded on the door and walls of this room for two days before the Night, trying to get in. It was Gumezinda's father, never a patient man, and he still isn't." Peeking through the door, Dimas's ten-year-old granddaughter nods solemnly. She remembers those two days well, and she believes.

But I wait for Dimas to give me the Big Wink, some sign that he knows this is a game, the Uranden equivalent of the Tooth Fairy and Santa Claus. Dimas is, in his time and place, a sophisticated, intelligent man who successfully deals with the hard work and harsh reality of daily survival. He fishes from a canoe, but with a Yamaha on the back. He owns just one cow, but he knows cattle like a Montana rancher. He doesn't seem to be a person who has the time or tendency to fantasize. But there is no wink, no sign. I think Dimas Castillo sincerely believes his ancestors are coming back to his house to be honored on the Night of the Dead; to eat his food, drink his Coca-Cola and see their surviving grandchildren, great grandchildren, brothers and sisters once again.

"When you die," I ask, "will you come back to frighten your children if their altar isn't adequate?"

"But that will never happen," he answers quickly. "Because I have given them so much. They will have the land, the nets, the boat. They will show gratitude for these things by creating magnificent altars for Gumezinda and myself, and we will accept them with honor." The ten-year-old nods again.

"And what food will you be looking for?"

Dimas thinks, then smiles. "Anything will be fine. And maybe some beer."

Gumezinda slides quietly into the room to put some of the new food on the altar. When I ask her what will happen to the eats after the Night is over, she looks at Dimas for permission to speak, and he nods.

"In two days we eat it ourselves. But it will have no taste because the spirits will take all the taste out of it tonight." Gumezinda, like her husband and family, believes.

The ritual on Uranden is not solely at the home altars. A small church sits on top of the island, right next to the community basketball court. The church has a loudspeaker system that can be heard throughout the island, and at 8:00 P.M. on the Night the people and spirits are called forth over that system. During the next hour the families arrive, slowly walking single file up Uranden's candlelit paths to emerge in the dim electric glow of the church courtyard. The fathers carry *arcos*, homemade latticework structures three or four feet tall, covered with marigolds, fruit, pan de los muertos and, if an angelito is involved, small toys. They carefully place the arcos around an altar set up against the church's courtyard wall while the mothers and young women kneel and pray. Most of the men stay in back, watching or talking quietly. Most of the children giggle at each other and me, or sneak off to play basketball in the big court just down the hill.

It is an occasion both solemn and social, halfway between a funeral and a church coffee hour. The praying women seem genuinely to grieve for their ancestors, yet nobody tries to get the basketball players back, or even cares that their shouts of "Gimme the ball!" and "Over here!" continually cut through the quiet night.

There are images I will never forget. The centerpiece of the altar is a sugar skull, not small like the tourist version but life-size, with an expression on its face of mild displeasure. A woman in her forties appears on the edge of the crowd, gently carrying an ancient-looking metal object in her hands. The men part, and she slowly threads her way through the kneeling women to the altar. She places the object on the ground and lights the material inside with a candle. It is an incense burner, obviously a village heirloom, and for a long time she blows softly on the coals, making clouds of sweet smoke that fill the courtyard.

The women stay kneeling during the actual service, conducted by island men because Uranden has no resident priest. At the end of the service the women all stand and move back to the edges of the courtyard, where their husbands are waiting. And left on the ground directly beneath the altar are two children, two little girls who have fallen sound asleep on a blanket at their mothers' sides. They look very sweet, as small sleeping children so often do. But given the event, the night, and the skull floating in the incense smoke just above their heads, they also look dead, like angelitos who have returned in spirit and body to drink Coca-Cola and be remembered. There is a sense of relief, a nervous laugh in the crowd when they suddenly wake, look around in embarrassment, and run to join their mothers.

•

A few miles away down the lake, Tzintzuntzan is entering hour four of the night-long cemetery vigil (*La Velacion*) that is the cornerstone of most Michoacan Night of the Dead events. Three hundred families sit quietly with their ancestors, sometimes praying or singing, but mostly just staring at each other or the graves. The tombstones have been decorated with dozens of marigolds and small yellow candles, with bigger white candles placed at the corners of each tomb. As on the Castillo family altar, some Tzintzuntzan graves also include the favorite objects or food of those below. One family has covered its grandparents with long white feathers that seem to float over the marble monument and glow in the flickering light; a beautiful, ethereal sight. And at any given moment there are two dozen tourists standing in line to see and photograph it.

Tzintzuntzan's cemetery is the death equivalent of Times Square on New Year's Eve. Tourists are everywhere, shouting to each other, laughing, kicking candles over in the dark as they stumble from grave to grave. A reporter from Michoacan television, wearing a canary-yellow suit, conducts interviews with the vigil keepers while visitors watch. The cemetery is separated into two sections by Highway 35, and since dusk that bisecting road has been bumper-to-bumper stop-and-go traffic. Five police officers try to keep vehicular order by constantly blowing their whistles. Horns honk and car radios blare in response. A different group of policemen keeps the civil peace, breaking up fights over parking places and "establishing a presence" with the drunk and near-drunk, many of them teenagers. Tour buses pull up every few minutes. Clutching bullhorns, the bus drivers shout to their departing passengers, "Don't forget the number of your bus, don't leave any valuables on the seats, and be back in an hour for the drive to Janitzio!" And off the visitors go, wielding Kodaks and camcorders, slogging through the deep mud that the graveyard's dark paths have become. When they find a particularly spectacular tomb or a picturesque local family, the tourists take snapshots of each other with the Local Color in the background to show to friends back home. And through it all the Tzintzuntzenos demonstrate remarkable powers of concentration. They rarely speak to the tourists or even acknowledge their presence, as if this massive herd of noisy strangers simply does not exist.

In the center of town nearby, thousands more tourists gather to eat, drink, and stand around. Along main street and even in the church atrium, taco and hot dog stands do a brisk business. Where Father

Cervantes and I sat and talked about faith and hope, a man is now selling Sno-Cones. Craftspeople work the crowd too, but sales are slow,
possibly because Tzintzuntzan's artists are only offering their traditional work tonight and not the cute death objects their customers
have read about in the Ministry of Tourism brochures.

"This is what I make," I hear a woodcarver say to a disappointed
shopper. "Not souvenirs. Those are in Patzcuaro."

Back in the cemetery, one of the night's big events is about to take
place. The Purepechan yacatas that looms on a hillside over the graves
has been covered with 1,500 diesel-fueled flares mounted in tin cans.
At 11:00 P.M. these *antotorchas* are lit, and the pyramid is illuminated
just enough so I can see from the graveyard that tourists are crawling
all over it too. (According to anthropologist Stanley Brandes, The Ceremonial Lighting of the Yacatas was the Ministry of Tourism's idea
back in the 1970s, to reinforce the pre-Columbian roots of the event.
When townspeople complained that the diesel oil was smelly and dirty,
the government substituted electric floodlights for one Night. But the
antotorchas were back the next year, not because the town wanted
them, but because the oil lamps "were more evocative of ancient times"
for the tourists, who were apparently under the impression that the indigenous peoples of central Mexico discovered diesel oil. It could be
worse for the Tzintzuntzenos, of course. There's room on the yacatas
for a hundred big diesel bonfires.)

The only other scheduled cemetery event happens at midnight. Father Cervantes celebrates mass from a makeshift altar in the middle of
the upper graveyard. Villagers kneel in front as tourists stand at the
back of the service and take advantage of this unique religious photo
opportunity. The only illumination besides candles and Instamatic
flashes is an old automobile headlight wired to a portable battery. It
glares over Father Cervantes as he glares over his flock, the visitors, the
graves, and not far away, the traffic jam, policemen, standby ambulance
and milling crowd. I don't know if he still thinks the scene before him
is strictly an expression of faith in the life everlasting. I do know he does
a brief, by-the-Book ceremony, and does not linger afterwards.

Across Mexico, especially in the urban areas, there are complaints
each year that the Day of the Dead is being overwhelmed by Halloween. Children go trick-or-treating now in Mexico City, wearing
Batman suits and similar costumes that have as little to do with the
Dead as the plastic habiliments worn by the kids in my neighborhood.
But what Mexican traditionalists really regret is that belief in the power
and presence of ancestors during this festival is disappearing along with
the traditions. I went to Tzintzuntzan because I was told the people

there still believed, or at least acted like it. Because of the milling throngs, that was impossible for me to determine in the Tzintzuntzan graveyard that night, whereas the faith of the people on Uranden was obvious. And yet Dimas and his fellow islanders didn't invite me to see their home altars and join their ceremony because of my winning ways. They have decided they want tourists too, a piece of the pie, and had been led to believe I could help, publicity-wise.

After the heartfelt ceremony here described, there was one other event on Uranden, down on the basketball court. It was "traditional Mexican music and dance," performed badly on electric guitars plugged into huge buzzing speakers. The concert, attended by the Deputy Minister of Tourism, selected officials and one depressed American, seemed to have all the authenticity of Mexico Night at the Knights of Columbus in Minneapolis. For me it was a sad affair, but I couldn't blame them a bit. A community that depends for part of its income on leeches harvested off the legs of young boys almost has an obligation to go after relatively harmless tourist dollars. I suppose I can always brag that I was there in the old days, when the Night of the Dead on Uranden was still "authentic," whatever that means.

Nor is it the fault of the Tzintzuntzenos that so many tourists—principally from Mexico City and Guadalajara, the very places Day of the Dead traditions are supposedly fading—choose their graveyard to see "a real old-fashioned La Noche de Muertos," as one bus driver described it. And if they try to make a few pesos on the deal it's understandable. Tzintzuntzan is a poor town of potters, carvers, and other craftspeople who have every right to merchandise the byproducts of their traditions. I can only hope that they don't lose sight of the purpose or the goal as my culture has—honoring the dead, becoming accustomed to death, believing in the power of the ancestors to affect us, if not physically, then at least spiritually and intellectually. While I stood in the graveyard that night, I thought of my grandfather, alone and unattended in dark Lakeview Cemetery in Seattle. And now when I think of Mexico, I think of a lady named Marcelina.

The grave of Marcelina Pichu Alonso is just inside the Tzintzuntzan cemetery wall, near both the feather grave and the highway. It's not a particularly outstanding presentation, just marigolds, candles, and a clean headstone. Marcelina died two months before the Night I was there, and was buried next to her sons. This is the first time in forty years that her husband, Juan Estrada Natorino, has kept the vigil without her. I see him standing alone, like a sentinel, in the shadows behind her grave. He is one of the very few people present in true mourning.

We chat, and to most of my questions he just nods. But he will talk about her.

"She was a good wife. Her life was not easy. She worked very hard."

"Do you feel her spirit here tonight? Is she with you now?"

"I believe she is with God," he says after a long pause. "And here?" He stares at me and is silent again. We stand together for a while, watching the crowd surge back and forth in front of us. A few people stop to peer at Marcelina's grave before moving on to the feathers. They look at Juan too, but turn away quickly. Unlike most of the other townspeople, he looks back. And there is an intensity in his eyes that isn't hostile, but I can see how graveyard funseekers find him a bit threatening. Other than his look, he doesn't react to anything. Behind us on the road there is a great deal of whistling, shouting, and laughing, but you would never know it to look at Juan Estrada Natorino.

For me, graveyards should be and usually are quiet, reverent, respectful places. So the Tzintzuntzan graveyard on the Night of the Dead seems like a grotesque insult to the people who are buried here, and their descendants and loved ones who have come to honor them. I am outraged, and I am wrong.

"Doesn't this make you angry?" I finally asked Juan Natorino. "The noise, all these people who have come so far just to stare at you?"

He is genuinely surprised. "Angry? Why should I be angry? I'm glad they're here. Tzintzuntzan is honored that they have come to see our tradition, to see our faith. It is an honor to Marcelina and my children, and all who are here."

I got up early the next morning to drive the three hundred kilometers from Patzcuaro to the Guadalajara airport. At 7:00 A.M., going through Tzintzuntzan for the last time, the town looked like an occupying army had just decamped after months in residence. Thousands of paper cups lay where they were dropped in the streets. Flies were already swarming around half-eaten tacos. Abandoned cars were everywhere. And on the road to the yacatas, I saw the ambulance with the flashing red lights in the same place it had been all night, waiting.

The graveyard was nearly empty by then. Smoke from a few trash fires drifted up in the morning light as the last families gathered up their blankets and candle holders and headed down the hill toward town, toward home. Driving slowly by, I could just see José Guillen's tombstone, and the stones of the Lucas family.

The Night of the Dead was over for the tourists and the people of Tzintzuntzan for another year. With one exception. Juan Estrada Natorino was still there, standing as he had all night long, with his memories, and his faith, and maybe, just maybe, with the spirit of his Marcelina.

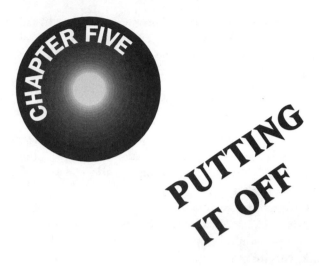

CHAPTER FIVE

PUTTING IT OFF

We seem to be afraid of two things. We fear dying because it sounds painful and upsetting, really quite unpleasant compared to, say, eating a pizza. And we fear death. But death itself isn't painful or traumatic. In fact, it's about as peaceful as you can get. If we define "live" as a biological organism that is not dead, and "dead" as just the opposite, then we all spend an extremely high percentage of eternity dead. By that definition, before I was born I was dead for a very, very long time, and it didn't bother me a bit. And after I die I will be dead again for what will probably be an even longer time, but that won't make any difference to me. My whole living existence will be exclusively the brief, intense period of time I actually spend standing up on the planet. And even then I'll invest quite a bit of my allotted living time lying down in a very deadlike way, probably six or seven hours a night. (The Dead, after all, are the most Perfect Sleepers, although given what's happening to them putrescence-wise you wouldn't exactly call it a Beauty Rest.) I'll even complain that I need more lying-down dead time and rarely get it. All those billions of years not being alive, and that two hundred thousand hours plus of near-dead sleeping haven't been painful or traumatic, so why should death be?

I don't know what there is about death (as opposed to dying) that frightens other people, but personally I have determined my principal fear. Boredom. I know it's a completely irrational perception, but being dead sounds like the most boring thing you could possibly be. Lying there with no books, no magazines, no television, nobody to talk to, nothing. Like a really awful Eternity Getaway at Club Ded. At least before you were born you had something to look forward to. You had a pretty important appointment marked down in your Eternity-At-A-Glance. "May 16: Be Born. Meet Parents. Eat, sleep, and cry. Begin growing up."

When you sleep, at least you go to sleep knowing that if you awaken in the middle of the night, there's *Moby Dick* on the bedside table, Don Ameche movies on cable TV, and perhaps someone asleep beside you just itching to wake up and chat.

But death offers none of these amenities. No appointments on the horizon, no crypt-side book, no disintegrating companions. And what if your feet start to itch? It would be agony. No, unless you speak fluent worm, you're stuck with itchy feet and no one to talk to, just staring forever at the underside of a coffin lid. I've seen quite a few coffin lid undersides in the last two years, and not one held my interest for more than a few seconds, much less ten zillion years.

I know I'm not alone in these feelings of boredom horror for two reasons. First, people are always buried faceup. There's absolutely no reason for that, except our subconscious belief that the dead down below have some kind of existence and would find it extremely unpleasant to have their noses eternally smashed into a coffin bottom. And that facedown they wouldn't be able to look at anything, like, say, the underside of the coffin lid. In fact, face-down burial in some places is used as a punishment for an evil life. And it was a standard technique for inhibiting potential vampires in the old revenants-under-every-bed days.

Some aborigine people of Australia even improved on the irrational horror of face-down burial with head-down internment, but only for special cases. Finding some of their British "protectors" in the old days to be not only less-than-perfect gentlemen but in fact vicious brutes, the aborigine leaders would go to the British authorities when one of these nasties died and ask if they could bury him "in the sacred tribal way, because we loved him so much and wish to honor him for all the wonderful things he did for us." The British suckers, believing themselves to be loved by all indigenous peoples everywhere, would buy this line. The aborigines would then take the body and stick it in the ground headfirst like a tent stake—though I presume without sharpening the head.

There was a spiritual reason for this fine trick. The aborigines, most aborigines, believe that during the Dreamtime forty thousand years ago, when the world began, the eternal spirits were created. These spirits cannot be destroyed, and no new spirits will ever come to be. So every human being is a manifestation of a particular forty millennia-old eternal spirit. And when that human being dies, the spirit survives and is inserted into a newborn child seven generations later, coming in through the fontanel, that soft spot on an infant's pate.

However, if a person is buried head-down, the spirit is trapped in the body and cannot escape to be reborn; the Fouled-Up Fontanel Flimflam. The aborigines were just making sure their British enemies would not return to plague the world seven generations hence, or seven generations after that, and so on. The British Empire may well have disappeared because the spirits of too many pukka sahibs were lifting their soles, rather than their souls, to heaven.

The second reason I know that others are terrified of boredom in the box is that some of the coffin lid undersides I've seen were illustrated. At a funeral home in Florida that primarily serves the Pensacola black community, I saw a lid with the Last Supper embedded in it. This particular Last Supper was certainly interesting, mostly because it was your basic Leonardo except that all the Supper guests were black men. But it still wouldn't have held my interest for anywhere near the time it would need to, no matter what race, creed, color, or national origin Jesus and his pals were. And I have to assume it's pretty dark inside a coffin anyway, so even though this Supper had been printed in bright colors, I doubt I would be able to see it when the time came. I've also seen coffins that featured photographs of loved ones, paintings of cute kittens, inspirational messages, and even pictures of forgotten movie stars, like the ones you used to get free in a new wallet. Imagine spending eternity being not quite able to see Doris Day looming over you. More agony.

The answer, of course, is video, and I offer this idea to any bright and resourceful entrepreneur who wants it. Install a TV set in the coffin lid, wire the set to a power supply and a small satellite dish up top (you could easily disguise the dish as a tombstone to fool would-be grave robbers intent on snatching your set), and you're in business. Selecting programming to watch for eternity would be a challenging but not impossible task. I'd probably eschew those shopping channels, because watching shopping twenty-four hours a day and not being able to buy anything would be almost as bad as just watching. You could keep informed with something like CNN ("More dead people get their news from CNN than any other source!") but the world news tends to get depressing and I should think being dead is already depressing enough. You want to find something to keep your spirits—or Spirit—up, like the Disney Channel. Better yet, select one of those channels that runs nothing but ancient television shows starring people like Jackie Gleason, Nick Adams, Ed Sullivan, Victor Jory—your fellow dead, in other words. Eventually somebody will come up with a cable channel exclusively for dead viewers (besides C-SPAN), featuring programming especially designed to appeal to the moldering audience and available on an eternal subscription basis. And the programmers won't have to worry about all that "interactive" business either, or any other television technological trendiness, like high-definition multichannel audio. Believe me, when I'm dead I'll settle for good old-fashioned low-definition coffin potato black and white with a coat-hanger aerial. And settle, and settle, and settle.

Until technology is ready for me, however, I'll just have to delay dying as long as possible. But boredom is a hazard of death delay too. Long ago someone said, "How many people wish for immortality who don't know what to do on Sunday afternoon?" I don't remember who said it, but he or she touched on an important point when one considers the efforts people all over the world make to put off death. The secret is not to delay your dying, the secret is to extend your living; not just existence but real living, with something to do and the strength and vitality to do it. And you've got a lot more time to try. At the turn of the century the average life span was forty-nine years; now it's seventy-six. Historically that's an unprecedented jump. It took from 3000 B.C. in the Bronze Age (when the average person died at eighteen) until 1900 A.D. for an equivalent increase.

Even though we're living longer, scientists have realized that we're living *older* longer, not *younger* longer. To extend youth, we're going to have to learn as much as we can about the complex, mysterious aging process, and then we may just have to start tinkering with that process.

•

The tinkering has already begun. Often the tinkerers are scientists with a very personal interest in the field. Oncologist William Regelson of the Medical College of Virginia put it succinctly in a *Chicago Tribune* article: "I'm sixty-five and I'm trying to save my ass. I can't wait around for some graduate student to save it for me."

Dr. Dan Rudman, at the Medical College of Wisconsin in Milwaukee, is one of the prime tinkerers these days, as well as a crusader for the treatment of elderly people so that they might live happier, healthier lives. Dr. Rudman is also an elderly man, albeit one who likes to play tennis for three hours on weekends. He's thought a great deal about the health and aging problems of the elderly. He says that when people got old and frail fifteen years ago they tended to be warehoused and forgotten, not only by society but by the medical community. "We tried to protect them in sheltered residences, but we felt that it was too late for any active medical examinations or innovations." But not anymore.

Dr. Rudman doesn't consider himself a life extensionist, but more of a life improver, working to make the last third of human life as beneficial as possible. Through evolution each species receives a certain maximum life span. And the genetically coded life span for humans is approximately eighty-five years, which Dr. Rudman thinks is about right . . . so far.

"It takes nine months for a new human being to be conceived and born, another fifteen years for that infant to be brought up to maturity. And then with the process of education and maturation, there's another several decades during which the aging members of the species are still extremely useful. I think the fact that we do have a maximum life span of about eighty-five years shows that even in our fifties, sixties, and seventies we have very useful functions to carry out, probably in protecting, guiding, and educating the next generation." Or in other words, evolutionarily speaking, we're long-lived because our children are a little dense and need our help. God bless the children.

The effort to find ways to make people feel younger longer isn't just for the benefit of the individual, it's for the educational benefit of society too. And the financial benefit. Rudman points out that although only 12 percent of the American population is over the age of sixty-five, they consume 50 percent of the medical services. But you can't carry out those later-life functions if you're feeling lousy, if you're weak and frail.

Rudman has heard the argument that weakness, illness, and the other common disabilities of the elderly are simply part of a natural process. Aging is a fatal disease, and some scientists (especially those who aren't trying to get grants to study aging) say there's not much to be done about it. Rudman argues that we are beginning to see that although natural aging certainly does have debilitating effects, many of those effects are the result of aggravated or accelerated aging that can be controlled or eliminated.

"Not that long ago we were taught that hearing loss was the inevitable result of the aging process. The older you get, the more those delicate mechanisms for hearing deteriorate. We know now that the process is accelerated by chronic exposure to noise. If you live for decades in a noise-polluted environment, your hearing will deteriorate more rapidly. The same thing is true of radiation. Lifelong exposure to continual low-level radiation accelerates the aging process.

"Shakespeare described old age in *As You Like It* as 'sans teeth, sans eyes, sans taste, sans everything.' Teeth? If you get a proper amount of fluoride when you're a child and reasonable dental care during adulthood, they should bury you with a good full set of teeth."

In fact, some of the effects of aging aren't negative at all, but protective. For example, after you reach age fifteen your brain cells lose the ability to multiply. The brain you had as a sophomore in high school is the brain you're going to have for the rest of your life. (Wait, the good part is coming.) Certainly that's unfortunate in some ways, but it also provides the mechanism for long-term memory. The only way you can hang onto things you learn for a lifetime is if your brain cells are stationary. It's why my fourteen-year-old son can never remember where he left his shoes, but I can. And part of our acquired and retained wisdom is knowing enough not to tell our kids any of this, or every time they screw up they'll offer the Brain-Cell Defense.

Dan Rudman's current research project, funded by the National Institute on Aging, involves seeking specific ways to make the last years of life better for elderly, frail men suffering from osteoporosis and related conditions.

"We found when we looked at the endocrine system, which is how hormones in the body operate, that the majority of older people have a partial or total deficiency in several hormones which seem to be very useful in younger people. Growth hormone is one, and the male sex hormone testosterone is another. With modern pharmacology and industrial breakthroughs these particular hormone deficiencies can be easily corrected. We can't give an old person a new set of eyes or new hearing yet, but we can restore some of the body's chemistry. We can literally take a frail, elderly person and give him a young person's endocrine system with a regular injection."

The beneficial effects of human growth hormone have been known for a long time. But until recently the only source was the pituitary glands of corpses, and the supply was understandably limited. All the available growth hormone was reserved for children with genetic problems like dwarfism. But now, through biogenetic engineering, artificial growth hormone and testosterone are finally available, even though currently they are quite expensive.

Dr. Rudman is in the next phase of his research, using patients from Milwaukee's VA hospital. From the initial tests, however, there's evidence that injections of biogenetically manufactured hormones have an almost miraculous effect on the elderly male subjects of the study, although Rudman is much too good a scientist to use the word "miraculous," especially about his own work. Three months after the beginning of treatment, patients had stronger bones, thicker muscles, and reported feeling better and especially stronger than they had in decades. And as long as they continued taking the hormones they continued to feel better. Unfortunately, as soon as the medication stopped they regressed, but some positive effects lingered. And the research continues. It's an important and extremely encouraging start toward using the gift Dan Rudman says our generation has received.

"This is the first century in which most of us can expect to live from age sixty-five to ninety-five. Previous generations rarely achieved that, but we will, and what we want is to figure out how to do it in the best way, the most significant meaningful way, and with the best physical and spiritual quality."

•

Dan Rudman is dealing with the treatment of a particular cause of aging—the inconsiderate tendency of the endocrine system to stop shooting us the gene juice we need after the age of thirty. Dr. Richard Cutler, a research chemist at the National Institute of Health Gerontology Research Center in Baltimore, has spent decades looking at the bigger picture: the causes of aging and the possible ways aging can be regulated. If you tell scientists in the various fields related to longevity that you want to talk to knowledgeable people about aging research, they all say, "Then you have to talk to Dick Cutler." Some of them say it enthusiastically, like Cutler is the aging messiah, and others say it like Cutler is doing this work just until his friends the space aliens take him back to Mars. Twenty years ago Cutler's studies debunking aspects of the "inevitability" of aging were cited at scientific meetings as precisely the kind of research that shouldn't be done. And then he had the audacity to be right.

On the way to Dr. Cutler's lab I stopped at Edgar Allan Poe's grave in a small church cemetery in Baltimore. It seemed right somehow, paying my respects to a man who was terrified of premature burial on the way to visit a man who thinks we all might be getting buried prematurely. It was raining hard in Baltimore that day, and even though the cemetery is surrounded by office buildings it seemed appropriately nineteenth-century; sodden and dismal, with sunken places in the ground where underneath the coffins had collapsed. Just the kind of place Poe would have enjoyed.

I stood at his grave for a while, looking at the raven carved into the stone, wondering which Baltimore city father had that bright idea.

("There will be a raven on my tombstone over my dead body!"—Poe.)
But you can only stare at a gravestone in the rain for so long, no matter
whose it is. And besides, if Poe's worst fears had come true and he was
buried prematurely, somebody would probably have heard him long
before I got there. So I took shelter from the downpour in the quaint
brick church. Only it's not a church anymore, now it's some kind of
meeting hall that groups can rent for special occasions. Inside women
were busy putting flower decorations on tables and a band was tuning
up on the altar/stage. Finally someone saw me dripping in the corner
and shouted across the hall, "If you're here for the bar mitzvah you're
early." A bar mitzvah, in Edgar Allan Poe's old neighborhood church.
Times change, Ed. There don't seem to be any nevermores anymore.

For Dick Cutler, times are changing too, and in his field almost all
the changes are good. Researchers and scientists in the life-extension
business have every reason to believe the next decade will be the most
exciting, action-packed years in longevity history, and one of the reasons is the work Dick Cutler and his staff are doing. He's a friendly-
looking guy with a frizz of white, wild hair. He has the kind of face that
makes him appear slightly amused much of the time. When I get to his
lab he's being slightly amused by his mice. He has a lot of mice, and although they look like your standard house rodents, at least some of
them are revolutionary, cutting edge mice. Because they are *old* mice.

"For most of human history people didn't live long enough to show
the signs of aging," Dr. Cutler explains, gently petting his mouse
Methusela. "There was very little cancer, Alzheimer's disease, stuff like
that. It was really a population of youth. And that's still the way it is in
nature. You don't worry about catching old fish or shooting down an
old duck. If you go out and study mice in the fields, you find there's no
old mice. They're killed randomly by their natural predators. So aging
in nature is rare, and it used to be rare in humans as well. What humans
have done is we've been able to lessen environmental hazards, allowing
us to live longer than we are essentially designed to live. We're really
designed to live to be about thirty. After the age of thirty, thirty-five,
everything slowly goes to pot."

And mice go to pot a lot younger, even without natural predators.
So where did Dr. Cutler get the old mice? Even though there aren't
many mouse-environmental hazards in his lab—Dick doesn't randomly
eat his mice, and none of his lab assistants look like mice-eaters either—
Dick's old mice are still very old, even for mice in the lap of luxury.
Why? The answer may help our children and grandchildren live to 150
and more.

Here's how. Although there is general agreement in the scientific community that some kind of primary aging mechanisms exist, nobody has yet satisfactorily identified any specific mechanism, or at least they haven't according to Dick Cutler. There are many theories, but generally scientists agree that the causes of aging are really the normal byproducts of metabolism and developmental processes that are essential to life. Or in other, simpler words, aging is a result of living.

Dr. Cutler presents an example. "As we understand more about the metabolic reactions that go on in our body, we see there is always a good part and a bad part. Like oxygen. Many organisms utilize oxygen because it's a very efficient way to gain energy. But you pay a price for that. Lots of energy, very efficient, but unfortunately in the generation of that energy there's all these reactive oxygen species produced called "free radicals." Unchecked, free radicals could easily destroy us, shorten our life span very quickly. But as a result of utilizing oxygen, our bodies have evolved defense mechanisms, so-called anti-oxygen DNA repair processes and so forth, to deal with free radicals. So a potential primary aging process would be the production of reactive oxygen species—like free radicals—as a result of oxygen utilization. And an anti-aging process then would be those processes that act to control or govern the levels of free radicals."

What? Well, think of it like a revolution in a small country, and that small country is you. The free radicals are the revolutionary army that wants to take over. The anti–free radicals are the loyalist army. As long as the loyalists can keep beating the revolutionaries, the country survives. But as time goes on the loyalist numbers diminish and the free radicals get stronger. One day the free radicals win a big one, and the country dies. So the oldest, most successful countries would therefore be those that have the best loyalist armies to beat the hell out of the free radical revolutionaries. So it is in living organisms, if Dick Cutler is right.

"The longer-lived a species is, the more you would expect those animals to have superior mechanisms or means to deal with free oxygen radicals. And indeed this is exactly what's been found to be the case. Humans are the longest-lived of all mammalian species and we have by far the highest levels of anti-oxygen, anti-aging processes in our cells. Now this is only correlated evidence. It doesn't prove the fact just because we have correlations."

But suppose you could clone a human anti-oxygen gene, call it maybe a super oxide (that's what Dick calls it) and then use that super oxide to provide artificial levels of protection against reactive oxygen species?

Sort of like an army of mercenaries brought in to beat the free radicals after the loyalist army has been reduced to four old guys in berets sitting in an outdoor café leering at the waitress. You could test the super oxide on a short-lived critter, say, a mouse. Might that not prove that longer life is connected to a creature's anti-oxygen levels? It would if you ended up with . . .

An old mouse!

Dick Cutler's breakthrough came about from looking for the right thing. He says most scientists avoid the longevity field because the aging process just seems too complex. But he wondered if there might be some relatively simple mechanisms that control the process, regardless of how the process itself works. Chimpanzees had something to do with it. If aging is genetic, and it must be, then theoretically chimpanzees and human beings should have approximately equal life spans, because genetically chimps and humans are 99 percent alike. But humans live twice as long as chimps, and chimps live twice as long as rhesus monkeys, and rhesus monkeys live twice as long as squirrel monkeys. The possible reason, Dr. Cutler wrote in the 1972 paper, was what he called the "longevity determinate gene hypothesis."

What, you ask, does this have to do with all of us living to 150? If Cutler is right that the processes controlling aging are relatively simple, then it follows that they can be manipulated in relatively simple ways. Jab some of the proper super oxides and other fancy stuff into Grandpa after his own body starts to lose the revolution, and you'll never get him out of that rent-controlled apartment.

Dick Cutler doesn't talk much anymore about the possibility of greatly increased human life spans. It was that aspect of his research that had some of the scientific community calling him a nutcase twenty years ago. He's also not thrilled about the possibility of getting letters that begin, "Dear Doc, please send ten gallons of that there gene juice you thunk up to Route 4, Box . . . ," etc. But in the safety of his cluttered office, he will admit to some "inching up" on increasing the length of healthy human life. And he has to, because his elderly father calls him regularly to find out how it's going and how soon the juice will be ready.

"We're not talking here about doubling or tripling the life span. My guess is we're talking five, ten years, something on that margin. And we really need to address seriously the question, not only the possibility but the advisability. There might be problems with retirement programs, social security systems. It has even been suggested that there would be more divorces. You'd be surprised how many negative aspects people can think of in terms of what might be the consequences, even if people lived healthier, longer life spans. But somebody needs to study the benefits too—economic benefits, like people paying taxes longer. And the benefits to society, creatively, scientifically, the human value of great minds that stay active longer. It's easy to think of the negative population impact, but I think the outcome will be that there will be more benefits than problems."

A friend of mine who used to do science reports on television was looking over her old scripts one day and came to a disturbing realization. In almost half the stories she'd done that year, the last paragraph of her narration included some version of the phrase, "only time will tell." Now I know what she was talking about. In longevity research generally, and for Dick Cutler especially, only time will tell. His mice get older every day, and every day they do is further proof that he's on the right track in his particular area of inquiry. And he's just one of hundreds of people all over the world working on different ways to make life longer, and long life better. Cutler says their scientific conventions are great fun to attend because they always check each other out to see if anybody looks dramatically younger than he did at the last convention. Dick threatens to get a face-lift and a dark brown toupee and scare the hell out of them someday. But if he waits long enough, he may not have to.

•

Ward Dean, a Pensacola physician who lives just up the highway from the funeral home with the Last Supper coffins, is as concerned with living well longer as Dan Rudman is. Some people in the scientific community think Dean, like Dick Cutler, is nuts; or worse, a charlatan. He agrees with Rudman and Cutler about a lot of things. Where they disagree is over the waiting. Dean thinks human beings could significantly increase their life spans now if they just knew what to do and were allowed to do it.

Ward Dean is one of the nation's foremost life extensionists, coauthor of *Smart Drugs and Nutrients, Biological Aging Measurement,* and other books. (And it should be pointed out now that aside from royalties on those books, Dr. Dean gets no revenue from his researches in the longevity field. He doesn't sell "Dr. Dean's Miracle Lozenge of Life" or anything else.) For all those people who want to try to live longer *now* and are willing to experiment, he is a true crusading hero. But he's a very low-key hero. I watched him make a rare public appearance before the patients of a chiropractor friend of his. The meeting was held one humid Florida night before a crowd of thirty people, ranging in age from twenty-five to seventy, that hung on his every word. And almost every word was what they wanted to hear.

"I define aging as the one fatal disease that everybody over thirty has caught, because after that we're all going downhill. And that hasn't changed for a long time. Once you reach fifty, your chances of living out your natural life span to eighty-five or so aren't any better than they were in ancient times. But even though right now the maximum life span is about 115 to 120 years, I see essentially no theoretical limit to how long we all can live."

Dr. Dean especially sees no limit to how long *he's* going to live. The next day I went to his house, the house of a man who practices what he preaches almost to the point of obsession. But I suspect Dean has never been a person to go halfway on anything he thought was important. For instance, he still has the three-thousand comic books he bought as a kid forty years ago, carefully wrapped in cellophane. How many of us wish we had done that, but never got around to it? Ward Dean did.

A former combat Marine in Vietnam, one day while being shot at he decided the infantry had distinct limitations, as far as being a rewarding profession was concerned. So he went to medical school in Korea, met and married his Korean wife, and returned to the United States. With a strong interest in life extension even before becoming a physician, he eventually opened a practice in Beverly Hills, advising the eternally-young-by-any-means-possible Hollywood crowd, although now he says he learned as much from them as they learned from him.

Dr. Dean exercises vigorously, is extremely careful about his diet, and takes eighty-five pills a day. Eighty-five. In one gulp. With a little bottled water. He explained to me what all the pills were for, but pharmacology was never my strongest subject so I got lost fairly quickly, especially since the only name I recognized was aspirin. But he certainly knows what they all do for him, including making him smarter, improving his memory, and giving him a good shot at living longer.

"There are drugs available right now which have demonstrated the ability to greatly increase the life span of animals, and we have every reason to expect the same drugs would probably extend the life span of humans." It's as simple as that.

What is not simple is acquiring the drugs he's talking about. Dean is a walking compendium, not only of drugs, but how to find them. If they're so beneficial one would think they'd be available at every pharmacy in America, but he alleges that because of one organization, that's not the case.

"The Food and Drug Administration is probably the greatest impediment to medical progress there is in this country. And the greatest impediment to life extension too."

"If they were here," I asked, "wouldn't they say 'Dean's a fanatic, don't listen to him'?"

"Sure they would, but that's because they don't take the time to read the scientific literature. The federal bureaucracies that control the health care environment in this country are probably going to prevent a lot of the great strides in longevity from being made. For example, the National Institute on Aging is the only component of the National Institutes of Health which is not directly focused on a particular disease. They're more interested in the sociological aspects of aging, user-friendly bus stops and that kind of thing. I attended a gerontological conference in Mexico several years ago that began with a singer singing a song that was dedicated to telling how wonderful it is to be old. And I thought, 'This is incredible! This would be like a cardiology conference opening with a song about how great it is to have a heart attack!' "

Dean's disagreement with the government is basically definitional. He thinks aging is a disease, a disease that can be cured, and he contends the government and too many physicians and researchers treat aging as if it's a natural process that must be endured.

"They try to separate aging people from older people who are sick, whereas I believe that it's almost impossible to find an older person who is truly healthy. Because if you look hard enough, it's easy to find diagnosable disease."

One of the ways to prevent disease and therefore increase life span is through diet. Most of the pills Dean takes are nutrients of some kind. He says the official recommended daily allowances of nutrients are designed just to prevent deficiency diseases like beriberi and scurvy.

"We do not know what the optimum doses for many of these substances are, just the scurvy-prevention doses. Those of us in life extension who are taking what some consider megadoses of nutrients are actually trying to provide the optimum amount of these various nutrients to optimize the biological cycles." In other words, should he really be taking forty-three pills a day, or 4,550 pills a day? He's not sure yet, and is testing the doses on himself.

And what of the argument that all his megadoses do is give him the most priceless piss in Pensacola?

"Absolute baloney. When they first developed penicillin, it was very expensive and the only way they could get a supply large enough was to collect the urine from patients who were receiving the penicillin. Then they would reinject it. Now you could say that these folks had expensive urine too, but clearly something was going on with that penicillin from the time that it went in until the time it came out 100 percent unchanged. I believe the same thing happens to these vitamins. And the studies of Linus Pauling and many other responsible scientists around the world attest to this fact."

Only time will tell, as they say, if Ward Dean is right about mega-doses of nutrients and the other life-extending things he does. He fully expects his grandchildren will enjoy healthy lives until they're 150 to 200 years old, in spite of the FDA. (In the year 2200 the value of Superman and Batman comics #1, both of which he has, should be about what the national debt is today.) And he agrees with Rudman and Cutler that even before any kind of biogenetically engineered gene juice is available to the public, regular folk can do a lot to prolong their lives through exercise and diet. Like the recent experiments in extremely diminished caloric intake. Paring subjects' food consumption down to six-hundred calories a day, with vitamin supplements, seems to have a distinctly beneficial effect on longevity. But, uh, only time will tell.

•

There's one other thing that affects longevity now, besides exercise, diet, and a paucity of bad habits. Spirit. Four years ago the Golda Meir Center opened in Clearwater, Florida. And standing at the door were the Leshners, Lil and Ace, retired New Yorkers who had moved to Clearwater in the mid-1980s. Lil had spent most of her working life teaching special needs kids in the public schools, and Ace was in sales and personnel. But now Lil and Ace were spending all their time working on Lil and Ace. Their kids were grown and spread around the country, and it was time for mom and dad to enjoy themselves. Above all, it was time *not* to die.

"I was reluctant to join Golda Meir at first," Ace says now. "Lil will tell you this. 'Why go there?' I said to her. 'It's for old people. I don't want to get involved with those old people.' I was sixty-six at the time. But just because I'm sixty-six doesn't mean anybody's going to lead me around by the hand. I continue. You work all your life and all of a sudden you can't just stop. Continue. There's a lot of things out there to do, a lot of things we haven't seen. Just continue. I'm not saying I hope to continue, I'm going to continue."

Part of the Golda Meir operation is the Life Extension Center, including a weight room, swimming pool, sports court and regular exercise and aerobics classes. That's where Lil and Ace went that first day, and where they still go every day. Lil says if they leave the house after 8:30 in the morning, they feel like they're late, even though there's no place they *have* to be.

Ace hits the weight room three times a week, Lil has exercise classes, and they both do stationary bikes, treadmills, and some aerobics. Ace says he's in better shape now than he was thirty years ago, and you better believe him. Lil says occasionally she gets a glimpse of herself in the mirror and she'll stop and wonder, "Who's that old bat?"

"My daughter said to me the other day, 'You know, we call you and tell you we're sick. You never tell us you're sick.' Not exactly true, but this place has kept us alive. Not alive, we weren't dying, but it's given us something that we didn't have the time to do before."

What they have the time to do now is a lot more than just riding bicycles and pumping iron. What they have the time to do is live. Ace recalls with considerable pain coming home from work one night many years ago and having his then three-year-old daughter ask him, "Who are you?" And by living life to the fullest now, both physically and emotionally, it's hard not to think they are also delaying death. Lil and Ace don't have time to get old, sick, and die, no matter how much of that is going on around them.

"Someone came up to me here the other day and he says, 'Ace, have you heard? So-and-so died.' And I said, 'Yeah? Where are you going for dinner tonight?' I'm not exaggerating, not being facetious. You can't sit there and brood about it. Life goes on. I can say 'I'm not going, I'm not dying.' If it happens, it happens, but I have plans for tomorrow."

"And we're not waiting for technology to take care of us, either," Lil says.

When they are done working out at Golda Meir, the Leshners take classes in pottery, basket weaving, and nutritional cooking. They usher at a local theater and do volunteer work at the Salvation Army. I talked to them a few days before they were leaving on a cross-country driving trip to visit their children. It's a grueling schedule, but Ace doesn't plan to keep it up forever. Just until the year 2020. He'll be 98 then, and plans to slow down. Just a little. "As long as he still keeps up with me," says Lil.

The Leshners are lucky. They have each other, the money to do most of the things they want, and basic good health. But they work very hard at their luck too. Keeping fit isn't easy, especially when you haven't any obvious reason to do it, and life would be so much more comfortable just sitting around the house watching soap operas and waiting for your children to call. It seems like that was the tradition in America for a long time, but there are more people like Ace and Lil every day.

In other cultures exercise and proper diet have been the principal way to delay death for centuries. I spent a morning in Chiang Kai Shek Square in Taipei, a huge open area circled by immaculate state buildings, including the opera house and a temple. It was very early, so I was the only one there. Just me and about five thousand Taiwanese doing their morning workout; some in groups with leaders, others off by themselves. I watched one gentleman for a half hour as he silently performed slow, graceful, precise moves in the morning mist. He was a bird for a while, then a cat, then maybe a tree sloth. I guessed he was an extremely well-preserved seventy-year-old. He was in fact eighty-six, and had been doing that particular exercise regimen for eight decades. For him, time had already told.

If avoiding death by delaying it was the human animal's top priority in life, then we'd all be like that Taiwanese gentleman, as well as Ace, Lil, and even Dr. Dean. In fact the world would be a different place entirely. The top speed limit would be twenty-five miles per hour rather than fifty-five on highways; the American Tobacco Growers Association would be two guys in gimme hats sharing a one-room office in Whipslap, Virginia, with the National Rifle Association; and each year the United States government would spend on heart research what it now spends on the military, because for most of us our chances of dying from heart problems are five times that of any other cause. You could buy artificial hearts and pacemakers at the drugstore and have them installed at shopping mall clinics.

Such is not the case. We spend our immortal years (12–40) not thinking about death, our middle years (41–60) trying not to think about death, and our later years (61–115) trying not to die. And somewhere in there many of us decide to "do something about it." The more energetic exercise, like Lil and Ace, or we quit smoking and drinking, or we always sit at an exit on airplanes. But a sizable group of people wait for the elixir of life, the miracle waters that will eliminate death without raising a sweat. Doctors Rudman, Cutler, and Dean say there never will be such a thing, but at best a combination of methods and treatments you can use to delay the inevitable, including all those things you can do right now. But we persist in our belief that if magic isn't in the air, it damned well should be. We are neo-Ponce de Leóns, searching for the Fountain of Youth.

•

It might therefore be enlightening to go where one Juan has gone before. Juan Ponce de León explored Puerto Rico, discovered and named Florida, and was the Governor of Hispaniola. But he will always be remembered as the man who *didn't* find the Fountain of Youth back in 1513. There's some confusion about whether that was what he was looking for in the first place. The fountain search isn't mentioned anywhere in his orders, which were then called patents. They imply his principal interest was finding gold, just like every other Spaniard back then with two boats and an astrolabe. But there's some evidence from the period that the Fountain of Youth was at least one of his real objectives. Perhaps sixteenth-century Spain had some similarities to the modern world. You couldn't get government money or corporate underwriting for what you really wanted to do, you had to apply for something else that was within the application guidelines and then slip your real interest in on the third page. And certainly in the sixteenth-century Spanish Call For Exploratory Proposals, *Find Gold* was application guideline numero uno. So Juan listed "Youth, Search for Fountain of" on the back page of his grant application to the private underwriters, under Tertiary Objectives and right after the résumés of his humanities scholars. Alas, Juan didn't find gold or the Fountain of Youth. Seven years later all he found was an arrow in his neck, an unsolicited contribution from a Florida indigenous person who'd had enough of these Spaniards. Juan Ponce de León made it back to Havana, where he died and was buried. Eventually his body was moved to San Juan, Puerto Rico.

Some scholarly opinion, plus a lot of popular belief, now contends that the place Juan was looking for and narrowly missed was Warm Mineral Springs in central Florida. Geologically, the Springs is an extremely deep collapsed sinkhole with caves and stalactites down below. (Therein may have been Juan's problem. He was looking for the Fountain of Youth when he should really have been looking for the Collapsed Sinkhole of Youth.) Some interesting archaeological discoveries have been made way down in Warm Mineral Springs, including the buried bodies of ancient area residents.

Sociologically, the Springs is one of those Florida places you pass by on the way to somewhere else that makes you wonder for a moment why anybody would pay real money to see an Alligator Skin Arts and Crafts Center or the World's Largest Cantaloupe. Warm Mineral Springs is a tourist attraction, in other words, but for those who go there, it is a great deal more.

For centuries the indigenous peoples of the area have believed that the waters of Warm Mineral Springs have miraculous healing powers. Historians assume Ponce de León somehow heard the rumors about the wonder of the wet, but his directions were faulty. He wasted a lot of time looking for the fountain in Bimini, and by the time he got squared away, he got it in the neck instead.

•

Four hundred years later, Colonel Bill Royal was more successful, but then he had an AAA road map. The colonel (Air Force, I think) heard the rumors too, and came to Warm Mineral Springs in the

1930s. There wasn't much around the place then. The bathhouse was a big wooden crate, and the owners were charging twenty-five cents a dip, although nobody was ever around to collect the money. But the colonel wasn't looking for amenities, he was looking for relief from bad arthritis.

When he got to Warm Mineral Springs that first time he slipped into his trunks in the crate, stepped out into the hot Florida sun, dropped two bits in the box, and proceeded to the water's edge. It was a historic moment for the Springs and the colonel himself. Expectant violins and a modest drumroll would have been appropriate, but all he heard were about ten million cicadas making that noise that's interesting the first time you experience it and becomes forever irritating within five minutes.

Colonel Royal entered the water. The bottom was slightly gooshy. The water was warm. It tasted like nontoxic industrial waste. And he was cured. (Trumpets up, dissolve to modern scene.)

Every day since then—especially after moving to Florida to be closer to his liquid salvation—Colonel Bill Royal has risen at dawn, gone to Warm Mineral Springs, and swum a mile. Then he sits in the sun, goes out for lunch, comes back, and swims another mile. And he says he's in perfect physical condition for a man of eighty-eight; no more arthritis or anything else, and it is the waters that have done it.

Many others have followed his lead. The day I visited the Springs the colonel was sitting in the water up to his navel, looking rather like the Caucasian Gautama Buddha of Liquid Enlightenment. And around him there were perhaps a hundred people in or next to the water, mostly elderly retirees, mostly foreign born. Elizabeth Hooker, who runs the Warm Mineral Springs Wellness Institute, says the place attracts a lot of people from Europe, the Ukraine, and other Russian spots where there's a tradition of "taking the waters."

"The water here is very similar to the waters of Odessa and the Black Sea," Ms. Hooker says. "Although I think this water is more powerful. Besides large amounts of most of the major minerals, there's also natural radon, which is found in few other places in the world. The water is also highly anaerobic, which means there's not much oxygen in it, so it negatively ionizes the body, which essentially balances the potential hydrogen or the pH of the body and staves off degenerative disease and for that reason, promotes longevity." I must admit I don't know if any of this is true, because I don't know what it means. But it sounds like Ward Dean could eliminate fifty pills a day just by knocking back an eight-ounce tumbler of genuine Warm Mineral Springswater.

Chris Sheehan is only thirty-four, but he says his daily dips have improved his skin and eliminated the dark bags under his eyes. It's the water's high sodium content he credits for helping arthritis sufferers like the colonel—"most people suffer from a sodium imbalance, and that's what leads to calcium buildup"—but he says the buoyancy of the water is also beneficial, because being able to move around more easily gets people to exercise more.

The people who believe in Warm Mineral Springs are fanatic about the place, so you can't judge by talking to them whether their daily dunkings are really rejuvenating or not. Like a lot of the other magic elixirs people use to feel healthier and delay death, the Springs may be a self-fulfilling fantasy. They work because their users think they work. That death-shall-have-no-dominion spirit the Leshners get from a full, active life, Springsians get from immersion. In death delay, I guess you do whatever turns you on, and doesn't turn you off.

CHAPTER SIX

A PAIR OF JACKIES

I once asked Buddhist priest Sogyal Rinpoche, author of *The Tibetan Book of Living and Dying* and a specialist in interpreting the Tibetan Book of the Dead for Western audiences, how he defined the moment of death. It's much more than a biological question. What constitutes the precise moment of demise has become a subject of controversy in our culture, with court cases cropping up all over the country regarding the ethical, sensible use of artificial life-prolonging technology. At the same time technology continues to make advances, to increase medicine's ability to prolong either life, or breathing, depending on how you look at it.

So I expected Rinpoche, a worldly, sophisticated man, to take some time with his answer. I'm about to hear the wisdom of the ages, I thought, coming face-to-face with scientific hopes for the future.

"It's simple," Rinpoche said. "You breathe out, and you don't breathe in."

Indeed. It may be just that simple, but he gave me the whimwhams nevertheless. And what was frightening about his answer is that it makes death such an easy, little thing. Although we rarely admit it, we want our death to be a Very Big Deal, both personally and for the people about whom we care. John Donne may have suggested poetically that we "do not ask for whom the bell tolls . . . " but at least he was thinking bells.

All too often the truth is just as Rinpoche said: You breathe out, and you don't breathe in. No bells. The bigger truth is that we are surrounded

by death every minute, every second of our lives, even when we're respir-
ing properly. Mere ceasing to breathe is just one of a million opportunities
you have each day to die. For instance, sitting on an airplane eating
peanuts I feel relatively safe, and at least statistically I am. But if I'm looking for something to worry about I can ponder that where I am in the
window seat I'm just five inches that way from a five-hundred-mile-per-
hour wind, not much oxygen, bitter cold, and a 35,000-foot drop. The
only thing separating me from that fate is five inches of airplane wall installed one Friday afternoon by a guy in Everett, Washington, who just
had a fight with his wife, had to change a flat tire on his way to work, suffered a painful hangnail in the process, and hates his job because what he
really wants to do is work in Flight Test, which from my few months as a
1968 Boeing clerk is where everybody in the plant thinks he or she be-
longs if only management would wise up. (He may be a swell fella, but if I
was going to put my life in somebody's hands, I wouldn't go to his hands
first.) Five inches this way, peanuts. Five inches that way, nobody but Superman gets out alive.

Similarly, I'm a fairly good driver (some would disagree) but each
time I take to the road I'm betting my life on the driving ability, not
only of myself, but of every single complete stranger going past me the
other way. One slip, one abrupt heart attack, one greasy steering wheel,
one cigarette ash dropped in the crotch by any of us, and I'm head-on
dead.

Then there's the natural world, full of beasts that kick, bite, scratch,
claw, maim and spit. In his book *Natural Acts*, David Quammen men-
tions in passing that if you live in the American Southwest, the chances
are extremely good that at least once each day you're six feet or less
from a black widow spider. And to this day I swim exclusively in swimming pools because in my childhood I watched a lot of underwater nature shows on television. On "Kingdom of the Sea," for instance, it
seemed like every time your host Colonel John D. Craig slipped on his
trunks and went into the bay, he got there just as schools of sharks, bar-
racuda, giant octopuses and moray eels were going by. Dip my butt in
real water? I said to myself then and now. Not a chance.

For the superstitious, those who think that avoiding places where
death has occurred is the same as avoiding death itself, I once read the
odds are extremely good that at least one person has died in every
guest room of every hotel in the world more than fifty years old. (I
have been unable to confirm this possibility with any hotel association
on the face of the earth. Most of them won't even tell you their standard procedure if a guest dies, as if someone passing over to the great
beyond whilst snuggled down in the old Magic Fingers bed is an

unheard-of occurrence.) Which means there are some famous hotels in Europe and Asia that are practically mausoleums, and yet it is the rare patron who even thinks about it, much less inquires. And if that's the case with hotels, can you imagine the ghosts lurking around every hospital room?

We can't protect ourselves from death's proximity, no matter what extreme measures we take. Reportedly Howard Hughes in his later years went to extraordinary lengths at an extraordinary expense to live in a germ-free environment. You know, the Howard Hughes who is now dead. So we choose to ignore the presence of death around us. Our various institutions eagerly assist in this deathly disregard, which is why no hotelier will tell me about room death rate, and no airline was interested in providing transportation on the *Trip of a Lifetime* project in exchange for credit. ("*Death* has been brought to you by United Airlines?" said the man at United Airlines. "I think not.")

Of course there are occasions when it's impossible to ignore death's ubiquitous presence. And when those occasions arise we perversely revel in them, but only for so long. A few years ago a man was waiting for a stoplight on a Seattle street that ran between a department store and a six-story parking garage. Unbeknownst to him, up on top of the garage an old gentleman was trying to park his car and lost control, accidentally hitting the gas pedal. He crashed through the barricade and plummeted one-hundred feet to the street below. But he didn't quite reach the street. He hit the guy who was just sitting there, killing both of them instantly. At least the old guy had 2.4 seconds to prepare.

From the newspaper and television coverage of this bizarre accident you would have thought Elvis himself had landed on a bus full of blind nuns with orphans in their laps. The news stories emphasized how unexpected sudden death can be, as if the reporters had just discovered death's unpredictable nature and were letting us all in on it. Had the old gentleman simply run into the other guy head-on in a freeway accident, they wouldn't have made page 12 together. That's a death we can imagine, a death we've seen, whereas getting nailed from above at a stoplight is not. "This Could Happen to You!"—and the obvious follow-up story, "Aren't You Glad This Didn't Happen to You?" and the follow-up follow-up, "How to Prevent This From Happening to You"—sold a lot of newspapers for a few days, before everybody chose to ignore death again, at least until the next time.

(My favorite unexpected true death story concerns the husband who told his wife he had fallen in love with another. "I'm taking my things and leaving," the rat said, and proceeded to do so. Heartbroken and despondent, his soon-to-be ex-spouse decided to end it all immediately by leaping from their fifth-floor apartment balcony. Which she did, landing on her departing husband and killing him. As I remember, she sustained a sprained ankle and a hell of a smile.)

While almost all of us ignore the proximity of death, most of us take at least some precautions. We wear seat belts and helmets, we don't put smoking objects in our mouths anymore, we buy child-proof caps for our potions. And we eschew needlessly dangerous situations. While there are some who bungee jump, mountain climb and alligator wrestle, there are a lot more who don't. But there are people who have to live in environments where the presence of death is not only continuous but obvious, people who are aware of the danger and find ways to live with it. They adjust their lives to the overwhelming death around them.

•

One day in a small English town in Derbyshire a tailor named George Viccars received a shipment of cloth from London. When he unpacked the box the cloth was damp, so the tailor hung it up before the fireplace to dry. A week later George Viccars was dead. A few days after that one of his landlady's young sons died, and then the man who lived in the house next door. And it wasn't long before twenty people a week were dying in the town. The year was 1665, the disease was bubonic plague, and the town was called Eyam (pronounced EEM).

"I think fear dominated life in this village in 1665," says John Clifford, who came to Eyam a decade ago and has made a careful study of the town's history. "Fear of neighbors, fear of the unknown, because they had no idea what caused the plague. They had the strangest theories. They thought it was divine wrath. During that summer the village boys had allowed some cows to get into the church. And the animals fouled the nave, creating a great mess. And so they said God's house had been fouled, it was only logical that God would punish them, and the plague was in fact a divine punishment for cows! Imagine!"

Eyam still looks much as it did then, a picturesque English village set in a valley, with green fields and farms on the hillsides and good, solid stone buildings stretched along the main street. And though Eyam doesn't get many tourists, as an example of the generosity and sacrifice within the human spirit in the face of death you could find few better places to visit. Mrs. Daniels, widow of the town historian, took me to all the high spots, from Viccars's cottage where the flea-infested cloth arrived, to a small enclosure of gravestones on a hillside above town. It was there, in the course of a single week, that Mrs. John Hancock nursed her sick family and then day after day dragged the bodies of first her husband and eventually their six children out to the field and buried them.

But the real story of courage in Eyam is not that a few townspeople survived unbearably horrible conditions and helped each other when they could. In London and surrounding municipalities there was a lot of that during a succession of pestilences. Eyam is a famous plague village because of a decision made by its residents.

Shortly after the plague began, Reverend William Mompesson, Rector of Eyam's Church of Saint Lawrence, and his predecessor, Reverend William Stanley, called the townspeople together for a meeting. There they made a proposal. Mompesson and Stanley wanted to create a *cordon sanitaire*, an imaginary line surrounding Eyam that villagers would not cross as long as the plague was present. In effect they suggested voluntarily quarantining themselves, voluntarily waiting for death rather than trying to escape to places where there was no plague. The proposal was adopted, and the quarantine was obeyed. In a village of more than 300 people, only two crossed the line and left.

More than three centuries later, John Clifford is still moved emotionally by that decision to forgo the only real hope they had of escaping the plague. "There was a saying at the time: 'The best means against the Plague is a pair of new boots used 'til they break.' But the people of Eyam knew they would have taken the plague seeds with them, seeds that would have germinated in Sheffield or Manchester or wherever. The death toll would have been horrendous, spreading 'round the North Midlands and possibly to Scotland. But as Christ had offered his life as a sacrifice for people he didn't know and places he'd never heard of, so they made a similar sacrifice."

And it was a sacrifice. By the time the plague was over in November of 1666, 260 people had died in Eyam, the highest percentage of the population anywhere in England. Mompesson's wife Catherine died, but her husband and two children survived. Mrs. Hancock survived too. As soon as the *cordon sanitaire* was lifted, she left for Sheffield to live with her sole surviving son, and forget.

The more I looked at groups of people who have to live with the constant, obvious threat of death, the more the question of escape became important. The people of Eyam could have escaped, but because of their Christian concern for their countryfolk they chose not to. At least some contemporary communities in similar situations also choose not to run, but their motivation is different. They are people who rise up and say they're not going to be pushed around by death anymore.

•

For those who live around Washington, DC, the Valley Green neighborhood in southeast Washington is the personification of urban hell; poverty-, drug-, crime-, and death-ridden. Nobody goes there voluntarily, not white, black, or any other color people. You go to Valley

Green only if you have to, and never on a weekend night. Locals say that's just plain suicide and you deserve what is sure to happen to you. A Washington policeman I talked to said, "There's no such thing as an innocent bystander in Valley Green. If you're there, you're part of it, or you wouldn't be there."

I can understand how he feels. Driving around Valley Green and the adjacent areas late one summer Saturday night, I saw dozens of people on the streets and none of them looked to me like they were doing anything "normal." No young couples strolled along hand in hand on the way home from the movies. Nobody was walking a dog or just picking up a quart of milk at the 7-Eleven. In fact, nobody was alone anywhere. I had a passing thought that one of the ways you could get a laugh on the DC police radio was to call in from Valley Green to report that you'd seen a suspicious person on the street.

To a naive white guy from the Northwest, everybody looked like a portrait on the post office wall. Clusters of men and women stood around parked cars, just stood there as if they were waiting for something to happen and even they didn't know what it was going to be. They filled the time by staring at me, my car, and my driver/protector, a former DC cop turned security guard named Jimmy Carter. Officer Carter is a black man who used to patrol in Valley Green and knows it well. Here and there he'd wave to a selected few. Others would pull up beside us, look in to see who I was, and then chat with Officer Carter.

They were amazing conversations to hear. Because of the accents, the slang, and what was being said, it was like listening to a foreign film in a language I barely passed in high school. A few recognizable words would surface, but not enough to get the gist of what was going on. And yet the sound of it was almost poetic, the high, fast rhythms of the street people playing against Officer Carter's slower, deeper cop cadence. And maybe it was my imagination, or the effect of the environment, but even in this banter I felt a sense of menace on both sides of the conversation. As there are no innocent bystanders in Valley Green on a Saturday night, there are no innocent conversations either. For a police officer assigned to work the area, it must be terrifying, and the temptation to turn into a complete hardass must be overpowering. You have to admire people like Officer Carter who still care about and even like the night people of Valley Green.

We stopped at the corner of Wheeler and Varney, a corner Officer Carter said was the most dangerous in Washington. There were a few people lurking about, but when we parked they moved back into the shadows a hundred yards away.

"It's because I'm wearing the security guard uniform," Officer Carter explained. "And where they went they can see us a lot easier than we can see them."

I got out and looked around. Deserted apartment buildings with boarded-up windows loomed up in the loud yellow riot lights that are standard Valley Green street illumination. It was very quiet. I didn't hear any gunshots or screams in the night, just the rumble of traffic a few blocks away, occasionally a laugh, and that's all.

Matthew Carey came out to see who we were and why we were there. Matthew is around thirty. He lives on the corner of Wheeler and Varney. I told him I was interested in places where residents felt threatened all the time. That's all it took.

"When we first moved here, it was great," he said. "We had all races, all kinds, everybody living here. Nice and beautiful. But over the years, the place just started going down. Government didn't care about any local problems on this side of the bridge. Especially after the riots in '68. So over the years, things got worse and worse. We couldn't go out the front door without having problems. I even got shot in my own hallway by a fifteen-year-old boy. And it was a twelve-year-old told him to do it. But the same boy that shot me killed another kid on top of my steps there. And he's gone for life now."

A place where the fifteen-year-olds have guns and know how to use them would seem to be a place worth vacating quickly. The obvious question to Matthew Carey is why he doesn't get out of Valley Green. I ask, and he looks at me like I'm crazy.

"This is my home," he says simply. But he didn't come out in the night to tell me how bad things are.

"We get enough of that in the newspapers. Valley Green this, Valley Green that. 'A shooting in Valley Green.' It could happen in a lot of places, but it's always saying Valley Green. Valley Green's 'where the action is.' Sure, because everybody who's looking for action reads the newspapers and comes here."

And is there anything he can do about it? How does Matthew deal with the perpetual menace around him?

"You come back tomorrow," he says. "Come back tomorrow and see."

Twelve hours later, Sunday afternoon, fifty yards from the spot where Matthew Carey presented his invitation to come back. Under the hot summer sun there are few shadows anymore, but then there's no more need for shadows. Nobody is hiding, at least nobody in this particular part of Valley Green. The abandoned apartment buildings with the plywood windows are still there, but in the light I see that only half the buildings around this long court are empty. The other half are alive with people doing normal Sunday things. Two men and a boy drag a bright new garbage can around, picking up the minimal trash and sweeping the blacktop in front of the buildings. Another five or six guys are playing basketball, a noisy, crazy version of H-O-R-S-E where making the shot isn't important, it's how bizarre a shot you try to make. Couples sit together on the front stoops, enjoying each other and the day. And through it all a dozen or more little kids run around, screaming and laughing, darting under the basketball players or teasing their watching parents on the stoops. There aren't many toys in sight, just one bicycle and a squirt gun with a thirty foot range, and the only playground equipment is the basketball and hoop. But when kids are with friends they don't need toys.

Sitting in her second-floor window watching all the activity, Mrs. Jacqueline Massey discharges a smile that could knock a cat off a fence. Two of the kids below are her three-year-old grandsons, she's related to some of the ball players, and everyone else is a friend. Like Matthew Carey, who lives just across the way, Jackie remembers when the scene before her seemed like an impossible dream.

"We used to hear gunshots every night, twenty-four hours a day. But now we don't hear it that often. That's why I'm smiling a little bit, because when I look out this window, I see some things that you cannot possibly see. I see everybody doing their own thing harmoniously. The children are playing, every one of those fronts have somebody doing something on it—nobody is arguing or fussing, there's no disorder here."

One of the reasons for the change in this corner of Valley Green is Jackie. Two years ago she realized that life can be, *must* be something more than survival in the face of death.

"I was passive. I didn't give a damn. I really didn't care. I left out my back door and came back in. And when tragedy struck, when somebody got killed, I said, 'Oh well, that's too bad.' Without a doubt and without an interest."

But one day that somebody was her own son, murdered by his best friend. "For some reason or another, that particular night they got in a fight over . . . what? I don't know. I still to this day don't know what it was. The night before they were the last two people I saw together. They stopped me, waved at me. They were *friends*. Then about three in the morning the police department called me saying my son had been killed. And that's how I found out."

Jackie has lost three sons; one dead, and two others in prison, including a twenty year sentence as an accessory to murder. One of the grandchildren she watches from her window will never know his father.

But partly as a result of his death, the son will know a peace his father never had, at least while he's growing up. Because Grandma decided not to be passive anymore. She created a community organization and through it she hassled the city bureaucracy to stop ignoring Valley Green, stop writing her home off as an unconquerable jungle. Perhaps most important, Jackie talked to her friends about what they could do to get their neighborhood back.

"One thing I learned is that communities are made of people, not buildings and material things. So it's the people who have to have the work done on themselves first. Then you can change the outside structure, the buildings. You can do just about anything that is necessary to make change happen. All you have to do is have a strong back and stand up for something other than the candy man. And you can't be afraid. Because fear, fear makes you a sissy. With fear you can't think. It just chumps you up."

Snack time arrives in the square, and Jackie's aunt carries apple juice and paper plates with mounds of garish orange cheese puffs downstairs to the stoop. The kids attack the food and soon everyone under four feet tall, plus one basketball player, has a face amplified by cheese puff dust. Out at the corner of Wheeler and Varney a traveling ice cream truck pulls up. In my neighborhood back home such trucks endlessly blare a tinny version of "Yankee Doodle," but here in Valley Green you buy your ice cream to the Supremes. Feeling the need to contribute in some way to the party, I open a charge account with the ice cream lady. From her window, Jackie organizes the actual buy, directing the neighborhood kids on their march to the truck, making sure they line up single file, bawling good-natured threats at the few adults who decide a little ice cream might just hit the spot right now and try to get in line before the little ones. Soon cheese puff-dusty kids are also extremely sticky. It has been a good afternoon.

"I'm living every day, and I'm not going anywhere," Jackie tells me when I go back up to say good-bye. "And my children aren't going anywhere either. I've learned. To live on earth just existing and being passive and letting things just take place, waiting for something to happen to you and hoping it won't, that's a pitiful way to live your life. Pitiful. I was a pitiful person. But not anymore."

It would be misleading to make Jackie Massey's part of Valley Green sound like some kind of urban paradise. There is still great poverty here. Jackie and most of the other families are supported almost entirely by welfare. And there's crime too.

Matthew Carey tells me they haven't taken the neighborhood back entirely. There are still a lot of car thefts by young teens, a problem the community organization doesn't seem able to solve. And in one sense the neighborhood is still waiting for something to happen, only now they're waiting for the government to fulfill its promise to refurbish the abandoned buildings and get some good new families in. As the community exists now, you still would be very foolish to hang around Jackie's courtyard after dark. She couldn't protect you from her window, but at least now she and her friends would try. That's a big difference. Surrounded by very real agents of death, Jackie and her neighbors have still significantly increased the quality of their lives, first by confronting their fears and then by confronting the cause of those fears. They've driven the agents of death away, if only a block away, and only for twelve hours a day. If there's a lesson she'd like everybody to learn from what's happening in her neighborhood, it's not to let yourself get chumped up.

The cop who said there are no innocent bystanders in Valley Green was wrong. There are thousands of them. They're not part of the problem, but they sure as hell are going to be part of the solution.

•

Compared to Falls Road in West Belfast, Valley Green in Washington, DC, has the feeling of a Kansas church social, even at night. Like Valley Green, there is poverty in West Belfast, devastating unemployment, a rapidly decaying infrastructure, and continual danger, but there is something else, too; centuries of religious and political hatred. "The Troubles" in Northern Ireland have taken hundreds of lives through the years and will probably take many more in the years to come. I'm certainly not qualified to delineate what the sides want or deserve in the conflict, other than to say that the situation in Northern Ireland is far more complicated than a religious dispute between Catholics and Protestants. I only know what I felt in a few days in Northern Ireland's Six Counties, and that was a palpable tension that permeates every part of human existence. There may be Catholic families living perfectly normal lives on Falls Road, and Protestants doing the same just a few blocks away. But walking West Belfast's streets, watching children who seem afraid to play in front of their own homes, passing armed and ready soldiers patrolling the sidewalks back-to-back so they can't be ambushed from behind, it is quite impossible to imagine anyone reacting passively to what's happening there. A whole chumped-up country.

The closest I've come to obvious death, or so it seemed at the time, was doing a television documentary in Normandy on the fortieth anniversary of D day, in 1984. Because the program had to be ready for broadcast on D day itself, we shot the piece the week before June 6 and then satellite-fed it home from London on D day morning. Which meant we couldn't include footage of the various heads of state, including the Reagans and Margaret Thatcher, when they held the official ceremonies on Utah Beach. But at least we wanted to see Utah Beach, as well as the reviewing stand where Ron, Nancy, and Maggie would be. So two days before the event we arrived at the Utah Beach parking lot, got the camera out of the car, and strolled down toward the water. Coming around the corner of the just-erected grandstand, we were suddenly confronted by a line of French soldiers, perhaps a dozen of them, who immediately threw the bolts on their machine guns and pointed them at us. The oldest one looked to be about seventeen.

There's something about being in the gunsights of a group of teenagers. Each kid looked like he was holding a 114-inch howitzer and just itching to try it out on a real target. And in that split second of confrontation I realized that if one of these youths did accidentally fire, the French government would probably give him a medal for taking out an American journalist.

The moment passed quickly. The officer in charge arrived on a run and told us in uneasy English that the beach was off-limits. They were trying to prevent terrorists from planting a bomb in the sand that would blow Reagan out of his Florsheims in two days' time.

In Belfast I felt as I had that day on Utah Beach, only the moment didn't pass. And there were similar situations at the many roadblocks the military and police have established in the city. As I drove up, young soldiers would point their weapons at me and keep them that way until the grim-looking interrogating officer signaled them to relax. That always happened as soon as the officer heard my American accent. Then he would smile and off I'd go. But I couldn't help wondering what the reaction would have been had I had an Irish accent.

If Jackie Massey was not in Washington, DC, but instead a grandmother in West Belfast who had done what she's done, she wouldn't just be the top name on a large file at the Mayor's office. She'd win the Nobel Peace Prize. Mairead Maguire did win the Nobel Peace Prize in 1987 for her work in Northern Ireland. With two others she's a founder of the Community of the Peace People. Like Jackie Massey, she was motivated by deaths in the family. In August 1976 a suspected IRA man was shot in the head by an army patrol. The car he was driving went off the road and hit and killed three children who were innocent of everything except standing in the wrong place at the wrong time. They were Mairead's sister's kids, and a few years later their mother committed suicide. At the children's funeral, Mairead took flowers off the grave and gave them to the IRA suspect's mother, "because I felt a deep sorrow for that family, and I believe that that young man was a part of the tragedy of Northern Ireland as much as the children."

Like Jackie Massey, Mairead deals with the threat of death around her by first finding strength and commitment in herself. "When we started off saying we want peace, we had a very vague idea of what peace actually was. We grew into the recognition that peace starts within one's own self. It means respect for every single human person, respect for the environment, and it means working to change your society out of respect for those with whom you differ.

"When I hear another story of young people going out and taking another life for a cause, I feel they've desecrated something beautiful, given by God. There *is* no cause worth dying for. But there are many causes worth living passionately for."

Mairead finds strength and inspiration in her Catholic faith and in the nonviolent lives of Mahatma Ghandi and Martin Luther King, Jr. Through a belief in the sanctity and sense of all people she has personally been able to overcome the desire for vengeance.

"We have here in Northern Ireland people like the hunger strikers, ten men who, from the depths of their convictions, feeling they had no other way to bring about change, gave their lives. Sadly, around their dying many other people in the community died as well. Sadly, there will be young people who will take their example and not only give their own lives, but take other lives. When people talk about giving their lives for their country, dying for their country, what they're really saying is they're prepared to go out and kill other people."

•

I don't know if Jackie McMullen has killed other people. He says no, but given the time and place we talked, he would say no regardless of what the truth may be. Certainly there are people who think Jackie is a murderer and terrorist, people who would kill him without a moment's hesitation if they had the chance. And there are others who think he is a hero.

I found Jackie McMullen through the Sinn Fein office on Falls Road. Sinn Fein is the political arm of the Irish Republican Army, headquartered in the floors above a Republican bookstore where I bought my son Ned a "Spot the Dog" book in Gaelic. You can walk right into the bookstore, but the floors above are something else. You need an invitation, and after that there are three different locked doors before you're actually inside. It may seem overly protective for what is a political party office, but then Sinn Fein is not your average political party. A few months before my visit a man gone mad burst into these same offices and killed three people before he was captured.

Dennis Greg, the Sinn Fein director of information, showed me up-stairs but certainly didn't offer to give me a tour. He didn't need to. The offices seemed familiar, just like the radical political party head-quarters of the late 1960s in the United States. There were three floors of small, cold rooms, filled with intense people and the smell of coffee kept too hot too long. The only difference was the faces on the walls. Where I had seen Angela Davis, Abbie Hoffman, and Bobby Seale twenty-five years ago, here were the faces of Irish heroes going back a century or more.

Dennis Greg took me to a windowless room on the second floor. He was in his mid-forties, with thick black hair and a guarded but accom-modating manner. You might not have noticed him in a crowd, except that something horrible had happened to the right side of his body. His right arm was useless, his right eye was missing. I made the assumption that a bomb had gone off, too soon, too near, but for all I really know he was in a traffic accident driving to his mom's. Belfast is a war zone, and war zones lead to sometimes foolish and melodramatic assump-tions about people.

I had told him I wanted to meet one of the people from Falls Road who had been involved in the struggles for a long time, someone who had faced death in the streets, and had gotten involved in some way. We both knew the kind of person I was really asking for: a soldier, the same kind of person Mairead Maguire was trying to reach.

"Tomorrow," Dennis said, after making a phone call. "His name is Jackie McMullen."

In the late 1970s the Republican prisoners at Long Kesh, a British penitentiary near Belfast, refused to wear prison uniforms or do prison work. They claimed they were political internees and demanded to be treated as such, as they had been treated earlier in the decade by a differ-ent administration. The British government refused. The confrontation escalated during the next three years. Protesting prisoners were fre-quently locked up twenty-four hours a day and not allowed to use wash-ing facilities, which is why it came to be called the No Wash Protest. In July of 1978 when Cardinal O Fiaich visited Long Kesh—renamed Her Majesty's Prison the Maze—he said, "I was shocked at the inhuman conditions in H Block. One would hardly allow an animal to remain in such conditions. . . . The prisoners' cells are without beds, chairs, or ta-bles . . . " The cardinal began negotiations to settle the crisis, meeting with the prison authorities. But six months later he admitted they were getting nowhere. So on October 27, 1980, a hunger strike began in H Block. Fifty-three days later the British appeared to give in. But the Re-publican prisoners' victory was short-lived, and they claimed the prison authorities had reneged on their promises. Republican inmate leader Bobby Sands began a second hunger strike and called for volunteers to join him. Of the three hundred inmates in the No Wash Protest, half volunteered, with the knowledge that this would be a strike to the death. One of those volunteers was Jackie McMullen.

I'm already in the small room in Sinn Fein headquarters when he arrives, an athletic-looking, shy man who reminds me of Clint Eastwood in his spaghetti-western days. He has the same slightly bemused stare, the same slow way of speaking, the same sense about him that he could be either your best friend or your worst enemy. And he achieves all these effects effortlessly. (Months later, the woman who transcribed the tape recording of my conversation with Jackie McMullen told me she just had to know everything about him. Although she is, I think, a relatively apolitical American with little interest in the situation in Northern Ireland, she found Jackie oddly compelling just by listening to his voice and hearing what he said. When I showed her his picture she looked at it for a long time, smiled, and walked away without speaking.)

Jackie was born and raised in West Belfast. When he was thirteen he decided to get involved in the Republican movement. "It wasn't as if I was outside the situation and coldly, rationally weighed up all the factors. It was as much to do with the area I was brought up in, the friends I had. It just so happened that at that time things erupted in Belfast and like everyone else around me, I got involved in it."

Involved enough that seven years later the British decided Jackie should go to prison for the rest of his life. I didn't ask him what the specific charge was, because I didn't feel I could, and I knew that whatever it was, he thought the real charge was being the wrong faith, in the wrong party, from the wrong section of the city.

Five years after he went into Long Kesh, the prison Republican leaders declared the hunger strike. "I put my name down. We knew the seriousness of it, everyone who put their name down for the strike knew there was every chance that it would mean death. I wanted to make sure in my own mind that I wasn't going to let anyone down, that if I did join the strike I would be certain that I could go through with it. That isn't to say I wasn't afraid or that it was an easy decision to make. It wasn't."

Jackie was one of a handful of men chosen to participate. Seven months after Bobby Sands began the strike, it ended. Sands was the first and most famous to die. He was followed by nine others. The surviving leaders, believing that the British were willing to let them all die, called off the strike. They gave many official reasons, but Jackie remembers how the men inside really felt.

"When Bobby Sands died and the government was able to weather that storm, we knew it was hopeless." Jackie McMullen survived the hunger strike . . . barely. He had fasted for forty-eight days, a day longer than Martin Hurson, one of the ten.

When we talked in the fall of 1992, Jackie was in the process of being released. He was a thirty-five-year-old man with a wife still in prison, not much of a job, and few prospects but to return to the very streets that contributed to his being sent to prison before. But he could never be anonymous again, not to his friends or foes. He was one of the hunger strikers.

"I think about the men who died, I knew some of them very well. They were just ordinary people, with faults like everybody else. Just ordinary people who happened to be born where they were born, in the Six Counties. If you could talk to them today, they wouldn't regard themselves as heroes, you know? They woulda laughed at ya had ya suggested they were heroes. What are heroes? Heroes are made by other people. In my own case, this may sound kind of funny, but I couldn't have lived with myself had I volunteered to go on the hunger strike for any reasons that had to do with self-glorification or making myself a hero. And none of 'em were like that.

"This country does tend to glorify people, and I don't think that's a good thing. If everyone was held by ties of loyalty to 'our glorious dead,' there could never be any end to it. Because people from all sides have died. I agree with Mairead Maguire—we should be more concerned with living for a cause as opposed to dying for a cause."

Toward the end of our conversation I suggested that Jackie and I walk up Falls Road so I could see it the way he does. He looked embarrassed, and Dennis Greg jumped in quickly to say that would be a bad idea. I realized why. In just three and a half decades, Jackie has seen more than thirty of his family and friends killed, and narrowly escaped death on the streets himself. His life has always been dangerous, but now with his fame each day on the street is even more threatening. Because now there are people within a few blocks of Falls Road who would particularly like to kill the Jackie McMullen they know by name and sight, people who hate him and are terrified of him. And there are only two ways he can live with that.

"I fear for my life, but I take precautions and I'm constantly aware of the dangers. But that isn't to say I'm terrified of death. It's just something I live with. My only other choice is to get up and walk away from here, leave Belfast, leave Ireland. But in my heart, I know I would be doing wrong. This is my home." Like Matthew Carey, Jackie Massey and the people of Valley Green, Jackie McMullen is not going to be pushed around by death, and he's part of the struggle to see that his neighbors aren't either.

It is not my place to take sides in what the British call "the Irish question." I talked to Jackie because he's a human being who was surrounded by death practically from birth. Then at the age when most of us have firmly opted for immortality he had to choose what might have been death for political reasons. The nature of those political reasons, at least for me, was and is unimportant. But I should also say I liked him. It will be hard for me in the future to read reports about IRA terrorists and not consider that I may know one, and I know him to be a quiet, intelligent man who more than anything else on earth desperately wants peace in the country he loves; a peace he has never known.

I won't forget the last time I saw him, leaving the Sinn Fein office, walking quietly but quickly up Falls Road; looking not like a hero nor a villain, but just an ordinary man trying to stay alive.

•

Finally, there is Mrs. Chhean Im, who did escape the deadly world around her only to discover that she could not escape the emotional impact of the life she left behind.

Mrs. Im lives in California now, with her daughter and grandchildren. The extended family has a Long Beach duplex on a relatively quiet street, far from the tourist-thick waterfront. The afternoon I arrived, the grandkids were watching cartoons on one side of the small wood-frame house, staring zombielike at the television set just like all American kids do. And on the other side of the house, Mrs. Im was sitting in the window, staring blankly out towards the street.

She is blind, or nearly so, and has been ever since a horrifying day back in her native Cambodia. Hiding in the forest near her village, she watched Khmer Rouge troops torture and kill her husband and all her remaining children. There's no physiological explanation for her blindness. In fact there are some skeptics who say that Mrs. Im and the more than two-hundred other blind, elderly Cambodian women who have taken refuge in the United States are faking their disability because it gets them more financial support from the American government.

I suppose that's possible. If Mrs. Im survived the Cambodian government, fiddling the American welfare system is probably not a big challenge. But having spent some time with her, the last word I would use to describe Chhean Im is "sly." Helpless, pathetic, terrified, yes, but about as sly as a lost child. And the psychological explanation for her blindness makes sense, at least to me. She has seen too much, and her subconscious mind has said, "Enough."

"I never had a problem with my eyesight before. But when they killed a lot of people, I started to have headaches," she tells me. "My eyes became blurry. There was no medicine, so I used salty water to wash my eyes. They became bloody, and I couldn't see. When I came here, the American doctors said I have a mental problem. I am thinking too much."

She stops, looks around at her living room. On the walls are images of her country torn from magazines, beautiful technicolor pages full of lush forests and rare beasts. And there are pictures of her family, formal portraits of her husband and children. She can't see them well, but she obviously feels them.

"I lost my husband, I lost my children. My heart is broken." And then she is gone, into herself, thinking again.

Since coming to America and getting glasses and medical treatment, her sight has improved slightly. But when there is any kind of threat to her family she loses her vision again. It's happened twice, when her granddaughter was harassed by gang members, and a few days before my visit, when a robber burst through the back door in the middle of the night. He took the little money they had and Mrs. Im's wedding ring. But the most traumatic moment for her was when he left. He told them not to report the robbery to the police or he would come back and kill them all. Mrs. Im has heard threats like that before. It's probably a significant step towards her psychological liberation that she ignored the warning and called the cops. The day I visited, her sight was coming back again, and she was eager not to blame America.

"I like the peace, the freedom and the peace here. The most happiness is the grandchildren going to school, to hear all the children come back home safe. But the television they watch. I don't want to see death in the movies, I don't want to see killing. I get scared."

She has tried to tell her grandchildren about her life before coming to America, about their grandfather and what happened to him. But she says they don't understand, they don't care. They are young Americans now, in the full blush of immortality. Even with the gangs in Long Beach, the children are almost completely removed from the realities of a life surrounded by death. In one way Mrs. Im is glad they will never be as terrified as she was, never feel the emotional devastation that she feels constantly. At the same time, though, she thinks people should know that such things happen. Because the more who know, the more who will decide to stand up and fight against the forces of death.

CHAPTER SEVEN

NOT DEAD, ONLY SLEEPING

> Though lovers be lost, love shall not,
> And death shall have no dominion.
> —Dylan Thomas

When writing about death you have to be careful or you can fall into a bottomless pit of pithy quotations, from the famous last words of the famous . . .

> "Get out! Last words are for fools who
> haven't said enough!"
> —Karl Marx's last words

. . . to just the deathly thoughts of everyone who ever contemplated "the perilous leap" (Milton), which is just about everyone. I usually dislike stories that begin with quotations anyway. The practice suggests that the writer thinks I'm not quite bright enough to figure out what his or her magnificent work is *really all about* so he or she has provided a little helper for me to refer back to during the more difficult passages. I've made an exception in this case because Dylan Thomas could have been writing specifically about Joe and Terry Cannon. They really have quite a simple story. Boy gets girl, girl gets boy, forever. And Dylan Thomas nailed it in thirteen words.

There are a lot of people like Joe Cannon in Florida, elderly Americans drawn to the sun from colder climates up north. "In the land of the cold and the windchill factor," as John Prine sings, they worked hard and sent their kids to school and then off into lives of their own. Then they got the hell out before one more pipe burst, either under the house or in the heart.

They say a Minnesota winter is the best real estate salesman Florida has, but I think there's more to the state's attraction for the elderly than just heat. Retired neo-Floridians have finished their life's work, but they are done with their life's hopes too. There's not a single place in the whole flat peninsula where you can climb a hill, sit on a ledge looking down into a green river valley, and dream great dreams of the future. And even if there were such a place in Florida, the climate isn't conducive to strenuous physical or mental activity. The hot, wet air clings to your body like mucous, daring you to make any quick moves. Beginners wait until nightfall for that damp cloak to go away. When it doesn't, they go back to bed in their air-conditioned rooms and ponder staying there forever. I should think if you've already done a lot in your life, Florida is a good place to do not much more. And when you don't have anything to put off until tomorrow, maybe it eases your fear that there might not be a tomorrow. Florida's just right for *really* getting away from it all, a state that offers no hope to those who don't need hope anymore.

There are exceptions, of course, even amongst the elderly residents. Ace and Lil Leshner at the Golda Meir Center hope each day will be enjoyable, and they work hard to see that it is. Colonel Bill Royal and the people who come to Warm Mineral Springs hope each day that the waters will conquer this ache or that pain. But of all the Floridian elderly I met, only Joe Cannon still dreams of something beyond a good dinner, a comfortable bed to sleep in, and hips that won't need replacing. Joe Cannon dreams of forever.

He's in his mid-seventies now, but he seems ten years younger. In old photographs he has thick, dark, finger-waved hair that makes him look like an insurance executive who leads a dance band at the VFW on weekends, like Wallace Stevens if he'd played sax and not words. The finger wave is almost gone now, but the white hair is still all there. Joe's got big, strong hands, and a walk that's careful but determined. He looks like a guy who's done some construction work in his time, and he has, in a shipyard during the war.

By trade he's a consulting engineer, although he claims to be the only consulting engineer in America nobody has ever bothered to consult. Joe reminds you of that old neighborhood guy you knew as a kid who always had interesting things in his pockets. Except Joe has always had interesting things in his mind.

I suspect his curiosity about how things work, and how they might work if you messed with them a little, is lifelong. They say Edison was like that, but Edison messed with the right stuff, and mostly Joe hasn't. Edison had the electric light, Joe holds the patent on a kind of flush valve. Throughout his life he's concentrated on subjects he's found interesting, whether they would pay off or not.

For instance, a long time ago he got interested in deviant sexual behavior. Theory, not practice. He read all he could about it, talked to some people, eventually gave lectures and counseled young couples. It was an odd sort of hobby for a man who felt the need to mark the "risqué" anecdotes in his autobiography with an asterisk, but Joe never promised to be consistent, just curious.

He's always been a frugal man, so he and Terry didn't need much money. They went to Florida every winter, the Bahamas once, and Europe three times. In Amsterdam Joe paid a prostitute twenty-five dollars for an hour of conversation—*just* conversation. Terry waited outside, and when Joe was done they went to dinner. That's Joe, and that was Terry too.

They met in Wisconsin, the lawyer's son and consulting engineer with little ability or interest in sales and marketing, and the tall, scrappy farm girl from Michigan with most of a good education. From the day they met until the day she died, there was nobody else in their lives, not even kids. Terry had an abortion before she met Joe, the result of a disastrous affair with one of her college professors. The abortion was badly done and she was thereafter incapable of having children. I don't know how Joe felt about it then. Now, forty-five years later, he's decided it was for the best.

"I know it sounds selfish, but I was just as happy I didn't have to share her with anybody else," he says. "See, you're not going to believe this, but I think I had the most perfect wife any man ever had. We never had an argument, not one. I mean arguments where you get nasty with each other and say unkind things. We had lots of differences of opinion, but we would talk them over. And she was correct on more of her opinions than I was. Terry was a much smarter person than I am, much higher IQ."

Joe Cannon is one of those guys who always knew how lucky he was in his marriage. He didn't have to find out the hard way after he was alone. He's never had any regrets that he neglected to tell Terry how much he loved her, because it was something he never neglected. But a married lifetime of happiness hasn't made the loneliness of widowerhood any easier. And if, in her absence, he's put Terry on a pedestal, he did that a long time ago in her presence. Now he can look at their life together almost objectively. She had an abortion, he was never much good as a money-maker, they didn't have many friends. But for thirty-nine years they were very happy with just each other. And then she died, and Joe Cannon took Terry off her pedestal and put most of her on ice.

In 1964 a Michigan junior college physics teacher named Robert C. W. Ettinger published a book titled *The Prospect Of Immortality*. Ettinger contended that technology and medicine had finally reached the point where human bodies could be stored indefinitely with little or no cell damage. The key was cryogenics—deep freezing—and therefore Ettinger's human freezing process was called cryonics. He wasn't the first to suggest suspending the deceased until a technologically better time. Science fiction writers had toyed with the idea, and almost two hundred years ago Benjamin Franklin wrote in a letter to his friend Jacques Duborg that he wished drowning victims could be embalmed "in such a manner that they may be recalled to life at any period, however distant." Franklin went on to describe the special kind of post-mortem immersion he would personally enjoy.

"I should prefer to any ordinary death, being immersed in a cask of Madeira wine, with a few friends, to be then recalled to life by the solar warmth of my dear country." Franklin had the right idea, just the wrong medium.

Instead of the basic pleasures of being pickled in wine with a few friends, Ettinger instead offered what he claimed was the first real scientific hope of eternal life, or at least continual resurrection. Because if it was possible to defeat the disintegration of putrefaction, then human beings could simply wait for the other, much more difficult half of the resurrection process to become a reality.

That second half of the process was the real gamble, not the freezing, because bringing people back might never be possible. Cryonics believers have to assume that someday human tissue can be repaired and rejoined cell by cell, first to reanimate the frozen, and then to eliminate what killed them in the first place. Philosophically it requires seeing human beings in very cold biological terms. Each person is a pattern of atoms, and what makes that individual unique is not the atoms (and not the soul) but simply the pattern. If the pattern is damaged, theoretically it can be repaired as long as the functional state can be determined by the damaged state.

The analogy cryonics fans use most often is the wrecked car. Wrap your Chevy around a tree and it ceases to function. But tow it to a Chevy dealer and a repair person can return the car to working order, albeit with a scratch here and there and maybe an irritating squeak when you turn left. But if you have the car melted down into a block of scrap iron and then take it in, you're going to be minus one Chevy. Similarly, if you reduce a human body to ashes, or put it where its sole function is to feed ground organisms, you lose it forever too. Ettinger's hope for the future made sense, as long as you were willing to think of yourself as a soft Chevy and the spark of life as being something that could be provided by biogenetic jumper cables.

Most people weren't ready for that possibility. I was in high school when *The Prospect Of Immortality* came out, and as I remember most of the nation's press reported Dr. Ettinger's theory as the loony ravings of a disturbed Science Guy who wanted to turn the nation's cadavers into Popsicles. His book was dumped into the bin with the UFO, Bigfoot, and Loch Ness Monster books and that was that. Three years later, Dr. James Bedford turned theory into reality by becoming the first person ever put into cryonic suspension. Bedford's apparently successful freezing didn't change the nation's attitude much. Even those who took the possibility seriously had many questions. Would the inhabitants of the future have any interest in defrosting the inhabitants of the past, even if they could? Sure, the first one will get thawed out, repaired, and go on to make millions of dollars on the twenty-first-century lecture circuit telling history students what Madonna was really like. But what about the third defrostee, or the hundredth, or the thousandth? And if the general public finally agrees that cryonics is a real possibility, what effect will fifty million resurrected immortals have on population control? Eventually, if the majority of the world's people are the formerly frozen, what's to keep them from saying, "That's it, we're the last earth generation, those wishing to have babies please go to Mars"?

But there were some people across the country who perked up like spaniels in duck season at Ettinger's hypothesis. They included a then fifty-three-year-old consulting engineer named Joe, and a nine-year-old boy named Carlos.

The center of the cryonics universe is now Riverside, California, home of the nonprofit Alcor Life Extension Foundation, the latest and most enduring of a succession of folk-freezing concerns that came about as a result of Ettinger's book. Alcor is located in an office park on the outskirts of town. At least it *looks* like the outskirts. Riverside may be one of those California towns that's nothing but outskirts. Next door is a car-customizing place specializing in vehicles for the movies. Parked out in front of that business is a 1957 hearse, a bit of cheap irony that nevertheless sets me up nicely for the Alcor Experience. How many of Alcor's drop-in trade accidentally go next door first?

Alcor's waiting room is very small, what you'd expect a moderately unpopular dentist to have. But then this is not an operation that concerns itself much with the comfort of the living who have to wait. Alcor is strictly for dead waiting.

"We don't say dead. We say 'de-animated.'" Thirty-six-year-old Carlos Mondragon is Alcor's president and one of the few paid employees. He's a gaunt, intense, friendly man who maintains a refreshing sense of humor about the cryonics business. Carlos has led hundreds of journalists, skeptics, journalist/skeptics and potential patients through both the shop and the philosophy behind it. He's very good at cryo-show-and-tell because he makes you think it's still just as exciting to him now as it was when he was nine. He isn't the least bit woowoo about what Alcor does, either; no mystery-of-the-ages stuff from Carlos. He describes cryonics and the philosophy behind it more as a series of redefinitions than re-animations.

"What's dead?" he begins. "To be declared legally dead, all it means is that some guy who has an M.D. after his name has given up and said 'Nothing more I can do. Adios. Beam him up.' Absolutely nothing magical about that. In most cases when it's done, it's simply that they've decided not to resuscitate the patient. You got an eighty-year-old woman dying of cancer in a hospital. She stops breathing. I guarantee you that 95 percent of the time they could get her back. They could keep resuscitating her until every bone in her chest is broken, and get her back for a few days, then a few hours, then a few minutes. But they're not going to do it. And they shouldn't. It would be pointless; pointless and cruel."

So cryonics is not freezing the dead in hopes that someday they can be brought back to life. It's freezing the living, and by that simple difference Alcor avoids a lot of problems, like the taboos in various cultures and faiths about mutilation of the deceased.

"I'm not crazy," Carlos says. "I don't think you can bring the dead back to life. I just don't happen to think our patients are dead." So Carlos and his staff doctors are really mutilating the *living*, just as tattoo artists and pierced-ear pokers do, and with similar consent. A family can't wait until Uncle Harry drops and then decide to have him cryonically suspended. By Alcor's rules, the potential patient must arrange the procedure him- or herself, usually paying for it through an insurance policy. At present the cost is between $35,000 and $80,000 for the various possible procedures, although who knows what kind of defrosting bill they'll hand you for re-animation in the future. Look at what it costs to fix a Chevy now, and re-animation sounds like it's going to take a lot more than two days in the shop plus parts and labor.

But Alcorians don't worry about re-animation. They concentrate on getting de-animation right first. Carlos leads me into the operating theater, where the de-animated as a doornail are brought for the treatment. And it's quite a treatment.

"I've been a volunteer on the team for the last fifteen of them that were done here, and I don't look forward ever to doing another one," Carlos says. "I know most of these people, and cryonics suspension is the second worst thing that can happen to you. The first is dying and not getting cryonically suspended."

It should not come as a surprise that dreadful things start happening to your body the moment after you die. Well, that's not precisely true. What happens to your body is dreadful only if you plan to use that body in the future. The first thing that occurs is that blood stops flowing—ischemia—and that starts biochemical changes taking place rapidly. To prevent that, cryonics patients are put on artificial life support in the field as soon after death as possible. They are also cooled a bit, and rushed to the Alcor table in Riverside.

"Once they're here, we try to mitigate freezing damage, and we do that by replacing as much of the water in the body as possible. By accessing the circulatory system with a heart-lung machine, we can replace the water with glycerol, a chemical that doesn't expand when it freezes. Then the patient is cooled down to dry ice temperature, which is 110 degrees below zero Fahrenheit. Then a few days later they'll slowly be cooled to liquid nitrogen temperature, about 210 below." And that's it, although Carlos is leaving out a few steps, but then you weren't planning on trying this at home, were you?

Just outside the operating theater are the diplomas and other honors of Alcor's "resident" physician, Dr. Donovan, famous for his deadside manner, according to Carlos.

"A couple of years ago the local health department bureaucrat insisted that we needed a physician on staff. We have two physicians on staff, as a matter of fact, but they're volunteers who come in when needed. But the bureaucrat said, 'You gotta have a physician on the premises twenty-four hours a day,' which was ridiculous. It's not like any of our patients are going to need a doctor suddenly. But it so happens that at the time Dr. Donovan was terminally ill, and we were getting ready to put him in cryonic suspension. He was a man with a great sense of humor. He told his family, 'After I'm suspended send all my diplomas to Alcor so they can hang them on the wall, and if anybody asks them if they've got a doctor on the premises, they can truthfully say yes.' "

Bureaucrats, not physicians, hospitals, or patient families, are the main pain in Alcor's rump. Cryonics is messing with death, which is not something elected officials care to have happen on their watch, as Carlos and staff learned with the interesting case of Dora Kent.

The eighty-three-year-old Ms. Kent knew that speed is of the essence for successful cryonics suspension. The more time nature gets to perform its dust-to-dust process, the more likely there will be permanent brain damage and physical deterioration. Ideally a patient would be hooked to Alcor's heart-lung machine the moment after death. Dora Kent had a lingering cancer, so she had plenty of warning about when the end was nigh. Just before she reached nigh, she came to Alcor, lay down on the operating table, and expired. Ms. Kent was a cryonics neuropatient, which means only her head was to be frozen. So after her demise a death certificate was signed by the volunteer physician present. Then she was decapitated and her sconce frozen in the standard manner. But shortly thereafter a deputy county coroner remarked to a reporter that he thought Ms. Kent's decapitation and freezing preceded her death, even though an autopsy of her abbreviated body showed the specific cause of death as "pneumonia" and not "no head." Knowing reporters as I do, I should imagine the young newsie drove back to his pressroom at a hundred and fifty miles an hour (you can do that in southern California) with visions of a Pulitzer prize dancing in his existing head.

"My God, you should have seen the headlines," Carlos says now.

The police response to the confusion was to take Carlos and staff out the door of Alcor in handcuffs, so they couldn't decapitate and freeze anybody else on the way to the station house. Then the coroner insisted that Dora's head must be decanted and autopsied too, which of course would play hob with her suspension and destroy any reanimated future she might possibly have. Alcor's attorneys fought the arrests and the neuro-autopsy, and won. The business end of Dora Kent now rests comfortably in the Alcor storage area across the hall from the operating room.

Just as that operating room is the only one in the world where every patient arrives dead (except Dora Kent) and leaves not dead, so Alcor's storage area is the only one in the world where the boxes of stationery, paper clips, and rubber gloves are right around the corner from twelve frozen heads and twenty-three frozen bodies. (At Alcor if you nautically ask, "Where's the head?" you could be in for a big surprise.)

You can't actually see the heads and bodies. They're stored in large metal containers called Dewars, named for the man who invented them. (Yes, the same man associated with whiskey. He apparently also designed the thermos-style container in anticipation of the outdoor professional football game, when his two contributions to mankind would be combined.) Dewars are essentially ten-foot-tall stainless steel thermos bottles without the plastic cups on top. There are four full-body patients in each Dewar, with the neuropatients bunched up in smaller containers.

"The bodies are in individual aluminum pods, wrapped in sleeping bags, head down for maximum protection to the brain, surrounded by liquid nitrogen." Carlos anticipates the next question, probably because he's heard it so many times.

"No, nobody's going to melt if we have a power failure. The Dewar is a mechanical device not dependent on electricity. And in a bad earthquake our only real problem would be that our supply of liquid nitrogen might be interrupted, in which case we'd have to have it flown in for a while. And should a Dewar seal fail, the liquid would boil off a lot faster than it normally would, which is why the patients are head down. But there's an alarm system both on the inside and outside to detect temperature changes, and there's somebody here twenty-four hours a day if the alarm goes off." Somebody besides Dr. Donovan presumably.

Alcor's system seems almost foolproof, even financially. There's a patient trust fund that is used exclusively for liquid nitrogen and other direct patient services, not to pay the rent or meet the payroll. Those basic operating funds come from donations to the foundation, which is why there are so many volunteers and so few paid staff. But even with all the safeguards, Carlos admits to the occasional nightmare that two-hundred years from now a cryogenics expert will say, "Gee, it's too bad those idiots back in the twentieth century didn't know to do 'x' so we could actually have revived these people. Get the dumpster." Alcor only has to perform half a dozen suspensions a year now. The rest of the time is spent on research, principally to combat what can best be called freezer burn on the brain.

"Our big question right now is are we preserving enough structure, memory structure in the brain to conserve the person's identity. We know that memories are physically encoded in your brain. How much of those memories could you lose and still be you? We're doing damage to the brain, we know that too, but it's not catastrophic damage. Still, there's a chance these people could be revived and not be themselves anymore. Or they could be severely retarded and physically disabled. And if that happens, then the whole experiment is a failure."

In most of the world's religions the possibility of some kind of existence after death is never called an experiment. An afterlife is 100 percent guaranteed, and the only question is how enjoyable that afterlife will be. Human beings can affect the answer to that question by the quality of their faith at the moment of death, their descendants' actions performing the proper death rituals, and/or most commonly by their behavior throughout life. Sinful living (however you define sin) and you go to hell, are tortured forever, or are reincarnated as a flea on the rump of a dead camel. But a good and righteous life gets you heaven, eternal bliss, or reincarnation as the person who owns a herd of camels but never has to clean up after them.

Cryonics, however, is available to anybody with the money and the circulatory system to handle it. Alcor makes no value judgments about how you lived your life. They don't even ask why you want to come back in the future. What you trade for cryonics' nonjudgmental stance is an absence of the kind of mortality hand-holding that religion offers. Cryonics might not work, it will be something of a miracle if it does, the future world may not want you, and when you see the future you may not want it. Nobody I talked to at Alcor, from Carlos to the guy who tops off the nitrogen, claims anything other than a slim chance for success, no matter how much you pray *or* pay. What they do emphasize is that a slim chance is better than no chance.

As far as nobody in the future wanting the frozen back, Carlos says, "*I* want them back, or my successor, or his successor. This is a volunteer mutual aid society organization; we're gonna want those people back because it's in our own interest. And I'm not really concerned as to what the rest of the world will think about that. I don't base the value of an individual life on popularity." So if all this is true, why isn't everybody in the world who can pay the freight signed up for the Big Freeze?

"I wish I could answer that," says Carlos, the devout believer. "I think the reason is that it's evolutionary—not revolutionary, evolutionary. Several thousand years ago human beings became aware of their own mortality, and in order to keep from going insane, in order to develop civilization, they had to find a way to deal with that. Most of us when we're adolescents realize at some point that we're going to die. And we find a little pigeonhole to stick that information in. Cryonics just drags your mortality out of that little pigeonhole in the brain and makes people very uncomfortable, because then they have to go through the whole thing all over of rethinking it. That's one possibility. Another is that by nature people hate ambiguities. We like things to be clear-cut, black or white, especially on an important issue like life and death. And cryonics makes for a big, ugly ambiguity."

As of this writing, thirty-five people have slipped into the Big Ambiguity, and a hundred more are ready when the time comes. Alcor membership is going up dramatically each year. According to an Alcor survey taken in 1991, 70 percent of the current members are men and 80 percent have college degrees (16 percent Ph.D.'s, 20 percent masters). The majority of present and future patients come from some kind of engineering background, especially (like Carlos) computer engineering. Politically, eight out of ten identify themselves as libertarians of some kind, and though generally not religious, several are Catholics, with a smattering of born-again Christians. Four generations of one family have signed up, and Great Grandpa's already on ice. He currently resides in Alcor's back room with a television comedy writer; a real estate investor; a cardiac researcher; Dr. Bedford, the original De-Animator; and a neuropatient named Terry Cannon.

•

Joe Cannon sits and gazes out over the lake behind his house in central Florida, sipping an orange juice made from his own oranges. The sun's just going down, and his property is glowing. Joe's pretty much of a loner in his neighborhood, just that eccentric old man down the road with the two old Cadillac de Villes parked out front. He says there haven't been more than five visitors to the Cannon homestead since he and Terry started living there a decade ago. Not many visitors, not much chance to talk about Terry. And if there's one thing you can say about Joe Cannon, it's that he's a talker.

"Cryonics was my interest at first. Terry accepted it, but she accepted anything I was interested in. And there's something about freezing and saving yourself, somehow it's a man's thing. You tell me 70 percent of the people in Riverside are men, I'm not surprised. But as the years went on, Terry became more interested, I think for the same reasons I was.

"Right near the end, I asked her, 'What do you want? Do you want neuropreservation, you know, just the head, or the whole body preservation?' Well, she had cancer, you know, three different kinds over a ten-year period. And she looked at me and said, 'Joe, if I have to come back with this body, I don't want to come back at all.' I never questioned it. I would have bent over backwards and sold everything I had if she had answered otherwise, even though we didn't have a lot of money, and the whole body was more than twice as much."

Cryonics was made for a guy like Joe. He read Robert Ettinger's book and it just made sense to him. Ettinger was using new technology to mess with an old idea, and that's been Joe's modus operandi all his life. But there were two other reasons Joe went big for Ettinger's theory. A self-described agnostic, Joe thinks cryonics is the only chance for continued survival, not just the scientific chance. "The kingdom of God isn't some spiritual roof garden! It's inside you!" as e. e. cummings's

Unitarian minister father once said. Joe would certainly agree with that, while at the same time admitting that occasionally he feels Terry's presence strongly in their home, helping him when he needs it. "All of a sudden I'll have this choice and I'll stop and think for no reason at all, which way to go. It usually turns out favorably, too."

Joe's other reason for embracing cryonics goes to the question of why anybody wants to come back. There are certainly a few cryo-candidates like Dr. Timothy Leary, the former Harvard professor, LSD advocate and video game designer, who now bills himself as a "philospher." In 1989, according to a report in the *Spectator,* Leary called all his followers together in a West Hollywood restaurant. There the good doctor and supposed convert to Hinduism announced that he had just completed the paperwork to have his head cryonically suspended by Alcor. Other than saying his mission is to popularize "new and shocking ideas" (the cryonics idea was by then a quarter of a century old) Leary's reasons for being frozen aren't mentioned in the article. But having spent one of the longer hours of my life trying to interview him, I would guess he wants to come back in the future because he can't conceive of a future without Timothy Leary. He plans to give the gift of himself to coming generations, starving for his insights.

I'm sure the majority of Alcor's membership isn't the least like Leary. For them, the attraction of cryonic suspension is the same as the attraction of time travel, the enthralling possibility that you can close your eyes and then open them two-hundred years or so in the future. I've always thought time travel as presented in science fiction is the one fantasy we can be sure will never come true. Because if someday the technology arrives to permit travel back in time, presumably the technology will continue, so that such travel will be possible from that moment through eternity. And given that inconceivable stretch of time, doesn't it follow that *somebody* would have returned to the 1990s and been identified as a future dweller? So either time travel is and forever will be impossible, or it will come to be so very far in the future, like 9,000,000 AD, that none of the travelers ever sees fit to come to the insignificant twentieth century. They must be real nice folks, too, to just let us die of heart disease, cancer, AIDS, and so on and not drop in with the medical insights they've developed. But if nobody is ever coming here from the future, that implies eternity has limits, that not long after 9,000,000 AD intelligent life will be eliminated from the Universe, or surely somebody from 18,000,000 A.D. would have come by, if only to see what fried chicken really tasted like. Either that, or future civilization will be so completely totalitarian and repressive that nobody will be allowed to travel back in time for fear of altering history, and all those other time travel problems science fiction writers imagine. Who among us wants to be part of a future civilization that has the will and the person-power to make any prohibition stick *forever*?

Cryonic suspension, then, is the only kind of time travel that makes the slightest sense now; a ticket to the future with the extra added benefit that when you get there you won't be dead anymore. This might be the deal of a bunch of lifetimes, so it makes sense that those who believe it can happen want it to happen so much.

Joe Cannon is, I suspect, in the rare third category of cryonics candidates, a person who is driven by neither ego nor personal curiosity about the future. The real reason Ettinger's idea so appealed to him is because it offered the slim possibility, not of his own resurrection, but of Terry's. And the even slimmer chance that he could be with her again. Joe Cannon is a man eternally in love.

"If Terry weren't frozen, I wouldn't go ahead with this," he says. "What makes me anxious for it to succeed is that someday I hope to continue on that wonderful marriage with her. That's what pushes me forward."

Joe is taking an even bigger chance than most cryonics patients. Because he lives alone in a relatively rural area there's at least a chance he will die alone as well. And if, in the Florida heat, he isn't found quickly, then cryonics suspension will be pointless. The same applies if he is found by people who don't know his wishes and instead of hooking him up to a heart-lung machine just zip him into a body bag and take the long way back to the morgue. Ideally Joe should pack up, move to Riverside and prepare himself to do a modified Dora Kent ("Nobody de-animates here again, ever"—Carlos) but he can't bring himself to leave the little house by the Florida lake.

"Terry and I built this home. She designed it, and we built it ourselves. And it's sort of a holy place to me. It isn't pretentious. In fact it's about a step above poverty level. But it has a closeness to me. There's too much of her here for me to leave, no matter what the reason."

To increase his odds, Joe has surrounded his bed with equipment solely meant to tell the world he's ready for the freeze. There's a monitor from a company in Massachusetts. If, in extremis, he pushes a button, a bell goes off in Boston and they call him back a minute and a half later. If there's no answer they dispatch the Florida medics immediately. When he sleeps, Joe wears a belt around his chest originally designed for babies prone to sudden infant death syndrome. If he stops breathing another bell goes off in a nearby hospital and the paramedics ride again. When they arrive, they'll find Joe's own personal heart-lung machine tucked under his bed, a bottle of Alcor-recommended medi-

cine his local hospital doesn't stock, and lengthy instructions printed
on a large sign on the wall telling the arrivees precisely what they have
to do, beginning with immediate cardiopulmonary resuscitation. And
Joe knows it all might be for naught.

"I could still go into town for groceries and be killed in a car wreck
coming back. So you play the averages and do what you feel comfortable with. I just hope they remember when the bell rings, it rings for
Joe."

Joe's preparation for his own future freezing is nothing compared to
his preparation for Terry's future resurrection. With the possible exception of Dora Kent, Terry had the best suspension possible. At her bedside in Wisconsin in 1987 were two Alcor doctors. After she was declared
dead, Joe doesn't think she missed three breaths before they had her
attached to a heart-lung machine and a sympathetic undertaker was
packing her in ice. She was then flown to Riverside and the suspension
process completed without any problems. So Joe knows that her
chances of coming back successfully are at least as good as his, and
probably better. And if that happens—if Terry returns, and he doesn't—
she's going to find a world prepared and waiting for her, thanks to him.

"Several years ago I took about two-thirds of everything I had and I
put it in an irrevocable trust. Nobody can touch that money, not even
me. It's for Terry. Alcor is the trustee, so they can use it to get her an
apartment, if such a thing exists then, and show her how goods are
purchased, just help acclimate her to this restoration of life. And if she
wants to live here in the house, I've arranged for a local realtor to rent
it, and for Alcor to be the manager of it, to keep it rented until the day
Terry gets back."

Joe knows of Alcor's concern about possible memory loss, so he's
prepared for that too. He's the star of a long videotape, telling his once
and future wife who she is, who he was and what their life was like together. And he's written and self-published a book, *Recollections of an
Average Man*, with 168 stories from his life and their marriage. He's
even considered the possibility of a third party.

"Because my suspension may not be as good as hers, there's a
chance that even though I die at a later date she may be re-animated
first. If that happened and if, five, ten, or fifteen years later I were re-
animated and I learned that she had found some man that she was just
delighted to be with, I would wish her well. I would make no attempt
to interfere with her pleasure."

Which is about the only thing Joe Cannon said to me that I thought
was crap. If Terry were the kind of woman to abandon the man who
talked her into cryonic suspension and then spent the remainder of his

life getting a world ready for her return, she would never have merited all his efforts and his continuing devotion in the first place. Years after her death, they are still a couple, not because of cryonics, but because, well, because though lovers be lost, love shall not.

I spent two days with Joe Cannon in Florida. Across the street from his home he owns a house he rents out to tourists in the summer. He let me stay there overnight, said he'd see me tomorrow whenever I wanted to get up. But around 6:30 the next morning I heard somebody moving outside, so I staggered to a window and there was Joe, peeking in. "Oh! You're up!" he said, just the way my grandfather used to shout, "Are you awake?" at anybody who was still in bed after dawn.

Joe was lonely and wanted to talk. He said he needed to tell me something, even though he was nervous I wouldn't understand, that nobody would.

We had breakfast and drank a lot more of his orange juice. And finally, after staring at me for a while, he talked about just how much Terry is a part of his life, even now.

"I didn't go to Riverside with Terry. I was just too exhausted. After she had been suspended—of course, only her head—the rest of her body went to a crematorium in California. And I was so upset with losing her that I told them to hold her remains for a few months while I thought of what to do with them. First I thought I'd bury her here in the yard where we had lived so happily for so long. But then I decided on something else. They sent me her ashes and bone fragments in a cardboard box. That was the hardest part of the whole thing, getting that box open. It took me all day. Then I got a large piece of pipe, about an inch and a half in diameter and ten inches long, plus a round steel bar just a little smaller so it could go inside. I took her remains and little by little I put them in this pipe. Then I rammed them hard with the steel bar, just like a druggist grinds things in a pestle. It took me four days, off and on, but eventually I reduced all her remains to a fine powder. Then even though they'd been sterilized to over two-thousand degrees in the crematorium, I wanted to play it safe so I put them in the oven at five-hundred degrees and baked them all one afternoon. Then I went to the drugstore and got some capsules, you know, like pills but empty, and I filled them with the powder that used to be Terry. And after that was done I started taking one with each meal. All except three. Those I put under her pillow, along with the down payment on a trip to Mars I bought her last year, ten dollars down— although I was hoping she'd be in the first flight—but she's probably not going to be back in time. So part of her is still sleeping in our bed, part of her is walking along with me every time I take a step, and part of her is cryonically suspended, waiting for the day when she'll be alive and able to continue her life. And I hope with me there to enjoy it with her."

What Joe Cannon did—what he's worried people will find repulsive— would be understood automatically by many other cultures around the world. And I think anybody who met Joe would understand it too, regardless of their culture.

The Alcor Life Extension Foundation has a fifty-page booklet they mail out and give to visitors to the Riverside facility. It's called *Reaching for Tomorrow,* and on the cover is a version of the "God Almost Touches Man" hands from the Sistine Chapel ceiling. In the Alcor version the man's hand is a frosty blue. Inside, the booklet covers what you'd expect, including lots of information about the tardigrade, a tiny animal that can be dried out and then rehydrated "like a backpacker's dinner" with no visible negative effects. Other beasts who have successfully endured freezing are also profiled, and there's a detailed report on how much the cryonic procedure costs, including "ice, 500 pounds, $62.00," as well as sixty cc of Maalox.

On page fifteen there's a picture without any identification, without even a caption to indicate why it's there. It's a formal picture of two people, a man and a woman. She looks emaciated and in great pain, but she still has a huge smile. She's gently holding the man's hand as if he's the one who needs reassurance. And indeed, he looks nervous and uncomfortable, like he's about to say something and what he's about to say is "get on with it."

The people are, of course, Joe and Terry Cannon, and if anybody needs a reason to hope cryonics works, they are it.

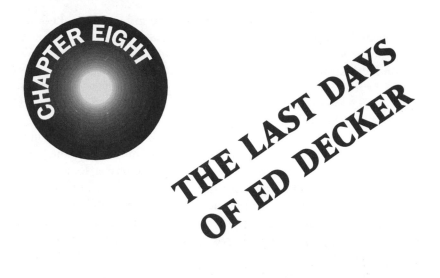

CHAPTER EIGHT
THE LAST DAYS OF ED DECKER

There was nothing special about Ed Decker. He had a normal American middle-class, twentieth-century white guy's life, with a wife, kids, jobs, a house. He was proud of some of the things he had done, and ashamed of a few others, and there were a lot of things that just happened without comment.

I didn't know him well. We met for the first time in the last two weeks of his life. After we'd been talking for an hour I thought I had a pretty good sense of him. Then he showed me a picture of a strapping, handsome man in a fire fighter's uniform, proudly standing in front of a fire truck.

"Is this your son?" I asked, even though the person in the photograph didn't look anything like Ed.

"No." He laughed. "That's me thirty years ago." And I realized I didn't have any idea who Ed Decker really was and I probably never would. There wasn't enough time left, and there wasn't enough Ed left either. I don't mean physically. Ed had both heart disease and lung cancer. It was just a question of which would kill him first, and Ed was hoping for a massive heart attack because he thought it would be more painful but a lot quicker. In those last days he looked like a good wind would blow him away. But a person doesn't have to be ready to run a marathon to be the person they are. It was Ed's emotional condition that made him impossible to really know by then.

He had two weeks to go, and he *knew* it. So in his mind I think he was reviewing his life, bouncing along the peaks, sometimes crawling through the valleys, and all but ignoring the flatland. Listening to a person recall his best of times/worst of times and find reasons and justifications for both is no way to judge him. It's the daily business of living that shows who we really are. A lot of mediocre actors can sound like Laurence Olivier when they're reciting the big, flamboyant speeches. The great actors reveal themselves by making the familiar something special, by making simple business unique. That was certainly the basis of Chaplin's art. And for Ed Decker, all the simple business was over.

We tried to get to know each other anyway. Ed realized it was too late to share his life with anybody new, but it wasn't too late to share his death. I was right on time for that, and for some reason he agreed to let me into part of it. People who knew him told me that like Joe Cannon, Ed was the kind of guy who loved to have listeners, and they were right. But not because he wanted the world to know he'd gotten a bum deal. He no longer felt the need to scream "It's not fair!" to anyone who would listen. I'm not even sure he thought his coming death *was* a bum deal. He wasn't pleased about it, but the hardest part wasn't knowing it was going to happen soon; the hardest part was waiting for it, having that fact dominate not only his every moment but every moment of his family as well. Like many of us, Ed would have preferred just going to sleep one night, breathing out, and then not breathing in. But it was his lot to live for a while with dying. Death was a palpable presence sitting next to him, like a rude party guest who shows up a half hour early, takes the best seat in the room and dominates every conversation.

Even though he hated the waiting, Ed was still glad that he would be able to say good-bye to those he loved. And he hoped the end would be easy—for him, for them. At the same time the process of dying both terrified and fascinated him. Ultimately I think that's why he decided to share his last adventure with me and a few other people. Because he was a talker, and this business of dying was certainly something to talk about. But he was reluctant to talk to his family about it because he didn't want to scare them, he didn't want to make his going any harder on them than it had to be. He wanted to share the terror and the fascination, and show somebody who wouldn't care much that he could handle them both. But Ed underestimated himself. To know him, even for a few weeks, was to care about him. You couldn't help yourself.

He was eighty-two when we met, and had been married for sixty-one years. Ed and Anne fell in love when she was twelve and he was sixteen, and they married five years later. They had been together ever since, the kind of couple that finishes each other's sentences but neither one gets irritated by it. She'd had a pretty rough childhood, an orphan raised by her aunt. I'd guess that the older, more experienced Ed was kind of a surrogate father for her. But that was a long time ago, and now they were equals in every way—or as equal as two people can be when one of them is obviously dying and the other one just as obviously isn't.

They lived in an apartment in Issaquah, a relatively small town about twenty miles east of Seattle. The apartment was relatively small too; one bedroom, a living/dining area, and a kitchen that would barely accommodate two people. Already that kitchen was used more for hushed conferences about Ed than for food preparation. It was just the right size for that.

Although hearing diminishes as we age, it's usually the last sense to go completely. That's one of the reasons so many religions have specific prayers to be whispered into the ear of the dying, and why nurses in terminal wards are cautioned not to say anything around the patient they don't want known, regardless of how unconscious or asleep the patient seems to be. So the dying are treated to a lot of whispered conversations in other rooms; people talking about present symptoms, future plans. I saw it happen to Ed, did it to him myself in fact, but he didn't seem to mind. Ed had lost almost all his vision years before. He knew when the lights were on. In fact he insisted that they be on all the time, because he still had a little peripheral sight. But if he couldn't hear you, and didn't sense you were near him, you weren't in the universe as far as he was concerned. Unless you were Anne.

The Deckers were originally from the Catskill Mountains of New York. Ed showed me a picture of their house, and I thought it was a shot of a Swiss chalet from their trip to Europe.

"Not Swiss. Bavarian," Ed said. He liked Bavaria, especially the beer. Rarely hard liquor for Ed Decker. He was a lifelong beer man who went to Munich and found Gott.

Ed had worked a lot of jobs. He was a construction welder, bank teller, fire fighter, police officer, and he and Anne ran what she called a boardinghouse and he called a hotel. "A hotel sounds classier. But Anne's right, it was a boardinghouse. We had a lotta land with it, though." The hotel was on two-hundred and fifty acres, with a lake out back. That suited Ed fine because he liked to fish. In his last days, when things seemed particularly grim, Ed would rouse himself by telling his favorite fishing story, about the one that almost got away. He and his then young son had been standing in a river fishing for trout for a long time. The boy finally caught a fish, held it up for his father to see, and said, "Is this the one you're trying to catch, Dad?" Ed would smile when he told the story and laugh his growly laugh. Sitting nearby on the couch Anne would laugh too. She'd probably heard Ed tell it five-hundred times since the day it happened, but she still laughed, especially then. Because Ed was happy, and at that time more than anything else in the world Anne wanted Ed to be happy.

One day that lake behind the boardinghouse, and fishing, led to what Ed became known for, certainly the thing he wanted to be remembered for.

"I was fishing with Bud Burston at the time, friend of mine. This was in the late 1940s on the lake at Kerhonkson, New York. Bud was a show doctor, a guy Broadway people called up when they had a show in trouble out of town and needed some gags. He wrote for radio too. And we got to talking about comedians, and I mentioned one guy and said, 'I can write just as good as that.' And Bud said, 'Maybe you can, but if you only have a few jokes you might as well give them away, you'll never get them sold. But if you can do it consistently, then maybe you can earn some dough. Pick a comedian,' he says, 'somebody you like who thinks like you, and write some stuff.' So I did, I picked Henry Morgan, who was very big on radio in New York at that time. And I sent my stuff off to him, just like a fan letter, you know, I said, 'Here's some material for you, free, gratis, for the years you've given me pleasure.' I was sucking up to him, see?

"Six weeks later I'm chopping firewood. Another guy and I got five dollars a cord. And I'm in town to pick up the mail and there's a letter from WJZ Radio, in green ink, I'll always remember, green ink, and under WJZ it said, 'H. Morgan.' 'Wow,' I said. My heart was pounding, and I opened it up and inside was a check for seventy-five dollars. And I'm killin' myself in the forest for five bucks a cord! From then on I was a comedy writer. Part-time. Wrote for Morgan for seven years, and then Bob and Ray and some others.

"Bob and Ray were amazing. I'd bring in a stack of stuff, they had these desks across from each other, and they'd take it and read it cold, and they had it right from the start; the characters, every gag. That was something. I just missed making three grand on the line Jack Paar gave after he came back from walking off the 'Tonight Show.' He was gonna use my line and pay me three grand for it, but when he walked out he said something else and I saw those bills just fly out the window."

Ed's comedy was based on looking at normal situations and turning them around just a little to show how ridiculous they could be. It's the kind of thing Jerry Seinfeld does now for more money per week than Ed Decker made in his entire life. But Ed didn't resent that. He got a lot of joy from contemporary comedians.

"I'll listen to these new guys, on these cable comedy shows, and hear lines I wrote in 1954. That's a kick."

Ed also liked to take advertising to its logical conclusion.

"There was this coffee, advertised that it was 97 percent caffeine free. So I created another brand of coffee that purchased all the caffeine from the real brand. My coffee was 97 percent caffeine, but at no extra price because we just hauled it away from the other guys. In trucks." Ed says he got in trouble with a few sponsors for making fun of them, but that was the only reason he ever had material rejected. "It was always funny enough."

All the time he was writing for radio Ed was still working at other jobs. Writing was never enough to support Ed and Anne and their children, but it kept him busy right up to the end. He was working on a book when he died, *Confessions of a Practical Joker*, he wrote a column for the local newspaper, and he'd recorded some story tapes for kids. *Grandpa Decker Tells Some Stories* was such a hit at the Issaquah public library that the tape wore out and they asked Ed to make another one. He was very proud of that, and proud of the award he got from the school system for teaching writing to eighth-graders at a nearby school.

"I got a letter from the kids, they sent me a valentine, a big thing, and they all wrote little notes. They were real notes too, not 'Mr. Decker, we're sorry you're sick, get well,' you know, all the same. Each one had their own little message in there. And one boy said I turned his life around. He was a problem child and a lot of it was his family, but he was getting poor grades and everything. And then he went up to an A student. I turned his life around." And at that moment, for the first time in our conversation, Ed Decker started to cry.

We get considerable joy from our life's achievements, but in the case of people like Ed, that joy is undermined by knowing that the good times, the good deeds are all over. And most of the highs have a low attached. Ed succeeded as a comedy writer, he thought, because he'd always been a smartass. But when I asked him if there was anything he regretted about his life, anything he wanted to do that he hadn't done yet, he was quiet for a long time, and there were tears in his eyes when he answered.

"I should have said I was sorry. If I could go through my teens and so on and be able to say I'm sorry. But that's impossible. That's really the only thing I regret, being a smartass when I didn't have to be."

And so I tried, feebly, to console him, and he promptly nailed me for it.

"There are worse things than being a smartass," I said. "Believe me, I should know. I'm sort of a professional smartass."

"So I hear," said Ed Decker.

Gradually our conversation shifted to the present. I said before that for Ed, all the simple business was over. But that's not really accurate. There was plenty of simple business to be done in his life, it just wasn't simple anymore, partly because he was almost blind, partly because his feet were in bad shape and his strength was gone. Getting around was very difficult. A lot of people are blind and/or infirm and have to deal with the inconveniences caused by their disabilities, but for Ed and those like him there is something else. Maybe it's a loss of motivation, a sense that tonight might be the night, so why should I try? Perhaps that's a danger of reaching Elizabeth Kübler-Ross's last stage, of Acceptance. Once you've accepted the fact that you're about to die, why should you be gracious about accepting any other problem, especially since each little pain, each time you need help going to the john, is just another reminder that time is running out? Acceptance can lead to self-ishness. Ed worried about Anne as much as she worried about him. Yet he would bark orders at her to get him something, do something, remember something he could not. And then he would catch himself and sink into a deep sadness.

I learned from Ed that reaching Acceptance is not like becoming a Shriner, where once you get there that's what you are. The afternoon before we talked, a new nurse came by to see him and mentioned cheerily that he had only been given six months to live but was lasting a lot longer. She wasn't being especially thickheaded and insensitive. Ed had been told many times he was terminal and had acknowledged the fact many times. So she thought she was cheering him up. But it was the first time in a few weeks he had actually heard the words, and it was like yanking the world out from under him. The next afternoon he was still shaken.

"I just had a CAT scan. They found that the tumor had reduced itself by 50 percent, so I was pretty happy about that. And I don't have any pain, which always seems to amaze them. I knew I didn't have a long time, but yesterday . . . I don't like those words."

You can see his point. To a man in Ed Decker's situation, "Congratulations, you're still alive!" may seem like an appropriate thing to say. But the subtext of the sentence is "And am I surprised!" Ed sensed that, and he resented it.

In the final days of almost all terminal patients, there comes a time when the emphasis shifts from the dying person to his or her care givers, the family and medical staff whose obligation it is to make those last days as good as possible. To describe the final days of Ed Decker without talking about Anne, their daughter Nancy, and especially the professional people who helped all of them, is impossible. Because in one sense Ed was lucky. Not only were his wife and family there for him when he needed them, but he was dying under the care of a hospice.

It wasn't his or Anne's idea initially. Anne went to their family doctor for a checkup and he suggested that it was time to prepare for Ed's care, that Evergreen Hospice up the road in Kirkland might be the way to go because Ed was terrified of being in a nursing home or hospital. He wanted to stay at home, and die at home if at all possible. But the physical and emotional burden on Anne would have been dangerous for her health. Like most hospices, Evergreen emphasized home care for the dying person and the family, but greatly assisted home care.

Anne didn't want to talk to Ed about it because "hospice" meant dying and at the time neither of them were ready to deal with that reality. Eventually Anne and her daughter Nancy told Ed they were "going out on some business," but instead they drove to Evergreen and took a tour. Anne actually felt guilty about misleading Ed.

"Oh yes, I felt very badly. Nancy laughed at me when I said, 'I lied to your father for the first time.' I didn't want to upset him. And then we found out what a beautiful place it was and what they could do for Ed. I thought God must be watching over us. So then we had to tell Ed. Nancy came up with me and I told him and he took it so well. I said, 'If you ever have to go there I could even sleep overnight. You know how I love to sleep on a couch.' And he said OK. Here I'd been so distressed about what he would think. I had told him a barefaced lie. Because we usually are truthful with each other or I say nothing, rather than get into a mess about it. We've been married a long time, you learn to talk and when not to."

So it was agreed. Ed would stay at home, and only go to Evergreen when the time came, if he had to. I wasn't there when the decision was made, but from talking to Ed months later I can understand why he accepted the hospice so easily. The reason people give for not visiting the dying is that they don't know what to do, and especially they don't know what to say. Hospital and hospice workers suggest you act normally and treat the patient as you always would, not ignoring the situation but not letting it change you either. And though I agree that the dying want to be talked to just like everybody else, I think it's also true that they want to be treated better than everybody else. They think they deserve it, and I think they're usually right. And better treatment of the dying is what hospices are all about.

The modern hospice movement began just about the time Ed was starting to knock out gags for Henry Morgan, although specialized care facilities for the dying have existed for centuries. In the Middle Ages hospices were places where travelers could rest on their journeys.

Mary Aikenhead, founder of the modern hospice movement, adopted the name for facilities for the terminally ill because she thought it reflected the proper philosophy of treatment for the dying. A hospice isn't the last place you go; it's a rest stop on a greater journey. But Aikenhead emphasized that the hospice isn't just a specialized medical facility. For the hospice experience to work the way it should, it is crucial to link the care of dying patients with community care and support in the home. Hospices aren't just for the dying, they're for the whole family.

Hospice care was first put on a scientific as well as philosophical basis in Britain. It makes sense that treating the dying requires special medical and personal skills if the patients and their families are to benefit. Nurses can get mired in ward efficiency, and doctors have to overcome all that training that teaches them any death is a failure. Once a patient is diagnosed as terminal and accepts the fact, that patient usually doesn't need or want a lot of the hospital routine other patients endure because they think it will help them recover, things like the early morning pulse taking and temperature reading. And as long as they're in the Acceptance stage, terminal patients can usually do without bright-eyed physicians taking tests and desperately seeking cures, as well as medical students who just drop by to listen to a really classic example of cancerous lungs. God help the medical student who tried to turn Ed Decker into a learning experience. Ed would have told him to take his stethoscope and marry it.

A disinclination to be inundated with cure-happy doctors doesn't mean the terminal patient wishes to abandon hope. The principal reason Ed was so upset by the "six-months nurse" was that he'd just had a successful CAT scan. He'd built up a little hope, if not for recovery, then at least for more time. She abruptly snatched that hope away. It made Ed even angrier because she didn't even realize she'd done it.

Staff insensitivity is another justification for the existence of hospices. Like most businesses, hospitals have slang expressions for various situations. But in the medical field, the expressions apply to people and circumstances that the rest of us find extremely serious.

In some hospitals, "the O sign" means the deceased has an open mouth, and "the Q sign" means his or her tongue is hanging out. Operations that kill the patient are called "therapeutic misadventures" and a patient for whom death is imminent is said to be "circling the drain." Telling that patient's family his or her condition is called "hanging crepe." And though such expressions sound brutally unfeeling to the public, I think it's unfair to blame hospital staff entirely for questionable sensitivity and taste. Spending sometimes decades of your life learning how to help people and then having to deal with people who are beyond help must be a very frustrating experience. A medical student once told me he was planning on going into pediatrics because "I don't mind kids, and your patients don't die as much."

Even in medical situations where death is common and the staff is prepared for it there can be emotionally traumatic situations. A friend of mine was one of the chief nurses at a facility for the study and treatment of a particular kind of leukemia. They were working with experimental chemotherapy that rendered the patient almost completely defenseless to any other disease. The mortality rate at this research hospital was near 100 percent—they offered patients a little time but not yet a cure. However, the fact that practically every patient was terminal wasn't what convinced my friend to leave after twelve years of outstanding work. She had adjusted to the high death rate by convincing herself that the medical research they were doing was a lot more important than any feelings of sadness or frustration she may have had.

Then one day a patient who seemed to be doing well suddenly died in the night. It was hardly a unique occurrence there, but the staff still couldn't figure out why he died until an autopsy revealed a strange fungus in the patient's brain. They finally traced the fungus to a potted geranium, a gift that had been left on the windowsill of his room. A man had literally been killed by a plant ten feet away, and my friend, the nurse, walked out. The sheer idiocy of that death was just too much for her.

At the same time, hospital staffs are made up of normal people (except the surgeons, of course), and we normal people out here in the nonmedical world shy away from the dying and dead, so why shouldn't people who work in a hospital do the same, subconsciously if no other way? Hospital workers have many of the same psychological reasons to dislike being around the dying as us civilians. Looking at terminal patients can't be that enjoyable if you harbor any fears about your own death, for instance. And they have work-related reasons too. Terminal patients are not easy to take care of, in part because they so often need more psychological support than nurses and doctors have the time or inclination to give, especially to a patient who is obviously going to "fail."

There is also the question of limited resources. According to a 1992 *Wall Street Journal* article, one in every seven health care dollars spent yearly in the United States is being spent on the last six months of someone's life. That same article begins by describing the forty-one days in intensive care of "Patient M," a ninety-year-old man with severe bilateral pneumonia, a fractured hip, and gradual respiratory, kidney, and heart failure. His doctor never thought he'd survive, and the doctor was right. But the cost to keep Patient M alive, the cost for respirators, heart monitors, antibiotics, sedatives, and X rays, amounted to $93,111.

Americans spend fifty billion dollars a year on critical care, and the elderly are the fastest-growing group of critical care patients. I assume that like the public, doctors, nurses, and hospital staffs think resources could be better allocated, and harbor at least some repressed resentment toward the dying for taking time and treatment away from people with a far better chance of survival. That resentment may be at a peak presently, because the technology now exists to quantify objectively a patient's survival chances.

•

I spent an afternoon in Washington, DC, at George Washington University Medical Center with Dr. William Knaus. A critical care physician for decades, in the mid-1970s Dr. Knaus began working on a computer system for hospitals that would display the survival chances, compared to a national data base, of every patient in a critical care unit. The system was eventually called APACHE, for Acute Physiology, Age, Chronic Health Evaluation. APACHE III has been available to hospitals since January of 1991, and it draws information from a statistical sample of 17,000+ patients in seventy-nine disease categories.

"This system is a response to the fact that when I went to a family, their question invariably was 'What are his chances, Doc?' And I knew that whatever I was telling them was so uncertain and so based on my own judgment that I felt very uncomfortable. Most physicians do. The APACHE system says there's a starting point."

APACHE actually does three things. It tells intensive care unit (ICU) staffs how they're doing, how well they have treated previous patients. It helps manage resources by telling the staff where they are being efficient and inefficient. And finally, in the Clinical Decision Support Module, APACHE helps doctors and nurses make decisions about continued treatment or life support of patients by providing the probabilities that a particular patient will survive his or her illness.

On an APACHE computer screen, Dr. Knaus showed me a graphic representation of a twenty-bed ICU, with the little beds in different colors.

"What you see displayed are two risk estimates, based on the national sample and similar ICUs. One is the patient's risk of dying before being discharged from the ICU, and the other is the risk of dying before leaving the hospital. Each of the beds is color-coded based on that risk estimate. Patients with a 10 percent risk of dying have green beds, 10 to 40 percent are in yellow, 40 to 80 percent risk of death is orange, and then greater than 80 percent is red. So what a doctor can do is look at this bed screen to see what his unit's like. If there are a lot of red beds, he knows it's going to be a bad day."

The doctor also knows if he or she is doing any good by seeing from the screen that a patient arrived with a 20 percent chance of dying, but three days later had a 60 percent chance of dying, or vice versa.

"What this enables doctors to do really for the first time is to separate out effect from benefit. We can do a lot of things to very sick patients in intensive care. The question is, what benefit is that having on them? Is it actually assisting that patient on a day-to-day basis in achieving the outcome, which for an ICU is saving lives? And the other thing the system enables a doctor or nurse to do is keep things in perspective."

Dr. Knaus pointed to a red (near-dead) bed.

"This patient is eighty-four years old, and the question is how much of a role should the fact that he's eighty-four play in the decision of how much treatment he should get. Let me emphasize that age is just one of the criteria for risk estimate in the APACHE system. And also that the system itself doesn't make decisions. It never tells a doctor what to do."

However, for a doctor trained to believe that survival is success and death is failure, the APACHE system certainly indicates where success and failure probably lie within the ICU on any given day. That can't help but have an effect on the staff's allocation of their *emotional* resources, and eventually the allocation of financial and technical resources as well.

Dr. Knaus agrees, and argues that there is a decided benefit to that use of APACHE.

"APACHE could be used for allocation of resources, *if* society decides that they want to begin making decisions about allocation based upon a patient's ability to benefit as opposed to their ability to pay, which is the way allocation's been done up 'til now in this country. The system can show that decisions were made for reasons of benefit to the patient, not arbitrarily, not because the patient didn't have insurance, or because she was black, or because he was poor."

Currently APACHE can only predict chances of survival, with no consideration of the quality of life for the one who survives. Dr. Knaus is working on models that will also predict functional ability, and when that APACHE arrives doctors really will be able to answer the "what are his chances?" question adequately. But I still wouldn't want to be a guy in a red bed. Or I'd want to be in a place where the beds were nothing but red; a specialized care facility for the terminal with a new definition of success and failure.

•

In Sydney, Australia, I visited a hospice called Sacred Heart. It's part of a huge Catholic medical center next door, but Sacred Heart is a very independent place. The hospice itself is in a big pink building on a busy downtown street, but in the beautifully kept gardens behind the walls you would think you were a thousand miles away from anything other than a big pink building.

Sacred Heart began in 1890, and through a number of locations and buildings it has always had about a hundred beds. But the nature of the care has changed radically, from a warehouse where the sympathetic sat with the waiting, to a place where "we don't add days to your life, we add life to your days," as the staff says. And like Evergreen hospice, many of the people under Sacred Heart's care don't stay in the facility but come in from their homes.

While the medical staff concentrates on alleviating pain and treating the nagging little problems like diarrhea and even hiccups that accompany some illnesses, the nursing staff specializes in making each patient feel like a special guest. They are true *care* givers, not pill givers and injection givers. All the patients I talked to mentioned that when they arrived at the door of Sacred Heart Hospice for the first time, there was someone from the staff waiting for them who knew their name and made them welcome.

Ian is a personable thirty-four-year-old man with an AIDS-related illness who has lived all over the world. Now he lives at Sacred Heart, a hospice that mixes AIDS patients with those suffering from cancer and other terminal diseases.

"My first day here, people greeted me at the door and said, 'Where is your partner? Where are your friends? Who's bringing you in?' I said, 'No, it's just me, kids.' I didn't have any family until I crossed the threshold here. And suddenly there was family. Because these people are now my friends. It's great, I'm very lucky. Yeah, I know, 'lucky' sounds a bit over the top, but that's the way I feel."

Britta, a Danish woman in her forties with cancer, agrees that the friendships she's made at Sacred Heart are the best thing about her situation, but at the same time friendships in such a place are difficult.

"We become friends so quickly because we have to, we haven't got time to fool around. And it gets hard, because the longer you last here, the more of those friends you lose."

According to Ian, being much younger than most of the residents has a good and bad side too. "A lot of women have said to me, 'Are you visiting, or are you here?' And when I told them they said, 'That's crazy, why?' And often they grab my hand. I mean, women don't just come up to you and grab your hand. But in a hospice they do that. They want to hear my story, which I've told fifteen million times. And then I'll see tears in their eyes. At the same time, I can tell it's hard on many of the people here to see someone as young as I am. They feel sorry for me, it depresses them, and depression is what everyone is fighting against so hard. And being a depressant for other people depresses me. Still, coming here was the best decision I ever made."

Sacred Heart is indeed a very special place, no more so than on Friday afternoons when all the residents have a party. The beer flows freely, you can smoke 'em if you got 'em, and a sense of joy pervades the building. The entertainment is provided by visiting volunteers, but the residents are invited to join in, and they do. While a seventy-year-old nun danced a sedate shimmy, I watched an eighty-six-year-old man do a music hall rendition of "Molly Malone" that would knock your hat in the water. He was accompanied by a roomful of very sick people singing "alive, alive oh" on the choruses as loud as they could. The message in the room was simple but touching: "We ain't dead *yet*."

Those who think people generally aren't affected by their own pending deaths, no matter what age they are, should attend a party like Sacred Heart's Friday bash. It's probably one of the few places on earth where the room is full of people who really aren't concerned with death, because they are so close to it and have accepted it. They're no longer worried about it—at least, not as long as the party is going on. And I could feel that in the room. These people have had one of life's last great questions *nearly* answered. As Nietzsche said, "the final reward of the dead—to die no more." *They know what it is like to die,* and at least on Friday afternoons, it's free beer and a sing-along. That knowledge allows them an escape from fear that is both eerie and mesmerizing.

For years Sacred Heart Hospice was directed by Sister Patricia Grantham. She eventually transferred over to the hospital side and is now the chief administrator there. Sister Patricia has seen life and death from both sides now, and knows the subtle but important differences between the acute care of a hospital and what she calls the apellative care of the hospice.

"I think the activity in the acute setting would drive me nuts if I was dying," she says. "There it's always go, go, go towards cure. Well, it should be, that's the purpose of a hospital. In the hospice it's go, go, go, too, but it's toward the person, the patient only, in terms of what they want to do, rather than being thrust upon them by professionals outside."

Oddly, hospices have suffered some from their success and reputation. Not every potential patient is as agreeable as Ed Decker was when the hospice alternative first comes up.

"It's strange, you know?" Ian told me. "When my doctor suggested Sacred Heart I thought, a hospice, my God, that's the place where people die. I can't go there."

Sister Patricia recognizes that many patients are like Ian. The very name hospice is frightening. It may mean "good death" to health care workers and the healthy, but the operative word is "death" for the terminal. That's why Sister Patricia prefers the designation "apellative care," why she also sees Sacred Heart and any good hospice as an educational facility as much as a care facility for both patients and staff.

"Education of the medical profession to understand that not everybody can have a cure of their disease, no matter what it might be. And for those we can't cure, we can still help, help them in a way that we staff members don't feel like failures."

Making the patient not feel like a failure is just as important. What is interesting about the care given in a hospice is how much success is based on what are otherwise trivial things, like meeting a patient at the door and knowing his or her name. Sacred Heart Hospital has rooms full of multimillion-dollar equipment for diagnosis, evaluation, repair, and recovery. Sacred Heart Hospice has a dog. That may not sound like much, but for people who are desperately seeking some normalcy in their lives, a pooch on the ward is a masterful touch that immediately says, "Things are a bit different here." (Evergreen Hospice in Kirkland says the same thing with a resident cat.)

But the small touches that make patients feel good about themselves and their surroundings aren't limited to an official greeter and one galumphing golden retriever. The women residents have their hair washed regularly and the men either shave themselves daily or are shaved if they so wish. Even though the residents may not feel their best, they always look as good as possible, and that's vital to basic self-esteem. The staff is also trained to be aware of pain, whether the patient admits it or not. And more than anything else, hope is never allowed to disappear entirely.

Except for an eye patch, Ian looks very healthy. But he has Kaposi's Sarcoma lesions internally, and when we talked he didn't know how extensive the cancer was.

"I'm petrified of what this thing is doing to me inside. But I don't think this is going to kill me. And I think I'm going to be one of the first people in Australia to get through to the other side, and be sitting there writing a book. All I have to do is survive another twenty-four

months. The pharmaceutical companies, the politicians, they're all looking for, maybe not a cure for AIDS, but something that will certainly
stabilize my condition. And once they've got something patented,
they're gonna be on the bandwagon to get distribution. Twenty-four
months. And that's what I'm hoping for."

A staff member told me she thought Ian had no more than a month
left, although they don't think in those terms, preferring to deal with
each day as it comes. I was glad I wouldn't be there for his death. Even
for the experienced staff of Sacred Heart, I thought the loss of someone that young, that bright, would be extremely sad and painful. Unlike Ed Decker, Ian had every reason to scream "It's not fair!" until the
last moment. But the people who staff hospices, many of whom initially dread the idea of working with the near-dead, say that the experience is not the emotional horror they thought it would be. It's often
the opposite. Although they certainly have down days and develop
emotional attachments to patients that lead to great sorrow when those
patients die, being able to give so much comfort to people who need it
so badly is tremendously uplifting.

"I don't know if this will make sense," one nurse at Sacred Heart
said to me, "but last night I sat with a man and just held his hand. We
didn't talk, we didn't do anything but just sit there in the dark for
hours. And this morning he was gone. I felt more privileged to be able
to do that for him, more like I knew why I became a nurse in the first
place, than I ever felt when I was working in an intensive care unit. It's
an honor to do this work."

I should think it is also reassuring on another level. I've never met a
funeral director who personally wanted a huge funeral when the time
came, and I've never met a hospice worker who didn't want to die in a
hospice when the time came. Being surrounded by good deaths must
be comforting, once you get used to being surrounded by death in the
first place. You know the good death is possible because you've seen it
happen.

From watching nursing staff work in both hospitals and hospices, it
seems to me that to be a good hospital nurse requires technical skill,
but to be a good hospice nurse requires a good heart. As a dying nurse
once wrote to her colleagues, "If you care, you can't go wrong."

Ed Decker's principal nurse from Evergreen Hospice was Diane
Stolock, a big blond woman with an easy style and an easy laugh. When
you talk to Diane away from the patient she refers to "psychosocial elements," "connectedness" and "the whole dynamics with the team involvement." She's obviously thought a lot about the philosophy of
hospice care and the different methods of patient management. But

that afternoon at Ed's apartment when she arrived to see how he was doing, Ed was not a patient being managed. He was her friend, and if you didn't know better you would have thought she was a Decker niece who just happened to be passing by and stopped in to test the new blood pressure cuff she'd just picked up at Sears. Their conversation wasn't special in any way, except again it was Diane paying close attention to what in different circumstances would be trivial matters.

"How are these slippers working here?" she asked at one point. "I was afraid that with your feet being swollen like that and coming out of your slippers that you might slip." Given Ed's trouble with his feet, slippers weren't just something to keep away from the dog. They were basic to his comfort and safety—one of those simple things that wasn't simple anymore.

It was fascinating to watch Ed's reaction to Diane, how he responded to her friendship and obvious sincere concern for him. I saw him become almost physically rejuvenated, like a teenager in love. He was more alive when she was there, even joking about his condition. He was more *Ed*.

"Are you exercising, Ed?"

"Yes, I go to the bathroom frequently."

"At the beginning it was very hard for Ed to acknowledge a lot about his disease process and what was going on," Diane said later. "It was very hard. All he wanted to talk about was his life and he didn't want to deal with the issues about his death. As he sees his body changing and getting weaker, he's been much more open. He's even talked about the kind of funeral that he would like to have and what he would like said at his funeral. He said to me, 'You know, on my tombstone, I'd like my name and then I'd like it to say, He Made People Laugh.' I think that says a lot about Ed."

Diane Stolock's job wasn't just to make sure Ed Decker was comfortable and emotionally healthy. Anne Decker's physical and emotional state were just as important. She and Ed were together a very long time and had recently been through the death of one of their two daughters. In many ways accepting Ed's death was just as difficult for Anne as it was for him.

"When I take her shopping," their daughter Nancy said, "sometimes I don't need anything and I'm waiting for her and I realize a long time has gone by, so I go up and down the aisles until I find her, and she's standing there staring off into space. When that happens I realize there's nothing else I can do for her, other than keep her active. But one other thing I can do is I can make my mother laugh. We all have a good sense of humor in our family; humor that's a very important part of dealing with something that's heavy."

"Ed and I talked about dying already," Anne said. "He was concerned about me. He said, 'Honey, will you be all right?' And I told him, 'I believe in God, and the thing that makes me able to take it is you're going to see our Judy,' our daughter who died two years ago. 'You're gonna see our little girl. And you're also going to see all of the little old ladies you wrote poems for these past years, all the ladies who loved the poems and put them in their Bibles or framed them. I'm sure they're up in heaven, too. But you tell them not to get overanxious when they see you. You tell 'em Anne is coming someday soon, so they better stay on their side, don't get too cozy with you.' And I made him laugh. So that ended our only serious discussion about death."

"They're not a really emotionally open family, they're somewhere in the middle there." A week after I met Ed the Evergreen team in charge of his care held its regular Ed Decker Meeting at the hospice. The supervisor for outpatient services seemed to be principally concerned with how the Decker family was doing generally.

"I mean, it's not quite the stiff-upper-lip school of thought," Diane said, "there's a little more emotional expression. But my sense is that they have really good coping skills, they're not so restrained that they're not dealing with things. I think they'll cope well when the time comes, when Ed does die."

Diane Stolock led the meeting, and present were a social worker, a volunteer who'd spent a lot of time with Ed and Anne, and a few others. Most of the meeting was nuts-and-bolts, discussing the effectiveness of the concrete things they had already done for Ed, like getting a hospital bed into his apartment. And they spent a lot of time trying to anticipate his needs for the near future. Anne's situation was discussed as if she was as much a patient as her husband. They all realized that Ed's dying was harder on Anne than it would have been for many people her age. Because her parents died when she was very young, Anne had little experience with the death of anyone close to her except her daughter, and Ed was with her for that.

"Anne isn't feeling well either; her arthritis is acting up this week quite a bit," Diane reported. "And that could be a real issue if Ed begins to decline fairly quickly."

At the time there was already some indication that he was going fast. Diane and the others had noticed an increased shortness of breath, possibly the onset of pneumonia, and he was becoming disoriented frequently.

"He begins to speak and then suddenly he'll say, 'I don't know what I was going to say,' and that's real new for him because he's sharp and quick. It's hard for him, he's getting so frustrated."

Although the family knew Ed would die soon, his rapid deterioration suddenly seemed to make that fact real for the first time.

"I took Mom out the other day," Nancy said, "and when we came back we looked at him and he didn't look alive. Mom went over and called him. She had to call him six times before he woke up. I was in the other room, and about the third call my hair started standing up on my arms. It was awful."

Nancy also worried that the father she knew wasn't there anymore. She couldn't see that he had any quality of life left except that he still had his wife and family around him. "But I wouldn't consider that that was a quality of life, you know?"

Anne felt it too, the beginning of the end. "So I've asked my dear friends, who believe in the Lord as I do, to pray for God to please take him home soon so he's not in any more pain, not distressed. I don't want him hurting mentally or physically in any way. I can handle it, I know I can. I'll be lonely, though."

Ed went into the hospice a few days later. Or as officially stated, he was "admitted to the inpatient center for symptom management." For an "inpatient center" Evergreen looks and feels, as Anne said, like a high quality motel. The one-story building is U-shaped, with each room opening onto a central courtyard with flowers and a little stream. There are family areas with fireplaces, and a kitchen where visitors can prepare their own meals and entertain each other. Evergreen has a real community feel to it, which in part comes from the way the hospice began. In the late 1980s local voters passed a bond issue to create Evergreen Hospice as a separate department of Evergreen Hospital next door. Therefore it is one of the few hospices in America built with public funds. Though occupancy was low in the first few years, by mid-1993 Evergreen was treating an average of sixty patients a day, either in the community or, now like Ed, in the fifteen-bed facility.

Once in his Evergreen room, the conversations with Ed were almost strictly to do with his comfort. He seemed to sink into that bed and become a part of it, although the old Ed would briefly emerge.

He had to take a bunch of pills one afternoon. It wasn't easy, and when he finally got them all down the nurse said, "Good! We got it done."

"What do you mean 'we'?" asked Ed Decker. It was a small joke, an old joke, but it showed that Ed was still in there.

It was his last joke. A few days later, after his family had a chance to say good-bye, Ed Decker died, quietly, peacefully, as he hoped to; not with a bang, but not with a whimper either. A week later, Anne cast his ashes into one of his favorite trout streams in the Washington Cascades, and except for memories and snapshots, it was over.

I previously vowed not to make value judgments on this Trip of a Lifetime. But watching hospices in action, seeing what Sacred Heart in Sydney did for Ian, what Evergreen did for Ed and Anne, it's hard not to sound like the chief lobbyist for the Amalgamated Association of Hospices. When I walked into the lobby of Evergreen once, it didn't smell like a hospital or death, it smelled like lasagna. Volunteer Jane Quirck has a great lasagna recipe and frequently mixes up a batch in the family kitchen. Given the choice, who wouldn't want to die in a place that smelled like lasagna?

If forced to I could probably find aspects of hospice care to complain about. In Sydney I saw a few people, both staff and volunteers, who had the irritating habit of speaking to patients as if a terminal illness suddenly turns you into a first-grader.

"How would we like a great big glass of water?" a volunteer using her best Mr. Rogers voice said to an eighty-year-old former engineer at Sacred Heart's party.

"I don't know about you," he answered, "but I'll have a beer." But she still didn't get the message.

And I suppose there's something a bit sad about the way hospices have replaced the support dying people used to get from their families. That certainly wasn't Mary Aikenhead's intent, or the intention of any hospice I know. Both the involvement of the family and sensitivity to the problems of loved ones are hallmarks of the hospice movement and very evident at both Sacred Heart and Evergreen. But for a family that wants to drop their dying off and walk away guilt-free, the hospice is a godsend.

At Sacred Heart I talked to Ian about a half hour after he had called his father. The two men hadn't spoken for six years, ever since the day Ian revealed he was gay and his father disowned him and sent him away.

"I called to tell him his wish had come true, that he wasn't going to have me as his son for much longer. I told him I was dying of AIDS. And he said, 'Are you calling me for my forgiveness?' So I hung up."

I've never met Ian's father, which is probably just as well for both of us. He wouldn't find our conversation pleasant. So it's impossible for me to know how he really felt about his son. But even with their long estrangement, even after the phone call, I think Ian loved him. He desperately wanted his father back in his life as it was coming to an end. And the reason I think that is because Ian was not his real name. He asked me to identify him as "Ian" so there wouldn't be the slightest chance that telling his story publicly would embarrass his father, a man I think deserves all the embarrassment he can get.

But Ian didn't. "I'd like him to see this place. I'd like him to see how I walked through the door here that first day, how alone I was. And I'd like him to see how strong I am now, how I can ring a bell at two in the morning and somebody is there. I'd like him to know that somebody cleaned me up when I messed the bed. He's not done any of those things for me, because he's been too afraid."

And if there hadn't been a Sacred Heart to become Ian's surrogate family, might the father have reentered his son's life? As a father of sons myself, I'd like to think any parent would do that regardless of what had happened in the past. All I know is that for Ian, Sacred Heart was there, and the father was not. And I know that somewhere in this world there is a father who should thank God for those people, the strangers who did for his son what he was unwilling or unable to do.

But Ian's story may not be over yet. I called Sacred Heart a year later to ask about some of the people we'd met. They told me that not long after we were there, Ian decided that if he was really going to have faith in his survival, he would have to leave. That same day he walked out the front door of Sacred Heart. When last heard from, he was living alone in a house on the beach near Sydney. Living.

CHAPTER NINE

GETTING RID OF THE BODY

Until I met Max, I thought that if you donated your body to science, science would find something to do with it. Certainly that was true in the old days. The ancient Greeks used the bodies of animals to learn about anatomy, and just hoped that the uterus of a dog, for instance, was about the same as the uterus of a human being. It's not, but for a long time surgeons thought it was, especially in the days when the titles "surgeon" and "barber" were interchangeable. They were wrong about a lot of other body stuff too, which must have led to some unpleasant surprises for patient and staff alike. In part it was their own fault. Dissecting deceased humans was thought to be uncivilized business, condemned by no less a source than the Bible: "He that toucheth the dead body of any man shall be unclean seven days" (Num. 19:16). Nevertheless, there were curious and conscientious physicians who delved into the odd human cadaver, until a Papal Bull in 1300 declared that anyone who cut up or boiled a human body would be excommunicated. Pope Boniface VIII was trying to stop crusaders in the holy lands from boiling down their fallen comrades so they could be more easily shipped home for a Christian burial, but the effect on the dissection business was disastrous nonetheless. Surgery, at least in Britain, was turned over exclusively to the more barber-inclined members of the profession, who apparently didn't care that their Greek-based knowledge of human anatomy included tails and ears on top of the head.

Body availability—and surgery—took a turn for the better in 1752 when the British Parliament passed a law saying executed criminals were not allowed to be buried and had to be dissected. That was easier legislated than done, because many criminals thought being hanged was enough indignity for one day. So they made sure their friends and family were present at the execution. After the drop these supporters would attack officials trying to remove the body to the doctor's laboratory and forcibly take it away. Consequently there simply weren't enough bodies available for the physicians who wanted them. William Harvey (1578–1657), who achieved fame by discovering that blood circulates, was physician to two British kings as well as a president of the Royal Society of Physicians and a lecturer on anatomy at the Royal College. But apparently even he didn't have the connections to get bodies. Harvey had to conduct some of his research by dissecting members of his own family, as did a number of other medical researchers and educators. (*Their* families, that is, not William Harvey's.)

The rise of private medical schools around 1760 made matters much worse. These institutions didn't have access to the late unlamented criminals, but to attract students they had to teach anatomy, and for that they had to have bodies. So a new industry arose in Britain and elsewhere, that of the "resurrectionist," (which probably looked a lot better on a business card than "body snatcher.") Startup costs were minimal. All you needed was a spade and a wheelbarrow. These enterprising people would provide bodies to medical schools for a fee, usually four guineas for an adult. Children were sold by length; six shillings for the first foot and then ninepence per inch thereafter. Naturally the resurrectionists got their stock from the place where all the bodies were, the graveyards. At least that's what they did originally. But the relatives of the deceased were naturally disquieted by having their loved ones dug up and sold. So they devised methods to protect them that were perhaps more realistic than simple faith in God's Wrath.

In slightly earlier times Shakespeare himself depended on such divine vengeance to protect his body. As it says on his stone in the church in Stratford, "Blest be the man that spares these stones, and curst be he that moves my bones." And at least for Bill it worked, because historically all parliamentary efforts to move Shakespeare's remains to Westminster Abbey or anywhere else have been thwarted by a dramatic reading of the tombstone. But Shakespeare was lucky.

A hundred years after his death more concrete defensive measures were needed, possibly because appealing to the religious convictions of a graverobber had come to seem naive to the public. A man who digs up bodies in the middle of the night, puts them in a wheelbarrow and delivers them around and about the town is not a man who is worried about being "unclean seven days." Chances are this was a relatively unclean individual right from the getgo.

So families developed elaborate stratagems to foil the resurrectionists before they could resurrect. Bombs were hidden in coffins, coffins were designed that were impossible to open, and trip wires were attached to guns strung over burial mounds. Because the awaiting medical staff needed the freshest possible "material" with which to work, the best defense against unwanted resurrection was always the passage of time. It was not uncommon in the early 1800s in British cemeteries to find family members standing constant vigil over graves for three or four weeks, until the relative down below was no longer commercially viable. The teeth of the deceased were still a hot item, because dentists used the teeth of cadavers to make dentures. (That may be the most revolting sentence in this book.) But I presume the time, trouble, and danger of digging up a body was such that only a resurrectionist with very low self-esteem would do it just for a few molars. A person has principles, after all.

Well, maybe not. Two gentlemen in Edinburgh—a city known at the time as the "Resurrectionist Capital of the World" because of the brisk body trade that took place there—thought of a way around familial and constabulary objections. William Burke and William Hare devised a simple shortcut in the entire process. They eliminated the middleMan, specifically God, by killing people themselves and taking them directly to their clients. Real freshness, no shovels, no irate relatives, such a deal. And I would presume that just as there are car thieves today who take special orders, say for a green Porsche 914 with CD player, Burke and Hare and their apprentices also took the odd special assignment from the medical schools; the eighteenth-century equivalent of "bring me the head of Alfredo Garcia." Eventually Burke and Hare's ingenuity came to be called "burking" in Mr. Burke's honor, and also in his honor—after he was captured, convicted, and hanged—he was dissected at Edinburgh University. The public viewed the hanging with pleasure, and in a rare display of ironic vengeance, was also allowed to attend the dissection.

The work of Burke, Hare, and subsequent burkers so horrified the British that Henry Warburton was finally able to get an Anatomy Act through Parliament in 1832. The act said that any unclaimed bodies could be turned over to medical establishments for dissection, which of course meant the bodies of paupers. At the same time the act abolished the automatic dissection of murderers. So as one writer pointed out, what had been a loathsome punishment for murder became an equally loathsome punishment for poverty instead. Nevertheless, the Anatomy Act drove the body snatchers out of business, except for the many who merely transferred their offices and wheelbarrows to the hospitals and medical schools and continued doing what they did before, only legally. Their profession was still not regarded highly by the population, however, which seems particularly unfair when you consider the medical advances made possible by the night labors of these dedicated bag persons.

Which brings me back to Max. From what I gather, Max's life in San Francisco was not brimming with accomplishment. Perhaps to make up for his lack of achievement, his last gesture was for the public good. He willed his body to science, in hopes that future generations might benefit from the medical knowledge gleaned from his innards. Except that when Max died his passing was due to a liver ailment brought on by bad habits. Science apparently took one look at him and decided there was nothing to be gleaned from his innards but innards. Somebody could use him, though. Max was sent, innards and all, to the San Francisco School of Mortuary Science.

The San Francisco School of Mortuary Science (SFSMS) has for decades taught young men (and as time goes on more and more young women) every aspect of the undertaker's trade. The school is appropriately located in a large, old funeral home on Divisadero Street. Inside the floors creak, the walls are darkly paneled, and an aura of aged gentility is everywhere. Decorating the paneling are photographs of past graduating classes, as opposed to shots of past granulating clients. There isn't a trophy case, but then I don't think SFSMS has a mascot or fields any teams. This is strictly vocational education. Upstairs in the quiet rooms where once the bereaved viewed the deceased, the Undertakers of Tomorrow learn the business side of the business: sales and marketing techniques, employee management, client relations, and so forth.

The principal hands-on instruction is in the basement, in the old funeral home preparation room. It is there students learn embalming and what the industry calls "restorative care." And it was there, one bright morning, I arrived to attend my first—and at least as a viewer, last—embalming.

The embalming instructor was Robert Yount, a mortician and SFSMS faculty member. He's a pleasant, straightforward man who was a music major in college, a budding concert pianist. But he needed some part-time work and a friend knew of a job that not only paid a hundred dollars a week but included an apartment as well.

"I wasn't even eighteen yet, and so I said, 'What's the job?' and he said, 'In a funeral home,' and I said, 'No, I don't think so.' But he insisted I wouldn't have to do anything with the bodies, just vacuum and answer the phone. And then I went to meet the funeral director. I expected an organ playing and this guy in a black suit and a top hat to come out, you know, John Carradine, but he was an energetic, bright, hip young guy. He talked me into the job, right on the spot." Four years later, with a music degree from California State University at Irvine in one hand and a formaldehyde bottle in the other, Bob Yount opted for the metal table rather than the three pedal Steinway. Now he's an energetic, bright, hip young funeral director himself.

(A friend of mine, an entering freshman at the University of Washington, had exactly the same experience at about the same time, only he heard about the job from his mother. Years later she admitted that the reason she pushed him so hard to take the work was that the only way you could get to his apartment in the funeral home was to go through the mortuary. She figured that even if he wanted to take girls to his room, no girls would go. "And she was right," he said bitterly.)

After a quick tour of the upper rooms, Bob Yount and I descended to the depths where the real undertaking is undertaken. In one small room off the mortuary I looked at the results of a student project. Laid out on a table were dozens of noses and ears. It can give you quite a start to be snooping around a mortuary science school basement and suddenly run into the nose and ear collection. But these were flesh-colored wax carvings I assume are used for restorative cases. And they didn't look that realistic to me anyway, although I admit that I'm so used to seeing noses and ears in context that laid out individually on a tabletop is no way to judge their believability, vis-à-vis the head.

"We have two possible subjects today," Bob said to me when I returned to the mortuary itself. "One is a middle-aged, slightly obese male who I understand the cause of death was a hepatic liver condition, complicated by alcoholism." (Max.) "Or we have a twelve-year-old girl who just came in. Which would you prefer to see embalmed?"

I don't ever want to meet the person who in such a situation would choose the young girl. But it does say something about our reaction to death and the dead that there was absolutely no question in my mind which "subject" I wanted to see. I was surprised Bob Yount even thought he needed to ask, until I realized that in his business there was no real difference between the two people. They were both dead, both going to be embalmed under the same harsh yellow lights in the same cold, off-white room by the same people. They were each pieces of work to be done, and as such were interchangeable as far as he was concerned.

In another time and place I think Bob would have the same emotional reaction to a dead child as I, but to do his job he mostly shuts down those feelings. The only analogous situation I've seen is television news photographers. Once they have the camera to their eye they stop thinking rationally or emotionally about anything other than getting the pictures of what's happening. On more than one occasion I've seen friends who are news shooters nearly get killed because they were rolling when they should have been running. In a sense, people who deal professionally with the dead are the same way. If you're in the cold room, you're today's problem regardless of who you are or where you come from.

But I wasn't able to make that emotional suspension yet. I wanted to know everything about this twelve-year-old. Who was she, what happened to her, why was she being used by students for practice, what the hell was the matter with her family that they allowed her to become an embalming class project? I could understand Bob Yount's apparent insensitivity though, because even before seeing Max, I didn't care much about his story at all. I never even knew his name—Max is just what I'm calling him because "the stiff" seems a bit callous.

Not for the first time I realized how much differently my culture reacts to the death of children from that of adults, and how strange those cultures seem, like some Australian aborigine peoples, for instance, who believe infants and children who die are simply eternal spirits not yet ready to be reborn. Strange and lucky, I guess, because convinced as they are that the spirit will eventually make a successful return to the world, they mourn their lost children very little. I will never be so fortunate, and so I knew I wouldn't be able to watch the embalming of a child. Max would be a lot less of a personal problem.

So Max it was. Bob was working with three students this particular day: Vivian, a bank worker who was laid off after thirteen years and had "always been interested in what happens after a person dies"; Donald, whose former job in the military included telling families of a death; and Ron, a "professional student" who had once gone to medical school in Mexico, worked in an Air Force lab, and had gotten a degree in computer science but found that work unfulfilling.

While Max waited patiently under a white sheet, Bob and his charges talked basic preparation theory. These were fairly advanced students—according to Bob, pupils don't make it to embalming until the second quarter—so I suspect a lot of the preliminary talk was for my benefit. But it was still enlightening to hear what a beginner hears, especially since the San Francisco School of Mortuary Science was one of the first trips I undertook on the death beat, and whomever they worked on was going to be only my second up-close-and-personal dead guy.

"Now as we discussed in school, the primary purpose of embalming is what?" Bob dutifully asked.

"Disinfection and protection of the public health," came the answer, quick as that. And then after a few more preliminaries, Max made his entrance. Bob flipped back the sheet, and there was this big guy lying there wearing naught but a blue-and-white serviette, about twice the size of a paper napkin.

He was quite, quite yellow. I wasn't expecting yellow, which is probably why I said, "My God, he's yellow!" Bob pointed out that because Max had died of liver complications he was perhaps a shade yellowish, yes, but that's what happens sometimes. Bob has seen a lot of jaundice in his time. Nothing to be alarmed about, he said, although it did present some restorative care problems. Before the family viewed the body, Max had to lose his tint. At least his head did. But that came later.

They went to work on him, shampooing his hair, washing him down thoroughly, cleaning the various spots on his body one might imagine need cleaning and disinfecting. And the odd thing was that after twenty minutes the fact that the dominant person in our little group was dead no longer dominated. For me Max became just another object in the room, like the embalming fluid pump and the rubber glove cabinet. I knew he was there, I wasn't about to lean on him or hang my lunch box on his feet, but that "wow, a dead guy" feeling went away quickly. It was, oddly, the way actors having a good show feel about the audience. If you are truly in character, you're aware of the audience and its reactions but only as a kind of mental peripheral vision. Your concentration is on the other players and your relationship to them, even though that audience is your reason for being. I was there to watch Max being embalmed, but my focus was on Bob and crew.

It had taken me twenty minutes to dehumanize Max completely. I still don't know if I could have handled the child, but it was no longer outside the realm of possibility. A special kind of professional dehumanization is part of the job, and it's also part of the job to philosophically, if not emotionally, deny it. Afterwards talking with Ron, I asked him how he related to Max, whether he thought of him as a human being.

"Definitely, definitely," he said. "I do think this person is a human being. He was born, he had some belief systems, he had culture, he spoke, he communicated. He exists." And at that particular moment I think he was completely sincere, even if it *was* precisely the right thing to say. But I had watched him sew Max's jaw closed and mouth shut by using a curved needle, bringing it out of the nostril and through the septum on the upstroke. I'll admit to being a complete beginner when it comes to the mortuary business, but could anybody do that and think the object they were working on was still in any way a sentient being?

Even though I had adjusted easily to Max's presence, or rather lack of presence, there were still tasks involved in his preparation and embalming that were difficult to watch. Probably because they looked quite painful, and we are so attuned to our own pain that it's difficult to separate ourselves emotionally from seeing painful things inflicted on others, regardless of their condition. So when they slid the eye caps—little plastic eye-shaped cups—under Max's lids so his eyes wouldn't cave in and look unnatural, I was off in the corner sucking on my teeth. And that wasn't the only time.

"This ear is starting to bleed clear. Is that ear, Ron?"

"No."

"As much of the whole blood as we can remove from this deceased prior to adding our preserving solution, the less discoloration problems we're gonna have. Let's help stimulate it somewhat with these forceps. I would suggest doing some massaging in the legs, too."

"Let's see if we can aspirate some of that bulk liquid."

"And look what we have here, a very nice carotid artery. Let's establish the jugular vein."

These are the kinds of things you hear around the instructional embalming table. It is not my intention to describe the whole embalming process step by step. First, I couldn't do it, and second, why should I? If people want to try a little home embalming, they're going to have to get the information from someone other than me. But there is a question that must be answered. Why does America, and only a few other nations, embalm in the first place? We may look at bone exhumation in China, or funereal goat sacrifice in Africa, and say those people are weird, but those people look at us and say, "At least we aren't taking the corpses of our loved ones and filling them up with chemicals." And they have a valid point.

Historically at least, embalming in America served a useful purpose. It was Abraham Lincoln's wish during the Civil War that Union boys who died in battle would be returned for burial in their hometowns if their families so desired, no matter how far those towns were from the battlefield. (This was the first time in the history of warfare that such a massive repatriation of remains was attempted, or so I'm told.) This meant many bodies had to be shipped long distances by train, and some kind of preservation was needed.

According to Bob Yount, a physician for the New York County Medical Examiner's Office named Thomas Holmes had done some research on embalming. He went out into the Civil War battlefields and embalmed the dead for a hundred dollars a body (which isn't that much less than what Bob charges for an embalming today. Dr. Holmes was no humanitarian, I suspect.) Because that was a lot of money during the Civil War, only the fairly wealthy could afford to have their sons embalmed prior to shipping, but Holmes did hundreds during the war nonetheless.

When Lincoln was assassinated, he became the first president to be embalmed. And as he lay in state, thousands walked past and saw how great he looked compared to the members of their own family they had seen in the days after death. From then on embalming was the thing to do in the United States. Every president since Lincoln has been embalmed (every dead one, that is) as well as now 60 percent of everyone who dies in America.

"Embalming," says Bob the Embalmer, "is defined as 'the preservation, disinfection, and restoration of dead human remains.' There's no law that says you have to be embalmed. But because of natural body processes, if we're going to view a dead human remains there are certain preparations that have to be accomplished, and embalming is one of them. As a consequence, embalming is really a convenience for the public at this point." So the only real reason to embalm is if the person is going to be viewed, or the burial delayed.

But what of that subconscious reason, the comforting thought that embalmed Uncle Harry will always be as we knew him, albeit down about six feet, but looking just like he's not dead, only sleeping? In 1992, Professor John Chew, Director of Funeral Services at Lynn University in Boca Raton, Florida—which certainly doesn't sound like one of your stereotypical Florida party schools, what with a director of funeral services—hit the news by announcing that after fifteen years of research he had solved the secret of Egyptian mummification and could preserve bodies for thousands of years. He had already tried the process on dogs and cats and pronounced it a success. But wouldn't you have to wait a thousand years to be really sure it was successful? Personally, I'd like to be there in 2994 when they're sifting through the rubble of Boca Raton and find a mummified schnauzer with the label "Chew" on it. "Wow!" the discoverers are going to say. "Back in the twentieth century when a dog chewed something up those people really got angry!"

Anyway, Professor Chew has begun signing people up for the process. And he says there are hundreds of people who are interested, just as there are thousands of people who think embalming lasts for a long time. That's one of the reasons they buy it.

Lincoln's body might have had something to do with the misconception about the lasting effects of embalming. People kept digging him up. The first time was in 1876, when some graverobbers tried it and nearly succeeded until they were foiled by Secret Service men. (Just how long do these guys continue to protect an ex-president?) And the last time was in September of 1901, when Robert Todd Lincoln, the late president's only surviving son, decided to embed Abe's coffin in two tons of concrete to discourage further illegal inquiries. The monument committee in Springfield, Illinois, where Lincoln is buried, had to exhume the coffin for the concrete process, and as long as it was up top, some present felt they should take one last look to make sure it was, indeed, Abe inside. (Apparently there was a nasty nationwide rumor that the real Abe was elsewhere.) The debate over whether to open up was heated, with Robert Lincoln strenuously opposed, but the "one-peekers" were eventually victorious. (What a surprise.)

Lincoln's appearance, after more than thirty-five years under Springfield, has been carefully described. But the bottom line, so to speak, is that he didn't look bad at all. According to one observer, he looked like an old saddle, but an old saddle that was the spitting image of Abraham Lincoln, right down to the mole and the coarse black hair. I assume the nation heard all about Lincoln's benign appearance, and that embalming received the credit for Abe's remarkable, albeit saddlelike, preservation.

When and if Professor Chew gets going on a full-time commercial basis with his mummification, and Chew's Mummification Centers open up across the land, Bob Yount implies you and/or your relatives will have a choice to make. Do you want to look good for just an hour, so your friends and family can say "My, doesn't (*your name here*) look just like he's alive?!" when they drop by the funeral parlor to pay their last respects? Or do you want to spend eternity looking like an old saddle?

"I can embalm someone now to last for years and years and years," Bob says. "By adjusting the strength of the chemicals I can preserve human tissue very easily, but to preserve tissue so it looks natural, so that it has pliability, that 'lifelike' look, that's another story altogether. Embalming is not a long-term process, it's a short-term process. Three days, five days, maybe a few weeks. Fifty years ago funeral directors inaccurately portrayed embalming as something that lasts forever. But that's changed, and now I think the industry is more forthright about the real purpose of the procedure." The public misconception hasn't changed entirely, though. There are still many people who think that embalming, like a diamond, is forever, and go for it even if they aren't planning to view.

That's not the only public misconception about the procedure. Bob and all three of his students told me one of the questions they are most often asked at parties of nonmortuary scientists is, "Is it true that you string the bodies up by their feet and then cut their throats to get the blood out?"—the Mussolini Technique. And the answer is no.

With the exception of Americans, most people in other countries faced with that decision—lifelike for a few days or the "leather look" forever—have chosen the third option, which is none of the above. A person dies, there's a service the next day, they all go to the cemetery, down he or she goes, that's it. But the difference between those cultures and mine isn't really the embalming, it's the viewing.

"If you take viewing out of the picture," Bob says, "there is no need for embalming. And American culture has very, very much solidified this business of coming and having a viewing of the deceased."

Why? "Psychologists, grief counselors, health care professionals, mental health people have pretty much consistently come to the conclusion that part of the grieving process can be accomplished through a physical viewing of the body. A finality. A period at the end of a sentence."

I'm not sure why our friends across the sea don't feel this psychological need to punctuate the lives of their loved ones by looking at them one last time. Or if they do take a peek, why they don't feel the body needs to be cosmetically rejuvenated for the viewing. But I would guess that the way other folk deal with the body itself has something to do with it. I spent time in Belfast with P. J. Brown, a family undertaker for many years. His place of business is his home, not some building downtown with metal tables, viewing rooms, coffin display areas, and a small chapel. And his principal professional tool isn't a scalpel or pump, it's a telephone.

When a client dies and Mr. Brown gets the call, he goes to the deceased in hospital or home and preps 'em where he finds 'em. Usually a good wash is all that's needed, just what Bob Yount and his students did first to Max. But Mr. Brown stops at cleanliness. He immediately removes the deceased to his or her own home, where the lying in state and the wake soon take place. The next day there's a "lift" to the church—whereby the late lamented is carried through the streets where he or she lived—and sometimes another lift to the graveyard. There's no time or need for embalming, and Mr. Brown doesn't have the facilities to do it even if he wanted to. (If a person is being shipped somewhere, Mr. Brown contracts out for embalming, but he says that happens very rarely. Northern Ireland, and Ireland too, are wee countries, and nobody has to go too far to get home.) Perhaps Mr. Brown's clients don't look as good as Mr. Yount's—don't look as "not dead"— but the deceased on view in his or her own home and own bed probably makes up for some of that, especially with a party going on around said bed. And as Mr. Brown says so well, "Why shouldn't they look dead? They *are* dead."

As a result of this different philosophy regarding treatment of the body, many Europeans and Asians think our embalming, viewing, and funeral practices generally are just further examples of American excess. And now Japanese excess as well. American funereal techniques, including embalming, seem to be one of the few things the Japanese want from us. They export cars, videotape recorders, and computers over here, and we send them the pump, the big needle, and coffins. Unless Japan has a really disastrous plague sometime soon, this exchange shouldn't have much effect on the balance of trade between our two great nations. Nevertheless, I can tell Bob takes some pride in the fact that the American funeral industry is doing its part. Recently three of his students, graduates of good old SFSMS, went to Japan to give embalming lessons, carrying along a training video starring Bob Yount and (I assume) others in very nonspeaking roles.

"And we make caskets like no one makes caskets here in the United States in terms of their quality, if you will, and how elaborate they may be. We are now exporting caskets to Japan."

Generally Bob Yount is right. There's no casket like an American casket. Frank E. Campbell's Funeral Home in Manhattan is probably the most famous undertaking establishment in America, in part because Campbell's has become mortician to the stars. They did Rudolph Valentino here in the 1920s and since then Judy Garland, Greta Garbo, and a lot of other big, dead names have been handled by Campbell's. (Recently they even embalmed the late King of Sikkim in the lotus position.)

Manager Bill Hartgrove showed me the top-of-the-line Campbell casket, and it was indeed a beauty. As everybody knows, a casket is really just a big, body-shaped box. But this box had a certain undefinable majesty. It was almost insolent in its assumption of elegance, like a Mercedes with all the options.

•

But in Ghana you can get a casket that looks just like a Mercedes with all the options. On the outskirts of Ghana's capital city, Accra, a man named Benjamin Quaye Sowah supports himself, his family, and fifteen workers and their families by making fantasy coffins out of wood. He inherited the business from his father, Kwame Quaye, a farmer and amateur woodworker who made his first fantasy coffin for a friend. Word of this remarkable box spread. Fortunately the friend survived long enough for many people to view Mr. Quaye's work, many people who then asked him to make similar coffins for them. And a very healthy little cottage industry was born.

The Mercedes is the biggest seller amongst the standard Quaye designs, often purchased for or by a man who never had a Mercedes but certainly wanted to have one someday. And now he will have one all his days. Other popular fantasy designs include elaborate boats for fishermen, rocket ships for kids, crabs for, I assume, crab catchers, various other assorted birds, animals, and even insects. Mothers are often buried in large chickens, based on the Ghanaian proverb *Akoko nan tiaba na enkum ba,* which means "The hen steps on its chicks but does not kill them."

Standard designs take about two weeks to complete, but Mr. Sowah also takes special orders. The day I was there he and the workers were putting finishing touches on a casket that looked just like a big Yamaha outboard motor. It was to be the final resting place for a fisherman who was the first in his village to own the real thing.

The cost for a Sowah fantasy coffin is approximately seven times the yearly income of the average Ghanaian. In relative terms that makes the $10,000 price tag for Mr. Hartgrove's top model, or even the $90,000 for Frank E. Campbell's full funereal works, look like chump change. But Mr. Sowah argues that almost all his clients die long after their coffin is completed, so they have had a chance to see it many times. They find great comfort in knowing that their families think enough of them to pay such a price, and also in knowing that they will be spending eternity in such spectacular surroundings.

"They die happier," Mr. Sowah says simply, and he has a point. How much is that worth, to a Ghanaian, to anyone? And though his coffins are quite wonderful, Mr. Sowah has no regrets that his works of art are eventually buried and never seen again. That delay between construction and expiration allows him time to carry the really good ones through the streets of his village, so they can be appreciated by the masses prior to delivery.

For most Ghanaians the delays of death are not between coffin purchase and demise but demise and burial. Even without the expense of a fantasy coffin, Ghanaian funerals are extremely expensive affairs, usually because they are so big. Just how big is discussed in a later chapter, but here's a hint. Getting the money together to put on a proper funeral, at least for the Ashanti people, can sometimes take a family three years or more. And that is not so convenient for K. A. Boiteng.

K. A. Boiteng is an inspiring man. He was born in a small highland village to extremely poor, hardworking parents. He doesn't recall having (or needing) a pair of shoes until he was eleven, and didn't know what reading was until about then either, because his parents were illiterate. But Boiteng, to quote a cliché, had a dream. So not long after he was eleven he put on those first shoes and walked out of his village. He was going to be somebody. Today he is.

Dr. K. A. Boiteng is the chief medical examiner of Kumasi, a post he has held for thirteen years and the zenith of his thirty-year career in forensics. His principal duties include performing hospital autopsies where needed, determining the cause of death when foul play is suspected, and doing blood work for the coroner. Generally speaking, though, if you die anywhere near Kumasi, Dr. Boiteng gets you. Despite his beard, he bears an unsettling resemblance to Uganda's former premiere loon Idi Amin, but fortunately that's where the resemblance ends. Dr. Boiteng is soft-spoken, direct, very sane, and often quite funny.

I suspect he has to have a good sense of humor. Being a man of science in a country of fetish priests like Nana Kofi Adu often places Dr. Boiteng in a difficult position.

"I recently did a case where a man wanted to be fortified against a shotgun because he feared an enemy was going to shoot him. So he went to a fetish priest, and for days the priest performed the ritual that would protect him. And when the ritual was done, it had to be tested, so they took the man out, stood him up, and shot him. Dead. And then they quickly buried the body. But the police were informed, so I went there and exhumed the body. The person who shot him was charged with murder and is now in prison for the rest of his life. They both believed, you see, and yet one of them is dead and one of them might as well be. It is funny, and sad."

Often however, Dr. Boiteng's science doesn't put people in prison but get them out, especially people like fetish priests who are accused of committing murder by sorcery. Not that many people die as the result of what he calls "ritual matters," but what occasionally happens is that people will use charges of ritual death for their own ends. If two families are feuding, for instance, and one family member dies of obviously natural causes, someone in the other family will still be accused of causing the death. The coroner then authorizes Dr. Boiteng to exhume the body and perform an autopsy, which proves what everyone knew in the first place.

"The average Ghanaian African believes that disease comes from two sources," Dr. Boiteng explains. "Death from natural causes, and death which they attribute to supernatural causes. If a person dies of typhoid fever, they will assert that as being natural. But if a young man or young woman dies, then they attribute this to witchcraft, juju, all kinds of things. 'At the prime of his life, he shouldn't have died, and that is the work of somebody in the family who has done that.' And I am called upon to show that it is not."

Although he's never written "death by witchcraft" on an autopsy report, Dr. Boiteng is careful not to say there is no such thing. He feels about sorcery rather like the French divine Abbe Arthur Mugnier felt about hell. When asked if he really believed in hell he answered, "Yes, because it is a dogma of the church. But I don't believe anyone is in it."

Dr. Boiteng says, "I say anything that has a name exists, but I don't believe it can have any effect on me, because I don't believe it. For instance, I developed gout. I know what caused it. But somebody came to me and said, 'Too bad, you stepped on some juju. Go see this man, he has very potent medicine for you. You'll be okay in three days.' I said thank you. I didn't go. I took my Colchicine instead. And when this man saw me walking three days later he smiled and said, 'Oh, good, I see the sorcerer worked.' But now I have gout again. So where is this juju I keep stepping on?"

Dr. Boiteng's grappling with science versus sorcery isn't limited to his own feet. When death by witchcraft is charged, often his more scientific explanations are rejected by the relatives. He told me of a case where a man prayed to a shrine for help with his cocoa farm. The shrine in this case was a river, and he promised the river that if his cocoa farm thrived he would make donations to the shrine. But according to the relatives he didn't do it, so the river killed him.

"His belly was distended, and his family insisted that it was the water from the river that had killed him. I disagreed, but they wouldn't budge. But talking to them I realized the dead man was a heavy drinker of palm wine. And the autopsy revealed that the actual cause of death was alcoholic cirrhosis of the liver. But the family wanted to believe it was the shrine. And they still do."

In some ways I can see a kind of sense in the family's position. Given the choice of believing a loved one drank himself to death or was killed by mysterious evil forces, I'd probably pick the evil forces too. I couldn't have done anything about them, but there might have been something I could have done to convince Uncle Al to stop drinking. I'd feel a lot less guilty about shrine death than 'shine death.

Unfortunately, the Ghanaians who would believe their loved one was killed by supernatural forces are also the Ghanaians who believe that such a death is inherently dishonorable and therefore get no solace from its unpreventable cause. Death by witchcraft, as well as death in labor, accidental death, and suicide, all mean a quick burial and no funeral. No funeral in my culture wouldn't be the worst thing that ever happened, but the Ashanti believe that in some ways a person's life is judged by the funeral he or she has. Which brings me back to how the Ashanti belief in huge funerals creates quite a problem for Dr. Boiteng.

He has to store the bodies, that's the problem. Most medical examiners have a fairly rapid turnover, but Dr. Boiteng has a building full of deceased persons waiting until their families have raised the money for a proper burial. The Kumasi government built a new mortuary some time ago, but the architect declined to consult with Dr. Boiteng or any other knowledgeable person about what mortuaries need. As a result Dr. Boiteng ended up with a facility suitable for mink farming and not much else. He refused to occupy it. And although he's been promised a new, adequate mortuary soon, Dr. Boiteng's present facility was built during British colonial days when Ghana was the Gold Coast. Not a lot of that gold was put into mortuaries, and not a lot has been put into maintaining them since then. Walking into Dr. Boiteng's back room, his equivalent of the San Francisco School basement, is like walking onto the principal set for a horror movie called *The Hideous Experiments of Dr. Zongo*. The walls and floor are streaked and decaying, water drips constantly from ancient spigots into blackened porcelain, and the lighting is half what it should be, casting a sour yellow pall over the room and everything in it. This actually looks like a place where embalming is done employing the Mussolini Technique.

On closer inspection, however, I saw that everything in the room was clean, orderly, and in as good condition as possible. Dr. Boiteng is a professional, doing what he can under difficult conditions. Everything about his back room reflected that concern for his work and his people, even the ancient old man lying alone and unattended on one of the four tables.

"My uncle's father," Dr. Boiteng explained. "He was 105. He's thawing." The old gentleman was, in fact, frozen solid.

For a long time Dr. Boiteng kept all his stored bodies in two big, rattling coolers that were installed by the British in 1958. The British colonial architect who designed the Kumasi mortuary apparently didn't have the time or inclination to delve into cultural attitudes of the

indigenous population, or he would have built in three times the
corpse storage space. "Hey, mate, if it was good enough for Bombay,
it's good enough for Kumazzzi" was probably the attitude at the time.
So the coolers were inadequate. Dr. Boiteng was especially worried
about the possibility of cooler collapse or a power failure. If his coolers
were down too long, he'd have a large and very unpleasant problem on
his hands. So recently he purchased a big freezer and a backup genera-
tor. On our tour of his facility, he opened his freezer door, and there
must have been fifteen people in there, solid as rocks.

But he still worried about the power. "If we ever have a power failure that lasts very long, I'm going to be on the phone a great deal," he
told me. And who he'll be calling are the elders of all the families who
have left their late loved ones in his care. Some of the freezer fellows
have been in Dr. Boiteng's mortuary for years, so I hope his Rolodex is
current.

When a family is finally ready to go ahead with a funeral, they inform
Dr. Boiteng a week or so in advance so he can bring the deceased out
of the freezer and defrost him or her. "In this climate, it takes about
three days," the doctor said, looking at his uncle's father with a "what
can I do, this is my life" expression. His uncle, who he called the Professor, also works in the mortuary, and while I was there he popped in
to see how Dad was coming along.

"The funeral is this Friday, you see," said the Professor, "and he
must be taken back to our village."

"No problem," Dr. Boiteng assured him. Although the Professor
has watched dozens of other people thaw out for burial, he said it was
still strange having his own father melting in the back room. I could
understand that.

I went back on Friday to watch the body delivery process. Because
Ghanaian funerals are traditionally three days long, many of them start
Friday night. That makes Friday morning an especially busy time at Dr.
Boiteng's. Recently thawed loved ones are constantly being carried to
and fro by the staff; tall, quiet men who wear big rubber boots and
blue smocks. Other deceased are lying on the mortuary hallway floors,
either in caskets or wrapped in white sheets. Meanwhile, outside Dr.
Boiteng's back door the families are gathering, and sometimes all hell is
breaking loose.

Dr. Boiteng's back door is so famous in Kumasi, tour buses occasionally pass by. It's the place where everyone must come to get their
bodies, so in a very real sense the back door is the first event of the
lengthy funeral process. For that reason a family doesn't just send
Cousin Kobi around in his van to pick up Grandpa, or dispatch an

undertaker with a hearse. The whole family arrives in full funereal re-
galia, and while the paperwork is being done inside—a process that can
take hours, depending on the number of bodies going out that day—
the families sing, dance, and grieve exuberantly. Five days a week, and
especially Friday, the parking lot out the back door looks like one of
those mine disaster scenes you see on television when the families of
the trapped miners first hear the sad fate of their husbands and fathers
below. The back door gatherers already know that their relatives are
dead. Sometimes they have known it for years, but an unknowing observer might think they too had just found out.

According to the police officer who is always on duty at the back
door, many of the male mourners are already liberally refreshed by the
time they reach the mortuary. "This can lead to 'incidents,' " he told
me, because liquor seems to make the men angry at death itself, a frustrating anger that causes them to get into fights with each other.

The fighting, and the anger, reach a peak when the awaited body finally does come out the back door, down the ramp, and into the family's care. Relatives sometimes fight for the honor of touching and
carrying the casket. Some of the men seem to be scanning the crowd of
waiting members of other families to make sure everyone present is
paying the proper respect. I was told by the police officer to stay as far
back as possible and look as quiet and respectful as I could. He didn't
have to remind me.

It would be misleading, however, to portray the Boiteng back door
doings as some sort of continuous riot. For every family that seems
emotionally out of control, there are a dozen others who wait quietly,
occasionally singing hymns. And when the body is delivered they make
no great fuss.

At one point that Friday morning, a small van pulled up to Dr.
Boiteng's back door, and five somber young men got out. They stood
at the bottom of the ramp and waited. Soon the mortuary workers
emerged above, holding a body wrapped in a white sheet. Two of the
young men ran up the ramp and took the body. It was their grandmother, and they carried her slowly and gently down to the parking lot
as if she were still alive and very fragile. One of the others jumped in
the back of the van and tossed out the spare tire that was lying there.
Carefully Grandma was lifted in, and they drove away. When they had
arrived at the back door three of the men were in the front, and two in
the back. But as they left, I saw only the driver up there. The other four
were on the bench seats in the back, taking their grandmother to her
final resting place.

One of the things all societies have to do is get rid of the bodies.
If the Neanderthal burial display in the Smithsonian mentioned in

chapter 3 is any indication, for human beings getting rid of the body has always been a lot more complicated than it might be, certainly a lot more complicated than what our fellow planet dwellers do.

Animals get rid of the body for two reasons. They don't want the body to foul the nest or to attract predators. That newly dead creature in their midst has *ceased to be* for its relatives in any way, except as a meal or a safety hazard. And though there are many cases of animals showing grief, including elephants, apes, and dolphins, even grieving animals get rid of the body in conventional, unceremonial ways. But apparently the earliest human beings, those hunter-gatherers whose lifestyle was in many ways more like the critters around them than that of their descendants today, felt that a body deserved more than simple disposal. Now, with no exception I know and regardless of religious beliefs, every human society on earth gets rid of its bodies with some display of respect, tenderness, and care.

I don't mean just some kind of funeral. Every body is gotten rid of and certainly not everybody has a funeral. Max had no funeral that I know of, just disposal in a pauper's grave. But during the time they were in control of his body and doing the initial steps to dispose of it, Bob Yount and his students showed Max respect and even dignity.

Rather than another demonstration of the human's ability to emo tionally complicate the simplest matters, I think the way we get rid of the bodies of our fellow citizens is a unique demonstration of our humanity. We take great care with the bodies we know, and our grief at death is often exaggerated when there is no body. Embalming may seem weird to other cultures, but it became popular in America because the Lincoln administration recognized how important it was for those people back home in the small towns of America to have a body to bury. I gave you my son. Please give him back.

Proper body disposal is so important to us that we have used how the body is gotten rid of as a punishment. There was no prohibition against holding a memorial service for a person executed for murder in pre-Anatomy Act Britain. The rule that murderers had to be dissected strictly went to how society would get rid of the body. And the protest when the Anatomy Act transferred that punishment to paupers was understandable. Because what really shows the human being's consideration for the dead is the care we take, not with the bodies of friends, but with the bodies of strangers.

Before he came in the back door on a slab, Max was unknown to Bob and the students. And Dr. Boiteng personally knows very few of his charges either. And yet he treats them all equally, with care, dignity, and an efficiency that is rare in his country's bureaucracy. His operation may look crude to an outsider used to immaculate, antiseptic facilities

and crisply dressed personnel, but Boiteng has a natural advantage over
some others in his profession. He knows where these people come
from. He knows the lives many of them have led, lives close to the
ground in small villages, lives on the edge hustling in the cities, lives
with only a few joys and many hardships. Dr. Boiteng doesn't deny the
existence of sorcery because it would be politically unwise for him to
do so, but I think he also knows that such a denial would be an insult
to many of the living and the dead. It would be disrespectful, and that
is something he tries very hard not to be.

My last image of him is not in his lab, mortuary, or office, but standing on the top of the ramp outside the back door that Friday morning.
He was directing his workers as they carried out the bodies, but between deliveries he would lean on the rail and watch the crowd below.
It was a big crowd, with a group of women singing "Rock of Ages" off
in one corner and the center area dominated by angry young men with
red headbands, watched closely by the police officer of the day.

Dr. Boiteng looked his people over with curiosity, but also I think
with sadness and love. He sees more bodies in a week than anyone else
sees in a lifetime. But he has not forgotten that someday his family will
be waiting outside that door. When he looks down at the people waiting now and those for whom they are waiting, he sees all the eleven-
year-old boys in small villages who weren't able to walk away and fulfill
their dreams. Although I suspect if I had the nerve to say that to him,
he would tell me I was being romantic and ridiculous.

•

Joye Carter lives and works in Washington, DC, five thousand miles
to the west of Dr. Boiteng. She is the first African-American woman to
become a chief medical examiner in the United States. But Dr. Carter
would be an extraordinary person regardless of her sex or race. That
she is a black woman who succeeds two centuries of predominantly
white men is just one of the many things about her worth noting and
admiring. It can't have been any easier for Joye Carter to achieve what
she has achieved than it was for Dr. Boiteng. They are both people who
by background, training, and sensitivity know they are the last line of
respect; the last people with a chance to treat their fellow human beings
honorably, courteously, regardless of how those human beings were
treated during their lives. And Dr. Carter, like Dr. Boiteng, feels that
responsibility. It is sometimes as simple as caring about strangers.

"You get to play all these roles," she said. "You get to play mother,
you get to play advisor. You get to counsel families on what happened.
You get to educate doctors on what should or should not have happened. It's the total job."

Like Dr. Boiteng, Dr. Carter also keeps mortal remains on the premises for a long time, but not for the same reason. Most of the people stored at Joye Carter's facility aren't waiting for relatives to take them away. They're just waiting for any relatives at all. There's not much spare land in Washington, DC, not enough for the burial of paupers' bodies. So DC law says that unclaimed bodies must be cremated after thirty days. And there are a lot of unclaimed bodies, so unlike most medical examiner's offices, Dr. Carter's has a crematorium that operates five days a week, all day long. She'd run it nights and weekends too, but the neighbors have complained about the smell.

The law tells her to get rid of the bodies as quickly and efficiently as possible, so theoretically after the unclaimed are cremated Dr. Carter is to have their ashes buried. But stacked up against the walls of her crematorium the day I visited were more than two hundred small plywood boxes, with a name and date written on the end of each box in black Magic Marker. Almost half the names were John or Jane Doe, and some of those dates were more than two years old.

"We give the police a lot of time to try to identify the next of kin or those that will be responsible for the burial," Dr. Carter told me. It's hard to believe the police of Washington, DC, have much time to find the next of kin of a nameless, homeless man who died in 1990, but Dr. Carter and her staff have hope, and occasionally it happens; a relative appears, looks at the photograph taken of each person before cremation, and a plywood box goes out the door with someone who cares about the person inside. And Joye Carter has had a good day.

"You often wonder as you're examining a homeless person, or a very elderly person who died all alone, if somebody somewhere knows something about that person. There might be family somewhere. You often see individuals who haven't had a bath in a couple of months, or died of malnutrition. Those things really bother me. They're so senseless."

Joye Carter first became interested in forensics as a ninth-grader back home in Indianapolis. She came from a farming area, so she was used to seeing the deaths of animals. When she got a job as a specimen gofer in the city morgue, it didn't bother her. In college she was a volunteer worker in the police lab. And then came medical school.

"What unnerved me more than being around death was to see somebody with an injury or a tumor that I couldn't help. I did an internship in clinical internal medicine, and I never left the hospital because I was taking care of my patients and trying to think of ways to make them more comfortable. A lot of them had chronic ailments. That bothered me more than actually dealing with patients."

So she decided to become a forensic pathologist, treating the dead. And that's how she sees it, too, not just processing corpses, but treating patients.

"I consider the patients that come into the medical examiner's office as just that; patients. I'm not hurting them, I'm learning from them. I'm helping their family adjust and learn."

Families do not always adjust well. These days, pulling the metal slab out of the morgue wall so the body can be identified by next of kin is strictly movie hokum. Now there is a photograph, or for families that insist on something more, a video camera set up in the morgue, and a secluded viewing room with a discreet guard. In their grief and anger, family members have damaged that room occasionally, but the ones Dr. Carter remembers most vividly are the people who leave vowing vengeance and return the next day on a slab themselves.

With places like Valley Green and similar neighborhoods, Washington, DC, is one of the most murderous cities in America. And the great majority of that crime is committed by black people against black people. The day I visited Dr. Carter she had spent the entire morning searching the bodies of seven black men shot in her city the day before. She was looking for bullet fragments, evidence of what happened and how it happened.

"Looking at what men do to other men, and just mankind, can be frightening," she says. "And yet you've got to get the job done." If you suggest to Dr. Carter that by choosing as her life's work the dead rather than the suffering she is avoiding the "life-and-death" decisions medical people usually must make, and therefore avoiding the failure other doctors endure, she disagrees strongly.

"Sometimes it *is* life or death if someone is accused of a crime, of perhaps a murder. We are supplying information that may well put somebody behind bars, or in a state where they have the death penalty, it could be life or death."

I don't want to make too much of the fact that Joye Carter is an African-American because in the daily performance of her job race has nothing to do with it. I was impressed by the small things she does to make life and death a bit easier for the people with whom she deals. Dr. Carter would be a caring advocate for the dead, a sympathetic supporter of their families, and an enthusiastic scientist in the cause of justice no matter what her ethnic origin was. But it's also important to say that Dr. Carter is a member of her community too, and Washington, DC, has the largest percentage of black residents of any major American city. She can't help but feel a special responsibility to her people and sensitivity for them, and she does.

"I can count on my hands the number of white victims of violent crimes we've had this year. Most of the victims are black. Most of the accused or perpetrators are black. We have a lot of people who just don't have any education, and they certainly don't have insurance. Those are medical examiner cases. My job in court is give an unbiased testimony of the medical fact. And that's very important when you're dealing with a black victim and a black defendant.

"It's also important to show that black people can do anything they put their minds to, if they have the chances that I've had for education, and perhaps some of the determination. People call me up and thank me for doing my job. My neighbors say, 'I'm glad that you're there.' "

Joye Carter is proud of the work she does getting rid of the bodies, and she should be. She is a splendid representative of two ancient traditions; women caring for the dead, and the community getting rid of the body. It may seem like those traditions have disappeared in the last few decades, at least in some cultures. One of the reasons most Americans under forty have never seen a dead body is because our communities don't deal with the deceased anymore. We hire experts to do that for us, experts who are much more efficient at removing the dead from our presence than, say, Belfast neighborhood undertaker P. J. Brown in his little truck, or the old town doctor in his horse and wagon.

I spent a day riding with Seattle's famed emergency medical service, Medic One. We went on fifteen calls, everything from a man shot down in the street and an elderly woman who had a massive heart attack in her home, to three or four cases of what turned out to be indigestion. And in each incident there couldn't have been ten minutes between the time the call first came in and we were there. Then, if the case required it, ten minutes later we were on the way to a hospital with the victim.

Medic One has saved thousands of lives because of the service's speed and efficiency. I certainly wouldn't argue that they should slow down a little so we can all get a good long look at the dead and dying. After all, they may come for me someday, and if that happens, I'd like them to leave now so they can catch me as I fall. But turning our bodies over to specialists we don't know, be they medical emergency teams or corporate undertakers, has diminished much of the tradition of getting rid of the body. Has it eliminated some of the care and humanity from body disposal as well?

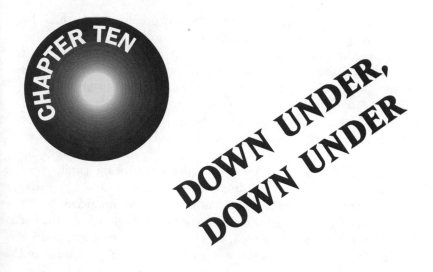

CHAPTER TEN

DOWN UNDER, DOWN UNDER

Tony Bonetti is wearing the kind of underpants I've seen in Sears catalogs from the 1930s; big white shorts, with a white vest tucked in, and thin socks held up by brown garters just under his knobby knees. And that's all he's wearing at present, lying on a metal table in the cool back room of a Sydney, Australia, funeral home. He's been dead for three days and embalmed for two, but he still has a hint of sprightliness about him. I can imagine at least two generations of Bonetti bambinos climbing up on those knees to hear stories about the old country, about the long boat trip to the new country, and how he and Grandma Bonetti struggled and saved and eventually opened the first restaurant in Sydney to feature real tortellini and a clam sauce just like home.

Tony Bonetti was eighty-six when he died, and in all those eighty-six years he never appeared publicly in his underwear. In fact, Tony never went anywhere in his skivvies outside his bedroom, unless it was a quick dash to the clothesline. Now two strangers gaze down at a sight not seen by any other human beings on earth except Grandma Bonetti and Great Grandma Bonetti, just as they themselves were viewed in previous years by other strangers in other places.

Only here there's a difference. The morticians who will prepare Tony Bonetti for his last appearance before the world aren't sepulchral men in lab coats and black, rubber-soled brogues. They are Linda and Michelle, attractive women in their mid-twenties, wearing spotless white dresses, aprons, and matching rubber-heeled pumps. Other than the fact that their white gloves are rubber and not cloth, they could be bridesmaids hovering over the reception canapés rather than morticians dressing a corpse. For that is their job. They're putting the final touches on Tony Bonetti's terminal image. They are the White Ladies.

Tony's face is already finished. Other than accident victims, old men rarely need much "restorative care," except possibly a bit of eyeliner. Tony died peacefully in bed, surrounded by beloved Bonettis on all sides, and his calm face shows he went gently into that good night. So all Linda and Michelle have left to do is dress him for the family viewing in an hour's time. Not that dressing an inert, fully grown person is easy. A shroud would be easy, but Australians, like Americans, aren't into shrouds, figuratively or literally. Tony will go to church for the last time as he always went to church, dressed in his best suit, with a shine on his shoes. That dark wool suit has been carefully cleaned and pressed for the occasion, his favorite tie chosen, and a new white shirt dangles from a hook intended for a jug of embalming fluid.

"All right, love, this is it," Michelle says to Tony, and the dressing begins. It may be because I'm watching, it may be because they are young and female, but Linda and Michelle seem particularly gentle. There's a tenderness to their touch unique to the back rooms of mortuaries I've visited, especially from Michelle. She handles Tony not like he's deceased, but rather like he's not feeling well and nervous about being dressed by beautiful women in strange rooms—which of course he would be if he knew it was happening. Michelle talks to him all the time too, taking him through the procedure as if he's a five-year-old getting his first real haircut.

"Upsadaisy!" Michelle says, lifting Tony's leg, handing his foot to Linda, and then slipping on a side of pants. She looks down into his face and smiles sweetly. "This is the easy part, love, it's the French cuffs I don't fancy. Lovely cuff links, though, it's a shame to lose them forever."

Pants secured, shoes on, Linda lifts Tony to a sitting position from behind as Michelle slips the crisp white shirt down over his head and the suit jacket around his thin shoulders, delicately taking his hands and sliding them into the sleeves. For a long moment, intent on their work, the two women wrap their arms around Tony in a sweet embrace. Then they slowly lower him down to the table for the last time. Grandma Bonetti herself couldn't have done it any more delicately.

That image, of gentlewomen hovering over the dearly departed and treating them dearly, has made the White Ladies Funeral Home the biggest thing to hit the undertaking business in Sydney since the horse-less hearse. After just five years in operation, the White Ladies have be-come a smashing success due to a simple idea that's still revolutionary in places where funerals are an "industry" and no longer a community ritual. Apparently a lot of Australians have discovered a preference for women handling their dead.

"We're especially popular with young children and babies. And the homosexual community, they also prefer women," Michelle says. "I think it's mainly because people see us as more caring, perhaps. They can relate to us better."

The assumption that women are just naturally more caring and ten-der than men (and won't stare at Grandma in her smalls and make re-marks) may be sexist, but for the huge funeral home corporation that owns the White Ladies, it's a profitable assumption nonetheless.

Women, especially the undertaker's wife and daughters, have always worked in funeral homes, to "do the ladies," as Belfast undertaker P. J. Brown says. And if the undertaker didn't have family women to help?

"We had a wee woman lived on our street here in Belfast, Minnie Hawkins you called her," Brown remembers. "And Minnie, Lord have mercy on her, she was the washer woman for the undertakers in the area. She done all the washing of the women. Anything that had to be done for the women, Minnie done it.

"But now we find that as years go on there, you can't get these women now. And ever since Minnie died, we've looked for another, but with no success."

If the Minnie Hawkinses are disappearing, the number of female morticians, embalmers, and funeral directors is increasing all over the world. They are reclaiming the societal role women in many cultures have always had, that of caring for the dead. But the White Ladies are among the first to exploit their gender aggressively for promotional purposes. Painted on the front door of the establishment is their slo-gan: "The Caring Alternative." And if the only real alternative here is women in white rather than men in black, that's more than enough for an ever-increasing clientele. When Tony's family arrives a few minutes later they are pleased not only with how Grandpa looks, but how they think he got that way.

"They did the child of a mate of mine a few months ago," says Tony's son, "a two-year-old boy who drowned. It was a very sad occasion. He was their only son. But what I remember from the funeral, there was this lovely young girl all in white standing by the grave. The funeral was over, we were all going back to our cars, leaving, and she just stood there with my friend's wife. She was crying, they both were, they looked like angels. I'll never forget it. That's when I said to my wife, 'When Dad goes it's those White Ladies who are going to handle it.' "

"Yeah, that was me," Michelle says later in the White Ladies' tearoom, behind an unmarked door just off the viewing chapel. "I try to do the children because a lot of the other girls here have got young kids, and I haven't. Kids are harder on them. Not that they're easy for me. I did the music for that one, and it was John Lennon singing 'Beautiful Boy,' and that did it, that broke me right up. I still can't hear it today.

"I cry sometimes, mostly for children. All the regular reasons, I guess. I think people should be happy at funerals usually, because I believe in an afterlife, and the deceased is going to a better place. So when I cry, it's usually for the families, and that's especially true if they've lost a child. I've had some in the business accuse me of faking it. And others have told me it's unprofessional, my job is to console the grieving but not join in their grief. Nobody here would say that, it's the men. And I tell 'em that's rubbish. I don't call myself a 'grief counselor,' none of us here are that pompous. We're just regular women who know what to do, and that includes knowing how to feel something for these people. As long as I can handle getting, whatdya call it, emotionally involved, it's nobody's business but mine and the family's."

And can she handle the emotional upheavals her work requires, at least the way she does that work? Michelle admits she's been fascinated by dead things since she was a small child. While the other kids in the neighborhood were bringing home kittens, she was bringing home dead kittens. And she liked reading death and funeral notices. So when there was an opening at the White Ladies, she quickly dumped her secretarial job and signed up. Her fascination continues, too. Ask most funeral home workers what they like best about their jobs and they'll recite the industrywide line about "the opportunity to help people in their time of sorrow and grief." And Michelle?

"I like it best in the back with the bodies. Just being in there alone, working on somebody. I suppose it's because I'm away from everyone. I can do my own thing. I just feel more comfortable. And I chat with them, as you know. Quite often I think they're sitting next to me talking, like if I hit someone accidentally, I'll always apologize. I talk to them like they're here, which in some cases, I think they still are."

Funeral home workers can become, if not callous, then certainly a bit larky about their work. We expect them to be as somber and reverent around death as we are, but really that's impossible, or they'd spend their whole lives looking like their clients. Around the White

Ladies, the back rooms can become quite frisky, with the radio blaring, some dancing, and the odd joke. (What do you call a funeral home in Japan? Jap in the Box. This is the only industry joke any of the dozen funeral home workers I've talked to has ever volunteered, and to be truthful, it came not from Michelle or any of her sister Ladies, but a guy at Forest Lawn in California who immediately begged me not to mention his name should I repeat it.) Michelle says the occasional frivolity at the White Ladies helps relieve tension, "or if it gets too much, you just walk outside and have a bit of a stress attack, then you come back in and someone throws something at you."

For Michelle, though, the problem is not becoming too callous, but just the opposite. "We're too compassionate," she says, "too close to them. We have had cases where you refuse to let anyone else help you. You just want to do it all on your own. You almost adopt them, sort of a maternal thing where you don't want to let them go. You can sit down, hold their hand, and talk to them for a while."

Michelle is a single person. Although her mother, a sheriff, is more than accepting of her occupation ("She'd like to be a White Lady herself"), Michelle finds that most young men don't understand her work or her passion for it. Except one potential suitor, who turned out to be entirely too enthusiastic for what she did, a guy she dropped like a rock. "Creepy, he was."

Michelle admits to going through a creepy phase herself. She lives just six minutes from the shop, and without immediate family nearby to spend time with, she was working fourteen hours a day at the table, even coming in on weekends. But she realized that wasn't healthy, and she's stopped doing that now.

"I do occasionally have to counsel the girls." Marie Westall, the former public relations executive who manages the White Ladies, walks a difficult line in hiring, trying to find young women who are compassionate but professional.

"You have to be completely sure that they're not getting too close. Because sometimes what that girl does at a service, just trying to help as much as possible, can be mistaken by the family as an intrusion. We're really not counselors, we're not grief counselors, we're really facilitators."

Besides emotional stability mixed with compassion, Marie is looking for something else in a potential White Lady; physical attraction. She's aware that there's a sexual aspect to the operation, that it's a "Freudian's dream business," as psychiatrist Robert Wilkins calls the White Ladies. Marie is, after all, an older woman who oversees pretty young girls handling naked strangers' prone bodies in small back rooms, a business description that certainly has other applications. And her favorite inquiry from a potential client did come from a new widow who wanted the White Ladies to bury her husband. "She said, 'That bastard was such a womanizer when he was alive, it's only right that women should put him in the ground when he's dead.' It was quite a lovely funeral, actually.

"I think that aspect of it, the sexual aspect, appeals to a lot of people, being terribly commercial about it. It's just a matter of commerce, really. If we had a very caring girl who wasn't particularly attractive, I'm not saying we wouldn't employ her, but if we had the choice, obviously we would employ attractive girls. Show me a business that deals directly with the public that doesn't do that.

"Part of that for us is because the relative who is arranging the funeral, they're doing it for their loved one who's just died, but they're also thinking about how they're going to be perceived as mourners. And it's a little like a wedding, you demonstrate how important the focus of the ceremony is by the nature of the ceremony itself. And my women in white are like bridesmaids in a way. We often have requests for women to be buried in their wedding dress. And the girls, nine times out of ten we find people who come to the White Ladies do want the girls to be pallbearers. They want to actually see the girls carry the coffin into the chapel, and lower people into the grave."

As a business the White Ladies doesn't emphasize the obvious sexual overtones of the operation. It's "the caring alternative," not "the leering alternative." If people want to see them as the vestal virgins they certainly look like, or something less vestal and virginal, that's up to the customer. But they had better not try to do anything about it.

"A few months back, twice in one week, we got late pickup calls, and when the girls arrived they found forty men and a lot of beer, but no body." Marie scowls at such prevarication. "I can't put my girls in jeopardy like that, so now all the clients know that if it happens in the night, a man will do the pickup. But once the deceased is here on the premises, he or she is entirely ours." No man works at the White Ladies, just Marie and her eight young ladies, and they do everything but embalm and dig the graves. They wash the white hearses, sell the white coffins, supervise the funerals themselves.

"Nonsense," says Bill Groves, a mortician with his own funeral parlor in a Sydney suburb called Picton. Sitting at his home bar nursing a modest gin and tonic before he goes to slip a dress on Mrs. Morrissey, Bill warms to the Australian funeral establishment's favorite topic of discussion. The White Ladies are a fraud, he says, because their success is based more on public relations than any difference in the quality of care or how that care is provided; specifically, who's actually doing the work.

Bill's business is obviously very profitable. His suburban home is spacious, and the immaculately kept grounds include a splendid gazebo in the middle of a wide green lawn (dotted with sample gravestones), a carp pond with fish big enough to tow small boats, and one of the biggest, cleanest home garages in Australia and the world. So it's not the White Ladies' success he resents. He thinks they are lying about how they do their work, and that reflects badly on funeral directors everywhere.

"They're a front, a front for the benefit of the big-time operators who own them; owners who would like to get into a certain clientele that wishes to believe that women are more caring. And you can tell that from the simple fact that the White Ladies claim they do everything themselves. Men can do things women are not capable of doing and vice versa. We are physically entirely different. You're not going to tell me that the White Ladies can go into a house and take a 230-pound man out of that house. I'd like to see somebody lift you and I down the stairs and out the window.

"I'll give you an example. We had a lady here. She was twenty-six stone—about 360 pounds. Not Mrs. Morrissey, she's quite petite. Another lady. I had to pump up the tires on the hearse before we went out and picked her up. I'm not as fit as what I was fifteen years ago, but by God, I don't do bad for my age. And I've got to take her downstairs, around corners, I can tell you there were times I didn't know if I was going to make it and any of my fellows with me either. How in hell is a lady going to do that? I can't prove it for sure, but I'm prepared to put money on it. There's no lady will lift a heavy, deceased person some of the places you've got to take people out of, you would never believe you would get them out. And believe me, there's no deader weight, you pardon the pun, than a dead body. I should know."

Bill has been lifting, carrying, and caring for the dead for fourteen years, having inherited the business from his father. He's a proper man for the Australian funeral business, because, like most Australians, he believes in having a good time whenever possible—a "regular bloke," according to his friends. Bill looks a bit like Stanley "My Fair Lady" Holloway, but he never worries about getting to the church on time. The Groves Funeral Home is an efficient, well-run business, one of the last of the independent, family-owned undertakers Down Under.

Bill is also something of a rebel. For one thing, he has a sense of humor. Right outside his mortuary is an old science class skeleton he picked up at a rummage sale; "a dissatisfied customer," he tells everyone, including new clients. And he still talks about the morning some coal miners showed up with the body of one of their young comrades, killed in a mine accident. Bill took one look at this group of young, hard-working men, grieving over their lost friend, and even though it was 7:00 A.M. he marched them right into the family bar and served whiskeys all around. And they thanked him for his sensitivity afterwards.

Then there's the way the Groves family lives. Funeral directors have resided above their parlors for centuries, but most of them maintain a distinct separation between the land of the living quarters and the business of the dead. But Bill's home and business are intertwined. His dining room leads directly to the mortuary, caskets are on display next to and sometimes in the family living room, and there isn't any Groves family car that couldn't and doesn't double as the car behind the hearse. Bill jokes that when he dies it's going to be very easy for his family. All they'll have to do is roll him down the hall. So Mrs. Morrissey is not quite a guest in their home, but she's a lot closer than the average cadaver at the average mortician's has ever come.

Michelle the White Lady would love Bill Groves's house, and if he didn't know where she worked, they could probably become good friends. Because like her, his life is his work, he cares about his clients, and he's just as critical of his male colleagues as he is of the White Ladies.

"It's nothing unusual for funeral people to hold their fingers up at each other as they pass and say 'four today, eight, nine funerals . . . ' bragging about the success they're having. As I said to quite a few of them, 'One of these days, one of those fingers you bring up will be you.' They don't want to see it like that. They don't know what this business is really about. This business is about helping people in their time of grief."

Bill's right, of course, and he's also right about heavy lifting. What he doesn't know or chooses to ignore is that the White Ladies have adapted their working environment to compensate for any physical shortcomings they may have. When Linda and Michelle were finished with Tony Bonetti, they moved his casket in beside the metal mortuary table. Where Bill and an assistant would have then lifted Tony up and placed him in the casket, Michelle just tilted the table, and Tony slid off into the box as neatly and easily as sliding a cheese omelet out of a skillet onto a plate.

The mortuary table isn't the only special equipment the White Ladies use because they are ladies. Their white caskets have specially designed handles to make lifting and carrying easier, and much of their other equipment has gears and cranks for raising and lowering deadweights. And the Ladies have learned to work together, using four or five people to accomplish some tasks that Bill would do with just one of his male workers. But Bill doesn't want to hear about that, because I don't think that's his real problem with the White Ladies. What he resents, bitterly, is the implication that just because they are women they *care* more than he does.

"The bastard who says I don't care is in for trouble."

Bill is fighting one cultural tradition at the same time he's one of the few representatives left of another. Like his father before him, Bill Groves is a member of his community who happens to be an undertaker, rather than an undertaker who happens to be in this particular community. Many of the people he buries are people he has known all his life. More than any other reason, families come to him in their grief because he's a neighbor who knows what to do. And whether he realizes it or not, his home/mortuary/funeral parlor is a perfect representation of that. People don't go into town to the funeral parlor to arrange for their loved ones, they go over to Bill's.

"I treat everyone who comes in the same way I treated my mother and my brother when they died," Bill says. "And once I lose that attitude, I don't want to be in this game." Bill is *community*, in other words, and the community taking care of its dead is an ancient cross-cultural tradition. So it's no wonder he resents the nine-funeral-a-day corporation undertakers, *and* the promotion-enhanced White Ladies— who are owned by the same corporation.

•

What Bill Groves doesn't realize or once again chooses to ignore is that traditionally the people in the community who dealt with the dead were women. In most preindustrial societies, if women don't actually bury the dead they are almost always the key figures in both burial preparation and mourning. As usual, the Greeks have a saying for it: "Women bring you in, women take you out." (There are a lot of midwives in this world, but few midhusbands.) The only real tasks for men in most funeral rituals are heavy lifting, digging, and saying those things required for the good of the soul of the deceased, because most religious authorities are still male.

In some traditional Greek villages, for instance, the female friends and relatives of the deceased immediately gather at the home of the dead, both to "protect" the body and prepare it for the rituals to come. Following extremely precise procedures that were established centuries ago, women of the community wash the body and dress it in new clothes. The feet are tied together, the jaw tied shut, and the hands are

tied over the chest, with a white cross placed between them. During
this time the women of the immediate family cry and sing sometimes
ancient laments. After the body is clothed for burial the women of the
village change into black dresses and black kerchiefs—becoming, I
guess, the Black Ladies. And only then does a man other than the deceased become involved. The priest is officially informed of the death,
and he orders the slow ringing of the church bells.

For the day prior to the funeral, relatives and friends watch over the
body. The visitors bring lighted candles, which they set around the bed
and in a large tray of flour by the door. And though both men and
women visit, when the men have paid their respects they go outside to
stand around and talk, as men so often do. But the women stay with the
deceased, singing laments and mourning with ever-increasing intensity.

Men, led by the priest, take charge of the funeral itself, after which
the women return to the house of the deceased to wash it thoroughly
and give away the deceased's clothing, "so that the soul will leave the
house." In this particular Greek ritual the obligations of the men other
than the priest are now over. But in at least some villages the female relatives are expected to visit the grave daily for up to *nine years* after the
funeral. During this time they are always in mourning, must wear
black, and in the case of the widow are prohibited from attending community events other than funerals. They cannot even shop, adhering to
rules that are strictly enforced by the community.

At the conclusion of the mourning period, the body is exhumed, ostensibly to see if the deceased has reached heaven. If the body of the
deceased husband has completely decayed and his bones are clean, he
has made the journey successfully. But if not, then the women of the
village clean the bones and kiss them. The bones are then put in the
town ossuary with all the other village ancestors, and the grave reused.
And only then does all mourning end; only then is the widow allowed
to rejoin the community completely.

Dr. Margaret Alexiou, a Harvard University professor who is an expert on rural Greek funereal customs, told me of one young woman
whose considerably older husband died less than a month after their
wedding. To escape spending the next third of her life in widow's weeds
removed from community life, she stood over his body and informed
the village women as they arrived that her marriage was never consum-
mated. It was probably a lie and everyone knew it. (He wasn't *that* old.)
And though attractive young widows with inheritances are seen as a
threat to community life (especially by not-so-attractive-anymore wives),
this particular woman successfully avoided her postmortem seclusion

because of her quick thinking, and because an unmarried young man expressed more than a passing interest in her future.

In many cultures around the world not only are widows on the loose a threat to the community, but all women are viewed as a threat to life itself. Death is the final physical act of one's earthly existence, an existence that began with the first physical act of being born. Though you are alone in death you are never alone in birth. There is always a woman with you, a woman on whom your physical survival depends for years to come. So it is not surprising that women have always been more closely associated with the physical nature of life than men. They give birth, they nurse, they menstruate, they are the receptacles in sex, and they usually live longer. Humankind thanks women for providing life, and three score and ten years later blames women for providing death. And that blame, both overt and repressed, seems to be reflected in a hundred different belief systems and funeral customs.

In the Judeo-Christian tradition it is the temptation of Eve that brings death and decay into the world. Similarly, a well-known Japanese creation myth concerns a brother and sister, Izanagi and Izanami. After an incestuous coupling, Izanami gives birth to the Japanese islands, and then dies.

> She was followed into the underworld by her grief-stricken brother/husband. She begged him not to look at her in her horrible state, but he could not resist a peek, and seeing her putrefying body swarming with maggots, he exclaimed, "What a hideous and polluted land I have come to unawares!" Thus shamed, the furious Izanami sent the Ugly Females of the Underworld after him with the order to kill him. Shaken by these events, he announced his divorce from her. In retaliation, Izanami vowed that she would strangle a thousand people a day in his land. He replied that he would set up fifteen hundred houses for childbirth in one day.
>
> *—Behind The Mask*

I doubt many modern Japanese are affected by this tale, although the Ugly Females of the Underworld conjures up an image that certainly lingers.

In some areas of China only married women are allowed to handle a corpse, because only women can do it without being adversely affected by the pollution of death, without their own "life essence" being depleted. Female hair is considered especially putrefaction-absorbent, so women hired for the purpose rub their heads on the coffin during funeral services, symbolically soaking up the pollution of the decaying flesh inside so it can't harm the menfolk.

On Taiwan I went to the funeral of Mr. Wen Shin Wei, held in a Taipei street because he was a poor man and his family couldn't afford a fancier location. It was a particularly noisy, tempestuous affair because Mr. Wei drowned. That meant the funeral had to be performed precisely according to the ancient rules or his spirit would spend eternity as a miserable, wandering ghost rather than a comfortable ancestor. And miserable ghosts often wander back home and create havoc in the lives of their descendants.

Three Taoist priests and a team of funeral advisors (all male) hired for the occasion carefully directed the events. And there were dozens of events. But one of the first was one of the most memorable as far as the relationship between women and death was concerned.

Mr. Wei had four daughters, but they weren't there when I arrived. In fact, hardly any women were in attendance at the start. Then I saw a group of women, including the daughters and Mr. Wei's sisters, coming up the street. They were all down on their hands and knees, like dogs, and all sobbing. A funeral advisor told me that this was to show the ancestors that they had unquestionable faith, as well as complete subservience to the spirit of Mr. Wei. But none of the men had arrived that way, nor did any of the men stay on the pavement throughout most of the service, as these women did.

Making assumptions about beliefs based on the observation of ritual events is dangerous business. Were these women somehow responsible for Mr. Wei's death and this was the penance they were required to do? I don't know. It's only accurate to say that there were so many ritual events in that funeral that you could spend the rest of your life trying to figure out what they all meant. Where was Mrs. Wei for most of this, for instance? And why were the only allowable active family participants in the ceremony those relatives who were younger than Mr. Wei when he died?

Women did play funeral roles other than as supplicants. Amongst the hundreds of prayers and chants, Mr. Wei's daughters were called forward for a kind of spiritual interrogation, making sure they knew all the things that had to be done to upgrade Mr. Wei from ghost to ancestor. And at one point they formed a circle around a huge pile of spirit money. The money was set on fire and the women began crying up to the heavens for their father to come get the cash, while their adopted brother stood handy with a sword in case another spirit tried to come and steal it.

Besides the canine entrance, however, the most striking event was calling forth the dead man's spirit. The principal prop for this ceremony was a multicolored cloth cone, perhaps eight feet high. Members of the family held parts of the cone and ran around in a circle calling Mr. Wei. The cone symbolically became the whirlpool that sucked him to his death. Eventually one woman—Mr. Wei's sister—went into a trance, and was thrust headfirst into the bottom of the cone. She stayed there for perhaps five minutes while a priest stuck his head inside above her and listened. I was told the trance indicated she was in communication with Mr. Wei, who would then speak to his assembled mourners through this female spiritual telephone. The crowd was waiting for his report that their funeral performance had been a success and he was now happily established as an ancestor. But according to the priest Mr. Wei declined the opportunity to address the crowd. His sister revived and went back to her knees.

When I left hours later, the priests were still chanting, the horns were still blowing, and it looked like a long night for the Wei party.

•

In the competition to blame women for the irritating fact that men must die, few cultures can beat the Bara people of Madagascar. Over the decades anthropologists seem to have attacked the Bara in packs, like wolves, so precise descriptions of every aspect of Bara life are available, especially funerals.

When a Bara man dies, his body is immediately prepared for burial by the women of the community. At the same time the men erect two huts, with an open space in between. When the huts and the deceased are ready, all of the village men go into one hut to sit around and talk, and all of the women take the body into the other hut to weep and wail. And there they stay for three days. But on the first night between those days the women come out into the space between the huts, singing and dancing provocatively. They are soon joined by the men, who have apparently decided that provocative singing and dancing is more interesting than continued sitting around and talking. The musical numbers become more erotic, and eventually there takes place what one horrified anthropologist called "promiscuous sexual pairing," behavior that is socially unacceptable to the Bara at any other time. The next night, they do it again.

On the afternoon of the third day the men attack the women's hut. In a pitched battle they "rescue" the deceased. Relays of young men then run the coffin up the Mountain of the Ancestors nearby, pursued by screaming young women trying to get it back. In their last stand, the pursuers form an all-girl barricade across the mountain path. The men are obliged to break through this red roverish impediment, using the coffin as a battering ram. The late lamented is finally buried in a mountain cave and everybody left alive trots back down the mountain to get ready for the party. There actually is a party some time later, called a Gathering, during which more promiscuous sexual pairing takes place and the village witches try to poison people. It sounds very much like a good time is had by all, after which Bara life returns to normal. Until the next funeral.

But what does it mean? There are two principal theories. Barans believe life is a balance between the sterile forces of *order*, associated with bones received at birth from the father, and the chaotic forces of *vitality*, represented by flesh received from the mother. Baran life is thus a journey "from mother's womb to father's tomb," because in death you are eventually reduced to just bone. In anthropologist John Huntington's theory of the meaning of Baran funeral practices, death is therefore a dangerous imbalance between flesh and bone. The frenzied sexual activity of those two funeral nights and the after-burial party is a symbolic attempt to restore some equilibrium through a shot of the old vitality.

Huntington's fellow anthropologists Bloch and Perry disagree. They argue that far from using sexuality to restore vitality, it is women's "obscene sexuality" that must be overcome before the soul of the deceased can be successfully integrated into the Land of the Ancestors. So the most significant part of the ritual is not the moonlit coupling, it is that moment when the men use the coffin to bash their way through the women and reach the mountaintop, something that has to happen before spiritual rebirth can take place. As Baran funerals proceed, they become more and more *male*. The sexual aspect declines, and only when the proceedings are all male, all bone, is the transitional stage of death complete.

One of the things all funerals must do is demonstrate that death can be overcome; that the death of one individual does not automatically mean either the death of all, or the end of society as we know it. For the Bara, if Bloch and Perry are right, victory over death means victory over women, and particularly victory over female sexuality.

•

Blaming women for death (or at the least finding them to be the usual suspects) is still found in so many cultures around the world that perhaps all *man*kind, no matter how sophisticated, has some lingering, unrealized resentment. Does Bill Groves really dislike the White Ladies because he subconsciously thinks they did in his dad and are out to get him? Of course not. But his distrust of women in hands-on roles in the funeral business goes beyond simple dislike of a group of white-clad female strangers fifty miles away. Bill has only one child, a bright, hard-working twenty-seven-year-old, the obvious heir apparent to the family business. Except that the family business is undertaking, and Elizabeth Groves is a woman.

"She can't handle it," Bill tells me confidentially. And though I don't ask, it's clear he's not talking about the heavy lifting again. In fact, Elizabeth and her mother are very much involved in the business now. The daughter does all the bookkeeping and keeps Bill's schedule, while Bill's wife Mary often prepares the bodies of women, using the same gentleness and sensitivity that Michelle displays.

If Elizabeth were to inherit the family business as her father did before her, she could hire any number of men to do the lifting, the same men Bill hires now. I suspect what he thinks she can't handle is the death *business* itself; she can't handle it emotionally. She can't perform that odd emotional separation that enables Bill and people like Bob Yount in San Francisco to function in the face of daily death. Or perhaps he is worried that she will perform it too well, and turn into the kind of corporate undertaker he loathes, the kind who brags about her turnover and refers to clients by the value of the coffin they bought. I'm sure to Bill that would be even more unseemly if the undertaker were a woman. Whatever the reason, although he is proud of his work and his success, and vociferously defends the societal role of the funeral director, Bill Groves still thinks undertaking is an unsuitable job for a lady, no matter what color she chooses to wear.

Saturday, a clear, bright day in February, Australian summer. In Picton, Bill is burying a thirty-seven-year-old truck driver who died after a long battle with cancer, while the White Ladies are burying Tony Bonetti miles away in Rookwood, the largest cemetery in the Southern Hemisphere.

Bill's trucker, Shane Richardson, had a lifelong dream. He wanted to drive a monster Kenworth, the truck of all trucks. But he died before he got the chance. So in Shane's memory his long-haul colleagues have rented a big Kenny to carry his body from the church to the cemetery as they follow behind in their own rigs. As a man who's done some professional long-haul driving himself, Bill has become known for his trucker's funerals. They present unique logistical problems—where do you park thirty-five semis outside a small village church?—but they have a certain raffish style that perfectly suits Bill's Australian sense of doing the right thing by your mates and having a good time while you do it. And in his black suit and suddenly serious mien, he is every inch the proper funeral director. Except at the moment the proper funeral director is hiding up a Picton side street in the hearse with Shane, waiting for a phone call.

Outside St. James Church two blocks from Bill, Mary Groves casually leans against a tree, watching the crowd milling around the church doorway. It's not the truck death crowd though, but celebrants from the wedding scheduled at St. James an hour before Shane's funeral. Inside the bride and groom are about to do the "I do's" and make their traditional dash to the parking lot. Finally the happy couple emerges, rice is flung, and the honeymoon minivan pulls away. The moment they are down the road and out of sight, and the rest of the wedding guests are turned toward the parking lot, Mary grabs the cellphone out of her purse and makes a terse call.

"All clear, Bill," she says. Bill immediately fires up the hearse and pulls out, making sure his route to St. James doesn't pass the newlyweds' route from it. Few people will know about this extra effort to avoid confronting a young bride at her finest hour with a reminder of her final hour. It is but a small touch of sensitivity, the kind of thing a neighbor, not an undertaker, would think of.

"Well," Bill says with a smile, "I knew Shane, but I know the bride too."

Meanwhile, in the Roman Catholic section at Rookwood, five elderly Italian-Australians and one grieving son carry Tony Bonetti to his final resting place, making grateful use of the White Ladies' specially designed coffin handles. Michelle and a colleague walk along beside, in stark contrast to the dark people in their dark clothing who have come to say good-bye. Michelle does indeed look like an angel, but a very efficient angel-in-charge.

Right before the graveside service, she nonchalantly strolls over to the cemetery groundspeople standing next to their backhoe fifty yards away. The gravediggers' shift ends at noon, and they're waiting impatiently to fill in the grave and be off home. Michelle smiles sweetly at the gravediggers, who leer back, but when she speaks there is a toughness in her voice I haven't noticed before. They notice it immediately, however.

"I'm not going to hear that engine start up before the last person has left the cemetery," she says, referring to the backhoe. "Am I?" It is strictly a rhetorical question, and the gravediggers take it as such. Michelle turns smartly on her white heel and returns to the graveside.

"You've got to watch those blokes like hawks," she whispers on the way.

The graveside service is brief. A dry-eyed Michelle holds the hand of Tony's eight-year-old great-grandson, not to console him in his grief but to keep him from running up and down the nearby graves. She knows the rest of the Bonettis have been prepared for this day for some time and don't need any soothing from her.

"I envy Tony," she tells me later. "For his good, long life, and his family, but more because he knows the answer now. Death is kind of this big secret, and I envy all of my people for finally finding out what happens. That's why I'm looking forward to dying. I wouldn't go out and shoot myself tomorrow, but I'm looking forward to it just to see what happens."

Back in Picton, the service is over and Shane's coffin is placed on a platform attached to the back plate of a Kenworth cab. Truckers stand around watching, smoking, offering Bill advice on the best way to strap the box down for the fifteen-minute trip to the cemetery. The funeral ritual has become a unique loading problem, and the truckers enjoy having the opportunity to get involved as something more than spectators. When all is ready, Shane's widow and somber, handsome ten-year-old son climb up in the Kenworth cab with the driver. Bill slides the limo with Shane's parents in line, and the cortege of Kenworth-hearse, limousine, trucks, and cars proceeds slowly through the village and down the road toward Forest Lawn Memorial Park.

An hour later it is all over save for one last event. The drivers return to their trucks and at a given signal pull the handles of their airhorns; a deafening truckers' equivalent of the twenty-one-gun salute that rattles off the low hills nearby and brings to a dead stop two other funerals going on nearby. In the first truck, the Kenworth, Shane's son has been invited up to honk the horn in his father's honor. Bill helps the boy up into the high cab and then stands alone ready to help him down again. The signal is given, the handles are pulled, and for the first time in a week Shane's son smiles.

I glance over at Bill, looking up into the cab, looking at that boy's sweet, sad smile. In the midst of that deafening blast, there are great fat tears rolling down Bill Groves's cheeks. And then there is silence.

CHAPTER ELEVEN

SAD MUSIC AND SLOW DRIVING

Americans are strange about funerals. I've asked quite a few people around the country to describe the best funeral they've ever attended. Without exception they've looked at me like I'm the kind of person who keeps body parts in jars of formaldehyde on his dresser. But if you ask the same people to describe the worst funeral they've ever seen, they don't hesitate for a moment to tell you all about it in detail. The minister was dull, some of the relatives didn't show up, the music was awful, the deceased looked like something straight out of Madame Tussaud's Wax Museum, and the funeral was scheduled on the same Saturday afternoon as the Big Game. How inconsiderate. Clearly the attitude of many Americans seems to be that the expression "good funeral" is an oxymoron, like "in-depth television interview" and "Super Bowl highlights." Funerals are meant to be suffered through. Period. And for many Americans that may very well be true.

Permit me, then, to describe my favorite funeral. I don't have dozens from which to choose. I hadn't been to that many plantings before getting the death beat, but I did at least go to one that was satisfying.

John was among the best young actors in America when he died of AIDS complications a few years ago. We'd been college drama students together two decades before, and in one way he's the reason I decided not to become a professional actor myself. Because even in college John was better than I knew I'd ever get, and he wanted it a great deal more. To be a successful actor you can't even consider the possibility of being anything else. I could think of lots of other things I'd be happy doing, and I eventually did some of them. One was to become a theater critic, so that eventually I reviewed John's performances. Knowing what a mediocre actor I had been, he was always most gracious about the irony of my reviewing his work. We were never friends, but I greatly admired his talent and professionalism.

Unlike me, John was a true theater man. Professional theater salaries being what they are, however, he also worked as a travel agent, and apparently was a very good one. And he was a Native American, a Nez Percé from eastern Washington. His various alliances had a lot to do with making his funeral what it was.

In the course of a lifetime we become part of many different communities. There's the real community where we live and the human communities of the people with whom we work and play. There's the church community, the poker players community, and of course that community made up of our extended family. Although for most people these communities overlap, with only rare exceptions the only thing all the communities have in common is that one person.

So it was with John. He was part of quite a few disparate communities, but the five main groups seemed to be the Native American community, the travel agent community, the theater community, the gay community, and his family. At his funeral, these five groups came together in the Indian Cultural Center in Seattle and created an entirely new entity; the John Community, a unique body with an extremely short, vital life, and just one task to perform—celebrating his life and mourning his death.

For two hours that's what hundreds of us did. The Native Americans danced and sang. Some actors who had worked with John told funny stories about him. A member of his immediate family spoke movingly about his life. It was the only funeral I had attended up to that time that I didn't want to end. And when it did end, I think most of us there felt better than we had when it began. And not, as in a lot of other funerals, because it was finally over.

As I left, the guy walking out behind me said, "Too bad John wasn't here. He would have enjoyed this. It was so like him."

"Wasn't he here?" said the woman beside him. It was a bit glib, but I knew what she meant.

John's funeral worked for many reasons. First, there was the coming together of his communities and that ebullient creation of a new entity solely in his honor and memory. Second, the funeral provided the opportunity to express sorrow at his passing, but joy at the life he had and especially the pleasure his work gave to others. Third, we who attended had something to do. We participated in the show, either as speaker, dancer, singer, or audience member. We didn't just sit there while trite phrases were lobbed out into the congregation by some mournful eulogist. We celebrated.

Finally there was no question in anyone's mind that this was precisely the kind of event John would have wanted. He was an excellent director too, and you could imagine him standing in the back watching the proceedings, taking notes for the next rehearsal on how to improve the show.

A funeral director told me once that one of the hardest things he had to do in his job was not laugh when the bereaved family said to him, "This is what Dad would have wanted." And the reason he felt like laughing was because in forty years in the business, "what Dad would have wanted" was *never* at odds with what the family wanted too. Nobody ever said to him, "We don't want to do this, but Dad liked it so we're going to do it anyway." In the defense of such families, the funeral Dad devises for himself in his last days isn't necessarily the funeral that works best for anybody else who attends. Often the dying person shoots too low, insisting that they don't want any funeral or something extremely simple. Modesty is a becoming trait, but it can play hob with funeral rituals that have to serve many functions besides quietly singing the praises of the deceased.

So I'll admit that "what the person wanted" is a problematic criterion for the successful funeral. I have to, because the worst funeral I ever attended was precisely what the person would have wanted. The departed had lived a very long life of tremendous accomplishments both as a business and social leader. He was one of the most impressive people I have ever known, a tough businessman who still believed his duty was to serve the public any way he could. He was scrupulously honest and always fair to his employees in an industry where treating employees like dirt was standard business practice. We who worked for him felt honored to do so. Yet his name was mentioned exactly three times at his funeral, as a fill-in-the-blank during a regulation religious service. If there was ever a life that should have been celebrated it was his, but his funeral was presented as a thirty-minute commercial for God in which he played a very minor role. He deserved a lot better. But it is only honest to say that throughout his life he had been a very shy man and had always avoided big, flashy events in his honor. A big flashy funeral would have been inappropriate for him and excruciating for his equally shy family. They got what they wanted, but the result was frustrating and maddening for those of us who needed to express sorrow and joy, to pay attention to this splendid man one last time.

I certainly believe that the wishes of the family should be observed. It's the reason I've not named this man and disguised him a bit. His family is still here and they're still shy. But sometimes what the family wants can be a damned shame for the rest of us. That's why the rest of us should do what we want to, by ourselves. So perhaps the final criterion for a successful funeral should be in two parts. First, a funeral should be what the deceased and his or her family wants. And second, a funeral should be what the deceased deserved. In John's case parts one and two were combined perfectly in the same ritual. But for the businessman they were not. We who wanted to celebrate him should have held our own event, something that happens these days quite often in AIDS funerals.

In one way it's probably unfair to use John's celebratory service as the example of a funeral done right. Half the people in the room were performers of one kind or another, and performers have a tendency to rise to ritual occasions. In recent years this has become especially true of the services for artists who have died of AIDS-related causes. There have been so many of them, for one thing, that arts communities have learned what works and what doesn't. And at least at the beginning, the celebrations for AIDS fatalities were often without benefit of family or body.

Bruce Vilanch is an Emmy award-winning Hollywood comedy writer and actor, probably best known as the man who helps Bette Midler be funny. A gay man himself, he has been to dozens of AIDS funerals and memorial services, and has become famous for his appearances at them. Bruce Vilanch is one of a handful of people who do stand-up comedy at these events.

"Most of the people in show business who die of AIDS-related illnesses were not family men. They didn't have particular attachments because their attachments were their friends. And so when they died, the family would come and say, 'He's ours now' and snatch the body away. They'd take him and bury him in Iowa somewhere. And his friends were left with nothing.

"So we began organizing what were first called memorial services, because that was what we really knew how to do. But in the course of doing them, we discovered that they were really celebrations; a way for us to say good-bye, to resolve his life and put a period on our relationship. And because the memorial services weren't traditional, not conducted by clergy or with the traditional trappings of a funeral, they could be whatever we wanted them to be. We weren't inhibited by having to be solemn."

Vilanch told me about his favorite such service, for an actor named Michael Murphy who had been a chorus boy years before. Like many with AIDS, Murphy had time to think about his service and what he wanted to have happen at it. And what he wanted was tap dancing. He wanted someone to sing "Once in Love with Amy" and tap-dance.

"So there we were in the Paul Revere Chapel at Forest Lawn, which is hysterical because the place looks like a movie set anyway, just like the Old North Church, with a Jonathan Edwards pulpit. You could get up there and do 'Sinners in the Hands of an Angry God,' but instead this choreographer gets up with his cassette deck, puts on Ray Bolger singing 'Once in Love with Amy,' and tap-dances. And the floor there is great for tap dancing, by the way, if you ever need a venue for your tap. It was quite wonderful, and everybody applauded."

As well they should. There are certainly places around the world where a funeral would be considered lackluster if it *didn't* have the cultural equivalent of tap dancing. Only in America it seems, and only for some people in America, are funerals required to be solemn affairs bereft of celebration, humor or joy. Why?

"Attention must be paid . . . " In Arthur Miller's *Death of a Salesman* that's what Linda Loman says to her sons about her husband Willie. "He's not to be allowed to fall into his grave like an old dog! Attention; attention must finally be paid!"

We often hear that funerals are for the living, and at least in my culture, it is true. In other cultures, in Japan, China, India, and elsewhere, the ritual performed for the dead has a direct bearing on where the spirit of the deceased goes next, like the street funeral for Mr. Wei in Taipei. In those places funerals are very much for the dead too. But regardless of culture, race, or place, *attention must be paid* in the proper way if the ritual is to succeed. What Joye Carter and K. A. Boiteng do that makes them special in the way they get rid of bodies is that they pay more attention than they have to.

There are others. New York City, unlike Washington, DC, where Joye Carter works, has spare land and an established pauper's burial ground, so unclaimed bodies are interred rather than cremated. Every morning a small ferry with twenty low-risk prisoners from Riker's Island and a half dozen jail guards crosses Long Island Sound to a place officially named Hart's Island but called Potter's Field, where New York has been burying its dead for a century.

The day's dead come in a truck an hour later. The inmates stack their plain wooden coffins three high in deep, long trenches dug by bulldozer; fifty bodies to a trench, three trenches per plot, with one white marker for each one hundred and fifty bodies. No service, no clergy, no tale of the death, just the trench, the boxes, the prisoners and guards, and fields dotted with more than two hundred and fifty white markers. Back at the jail, burial detail is considered a privilege because it gets you out of the joint, into the sun. But the nature of the work still has a sobering effect on the men who do it.

"I thought about the fact that where I come from I've seen guys get killed under dubious circumstances and there's nobody there to claim them," inmate Michael Hicks told me. "They wind up here. I thought about how I grew up, it could have been me. If your parents don't know where you are, you're coming here."

His coworker Moses McKoy said his eight weeks on grave detail have been "a hell of an experience."

"It's touching at times, and it was bothering me the first couple of days, but now when I go home I wouldn't mind working around here, because the money's good and my fear is just about eliminated. I know one thing, though. When I go out there's gonna be flowers and organ singers and ministers and people jumping up and crying."

"I figure I do it better than the next guy because I'm a little more caring about it. I feel I give a decent burial." So says Cemetery Officer Hugh Conroy, the man in direct charge at Potter's Field the day I was there. He's been a cemetery officer for eight years, and has buried more than five thousand of the estimated eight hundred thousand people on the island. At first the work bothered him, but he got used to it, and now the hardest part of the job isn't burying the bodies, it's training the men who bury them.

It's difficult to imagine a more ignominious departure than being dropped in a trench by strangers, with one hundred and fifty other strangers, on a barren island forty-five light-years from Broadway. But at least Conroy and company do something to pay attention, something as simple as knowing who is where. New York City keeps detailed records of the names (if they have names) in each plot, each trench. And even if the deceased is a John or Jane Doe, the city keeps a morgue photograph for every box. The day I visited the island we shared the ferry with a hearse on the way out for a disinterment. A relative had arrived from California searching for her lost brother. And she found him, or the city found him for her, in plot 225. She was taking her brother home, as soon as Hugh Conroy and his men found the plot, the trench, the box, and dug it up.

Conroy disinters an average of three people a week, a very small percentage of the number he buries. But at least it's something. Like Joye Carter saving her cremated remains, Conroy retains for his lost, often nameless dead the only thing he can give them: hope. He doesn't just get rid of the bodies.

Getting rid of the body is the only thing a death ritual *has* to do for the public good. Everything else is an elective. The way we choose those electives, prioritize, and then implement them says something about us, about the things we find important in death *and* life. For John and his communities, it was celebration. For the businessman and his family, it was decorum and propriety. For Officer Conroy, it is the only thing he can do. In my part of American culture, bereft of much funeral tradition, there's a wide range of options. That could be a reason for the general dissatisfaction with American funerals as they are done today. We have too many choices and too little cultural background and information on which to base decisions. So as part of this Trip of a Lifetime I went to three funerals where the events are dictated by sometimes rigid tradition; funerals where the choices are extremely limited, but the social rules are precise. And in each place I expected one thing, found another, and found that it seemed to work for the participants.

MARGUERITE JACKSON McCLAIN

"There's a funeral home in Pensacola, Florida, with a drive-through window."

"That's false."

"No, it's true."

This witty exchange took place on the American game show "Hollywood Squares" back in the 1970s. Sitting in his Pensacola home that day, Willie Junior smiled his brightest smile. As owner/operator of the new Junior Funeral Home, Willie was trying to break into a market already tightly controlled by two old, prominent competitors. The difficulty with starting a new funeral home is that you don't have many funerals going on, so no potential clients can see your operation. Willie needed to find a device that would get curious Pensacolans to come by. He needed to build traffic, and that is literally what he did. One of America's few drive-through funeral parlors was born, "Hollywood Squares" followed, and Willie has been doing nicely ever since.

"Sometimes when I'm down here on Sunday getting caught up on my work, I see tourists going around the building. All day long. Tour buses, too. I received mail from all over the country when we got the 'Squares,' and there was one lady who wrote me a letter and told me she thought I was a little sick. I didn't write her back."

Willie Junior isn't a little sick. He's a lot smart. Willie is a refreshingly straightforward businessman who got into the funeral industry because the father of a school friend was a mortician. Willie was a poor kid, and he couldn't help noticing that his friend wore new suits, drove a new car and had a diamond ring. "That's for me," said Willie Junior.

Nowadays, even though Willie still has the window, that's not why the grieving hire him. They choose Willie because he's become a part of the community—an elected county commissioner now—and he runs a good operation.

"The drive-through window is strictly promotional. We do not market it. If a family comes in, they are aware of it and they can use it if they want to. We will let them, but we don't bring it up." The people who do use Willie's Window often have ambulatory members in the family. Even though Willie's has ramps into the chapel, the window is a convenience for those who have trouble getting around.

So why was there someone in the window the day I was there? Because Willie knew I was coming to see somebody in the window, that's why. If the family he asked had refused, he was fully prepared to have one of his workers go in the window box and lie very still for the media. But the kin of Mrs. McClain said it would be okay. So when I drove up to pay my vehicular respects, there she was.

The window itself is more like a drive-up banking window than a fast-food or laundry drop-off window. It's large, rectangular, and set into the red brick side wall of Willie's big square building. I suppose it's as decorous a drive-through funeral parlor viewing window as a drive-through funeral parlor viewing window could be. Thankfully there aren't any billboards over it, no "this way to see the body" stuff. There's just a small sign a hundred feet away next to the street that says "Junior Funeral Home," and underneath "Viewing Window & Parking."

In the window, Mrs. McClain was a proper-looking black woman forever in her late forties, wearing a pretty white dress accented with the kind of pink corsage young ladies wear to the prom. She looked more like a prom chaperone, with as fiercely determined an expression as you can have with your eyes closed. And though her eyes were closed, she was wearing her glasses, which told me that in life, Mrs. McClain was a lot more interested in seeing than being seen. I could just tell from looking at her that she had taken very little guff from anybody in her life and had boxed more than a few ears. I felt guilty sitting there, motor running, staring at her. This didn't look at all like a person who would have agreed to be put in a window for the amusement of tourists and writers.

Looking at Mrs. McClain or her equivalent was all I planned to do at Willie Junior's: drive by, shake my head sadly at the crassness of it all, and get the next plane home. But after the viewing I stopped long enough to thank a member of the family, a handsome young man with a soft voice and softer Southern accent. He invited me to stay for the funeral in a half hour's time. His request was more than courtesy, I think. Someone, that young man, or maybe Willie, realized I might be getting a false impression of how they do things in Pensacola, especially if the window was my only funereal call. They didn't say that to me though, because I was already saying it to myself. There was something about Mrs. McClain that commanded more attention than I had paid. So I became part of the community of Elder Marguerite Jackson McClain.

Willie Junior's chapel is a large open space with room for hundreds of people on nice wooden pews. There's a wide platform up front for the speakers, and a piano off to the left. By the time I got inside a woman was making that piano work hard. The house was less than half full, not a great turnout in such a big room, but those who were there were singing with spirit. "Soon and very soon, we are going to see the King" was the lyric, not a dirge but almost a march. The casket had been moved to right under the podium and was still open. Some of those arriving would go up and stand for a moment with Elder McClain, but most just took their programs, went to their seats, sat, or sang. It was as much social occasion as ritual for these folks, people saying hello, hugging, talking about life in general.

The doors behind the podium suddenly opened, and many more people began pouring in; family and friends I assume, including Elder McClain's sisters and her son. They had been waiting in Willie's back rooms to make an entrance. They filled the chapel quickly, with the family in the first few rows. Two of Willie's workers quietly closed the coffin, covered it with flowers, and disappeared into the staging room just off the lobby where the staff can watch the proceedings without being part of them.

At the start the crowd was neither joyous nor somber. They acted the way people do at the start of a normal church service. And they were dressed that way too. The older men, usually sitting alone and usually very quiet, wore traditional black suits. They were the only somber ones. Most of the women were in very bright colors, flowered prints and big, dashing hats. They looked full of life and they made the room seem that way. I was reminded of the Chinese, who believe the proper color of mourning is not black but white. That makes sense to me. Where there is death and contemplation of the life beyond, light should be reflected, not absorbed.

The proceedings began with scripture readings and prayers from four male ministers who sat behind the podium.

"I am the way, the truth, and the light," said the oldest one, a gray eminence, and the congregation agreed. In between the prayers a small choir sang, the pianist forcefully leading five women and a man through the musical glory of God, with much assistance from the house.

At one point a woman rose from the second row and came forward to stand next to the piano. She was wearing a wonderful white suit and hat, both covered with big black polka dots. And she had that same look of fierce determination I had seen outside through the window.

The room went very quiet as she stood there, looking at us through her big eyeglasses. I suspect for these folks the funeral up till then had been a standard ceremony, with the expected songs, prayers and readings. But this appearance from the audience was clearly something special.

She spoke with a shy, soft, determined voice. "Marguerite asked me to sing this song today in God's glory," said the woman, "and I told her I would. I'm gonna do my best, but if I don't complete it, well . . . " and her small voice trailed off into silence. Then the pianist hit a chord, the lady in the polka dots began to sing . . . and it was glorious.

I've learned how to live holy,
I've learned how to live right,
And I've learned just how to suffer,
For if I suffer, I'll gain eternal life . . .

Her powerful contralto filled the room, filled the world, and the more she sang, the closer she moved to the coffin. This was no professional singer hired for the occasion. It was Elder McClain's sister, Mrs. Gwendolyn Johnson, up from Okeechobee, Florida, where Willie told me she's the soloist in her church choir. And indeed she suffered as she sang, with tears in her eyes but the sound still pouring out of her.

By the time she finished she wasn't singing for us anymore, she was singing for her sister and herself, standing flat-footed by Elder McClain, shooting that message into her own heart and her sister's soul.

No more trials, no more heartaches,
No more pain, she's seeing Jesus! Amen!

Sister Johnson made it through and sat down with the family, taking their hands. It was a magnificent moment, and a real tough act to follow. Or so I thought.

There was one other person seated behind the podium besides the four ministers in their black suits. She got up then. Pastor Eddiemae Layne was wearing all white, from hat to shoes. A tall, commanding presence, she looked like a beacon, a lighthouse for souls adrift and heading toward the rocks; precisely the look she wanted, I suspect.

"I have to begin with an apology," she said quietly. "I might not be as brief as I ought to be, because Elder McClain and I go back a long ways, and this is the last opportunity. So if you don't mind I'm gonna take my time, and say what I want to say." It was exactly the kind of thing a eulogist would say to terrify 98 percent of the assembled at other funerals I've attended; funerals where the principal unstated question running through the crowd is "When will we get out of here?" But not at the services for Marguerite McClain. Pastor Layne knew her audience, and knew her ability to hold them.

She started slowly, telling the tale of Elder McClain's life and death as all successful funerals tell the tale in some way. Marguerite McClain had been a preacher, a Sunday school teacher, a "prayer warrior." When Pastor Layne visited her in the hospital during her fight with cancer, Marguerite wouldn't let her leave until they had prayed together.

"You had to pray your way out of her room! She was *right* with her God!"

Eventually Pastor Layne got to her subject for the day. With a text from Philippians, it was "if you live in Jesus, to die is *gain*."

"What would happen if we couldn't die? Suppose we couldn't die! Do you know what it would mean not to die? If we couldn't die, the blind man would remain blind. If we couldn't die, the paralyzed would never walk! If we couldn't die, that aging heart would continue to ache, and never be healed! Glory be to God! Hallelujah!"

When she really got into it, got her rhythm going, she brought that crowd of three hundred people along with her like we were cattle and she was riding a big smart horse named Jesus. Together they were leading us into the corral. She'd hit a peak—"So dyin' ain't bad, y'all, because there is something after death! Hallelujah!"—and then she'd swoop down into the valley and immediately start climbing to a higher peak. Eventually she was singing her text as much as speaking it. Many in the audience were singing along with her, like a parenthetical Greek chorus trying to make every word important.

"We die to gain a better body! (Amen!) A glorified body! (Glory!) A resurrected body! (Yes!)" And intertwined through it all was Marguerite, whose body was in the coffin before the pulpit but whose spirit flashed around that room like lightning.

"Many times I thought I couldn't make it, but she stood right there and said, 'Hang on in there, Pastor!' Elder McClain was like Isaiah, she constantly pointed the church to brighter days, better things in the future. Some of you don't know about our church but—hallelujah!—we went through hell and high water to be where we are!! We needed people like Elder McClain. She didn't just talk to the Pastor! She talked to the church!"

It was a breathtaking performance, and yet as heartfelt as any eulogy I've heard. It wasn't all cuddles and God, either, there was some grit to it. Pastor Layne and Elder McClain had founded a church together. Two strong women, both not used to taking guff, so I suspect their relationship had its heated moments. Pastor Layne said as much.

"Yes, you know it, we had our ups and we had our downs. We had our ins and we had our outs! But by the grace of God we hung in there!" Pastor Layne won, of course, because she survived and survival is victory. But not if to die is gain. From her eulogy you would have thought the winner was Elder McClain. She was going to see Jesus first, and that was the biggest victory of all. A wonderful thing had happened to Marguerite McClain. She had died, and you could almost believe Pastor Eddiemae Layne was jealous.

Like the businessman's funeral I found so disappointing, this one also became a commercial for God. But this time it worked, because the clear indication was that pushing the faith was precisely what the deceased did all her life and would have expected at her funeral. And it also worked because when she was rolling Pastor Eddiemae Layne could have sold Jesus to the OPEC ministers.

"Now the Lord is preparing a place for us, a mansion, but you know you can't get it unless you die. (No!) You got to die to get that heavenly home! (Glory!) Glory be to God! (Amen!)"

Pastor Layne finished with "Praise God, if you don't have it right, get it right!" Then she apologized again for going on so long. She wasn't preaching to us anymore. As the singing sister before her, she was really talking directly to Marguerite, and her voice had dropped to almost a whisper.

"I'm like you, I hate to give her up. We just hate to give her up, but we've got to. All we can do now is make preparations to meet her, because we have to give her up."

Pastor Layne sat down, and the four ministers gravely shook her hand. Two of Willie's workers reappeared from nowhere, carefully removed the flowers from the coffin, and opened it. I almost expected Elder McClain to have changed somehow, expected her to be smiling. But she looked as fierce as ever. It was the rest of us who had changed.

The pianist began singing "Onward Christian Soldiers," everyone joined in, and the front rows stood. I thought it was all over, but as people began to file out they turned and came back up the central aisle of the chapel. Slowly, one at a time, they walked past the coffin. A few women cried when they looked into Elder McClain's face for the last time, but only a few. The rest of the congregation just looked, as you would look at your own sleeping child. Sister Johnson stood looking down a long time, smiling, nodding, saying good-bye to a lifetime together. She put her hand on Marguerite's shoulder for just a moment, and walked away.

When everyone had filed past once, some female members of the immediate family came forward again for a last farewell. Willie Junior suddenly appeared and came with them, helping each woman from her seat, supporting her as she stood there, then gently guiding her back. It was the only moment of great sorrow in the whole day. There had been tears throughout the congregation, throughout the service, but nothing like the grief expressed now. "Letting go" is an expression I've heard a lot, talking to people about death. I saw at the end of that funeral that often letting go is no easier for the survivors than it is for the dying.

Sister Johnson didn't join her siblings for that final visit. She stood at her seat and watched. When they were done she followed them towards the back door out of the chapel behind the podium. Willie and his workers were closing the coffin by then. Gwendolyn Johnson glanced over, saw the lid come down, and dropped like a stone to the floor. Eddiemae Layne was the first one to her. She wrapped Sister Johnson up in her long, white arms, and helped her to her feet. Then they were gone, and I never saw either of them again.

I can't think of a single thing I had in common with Marguerite Jackson McClain. Religiously, socially, geographically, and ethnically we were worlds apart. And yet I left that funeral wishing I had known her, and proud that the fine, devout people who did know her invited me to join them for their celebration of her faith. What was said at the service and what happened at the end of it were obviously contradictory. If her family believed that "to die is gain," really believed that Elder McClain was in heaven with Jesus while they sat on earth at Willie's and sang her praises, then there should be no reason for such devastating grief and sorrow. Just joy. And yet there was joy, and true belief, and grief as well. Pastor Layne said it, and I guess she was right. No matter how devout we might be, we just hate to give her up, but we've got to.

EDMUND ODIATUO AMOAKO

Kumasi is the second largest city in Ghana, after Accra. It's a noisy, busy place in the south central highlands of the country, four hours up a sometimes good, sometimes nonexistent highway from the capital on the coast. There's a university in Kumasi, a big football stadium, and architectural remnants of British colonial rule everywhere, from mansions

and military facilities to Dr. Boiteng's decaying mortuary. Ghanaian
military troops and police officers now occupy the barracks where once
Her Majesty's Finest used to spit shine their bagpipes.

The rain forest isn't far away, and at any time circling over Kumasi
are hundreds of huge vultures that never seem to land. (This is not a
complaint.) Little lizards are everywhere too, but they disappear when
it rains, possibly into your luggage. I asked a resident what they were
called and he said "li-zards" very carefully so I would be sure to understand him. The lizards and the vultures are about the only critters you
can see in Kumasi outside the town zoo. That came as a distinct disap-
pointment for an American kid prepared by television to believe that
any place in Africa south of Cairo there are elephants, lion prides, and
wildebeest just waiting for Richard Burton to come back so they can
eat him. Either Richard Burton.

With no colorful beasts to watch, the people of the area watch each
other. They do this in a special way, using what Paul Goodman called
the "open look." Goodman was talking about cats, and indeed, cats
and Ghanaians both have that open look, which is free of emotion, neither dominant nor subservient. Using that look, a cat comes at you as
an equal, and so do Ghanaians. I don't think there's a road in the
greater Kumasi area that has less than a dozen people standing at the
edge twenty-four hours a day, shooting that catlike look at the cars
going by.

Many of the people in Ghana move like cats too. The men never
seem to put their full weight on the ground. The often-beautiful women
have the same combination of intelligence, sleekness, and cuddliness
that you find in the best cats.

What cats don't often do that Ghanaians do all the time is argue
with each other. Exactly like the Georgians of the former Soviet Union
with whom I spent a few months, there is nothing Ghanaians like better than getting many people together in a small place and shouting. I
went to one soccer match in the stadium, and there was constant
shouting from the stands. But not, as in America, towards the field.
The fans were shouting at each other, and the game was secondary to
that experience. They were having a wonderful time doing it, too, even
though when the game was over one of them had to ask *me* who won.

What dominates Kumasi economically is the market, a huge complex of small three-sided sheds by the railroad tracks in the center of
town. You can purchase just about anything you want in the Kumasi
market, and a million things you don't want. There must be a hundred
and fifty little stands selling toothpaste, for instance, yet I never saw a

single person either buying toothpaste or carrying a just-purchased tube. I suspect toothpaste is a big item not because of customer demand but because there's a lot of toothpaste available to sell.

The market is run unofficially by a group of women who are true queens of their particular product area. There's a fish queen, a calabash queen, a household appliances queen, presumably a toothpaste queen, and so forth. They are not to be messed with. One year the government tried to strip the queens of their power. The queens responded by shutting the market down cold, which shut down the city, which shut down an area for two hundred miles in any direction. The government gave in very quickly.

One of the queens is in charge of a small, select group of people who sell cloth to wear to funerals. In some cultures her product area would put her very low on the power totem pole amongst the queens. But not here. Because Kumasi is the center of the Ashanti administrative region, what was the Ashanti kingdom until the British deposed the king, or *Asantehene,* in 1896. And as I have said, the Ashantis and many of their fellow Ghanaians believe funerals are extremely important affairs.

The principal weekend social thing to do in Ashanti territory is go to a funeral or two. It's not just the Ashanti who do that, either. Near the market in Kumasi is a tiny restaurant called Baboo's where you can get the best cheeseburger, hot dog, and grilled cheese sandwich in town. (The Ghanaian competition in this area of cuisine is not fierce.) And whenever Baboo's is open there seem to be American Peace Corps folk in there, either starry-eyed youth just arriving for their stretch or scrawny old people leaving after a year or two, plus those in the middle of a hitch who have been "up-country" for months eating foofoo (you don't want to know), planting cocoa farms, teaching, or if nothing else giving the local population gung-ho American-style encouragement. One Corps youth in his late twenties, the son of a wealthy Wisconsin burgher, told me what he and all his Peace Corps friends did for entertainment besides eat burgers at Baboo's. They went to Ashanti funerals, interested not in anthropology but refreshment.

"Free booze," he said. "And a band." And of course you can pass off this cheap date as a cultural, anthropological inquiry. It looks good in the postcards to home.

To attend a funeral you have to be properly clothed, which accounts for the dozen stalls in the Kumasi market selling *adinkra* cloth. Usually it's cloth made originally for other purposes, including holding flour. The cloth is stitched together and then dyed and redyed until almost black, although I've seen dark red adinkra cloth too. (For the extremely traditional, the funeral attire you wear depends on your relationship to the deceased and how long he or she has been dead. So a second cousin once removed on the mother's side of the dead person's family would have to wear different colored cloth on the second day before burial from the cloth a nephew on the father's side would wear the day of burial.)

After dying, the cloth is stamped by hand with symbols. Only cloth so stamped is real adinkra cloth, a tradition going back at least to the early 1800s. The Ashanti have always had a relationship with the Muslims of northern Ghana, although that relationship hasn't always been friendly. (Ashanti still refer to their northern brothers as *donkor,* which is the word for "slave.") The Muslim influence can be seen in some aspects of Ashanti culture, and the theory is that the original adinkra symbols were from Islamic writing. There are now hundreds of these symbols, each connected to a saying, parable or belief. One symbol, for instance, looks like goat horns, and is. It means "goat horns and love are somehow linked," although what that means is beyond me. What looks to me like a Maltese cross is a butterfly and means "the family is always interested in the body of the dead." My favorite adinkra stamp is a relatively new creation that looks like a Rorschach test. In Twi, the Ashanti language that's done as much for the vowel as Celtic did for the consonant, it is *Bomokyekye firi nsuo ase bekase denkyem owua yen ngye no akyimie,* or "When the hippopotamus surfaces and says that the crocodile is dead, you shouldn't argue." It's one of those expressions that loses nothing in translation.

The market for stamped adinkra cloth is so big, especially now that people are wearing the cloth to social occasions other than funerals, that not far from Kumasi there is an entire village named Ntonso that produces little but adinkra cloth and associated funereal materials. Artists and seamstresses from Ntonso supply most of the stalls in the Kumasi market, but you can go to the source for special orders. On warm days the Ntonso streets are covered with drying cloth. Women dye more fabric over fires in big steel drums or sit at sewing machines putting together small pieces of recycled cloth. On the sidewalks, looms with thread stretching the entire length of the block are manipulated by weavers making strips of *kente;* bright, multicolored threads woven tightly together that are used to connect pieces of adinkra. And in the courtyard of his house Mr. Nsiah sits and carves adinkra stamps.

Joseph Nsiah was a cocoa farmer who made stamps as a hobby. He started to make more money from the hobby, and the work was much easier, so for the last thirty years carving the stamps out of calabash shells has been his work. Most of that work is on standard designs, but he's especially proud of the stamps he's designed himself, like the wise spider, Ananse, who is the hero of much Ghanaian folklore.

His carved stamps usually go around the corner to Kwame Tawiah, the foremost cloth stamper of Ntonso. Mr. Tawiah's father was a chief of the village, but because Mr. Tawiah was not the oldest son, he didn't inherit the job. And to keep him from becoming a threat to his older brother who did, Mr. Tawiah was not allowed to go to school or learn to read. At the age of twelve he was apprenticed to an adinkra cloth stamper, and that's what he's been doing ever since; more than sixty years now.

I bought a stamp from Mr. Nsiah—*gye nyame,* which means "without God," as in "We can do nothing without God"—and brought a cloth for Mr. Tawiah to stamp for me. Stamping didn't look that difficult, although I suspect it's much more difficult than it looks. Mr. Tawiah doesn't talk a lot while he works on a cloth. He told me I'd picked his favorite stamp, and that he likes to go to funerals to see his work on display. Other than that he just did the job. It took twenty minutes, and the cost was around five dollars.

Both gentlemen are elderly now, and both are engaged, with no pun intended, in a dying art. Cloth manufacturers outside Ghana now make machine-printed adinkra cloth that has the added advantage of permanency. The ink Mr. Tawiah uses is water soluble. He doesn't switch to a permanent ink because he's always done it the other way. So if you wash one of his creations you have to have it restamped. His business is down from twenty years ago, but at least there are apprentices who are interested in carrying on hand stamping. Mr. Nsiah, however, is the last stamp carver in a village that was once one of the two centers for adinkra stamps in the country. Other than visiting anthropologists, his fellow Ghanaians seem to take little interest in his art or its survival.

In some ways the lavish Ashanti funeral is endangered as well. The expense and complexity of the event is such that urban dwellers are starting to have more American-style funerals. I was told that I'd be hard pressed to find a good, traditional Ashanti funeral in a big city like Kumasi, but if I went to the rural villages I'd find dozens of them. I found just one, but it was the biggest death ritual I'm ever likely to attend.

There are apparently three different villages within the Ashanti empire named Assamang. Edmund Odiatuo Amoako was from the one two hours southwest of Kumasi, a short distance up the road from Nana Kofi Adu's Mensase. The Amoako Assamang probably has five hundred residents. There's one wide main street, two side streets, then a few alleys, and suddenly you're in the rain forest that comes right to the edge of town. The Ashanti are known for never clearing more land than they need, and Assamang is a perfect example of that. What sets the village apart from some towns of similar size in the area is that Assamang has electricity, a direct result of the influence and ability of the late Edmund Amoako.

He was born in Assamang of royal blood, educated and raised there, and eventually left the village to join the army. According to his son Fred, an Accra public relations man, Amoako distinguished himself in several minor battles, and rose to the rank of warrant officer. When he wasn't fighting he ran a large post exchange and food service until he retired from the military and became a security officer. That's what he was doing when his heart suddenly stopped at the age of fifty-nine. He was a powerful man, personally and professionally, and that's how he successfully lobbied the government for electricity for his home village.

Edmund Amoako came home to be buried by the people who traditionally are responsible for his death ritual. The Ashanti say, *Ayi, woso no abawabwa*—"Everyone helps to carry the burden of the funeral." Although the elders of Amoako's family, what are called his *abusua panin,* are directly responsible for preparing his body for burial, organizing the funeral and making sure that the rituals are properly held, the entire village must contribute as well. The Amoakos had lost a family member, but the village, the community, had suffered a loss as well. When I arrived on the Friday afternoon of his weekend farewell, the streets were already full of people getting ready for the event. Mostly they stood and stared at those of us who were arriving. Like cats.

The first two things that happen at a traditional Ashanti funeral are the preparation of the body and the wake. At least that Friday night in Assamang these two events took place simultaneously, right next to each other. Warrant Officer Amoako's body had already been collected from Dr. Boiteng. He was lying in pre-state in the central courtyard of his mother's house on a beautiful brass bed rented from the Last Respects Funeral Accoutrements Rental Company in Kumasi, one of the oddest little businesses I've ever visited. They have ten funeral brass beds in constant use, garish-colored floodlights that attach to the beds ("and look just like candles," the owner informed me), and gold jewelry to give your deceased that wealthy look.

Right outside the door of the house where Amoako lay, the wake had begun. It was lit by one painfully bright neon light that made everybody look blue and bizarre. The wake's principal activity was dancing to a very loud, fast band. If I didn't know better I would have thought this was some kind of village celebration and certainly not the first event of a ritual for the dead.

But inside the house, thirty feet away, there was a dead man. His male relatives gathered around the bed, pulling makeshift cloth curtains so they—and he—couldn't be seen by the dancers outside. The actual preparation of the body was performed by the dead man's son, Fred Amoako, assisted by a young man in a T-shirt from Last Respects Rentals. While Fred and Mr. Last Respects worked, the other men shouted at each other and stared at the deceased. A dozen rented gold bracelets were put around his wrists. Gold rings were placed on his fingers. Then the body was covered with a beautiful brocade quilt of blue and gold that looked like it just came off the second best bed in the palace at Versailles. After some effort, the dead man's arms were placed in the proper position on top of the quilt, and a white handkerchief put in his clasped hands. They rubbed a kind of salve on his face, presumably to give it that lifelike look, and finally Edmund Odiatuo Amoako was ready to be seen.

When the curtains were removed the men began marching around the bed. Each man held his hands up in the two-handed, two-fingered victory sign made popular first by Churchill and then later by Richard Nixon. Like adinkra stamp designs, this "symbolic salutation" has a meaning; specifically, "We are all of one family."

Then it was the women's turn to view the body, and where the men were stolid, the women wailed and sobbed hysterically. Their arms were stretched out toward the body, a salutation that means "I am left alone without you." Amoako's mother, a very old woman wearing bright orange cloth, shouted at her dead son angrily, waving her fists in the air over his body as tears rolled down her cheeks. Next to her the dead man's widow was far less demonstrative but no less distraught. She was a small, young woman with dark circles under her eyes—a second wife, I suspect, because she didn't look that much older than son Fred. She stared quietly at her husband, with her hands symbolically covering her breasts ("Who will feed my children now?")

The other women seemed more angry than sad. But Amoako's widow acted lost and very afraid, and I felt sorry only for her. Apparently I was the only one who did. Dan Mato, an American art historian and anthropologist who has been studying Ashanti funeral customs for decades, told me later she had every reason to be afraid. The Ashanti are a matrilineal society. Power and inheritance come exclusively through the mother's side of the family. Therefore, with her husband dead, his family was under no obligation to her. Widows (and widowers) have no rights once their spouse's body is in the grave. The Amoako abusua panin had the choice of taking care of her or sending her back to her own family with nothing to show for her married years but memories. In this particular case, they eventually gave her a room in their house. But her presence at the funeral seemed to me more an expression of toleration than sympathy.

For the first and not the last time that weekend, I considered the sincerity of the deeply grieving people before me. Some of these women who were now not able to stand because of their grief I had seen dancing outside the house less than an hour before. At the same time, Fred Amoako was standing on a chair across the body from me, using my camera to take pictures of his family in mourning. While dressing his father and then watching his grandmother, stepmother, and sisters collapsing around the body, Fred had been a rock. As the oldest son, the specific organizational details of this massive funeral were his responsibility, and he'd already told me it was a lot tougher to put a funeral together than he expected. The way he stood on the chair snapping away you would never have guessed he was the dead man's son and heir. Except suddenly he was sobbing, as if the scene before him had come into some kind of brutal focus all at once. Fred wasn't faking anything for ceremonial reasons. For one thing, I was the only one who saw him back there, and he didn't know I was watching. Still sobbing, he continued to take pictures. When I saw him outside later on, he was a rock again. So perhaps as part of their death ritual the Ashanti purposely put themselves through vast mood swings, and the sorrow is just as heartfelt as the joy.

The next morning Edmund Amoako was still lying in state on the brass bed in his mother's courtyard, but now he was covered to the neck with a white sheet. Baskets of flowers had appeared around the bed. One card I saw on a particularly lavish floral arrangement said in English:

From: Children
To: Beloved Father
RIP

The wild dancing outside of the night before had become much quieter, more traditional dancing inside, directly in front of the bed. Half of the fifteen dancers were wearing white T-shirts that said Presbyterian Women's Fellowship. I believe symbolically that means they were members of the Presbyterian Women's Fellowship.

At a table in the corner there was now a man of the cloth, an older gentleman in the standard black suit and clerical collar. He didn't have any function that I could see. He was never called upon to speak, and may have come along just to drive the fellowship ladies up from Kumasi and back. He maintained the same expression of bemused embarrassment for five straight hours.

The rest of the courtyard was jammed with people sitting in folding chairs or standing against the house walls, staring not at the deceased but at each other. Edmund Amoako's mother was back in a dark corner, surrounded by the same women with whom she visited the body the night before. Usually she just sat, but occasionally she would begin weeping and the women around her would comfort her. The widow was nowhere to be seen.

The dancers finished and we sat there for a long time. New groups of mourners would arrive and one of their members would stand in front of the brass bed and speak for a few minutes, and then they would sit down too. Finally a group of women arrived carrying gifts for the deceased and his family on their heads; pillows, rugs, bottles of schnapps, and many white handkerchiefs. Some of these things were placed on or next to the body, and others disappeared into the house.

When the gift giving ended, the men rose and once again put up sheets so Edmund Amoako could not be seen. Behind the curtain, the coffin was moved into position next to the bed. Fred and others removed the jewelry from the body and handed it to the man from Last Respects, who did an unobtrusive inventory check before packing it away. They took the sheet off that had covered the body, and I saw with surprise that Edmund Amoako was wearing white Bermuda shorts. While he was re-covered with other cloth, the original sheet was ripped into strips that some of the men then tied around their heads, a symbol of grief but also something that can only be worn by members of the dead man's matrilineal clan.

With the help of a few others Fred lifted the body of his father off the bed and put him in his coffin. He carefully arranged the white handkerchiefs around the body. Traditionally they contain gold dust to use for purchases in the spirit world. Like many cultures the Ashanti believe that death is merely a transition to another place where the spirit of the deceased continues to live. They believe their ancestors do get directly involved in the affairs of their surviving descendants. And that's one of the reasons for such grand and complex funerals. The spirits must be sent off properly, or they become unhappy spirits.

The curtains came down again, and for the last time a member of the abusua panin told the tale of Edmund Amoako's life and death. Then the coffin was moved to the center of the interior courtyard and we all went outside for the party.

At one end of Assamang there is a huge field, bordered on one side by an elementary school and on three other sides by forest. Hundreds of rented folding chairs had been placed around the field, and by the time I got there hundreds of people were in them, people who had come from all over Ghana for this event. Ashanti funerals are meant for paying attention and mourning, but they are also an important opportunity for people to socialize. Relatives come long distances, and a funeral is often the only time in years they get together. And at least at the Amoako funeral, the field was the place to meet and greet.

The family elders sat at one end, shook hands with everyone who arrived, and took their money. It is a tradition at these events that guests pay hard cash as a tribute to the deceased, and if the donation is too small the elders think little of ridiculing the guest. (Perhaps the young, freeloading Peace Corps guy is beyond ridicule.) So it's not just "drop your money in the box and move on" donating. When I walked up and handed the three funereal accountants my cash, it was carefully counted while I stood there. I received a signed receipt, and then we shook hands all around. I was told that later on in the week the family gathers and carefully counts the money to see if they've broken even on the funeral.

At the field party there was more dancing, more gift giving, and a few speeches over the loudspeakers. Then as dusk fell, a group of young men took the coffin from the house and walked it through the village a last time. I had been warned to stay clear of this lift, because traditionally the young men are very angry. They yell at each other over the coffin, shouting threats against death. Some try to keep the coffin from its destination, while others push it forward.

Because he was of royal blood, Edmund Amoako was entitled to be buried in the graveyard hidden in the royal forest at one side of the big field. No commoner may enter that forest, and certainly no white guy from Seattle. So the last I saw of Edmund Amoako he was going down the path into the thick trees, while his uncle brandished a folding chair at me to make sure I didn't follow.

For me the death ritual ended there, but not for Edmund Amoako. The next day they sacrificed a goat, both in his honor and to feed his family, which is not allowed to eat during the three days of the funeral. And there would be other ceremonies over the following months and even years, especially forty days later when he officially became a spirit, a *saman*, and arrived at his new residence, or *samano*. That forty-day period also gives the organizing abusua panin time to make the social adjustments within their family and lineage necessitated by his death.

Because one of the things funerals often do is begin the reallocation of roles the deceased played during his or her time on earth.

We don't just acquire objects during our lives that can then be doled out through a will. We also take on roles and responsibilities; as parent, child, sibling, boss, friend. When we die we create a hole in the fabric of society because those roles are suddenly vacated. The size of that hole depends on how important we were to the rest of the community when we died. The anonymous people buried in New York's Potter's Field create very small holes indeed, whereas the hole in society created by the death of John Kennedy, for instance, was immense. But regardless of the size of the hole, it must be filled by the surviving members of society if that society is to continue. And not only continue, but continue with a reaffirmation that life goes on—the victory over death the Barans (possibly) see as a victory over women.

Often it is a funeral ritual that firmly establishes the repairs in progress. The minuscule societal holes of the Potter's Field dead are filled by the simple recording of their locations and the continuing hope that someone, someday, will come for them. The bigger the hole, though, the more difficult it is to fill. As I recall Lyndon Johnson was sworn in as president twenty minutes after Kennedy was declared dead. But in the nation's mind, he wasn't really president until the funeral was over and Kennedy's eternal flame was lit. And I think some political scientists would argue that it was many months before Johnson was really able to assume the power and image of the presidency. After Richard Nixon's symbolic death in 1974, Gerald Ford never did achieve the office for much of the country. He was always "that guy in the White House." (Ironically, Betty Ford became the First Lady almost immediately, thanks to the force of her personality and the absence of Pat Nixon's.) Sometimes, for some people, the hole in society created by a death can never be repaired. We may laugh about the Elvis sightings reported in the tabloids, but there are thousands of people who refuse to believe Elvis is dead and cling to rumors he lives. None of those people thinks his appearances in shopping malls are the manifestations of a wandering spirit, either. It *is* Elvis.

In the case of Edmund Amoako, his son Fred will never have another father. But the funeral was a demonstration that Fred's loss was manageable. Fred was able to run the event successfully without his father's help, and the elders were there and would continue to be there to provide whatever pseudoparental support he might need (although Fred is in his thirties and won't need much). And because of Ashanti beliefs in the continued existence of the spirit, by holding such a proper

funeral Fred can assure himself, if he so wishes, that his father will continue to guide him in ways he might not recognize.

The funeral of Edmund Amoako was a roaring success, and I do
mean roaring. I've left out a number of events that occurred (believe it
or not), including a considerable amount of drinking. The schnapps
flowed freely during the two days I was there. Even though the family
must fast during the entire ritual period, they are practically required to
drink. When I asked a member of the Amoako abusua panin why the
young men carrying the coffin to the royal forest seemed so angry, he
answered simply, "Because they were drunk."

However, it would be misleading to characterize the events I saw in
Assamang as some kind of drunken revel that incidentally involved a
burial. The grief and joy expressed for Edmund Amoako were sincere,
even if some people's sincerity was alcoholically enhanced. And just as
in the funerals of my actor acquaintance John and Marguerite McClain,
the majority of the people left Assamang that day feeling better than
when they arrived; not for reasons of refreshment, either. All those
things a funeral must have, we had seen and been a part of, with the
added assurance that we had helped get the spirit of the dead man to a
better place. We did exactly what Edmund Amoako would have wanted
us to do because it's what every Ashanti wants. On the simplest level
the Amoako funeral was a job that had to be done. Therefore it provided the basic satisfaction for hundreds of people of getting up and
doing that job well.

•

I felt a similar sense of accomplishment at the one Buddhist funeral I
attended in Osaka. And like the McClain ritual and its drive-through
window, the Japanese ceremony started strictly as an opportunity for
me to "view with dismay" as well.

One day some years ago I saw an American television news report
about those wacky Japanese. There's a funeral parlor in Osaka, the report said, where you can see just what it's like to go to heaven because
the funeral makes it look like that's what the coffin is doing. And then
there was hazy video footage of a coffin rolling through an arch made
out of laser lights projected through a dense fog. The music in the
background was strictly New Age Ethereal. As the coffin disappeared
into the mist, the reporter informed us that many Japanese loved the
new laser funerals because they were technologically advanced, but
that some older Japanese missed the traditional Buddhist funeral and
thought what they were doing in Osaka was "too flashy." End of report, hah hah hah.

RIGHT: Host and hearse, Grave Line Tours, near the site of the Divine Demise, Hollywood.
(Barry Stoner)

BELOW: Fetish priest Nana Kofi Adu at his shrine, Mensase, Ghana.
(Barry Stoner)

ABOVE: The stone tent final resting place of Sir Richard and Lady Isabel Burton, Mortlake Cemetary, London, was erected in Mortlake because Lady Isabel couldn't get her erotica-collecting husband into Westminster Abbey. The unseen picture window faces the brick wall, just as in a bad hotel.
(Barry Stoner)

LEFT: The priest of St. James Garlickhythe Church, London, and Jimmy Garlick, Britain's only indigenous mummy. Jimmy was found buried under the altar and now resides in the belfry. He hasn't missed a service at St. James for 300 years.
(Barry Stoner)

ABOVE: Children of the Lucas family pretend to clean Grandma Lucas's grave for the Night of the Dead, Tzintzuntzan, Mexico.
(Barry Stoner)

RIGHT: The home altar of the Castillo family, ready for ghostly Night of the Dead snacking, Uranden Island, Mexico.
(Barry Stoner)

ABOVE: Mrs. Chhean Im and her descendants, Long Beach, California.
(Barry Stoner)

RIGHT: Perhaps the world's only 75 horsepower coffin, at Benjamin Sowah's Fantasy Coffins, Accra, Ghana. The wooden Yamaha was commissioned by a fisherman who was the first in his village to own the real thing and didn't want anybody to forget that.
(Sue McLaughlin)

RIGHT: Mr. Carlos Mondragon, photographically deanimated, standing before a dewar containing four physically deanimated people, at the Alcor Life Extension Foundation headquarters, Riverside, California. (Barry Stoner)

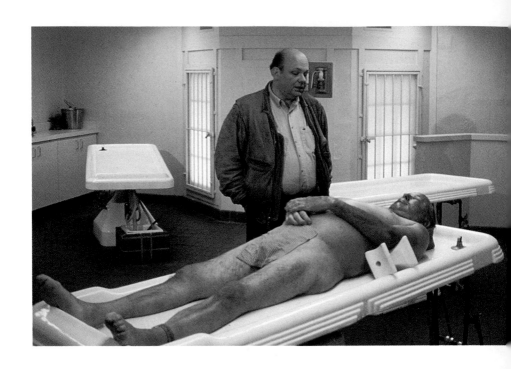

ABOVE: The author (left) and "Max"—San Francisco School of Mortuary Science. (Barry Stoner)

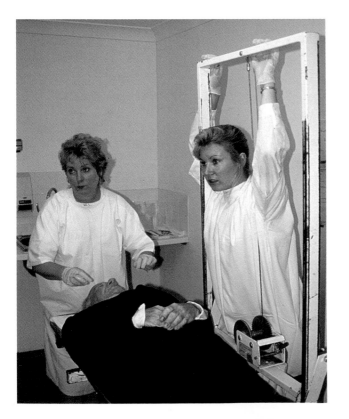

LEFT: White Ladies Linda (left) and Michelle about to crank Tony Bonetti into his coffin for a last viewing, Sydney, Australia. (Barry Stoner)

ABOVE: Edmund Odiatuo Amoako lying in state in Assamang, Ghana.
The brass bed, jewelry, and blanket were provided by the Last Respects
Funeral Accoutrements Rental Company, Kumasi. (Fred Amoako)

LEFT: Archbishop Dionysius Behnam Yacoub Jajjarvi, the Syriac Orthodox Patriarchal Vicar of the Holy Land and Jordan, at St. Mark's, Jerusalem.
(Barry Stoner)

BELOW: Remembrance in action: one of many plaques in Postman's Park, London, commemorating a heroic Victorian death. (Barry Stoner)

WILLIAM DONALD OF BAYSWATER · AGED 19 RAILWAY CLERK · WAS DROWNED IN THE LEA TRYING TO SAVE A LAD·FROM A. DANGEROUS ENTANGLEMENT OF WEED · JULY 16 · 1876 ·

I bought the concept, and went to Osaka to see it; old traditions dying because modern people want more flash and less feeling. And I found that the American news report (and every other story I've seen and read about the laser funerals) was at best misleading.

Gyokusen-in looked like anything but a funeral parlor from the outside. The lights and chrome seemed more suitable for a trendy computer software firm or perhaps even a disco, or whatever discos are called now. In fact the building used to house a huge bowling alley. But since March of 1991, when the laser funerals began, the green and silver building in an Osaka business district has become the city's, and perhaps Japan's, most famous funeral parlor.

Inside, employees leapt to their feet and bowed as I entered. Off to the right of the entrance was a display area for funeral gifts sold on the premises, everything from cheap boxes of candy to electric appliances and toiletries to porcelain and furniture worth thousands of dollars. In the back of the ground floor was a snack bar right where the bowling snack bar was, I suspect, and selling some of the same snacks. The ceilings were low and furry and the walls gray, neither joyous nor solemn. The whole feel of the place was like that of a very modern hospital, one of the new ones where you don't actually see anybody who has anything to do with medicine until you get out of the elevator somewhere upstairs.

A young lady took me somewhere upstairs to a room half as wide as a football field is long, with a high ceiling on one side that got lower and lower as you moved towards the other side. It was definitely a bowling alley ceiling, and from it I was able to figure out where the shoe rental desk was, and the ball rack, and the alcove off to the left where they put the video games.

None of those things were there anymore, of course. The ball rack area was an open space with a nice hardwood floor (I didn't ask, but it looked like recycled bowling lanes to me) and down where the pins used to stand and fall there were six small Buddhist chapels side by side. The chapels were in different colors and themes, but the basic religious nature of each was identical. And in chapel number 1 were the family and friends of Mr. Osama Fujii.

Mr. Fujii was a noted educator who lived a long and successful life. Most of the guests at his funeral were his fellow education administrators, serious-looking men in black suits with briefcases at their sides. The principal family participants were the Fujii daughters, led by the eldest, Mrs. Atsuko Kiyou. When I arrived, the services for Mr. Fujii were already in progress.

That does not mean Mrs. Kiyou was just strapping her dad in for the
big laser experience. What not a single American news report had mentioned about the laser funeral is that it comes at the end of a very traditional Buddhist funeral. In fact, according to Mr. Tomikawa, general
manager of Gyokusen-in, it can't come at any other time. He will not
allow families to purchase just the laser part because he says that
wouldn't be proper. Ten percent of the families who use his establishment for funerals do so *without* opting for the laser. It's an option, a
part of the package you can include or exclude, just like Willie's Window. Well, not exactly like it, because Gyokusen-in actively markets the
big laser finish with television commercials. Even Mr. Tomikawa
couldn't hide his astonishment that anyone would use his establishment and not want the laser ride.

"We did 1,700 laser funerals the first year," he said with obvious
pride. "Eight in one day; that was a record."

The laser service is also not just something made up to give Japanese
funerals a flashy finish. It has a ritual ancestor. Most Japanese funerals
used to take place in private homes. And at the end of those ceremonies, the coffin would be carried through the streets to the nearest
cemetery, exactly as in the Irish lift and for the same reasons. But as
space became more valuable and homes became smaller, funerals were
moved to places like Gyokusen-in. A lift from Gyokusen-in to the cemetery would be a fifteen-mile hike, mostly past factories and pachinko
parlors. That's the case with most of Japan's more than three hundred
funeral halls.

So Mr. Tomikawa, and his boss Mr. Saito, developed the laser lift as
a replacement for the lifts of the past. And they decided to re-create a
near-death experience because the Japanese are very intrigued by near-
death experiences, and doing *something* fancy made more sense than
just picking up the coffin and walking it around a little inside the
building.

According to Mr. Tomikawa, there is also a practical reason for the
laser lift at the end of the traditional service. For funerals that are sticks,
the lift is the carrot.

"For many Japanese funeral services, people come because it's a civic
obligation to be there to send people off. So they just offer incense,
and then very quickly they go home. No dignity, no sense of worship-
ing this dead person. But sending off the deceased is an important part
of the ceremony. Now they stay to see the laser part, and that makes a
better dignified ceremony. Otherwise, two minutes of incense and
they're gone." It's a basic rule of show biz, actually. Always put the
biggest act last on the bill. (And another basic rule as well: Make 'em

laugh, make 'em cry, make 'em wait.) Mr. Tomikawa wouldn't invoke show biz. He would argue that he's just using what he learned at his previous job running a large wedding hall. Nobody leaves a wedding early, because the "I do's" are a natural finish that must to be seen. In the case of his funerals, the obvious finish isn't "I do" but "I did," or perhaps more accurately, "I go."

Mr. Fujii's traditional funeral at Gyokusen-in seemed very traditional indeed. Prayers were said, the tale of the life and death was recited, and incense was lit. Mrs. Kiyou and her sisters, dressed beautifully in black kimonos, were very somber, but there was no obvious display of emotion on their part or anyone else's. At least during the forty-five-minute traditional service the only odd thing about the Fujii ceremony was the presence of a flat little yellow car, parked in the alcove against the far wall of the building where I assume video games were once played.

After small gifts were presented by the family to the funeral guests, pallbearers took Mr. Fujii's coffin from the altar. But they didn't head for the hearse. Instead, Mr. Fujii was taken up to that mysterious alcove and placed on top of the flat yellow car. A worker opened the lid and Mrs. Kiyou and the other family members placed flowers inside around the body of Mr. Fujii. Then, and only then, did I see her cry, very quietly.

"We don't show sentiment like other people," Mr. Tomikawa had told me. "It doesn't mean we don't feel grief. If someone young passes away, many people cry and weep. But by the time we have a funeral service, two days have passed. So people more or less are suppressing their grief. Maybe when they get home, when there are no people watching, they will cry. But for us, grief is a very private thing."

After placing the flowers in the coffin, the lid was closed. Then somebody who looked like a construction worker appeared from nowhere and picked up a long handle attached to the rear end of the yellow car. A priest sat on a folding chair on the front of this four-wheeled catafalque, while Mr. Fujii's daughters and other kin formed two lines trailing behind. As the construction worker began pushing the coffin slowly along the floor, the lights dimmed. My fellow funeral attendees and I gathered along the inner edge of the hardwood runway just as music filled the hall.

Mr. Fujii began his last ride. Forty yards away at the other end of the hall, dry ice vapor began pouring out of ducts attached to the floor and ceiling. There was a slightly audible hiss. Then green laser lights cut through the fog, forming the arch. Mr. Fujii and company moved slowly towards this arch. When they were twenty feet away, a very bright white light suddenly hit the priest, coffin, and pusher head-on.

The music swelled, the funeral party was engulfed by the vapor curtain, and they all disappeared.

On the other side, the coffin kept going straight on down a ramp into a hearse in the garage below. The family stumbled around a bit trying to figure out where they were and where they should be. But we guests couldn't see any of that. For us it really did look like the traditional near-death experience. And Mr. Tomikawa was right. As soon as Mr. Fujii went through the arch, the business guests picked up their briefcases and trotted out rapidly. But the laser had held them to the finish.

Afterwards I talked to Mrs. Nakamura, whose mother was lasered away last year. Her mother had never seen the television commercials for Gyokusen-in, so it was Mrs. Nakamura who decided to get the full package. And she didn't regret it.

"We were very happy to have the funeral service here in dignified ways. Some of it, like the dry ice, is a bit showy, a bit flashy. But still the overall effect was very moving. Worth the money definitely, because it was the last ceremony for my mother, and having a great ceremony was quite important."

The laser funeral is partially a sales gimmick, and it works very well for that. But like Mr. Sowah's fantasy coffins in Ghana and Bruce Vilanch's tap dancing, laser funerals also make people feel better, both the dying in anticipation, and their descendants in reality. None of those other things funerals must do is adversely affected, either. Attention is still being paid, just in different ways. So the obvious question is, why not? And why should anybody else mind?

Which leaves for me that drive-through window. The family of Marguerite McClain overcame it, they didn't work with it. And I think Willie Junior understands that. Mr. Tomikawa told me he certainly plans to have a laser lift at his funeral. Mr. Sowah in Ghana has already done the rough designs for the fantasy coffin he's planning for himself, although he's a bit secretive about the actual nature of the box. If Bruce Vilanch doesn't have something like tap dancing when he goes, it will be a major surprise to his friends—probably the only way he could surprise them. And does Willie Junior plan to spend some viewing time in his own window, being photographed by people out of their tour bus? Hardly. He plans to overcome it, and everything else.

"Mr. Junior will not even have a funeral," says Mr. Junior. "My wife or daughter will run a little notice that there will be a graveside service. I just want a chaplain. No preachers, no funeral program. And the chaplain will say, 'We've gathered here today to pray for the soul of the departed. We therefore now submit his body to the ground, earth to earth, ashes to ashes, dust to dust. That concludes the Willie Junior funeral services. Return to your cars.' And that's it.

"Death is personal and I shouldn't have to share it," Willie says, "because if it hadn't been for all those people who would likely show up at my funeral, I wouldn't have been dead in the first place. They probably worried me to death."

Nice try, Willie, but it's not going to work. If I'm still around and I hear about it, I'll mourn for you, and you can't stop me. And maybe I'll play a little Ray Bolger too.

CHAPTER TWELVE

FOUR FAMILIES

Five years ago the relatively young wife of a coworker of mine developed a mysterious illness. They went to dozens of doctors all over the country, and she had many different kinds of treatments, but nothing worked. Over the months she grew steadily weaker. Even though we had plenty of time to prepare for the end, her death when it finally came was unthinkable, and the injustice of it maddening. She was a supportive, understanding, independent woman, and as far as I could tell a wonderful mother, with two great kids; a tall, shy, teenage boy, and a twelve-year-old girl who already had the essence of her mother's intelligence, charm, and simple beauty.

At the funeral, when that young lady walked slowly up the center aisle toward the coffin dressed all in white and carrying a small bouquet, it was more than most of us who knew her mother could watch. She was on the verge of womanhood, and yet I remember her at that moment as seeming very young, utterly defenseless, and alone. There is nothing sadder in my culture than the loss of a parent with young children, unless it is the loss of a child.

Nothing good came of that death, but in one way generations of kids may benefit from that young mother's passing. When she died her daughter was a seventh-grader at St. John's School, next door to the church where the funeral was held. It was a rough time just then at St. John's. Another parent and a student also died that month. As most schools do now when such tragedies happen, St. John's brought in

professional counselors to help both kids and teachers deal with their
confusion, fear, and grief. But many of the staff felt that the school
should be doing something more. Grief counselors were perfectly able
to administer a kind of emotional first aid, but they helped only in the
immediate crisis. They were fire fighters, and what the St. John's faculty knew they needed was a basic understanding of fire prevention—or
at least preparation.

The result of the deaths and the teachers' concerns was "A Time to
Live and a Time to Die," a six-week-long "instructional unit" that every
St. John's fourth-grader would henceforth go through. Using class-
room discussion, assigned reading and even art projects, kids were encouraged to think about dying, death, grief, loss, and the life beyond.

"I've thought about death a lot because my grandma died and my
grandpa died and my really little cousin died. And it's like something I
can't get away from."

"My grandpa died when I was like four or five, and I never got to say
good-bye to him. And I never even got to go to the funeral, so I
thought about death a lot. And my mom never said anything about it
so I felt a little scared before that."

Four years later I listened in on the last day of death study in Kate
Brune's fourth-grade class. Recess was coming up soon, and after that
maybe a story or math. But first Kate's kids were thinking about the
deaths they had experienced, and how they felt at the time and since.
It's likely nobody had ever asked them about such feelings before, and
barring tragedy no one would be asking them again for a long time.
Their answers were sometimes confused and confusing, sometimes
even cute, and occasionally frightening.

"I feel like I want to die right now so that, um, cuz it's like I've
heard about other people, like they saw a white light, and I just want to
experience it for myself."

Kate Brune didn't leap for the skylight when confronted in class by a
sweet young girl who said she wanted to die. Kate had led a lot of death
classes by that time.

"So," Kate said calmly, "it means you're not afraid, but that doesn't
mean that you want to turn around and die right now, does it?"

"Well, yeah, but like when I die, I'll be pretty happy."

"Okay," said Kate. "All right."

Later on she told me that when "A Time to Live . . . " first started,
she was surprised at how much her students had already thought about
death.

"A lot of them have experienced the death of grandparents and pets.
And I think for them basically at this age it's a lot of the pet sort of
thing. And I think they actually grieve deeply when they lose a pet."

The St. John's death unit doesn't just ask kids to think about their grief at the deaths of others, however. They actually have to contemplate their own deaths, something that isn't easy no matter what your age. And as often happens, that really means contemplating your life relative to its end.

In the six weeks preceding my visit, Kate's students had already written their own wills, listed the special talents they had that other people were likely to remember, and composed lists of the crosses they had to bear in life. The wills and borne crosses are intriguing glimpses into the fears and burdens of the nine-year-old American in the 1990s.

THE CROSS I BEAR IN LIFE IS . . .

- I have a basketball game the same day as track practice.
- My cat Henry died.
- Walking to school because my sister hurts my feelings.
- The fact that my parents live apart and when they are together they argue harshly.
- People will not pick me when we play basketball.

LAST WILL AND TESTAMENT

- Three-quarters of my money to Mina. I want to be cremmated with the rest of my money.
- My bear will be buried with me. My blanket will be buried with me. . . . Every thing else goes up for grabbes.
- My dear cat Casey goes in trust to my sister Lauren.

The day I went to Kate's room at St. John's they were doing the last in-class project.

"What we're going to do is I want you to make your own gravestone."

"YESSSSS!" Kate's kids answered, as if she had just announced a field trip to the ice cream plant.

"You need to think about it first, because I want you to write your own epitaph too," Kate added, writing "epitaph" on the blackboard in a practiced hand. And as she handed out big gray or white sheets of paper, she cautioned, "Leave the death date blank! No predictions!"

Somehow it was odd watching a room full of kids thinking about the one last thing they wanted to say to the world. They weren't as loquacious as I thought they'd be, but nobody was "not dead, only sleeping" either. Perhaps as a result of the previous six weeks' discussion and work, these kids knew that dead is dead, so they didn't need to waste valuable tombstone space trying to convince themselves (or anyone else) otherwise. Instead:

HERE LIES . . .

- a wonderful dreamer!
- a cheerful thinker
- a funny guy
- a good sport
- a person of outer space.
- the best baseball player on earth.
- a guy who had great times.
- a friendly athletic smart man.
- a person who had no special talents except the talent of love.

As far as no predictions, many St. John's students couldn't resist including the year of their death. They were all pre-ancients, with an average estimated life span of 108. That's not counting Jessica. She plans to be with us until the year 2,000,054.

Picking that last message to the world and writing it on construction paper cut into the shape of a stone took just twenty minutes. And when the bell tolled for them, it meant recess time. Death was over for another fourth grade, for another year.

Is death as an "instructional unit" working at St. John's? That's hard to say. Unlike math or language arts, death arts doesn't have a final exam with test scores to compare against national norms, or abnorms, or any of the other kinds of statistical data that modern education finds so enthralling. Success at St. John's is strictly subjective and attitudinal, especially for the half of the instruction that asks students to consider their own deaths. And admittedly, as a Catholic parochial school St. John's has an advantage over a public school when teaching and talking about death. Kate Brune had the opportunity to pitch the glory of her faith's heaven. God and His wonderful domain have taken the sting out of death for many people for many millennia now, and a class of fourth-graders wasn't about to change that. If my son Ned's public school tried a death instructional unit and his teacher even mentioned heaven, parents and their ACLU lawyers would instantly rise up to smite her. Lists of crosses to bear? We bear no crosses in the American public school system. There the teacher's answer to the obvious kid question "What happens after death?" is "I'm not at liberty to say. Ask your parent or guardian."

Kate's kids, however, heard about a heaven as concrete as Yankee Stadium. There's no question its existence contributed to their diminished fears, if indeed their fears were diminished. The kids told me they weren't as afraid of death as they had been before, but they knew that's what I wanted to hear. Most nine-year-olds haven't yet reached the age where they try as hard as they can to say what you *don't* want to hear. At age nine they still try to be a little accommodating to us adults, bless their hearts. And like all personal death preparation, adult or child, an individual really doesn't know how effective his or hers has been until it's put to a real test; an Ed Decker test, a Jackie McMullen test, a Chhean Im test. Once again, only time will tell, and I hope that time is a long way off for all of them; at least until 2,000,054.

For the other part of St. John's death unit, learning how to cope with the loss of friends and relatives, Kate and her colleagues have some indication that their work has been successful. Because of Miss Suzy. She was from New York, where she worked as a nanny for Dudley Moore, and came to St. John's two years ago to be a preschool teacher. Not long after she arrived she also became playground supervisor during the lunch hour. So she got to know every child in the school, and they got to know her as a friend rather than as their teacher. Kate says she was their "mentor, their soother, their comforter."

A year ago, Miss Suzy was diagnosed with the AIDS virus. She died a month before I visited Kate's class. In a school less prepared to deal with death, the lingering illness and ultimate loss of such a young, active, powerful presence would have been devastating. And although the St. John's community mourned her passing deeply and continues to do so, they dealt with that loss in mature and positive ways. The student body didn't have to be told to mix their grief with a celebration of Miss Suzy's life. They did it automatically.

The day I visited St. John's I looked at a display in the hallway in Miss Suzy's honor. The kids had written notes to her, thanking her for spending part of her life with them, remembering the great things she had done for and with them. And she had written back to them before she died. In the middle of the display were two sad, wonderful letters:

MY HERO!

My hero is Ms. Suzy because she has showed almost every one in our school that you do have to die sometime in your life and I think she took a stand by not just running away from St. Johns by staying and telling that she has aids, now she is in the hospital and nobody but me believes that she will get well! I believe in her!!

POST HUMOUS
by Patti Tana

Scatter my ashes in my garden,
So I can be near my loves.
Say a few honest words, sing a gentle song,

join hands in a circle of flesh.
Please tell some stories about me
making you laugh. I love to make you laugh.
When I've had time to settle, and green
gathers into buds, remember I love blossoms bursting in spring.
    As the season ripens remember my persistent passion.
And if you come in my garden
on an August afternoon
pluck a bright red globe,
let the juice run down your chin and the seeds stick to your
    cheek. When I'm dead I want folks to smile and say,
That Suzy, she sure is some tomato.

St. John's original plan was to prepare kids in an educational way for dealing with death before they came up against the real thing. At least this year, because of Miss Suzy, it didn't happen that way. But what did happen before and after her death was certainly a vindication of the program.

Perhaps St. John's and the other schools across America doing units like "A Time to Live and a Time to Die" are pioneering an approach that will spread and grow. As life is now in my country and most countries, we don't think of death until we are confronted by the real thing. We usually don't even have the opportunity to learn from others' experiences. Asking a family how they are dealing with the death of a loved one just isn't allowed socially. We prefer to bring over a tuna casserole instead. And there is so much we could learn from each other.

In this Trip of a Lifetime I met four families with little in common except that they were all trying to deal with the past or imminent future deaths of children. The death of your child seems horrible enough, but for all four of these families there were circumstances that made the situation even worse. And yet the families had found ways to cope. They had discovered a strength in themselves that in some cases they never knew they had. And they got that strength from very different sources.

THE AL BAROGHOUTYS

Once you see the farmland of the West Bank in Palestine, you can't imagine why anyone would fight for it, much less die for it. Those dry, rolling hills look like the only thing they have produced for thousands of years is a bounteous crop of washing machine-size gray boulders, millions of them. Besides the occasional gnarled tree, nothing seems to be growing out of the ground. And between the ancient Palestinian villages and the modern Israeli settlements that perch every ten miles or so, nothing has been planted either. The West Bank looks as inhospitable as Arctic tundra, even though the temperature is frequently in the eighties or higher.

Saleh Abdulla Al Baroghouty and his wife Farha Rabah Ali live in one of those Palestinian villages. They look like the Arabic versions of Jack and Mrs. Sprat. He is a small, wiry man with a fierce mustache who always seems on the verge of leaping up to do something dramatic. She is a large woman, sightless in one eye but with a round, red face that makes her look like the Generic Peasant Grandmother. In another time and place I could easily imagine her spending most of each day in the kitchen cooking dumplings and telling fairy tales to the wee ones.

The Al Baroghoutys appear to be in their eighties, but given the harshness of their life I wouldn't be at all surprised if they were twenty years younger. I suspect they don't have a year of schooling between them. Their wisdom comes entirely from living very close to the land, as they always have.

Their farm is just a few acres, with chickens, no obvious crops, and a white horse that is Saleh's pride. A young man in the village told me Saleh can't ride but thinks he can. As if to prove his point, at that moment Saleh came whooping around the corner on his horse; not riding the steed so much as being carried along by it, like a lion riding an elephant in the circus. The horse was clearly in charge and having a wonderful time bouncing this elderly man around the streets of the village.

The dozen people standing around with me watching Saleh's Charge began to laugh, but it says something about the old man that they made sure he didn't see them laughing. I suspect he has never been a person with whom to trifle. And Farha is no roly-poly granny either. She can shoot an intense beam out through her one good eye. I saw her stop an escaping grandchild dead in his tracks fifty yards away with that beam. Saleh and Farha Al Baroghouty are tough, hard people with very little, who have had to fight all their lives for the little they have.

Their struggle has produced many deaths in the family. Saleh's father is buried behind their home, perhaps the only male Al Baroghouty to die of natural causes in a long time. Most of the rest of Saleh's people disappeared years ago. Farha's grandfather was a fugitive from the Turks. For years he lived in hiding in a cave, but the Turks eventually captured him. He was decapitated on the spot, and Farha insists that as his head rolled away, it said, "There is no God but Allah, and Mohammed is His prophet."

Farha had three brothers. One died from a bullet wound in the leg. It was a superficial wound, but the bullet wasn't removed for fourteen days. When they finally operated, he was so weak from infection and loss of blood that he died during the operation. Another brother died on a pilgrimage to Mecca. The third brother has been in prison in Syria for more than four years with little hope of release.

Then there are Saleh and Farha's children, sons Ribni, Nibugh, Abdullah, Omar, and Nahil, and daughter Hanan. Nahil has been in prison for fifteen years, while Omar and Abdullah are serving their second sentences inside, for a total of ten years now. But at least they are alive. Ribni and Nibugh are dead, killed in the struggle. Only their daughter, Hanan, is home, and only because they paid a fine to get her released from prison after two years. Saleh and Farha Al Baroghouty are surrounded each day by orphans who are their grandchildren, constant reminders of the sons they have lost.

"I am shock-resistant," Farha tells me. "I accept anything from God, because anything He brings is good. My brother's death on the pilgrimage was a loss, but he almost died years before that in battle. By living those extra years, he was able to become the father of four children. So God was good to let him live long enough to have his children. I feel death has to come so I accept it, but the separation is what is hard on me. When I am alone, I cry a great deal. But not in front of people."

The Al Baroghoutys get strength to face their tragedies from their love of God. But they also get strength from hatred of their enemies. Before they would talk to me I went through many other people to prove I wasn't a spy from the Israeli secret police. And after that Saleh was eager to walk his American guest around town and show him the exact sites of Israeli army "atrocities."

Using the power of hatred and the contemplation of revenge to cope with grief may seem appalling to some people, but there's no question it happens, and happens frequently. For the Al Baroghoutys it seems to work. Farha and Saleh say they have not had happy lives. "From the day we were born, our life was hard," he insists, and there is little around to contradict him. But they have been able to accept the loss of their children and even find a kind of comfort and pride in the ways they died.

"I'm not sad my sons are gone," Farha insists. "They died honorably. They didn't die as spies or thieves. They died as martyrs who were defending their country. And that's how I wish to die. I prefer to be murdered in the path of liberating my house, my country, my dignity. One cup of dignity is better than a house full of money."

Her husband agrees. "I would like to die as a martyr in God's path."

They are grandparents in their last years, and yet their notion of the Good Death is not a quiet farewell, lying in bed at home with the surviving family around. They wish to die as their sons and brothers died, in battle. Using hatred as a source of emotional strength requires a lifelong sacrifice. The Al Baroghoutys have never and undoubtedly will never know any kind of personal peace or joy. They are captives to the emotions that death and hardship have fostered in them. And that is as sad as the deaths of their children.

(A postscript to their story. Some months later I sent them a letter of thanks and a small gift for talking to me. It was returned with the indication that no such people existed in that particular village. Saleh told me they had lived there for most of their lives.)

THE SHAYS

The rules for flying the American flag include a prohibition against displaying the colors at night unless the flag is somehow illuminated. But above the front porch of a house in Linthicum, Maryland, not far from Baltimore, an American flag has been flying continuously for almost twenty years now.

"It's going to keep flying, too, and I dare anybody to say anything to me about it. There it stays. My flag, my country. It's going to be right out there, winter, summer, night and day, until they come up with some kind of information about my son."

The speaker is Sara Frances Shay. She's no aging 1960s radical clinging to the antiwar movement and the slogans of the past. She's a teacher and a homemaker, an ideal representative of the American middle class, with a nice home in a nice suburb, a loving, thoughtful husband, and two grandsons who enjoy her company. The Shays live comfortable lives, pay their taxes, drive American cars, and go to church on Sunday mornings. And yet I'd be willing to bet there's a fairly thick FBI file not far away in Washington, DC, with "Shay, Sara Frances" written on top. Because more than anything else, Sara Shay is a mother who has lost a son.

"Donald was a good boy, an amiable young man who did well and didn't give us any problems, made good grades in school, was an Eagle Scout. He had a lot of sense, a sense of humor. He was good-looking, with a lot of friends. I make him sound like he was a perfect person. He wasn't, but he was certainly a good son."

In the early 1960s Donald Shay, Jr., went on a Scout trip to Colorado. While there he visited the Air Force Academy, and the place and people so impressed him he decided on his own that he wanted to make the Air Force a career. So he came back to Linthicum and worked very hard in high school, both physically and academically. He wanted the Air Force Academy so much he didn't turn out for lacrosse, because he thought if his teeth got knocked out he might not be accepted. And when he graduated, he received a senatorial appointment to the academy. It was a big day for the Shays.

"He was the youngest man there, just barely made it agewise. And I guess by the time he graduated from the academy, he was glad that he'd gone. He told me, 'I think maybe this is a good place to say you have been.' "

He went straight into flight training after that, graduated in 1967, and two years later Major Donald Shay was sent to Vietnam. Before he left, his mother gave him a journal to keep, and he gave her a warning.

"He said that if we heard anything, not to believe it unless an Air Force officer came to the house to tell us. So one night around 6:00 this Air Force officer knocked at the door and identified himself and said he'd like to come in. I said, 'Well, come in, but I don't want to hear what you have to say.' Why would he come if he didn't have some bad news?"

At the time the news wasn't as bad as it could have been. Donald was the navigator of a two-man photo reconnaissance plane. And it had disappeared on a mission. There was still a strong possibility that the plane and the two men would be found. The Shays were shocked and numb, but they had hope.

That was the last Sara Shay ever heard about the fate of her son. Nobody came forward who saw the crash, no wreckage was ever found, no sighting in a POW camp was ever made. It was as if Donald, pilot Daniel Ott, and their plane just vanished from the face of the earth. Or so Sara was told. To this day, more than two decades later, she doesn't know what happened to that plane or the men in it. She is sure of one thing, though. Somewhere, somebody knows.

I think Sara Shay and her family might have let it go then. They might have accepted Donald's loss completely and moved on, had they been treated honorably by people they thought they could trust to act in the best interests of their son. But the American government, and especially the military, made two mistakes with Sara Shay. First they said, "Don't call us, we'll call you," while they tried to find some evidence of what happened. And then, when it was officially decided Donald had been missing in action for so long he must be dead, they thought they could just close his file, pat her on the head, and she'd go off and mourn any way she wished. Perhaps that's what "military families" were supposed to do, but the Shays weren't a military family. They were a family with someone in the military, and that's a big difference.

Especially after 1974, when American troops left Vietnam, that war was something my country tried diligently to pretend had never happened. People like Donald Shay, Jr., became just one of those unfortunate tragedies that occurs in military conflicts; difficult for the families of course, but unavoidable. Ironically, the government made the same mistake with Sara Shay it had made with the North Vietnamese. It underestimated her ferocity and her determination.

Sara didn't wait by the phone for their call. And when it came and they said, "He must be dead," she didn't go away. She got very, very angry. She discovered that people who knew something about her son had been ordered not to speak to her. She learned that the government, *her* government, was withholding other information, like eyewitness reports of a man walking away from an otherwise unidentified plane crash; a crash in the right general place and time.

A friend of mine contends that the only way for a parent to deal with the bureaucrats in a public school system is by using the "baseball bat technique." They have to know that every time they do something stupid to your child, you will be there twenty minutes later with a baseball bat, looking to enlarge a few heads. Sara Shay took a bat to the military bureaucracy. She helped found the National League of Families. She went to Thailand and Laos herself seeking information. And she became very well known on Capitol Hill.

"I was in Congress one day with another friend, another MIA mother. We were distributing literature. And I sat down in the hall for a few minutes. This congressional policeman came up, just chatting with us, and said, 'What are you all doing today?' We told him, and he said, 'Let me tell you something.' And he told me a story about how he almost got left behind at the end of the Korean War because his name wasn't on some list. 'So don't ever quit,' he told me. 'Don't ever quit.' "

And she hasn't quit, even though everyone has not been as supportive of her quest.

"People like us were given the opportunity to have a memorial service. There's a section in Arlington Cemetery set aside for the missing in action, and a lot of people have done that. It kind of eases their minds and it puts an end to a lot of things. For a long time, my feeling was that by doing this, I was agreeing with the government. You know, he isn't alive, so I'll go along with you and have a memorial service. And I wouldn't do it. I said that to a returned POW. He was very much upset.

He almost cried. He said, 'That isn't fair to him for you to take that attitude.' I said, 'Well, it's fair to me, and it's fair to him in some ways, because we're not giving in.' But I've often thought about it.

"There's an old family cemetery back in the country where an ancestor is buried who was a POW in the Revolutionary War. I've thought if there was any way in the world I could ever make Kissinger and Nixon and Carter and Ford show up down there, I'd have the service. Especially Nixon, except I wouldn't want to see him."

The Al Baroghoutys mitigate their grief over lost sons by transforming it into hatred and a desire for vengeance. Sara Shay transformed at least some of her grief over her lost son into anger. In the terms of a funeral ritual, with no body to bury she concentrated all her efforts on having something to do; not singing songs or reciting parables, but getting a body. She realizes that quest helped her personally deal with Donald's disappearance and probable death. But she thinks her anger and the governmental sensitivity it inspired—as well as the anger of the other MIA families—also helped the country.

"We forced the government to do something about a problem that they should never have ignored in the first place. And I don't think they will ever ignore it again. So I guess maybe that's helped in some . . . lonely moments. But nothing would take the place of losing a child."

As a consequence, direct or not, of people like Sara Shay, the military is now actively pursuing and implementing new methods of registration and identification of every member of the armed forces. Before the American Civil War the identification of fallen soldiers wasn't considered that important. Around the world a mass grave for battlefield dead was common practice, and you knew who was in the trench by who didn't show up after the battle. But Lincoln insisted that the Union army try to identify and individually bury all Civil War battle dead—part of the same program that led to embalming's popularity in the United States. By the turn of the century soldiers were buying their own dog tags, and in 1906 the War Department officially adopted the dog tag program to identify military personnel. But the dog tag isn't a positive means of identification, it's presumptive, a personal effect that can become detached from the body. And it can't help in cases of incinerated or fragmented bodies. The same is true of fingerprints and dental records. Dental records are especially a problem these days, because fewer and fewer military personnel have much identifiable dental work anymore, thanks to water fluoridation and elementary school brushing and flossing indoctrination.

The solution to battlefield ID problems may come from a laboratory in Washington, DC. There, Major Victor Walter Weedn and staff are working on efficient ways to collect and store DNA samples from every member of the armed forces. Each person's DNA is not only unique, but it is in every cell of the body, unlike say, teeth.

Major Weedn already has one success. In part due to limited DNA identification, Desert Storm was the first military conflict in American (and quite possibly world) history without a single unknown casualty, at least on the winning side. By the year 2000, the military hopes that every member of the services will be represented by two bloodstained cards, vacuum-sealed in a metal foil package in a government freezer.

Major Weedn is both an attorney and a physician, a forensic pathologist. He could probably be making five times the money he makes now outside the military. But in a way he's very much like Sara Shay. Where she is dedicated to finding and identifying a single person, he is dedicated to finding and identifying all people. He wants to do whatever possible to make sure there are no more Donald Shays, and therefore no more Saras either.

Major Weedn: "For the individual soldier it's of tremendous importance that he may know that if he pays the ultimate sacrifice that he will be remembered, and his remains will be returned for proper respects to be paid."

Major Weedn's lab is also working on identifying remains from Vietnam.

"We have several cases of MIAs, skeletonized remains of 'believed-to-be's.' And we will compare the DNA from the skeleton to that of the family and try to come up with a match. And then we can say that this individual is this soldier, and hopefully come to some point of closure to allow the healing process to begin in those families."

I spent a Sunday with the Shays. Church in the morning, then dinner, and finally a visit to the Vietnam Memorial with the family; Dr. and Mrs. Shay, their daughter Mary Rutledge, her husband and two sons, Donald, fourteen, and Macon, eleven. Macon had never seen his uncle's name on the Memorial, or the special mark next to it. Most of the names on the wall have stars next to them, but Donald and other MIAs have a small cross—a cross Sara Shay insisted upon.

"When they came up with the concept of that wall, the people behind it came to the National League of Families Board and talked to us about it. We said, 'We'll never agree to having those names put on there if they're just listed as killed in action, because that means that they'll never do anything about finding them.' So they asked if the marker could be different, to indicate missing, and should they ever be found, it could be changed. And we said, 'Yeah, we'll go along with that.' "

When the weather's good, Sunday is a very busy day at the Vietnam Memorial in Washington. In the crowd the Shays looked like just another family of tourists, working their way along the wall. But this family knew precisely where it was going. The section for 1970.

+DONALD SHAY JR.   +DANIEL OTT

For the relatives of most of the 55,000 people named on the Vietnam Memorial, the wall was a relief. At last it brought an end to America's attempt to forget the war, which was understandable, and forget the men and women who served there, which was unforgivable. If anything could be said to be enough paying attention to those who died in Southeast Asia, for many the wall was finally it.

Macon Rutledge's parents hadn't even met when his uncle disappeared in Vietnam, so there's no reason Macon should feel any kind of personal loss. But there is a power in grief that is transmitted through the grieving. Macon may not have known his uncle, but he knows his grandparents, and his mother, and he senses what they feel. Standing there at the wall that Sunday afternoon surrounded by tourists from all over the world, Macon suddenly began crying. And all he could say was the same thing Sara Shay has been demanding to know for more than twenty years.

"What happened?" Macon asked, staring down at his uncle's name.

No one could answer him, of course. All they could do was give him consolation, and love, and the shared strength of the family. The Shays have a lot of experience doing that. Granddad wrapped his arms around Macon, hugged him, and they all walked away from the wall, together.

The Shays feel great sympathy for the others who lost people in that war. I'm sure they're happy those people have a way to honor their dead. At the same time, the Vietnam Memorial will never be enough for them, because it can never answer a simple question.

"I've never felt any guilt about not grieving any more," Sara Shay had told me, "because I'll grieve until I die, as we all do. And sure, you never give up hope. They're still working on this, they have information they haven't investigated, we found that out. But it's pretty long odds, pretty great odds."

Some day Major Weedn may call on Sara Shay with news. He may be the officer who shows up at her door, asking to come in. It's unlikely, but unlikely things happened because of the Vietnam War and they continue to happen. Major Weedn will not find a family that's been waiting all this time to begin their healing process. The Shays are strong, intelligent people, and they haven't let Donald's disappearance destroy their lives. He once told his mother that what drove him nuts at the Air Force Academy was that you couldn't get anybody to talk about anything but airplanes, and there was a lot more to life than that. The Shays know there's a lot more to life than Donald.

I hope Major Weedn does come to call, because Sara Shay and Macon Rutledge deserve the answer to their question. And then maybe the three of them, Sara, Macon, and the Major, can take that American flag down together. But I would guess that flag will stay there, no matter what happens, for as long as Sara Shay lives in that house.

THE MARTINS

Eugene Martin was a soldier killed on duty many years ago, as Donald Shay may have been. But there the similarity ends. Eugene was killed when a bomb exploded prematurely. He was eighteen at the time, and he was making the bomb. Eugene Martin was a soldier in the Irish Republican Army.

I didn't know about Eugene when I went to the Northern Ireland village of Moy to see his father. I wanted to talk to Benny Martin because he's a small-town Irish undertaker. Even more than Bill Groves in Australia, Benny Martin is a member of his community rather than the mortician on the corner. In almost forty-five years in the business, I'll bet Benny hasn't buried more than a dozen people he didn't know personally, or at least know their families. I was interested in hearing about wakes, lifts, life, and death over the years among the rural Irish peasantry. I was looking for "cute," I guess, an Ireland that may have existed only in MGM movies with Barry Fitzgerald.

Sitting in his family room in Moy, in a modern farmhouse surrounded by green fields, Benny obliged my Irish fantasy with stories. He told me about the funeral where the son of the deceased poured a dram of whiskey in his father's mouth right before the coffin was sealed; about the wake where a man untied the rope that held his dead mother to her bed so that she suddenly sat up and by so doing cleared the room; and about the lift where the deceased was propped up with a cigarette in his mouth because that's what he would have wanted.

"But those things happened years ago," Benny said sadly. "All the neighbors rallied around the people, went to the wakes, stayed with the family, helped them. All the work on the land would cease for the duration of the time that person lay in state until they were buried. But now all that has changed. Somebody could be dead in a house and somebody else working in a field next to it. There are people who go to funerals and don't go to wakes.

"It's because the public has become polarized, because of the Troubles. Fewer Protestants will attend Catholic wakes, Catholic funerals.

Catholics don't bother to go to Protestant wakes either, unless the departed was a near neighbor. They don't want to talk to one another, they don't know who they may be sitting next to. There have been so many tragedies. Too many wakes, too many funerals, it's easier and safer not to go to any."

In Northern Ireland every discussion seems to come back to the Troubles. And for Benny Martin that means every discussion comes back to his son Eugene. Sara Shay can't tell the tale of Donald's life and death. Benny Martin can't do anything else.

"My son died on Monday evening, May 13, 1974, with a comrade of his, Sean McKearney from Moy. Both were at school. My son was studying to become an architect. For some months previously he had been harassed by police and British soldiers. He was arrested and accused of doing some misdemeanor in Moy at a telephone exchange. He was taken to the local police barrack and beaten up. He was released the next morning and came home and explained to us what had happened. He was a very quiet fella, wasn't actually interested in politics at all."

Some time later, Eugene Martin was charged again with causing destruction and being disorderly. With his father, he fought the case. The charges were dismissed by a judge who said he knew troublemakers when he saw them and Eugene wasn't one of them. But if Eugene had been publicly vindicated, he had also been personally politicized.

"My son left the court that day, and he says to me, 'Dad, my talking days are over.' And he became involved. I tried to talk him out of it, but all young fellows at that time and even today with the abuse they've gotten, they can't be stopped. Eight months later he was dead."

"If you had been his age, would you have done what he did?"

"I probably would, yeah. I would."

Long after I visited Benny I went to a grief therapy session. Two of the people in the group reminded me of Benny in the way they managed their grief. Joanne had lost her nineteen-year-old son Carl in a car accident three years before, about the same time Rita's husband Dale died after a long fight with cancer. And in each case the women had adopted the life of the person they had lost.

"If anyone had told me a year before that I would be climbing mountains, I wouldn't have believed them," Rita told the group. "And I'm going kayaking next week. It puts me close to Dale again, doing these things that I wish he could come back and do with me now. But he's with me—he's with me every step of the way, I know he is. Everything that Dale liked I'm into now. It's as if once he left this earth, that's the part he left behind. He sent it back to me to say, 'You're missing this. You better get up there and out there.' "

Joanne's adoption of her son's life was more emotional than physical, but no less therapeutic.

"Before Carl and since Carl, I don't feel like anybody has ever loved me so unconditionally as him. I gave him my heart. And after he died, I thought the only thing I could do for myself is do what I did for him. And that's to love me and take care of me and give me the best life that I could give me because that's what I did for him. My life isn't remotely like it used to be. It seems like my life is more like Carl's, and I really loved his life."

Joanne and Rita chose to assume aspects of their loved one's lives, a choice that seemed to have helped them both immeasurably. Benny Martin didn't have much of a choice. He had himself been politically active in the Irish civil rights movement in the 1960s, so he was already known to the authorities as a fervent supporter of the Republican cause. He had become the unofficial IRA undertaker in his area, and IRA funerals had become very public, newsworthy events over the years. And he was the father of the dead terrorist, Eugene Martin. For these reasons, powerful forces assumed Benny had replaced his son as the enemy to be harassed. Seventy times since Eugene's death Benny's farm has been raided and searched by British army units, looking for weapons caches or IRA fugitives.

"I'd wake up in the morning, look out my bedroom window and there'd be helicopters landing in my field with dozens of soldiers pouring out of 'em. They've never found a thing because there's nothing to find. But they keep trying."

And that's not all. Benny and his family have had shots fired into their home. Four of their dogs have been killed. On quite a few occasions Benny has been called out to pick up a dead man and instead found men waiting to kill him. He's had some very close calls. And if, in one way, Eugene is partially responsible for putting his family at risk, Benny thinks Eugene is also responsible for the family's survival.

"I think I have a son protecting me from heaven. And I am never afraid."

Every Sunday Benny visits Eugene's grave in the cemetery in Moy. It's a neat, orderly place behind the church, full of small, ornate stones next to carefully tended paths. There was a strong, cold rain falling the day Benny and I went, but Benny didn't seem to notice. We walked straight to a far corner of the graveyard, to what he calls "the Republican plot." And there was Eugene, and his friend Sean McKearney, and

three other members of the McKearney family who have died by violence in just the last few years.

To the left of Eugene's grave, just outside the Republican plot, is a
vacant space. That's where Benny and his wife will go when their times
come. He wants to be buried next to his son. But there's another reason, just the kind of sensitivity you would expect from a man who is
politically active, but also a member of his community in the burial
business. Benny says that when there are future Republican commemo-
rations for Eugene and his IRA comrades in the cemetery, some people
of Moy might object to crowds trampling their ancestors' graves. So
he's taken the most likely place for people to stand. If it's to honor
Eugene, Benny won't mind being walked on. But significantly, he
doesn't want to be in the Republican plot itself. Although he didn't say
it, his implication was clear. Those spaces are for heroes, like his son.

Eighteen years after Eugene died, Benny Martin still mourns, his
grief made more painful by the knowledge that much of the world
thinks Eugene got what he deserved. Eugene was indeed a terrorist.
But for Benny he was first a son; a quiet young man who "loved doing
coffins, loved coming out doing funerals, a lovely-looking fellow who
got on well with the ladies. He had a great way with people." So Benny
consoles himself and alleviates his grief by telling the tale of Eugene's
life and death, trying to let people see Eugene as he did. And because
the harassment that he thinks led to his son's death continues, for
Benny that tale hasn't ended yet, and may never end. The forces that
are trying to destroy the Martins are, in an odd way, giving them a
great gift. They are keeping a son alive for a father who misses him
dearly.

THE VICKS

When I met Coogan Vick for the first time, she was seven, and her
chances of ever seeing eight were very slim. Coogan had the worst kind
of leukemia there is. Her parents, Kathy and Randy, thought she'd
caught the flu from her sister. But the flu didn't go away. Kathy Vick
said later, "The leukemia came on very quickly. Within a three-day period she went from being just kind of a sick kid with the flu and some
swollen lymph nodes to a kid who couldn't swallow and couldn't talk.
Her liver and spleen were extremely bloated. All of us felt that she
might not make it."

Although Coogan survived that initial crisis, when we met a few
months later her white cell count was unstable and there was no way of
telling how successful her recent bone marrow transplant would be.
Even so, she seemed full of life that day in the leukemia ward of Fred

Hutchinson Cancer Research Center in Seattle. Coogan was a smart, perceptive, scrappy kid, the kind who could drive you nuts, break your heart, and crack you up all within five minutes, and know she was doing it.

Watching her play with her troll collection, entertain guests, and gas with the nurses all at the same time, it was hard for me to believe Coogan was even sick. Except she was completely bald, very pale, and there were tubes running in and out of her like eels. White-coated staff came and went constantly, checking dials, injecting fluids into the tubes, sometimes just standing in the doorway and looking at her.

If I needed any confirmation that Coogan was a child in great peril, one glance at Kathy Vick's face that day in the hospital was enough. By her smile and her ease, she might have been hosting Coogan's eighth birthday party. Mother and daughter laughed at private jokes together. She let Coogan boss her around a little for the amusement of the visitors. Kathy chatted with a visiting friend about life in the neighborhood, mutual acquaintances, anything but Coogan. But in her eyes there was anger, and terror, and overwhelming fatigue. She was living through every parent's worst nightmare. That is very hard to hide, especially from another parent.

"Sometimes I thought I was in a dream and I couldn't wake up," she told me later.

On that first visit Coogan and I talked mostly about television. Her favorite show was "Star Trek: The Next Generation," and her favorite character on that show was Data, the android officer who's a cross between Mr. Spock and a file cabinet. It was spring, and the television season had just ended with Data in some kind of jeopardy that wouldn't be resolved until the start of the new season in the fall. So Coogan and I talked about Data's situation, because it was about the only interest we had in common. I started to say something like "I guess we'll find out what happens in September," and caught myself. It was very likely one of us wouldn't find out. So I just stopped dead, not knowing what to say next. Coogan smiled at me pleasantly, and went back to her trolls.

"This all started coming around at Christmastime," Kathy Vick remembered, sitting at home later with Randy and her daughter Alexis, who's fourteen. "And I found myself wondering, 'Should I take these presents back? Is she going to be here?' And then I stopped worrying about that and just dealt with the day-to-day."

Randy: "But I think one of the important things we did is we never gave up on our future goals. We kept making long-range plans as if Coogan was going to be there."

"But that was you making us do that," Kathy told him, "because I wasn't quite ready. I was glad you did, because that kept a lot of my hope up."

It was a typical exchange for the Vick family. Because of Coogan's condition they had developed a perfectly understandable fear of the future. I felt that same fear around Ed Decker in his last weeks, too: a stifling, painful sensitivity to thinking about anything more than a few days away—not just the patient's condition, but even life's simplest plans. But one of the Vicks decided to overcome that fear, and by so doing he brought the others along. And the more I listened to them talk about what they were going through and how they were dealing with it, the more it became obvious that the Vicks were discovering a great strength in themselves, not as individuals necessarily, but as a *family*. More than the Al Baroghoutys, or the Martins, probably like the Shays twenty years ago, the Vicks were facing the ordeal of Coogan's possible death *together*. Their personal hope and courage had combined to give them all a greater ability to cope than each of them would have had individually.

Which is certainly not to say it was easy for them. No matter how grateful you are to be able to draw strength from others, you can't escape the discouraging thought that it's because you don't have the strength yourself. Kathy said once, "I would have liked to have thought that all the traveling and all the work, and the introspection that I've done to grow personally would have helped me handle this, but I don't think anything really prepares you for facing the helpless feeling, and the not knowing. Looking back, had I known everything we were going to have to go through, I don't think I could have handled it when I first learned that she had leukemia."

The Vicks had one advantage in dealing with their crisis over the other families I've talked about. The Vicks still had Coogan. Her unique strength was strength itself, manifested in her complete and unwavering belief that she was not going to die.

Kathy will always remember the day she tried to tell Coogan what might happen. "I said to her very carefully, 'You know, Coogan, there are some kids who don't live through the type of leukemia that you have, and it's possible that if you don't have a bone marrow donor that's a match, your odds go down. That it's possible you will die.' And she looked at me, and it was just like with crystal clarity, she said, 'I am not going to die.' And it was a believable statement. She has steadfastly throughout the whole thing said, 'I'm not going to die.' And I found myself drawing strength from her, and her determination."

"You had to be kind of careful what you said around her," Alexis remembers, "because if you said something wrong, she'd jump on you. I was explaining to a friend about the Make a Wish Foundation, how it's to help kids who have life-threatening diseases go some place where they want to go. Coogan heard me and said, 'My disease isn't life threatening.' She likes to make you say things right."

She also liked to win, and, as Kathy said, "stay with the winners." The second time we met, Coogan and I talked about the other patients on her ward. Coogan was in an area of the hospital where the mortality rate was around 90 percent, but everyone she told me about was someone who had made it, who had survived and recovered enough to go home. When I asked her about the others who never went home, she said she didn't really know any of them. It was a lie, of course, and we both knew it at the time. But we also both knew why she said it.

"I guess I'm that kind of person," Coogan explained. "I always want to win in games and stuff."

"So you never thought you might not make it?"

"No, I didn't."

And I believe her. For a while the Vicks thought Coogan just didn't understand how serious her illness was. But ultimately I think they realized they were underestimating Coogan, not something it's advisable to do. Without training, without preparation, their small, weak, almost defenseless child willed herself to live because that's the only power she had left to use. Doctors controlled her body, luck controlled her future, but willpower was still hers, and she wielded it like a . . . baseball bat.

She succeeded, through the force of that willpower and the generosity of her sister. Although the chances of a successful bone marrow match within the immediate family are only about 25 percent, the Vicks were very lucky. Alexis and Coogan were as perfect a match as possible. The transplant was performed, Coogan's white cell count finally stabilized, and she went home.

Kathy: "Coogan felt Alexis was getting real roughed out. She saw that during the first six weeks at the hospital, we'd send Alexis on errands, you know? 'Go to the cafeteria, get this, go do that.' Alexis wanted to be helpful, but she really couldn't do a lot. And Coogan said, 'Well, she really did more than anybody else could have. She saved my life, and she didn't have to.' "

The last time I saw Coogan Vick, she was thanking her sister by drenching her with one of those industrial-strength squirt guns. It was a beautiful sunny day on the Vick front lawn. Coogan and Alexis were running around like mad, screaming with laughter. Eventually they

joined forces and turned on Randy with a liquid vengeance that was inspiring in its ferocity. Coogan was winning. Again.

Inside the house, Kathy and I talked about the future. With the kind
of leukemia Coogan has, her prognosis is better than 50 percent. And
every month she survives improves her chances. But even with her
daughter home and happy, Kathy was still living day to day.

"Maybe I'll be able to laugh again, like I used to. Maybe I'll stop
holding my breath and stop looking over my shoulder a year from now,
but there's still some hurdles in front of us. I feel extremely protective
right now. I . . . I hope I can see her when she's sixteen years old and
wants to drive a car. I'll be terrified, but I hope she lives that long."

At a critical moment in the previous six months, the Vicks realized
that if they were going to survive Coogan's illness as a family, as well as
be in an emotional state where they could help their daughter, they
would have to stop trying to hold onto her. They would have to accept
whatever was going to happen, and let go.

"I felt an enormous amount of strength when I let go," Randy said,
"knowing this was either going to work or it wasn't."

Kathy knew the exact moment when it hit her. "I was standing in my
kitchen. Everybody else was gone, and I just started crying and yelling.
I'd never done that in my life, just started screaming."

As individuals and as a family, people who have been through the
anguish, the uncertainty, the letting go and the taking back will never
be the same. They couldn't possibly be. Kathy worries that Coogan has
regressed emotionally in some ways. She's been the center of attention
for so long, she has come to expect it. Coogan was always bossy, and
that has certainly not diminished. And Coogan agrees. "When I was in
the hospital, I had control over everything," she told me, with the clear
implication that she wouldn't mind maintaining that status forever.

In other ways Coogan is extremely mature. She could probably pass
the entrance exams of a lot of medical schools. Her instinct for recog-
nizing when somebody's "jerking her chain," as her mother says, has
improved. Coogan doesn't suffer fools much anymore, not that she
ever did. She's gotten to know herself and her strengths and weaknesses a lot better than most seven-year-olds. And she and her mother
have, if you'll pardon the jargon, bonded in a unique way.

Kathy found that bonding encouraging, but a bit weird. "I sometimes ask myself, 'Would I have ever had the opportunity to get to
know her the way I do now had she not gotten sick?' Which is sort of a
gruesome thing, I suppose. Is that what it takes to really get to know
your kid?"

All the Vicks have learned one other thing from the nightmare they've been through. They don't sweat the little things anymore. Life is full of annoyances, but that's all they are—annoying.

Kathy: "People have told me how much calmer I've become, clearer in my communication with them and my ability to listen and to be with them. And maybe part of that's all the time we've spent being with Coogan and being with each other, and really having to pay attention to feelings and emotions. Which are what's important."

Attention must be paid, not just to the dying, but to everyone. The Vicks, the Al Baroghoutys, the Shays and the Martins have all learned that the hard way.

CHAPTER THIRTEEN

DID YOU EVER HAVE THE FEELING THAT YOU WANTED TO GO?

One of the more ridiculous accusations of recent times is the charge that someone is a "control freak." It's like accusing a person of breathing. "I don't trust that Roger. He breathes a lot." We are all breathers *and* control freaks. Some of us just hide it better than others. And perhaps some of us are overly meticulous in the control we exert, especially over people who are likely to accuse us of being control freaks. But just as every human being needs to be in control of something, sometime, society has always needed people who go that extra mile and want to be in control of everything, all the time: controllomaniacs. Leonardo Da Vinci was a control freak. So was Queen Elizabeth I. Franklin Delano Roosevelt was a big control freak, and Eleanor too. Mother Teresa is a control freak. I'm sorry, but she is, and you know it. And so are the guys who come to fix your telephone, your hot water heater, and your appliances. (You don't think they are? When's the last time *you* controlled when they got to your house?) There is no situation involving human beings that every human being involved doesn't want to control.

Sometimes we are able to obscure our efforts at control. We pretend to offer control to the other party—"I don't care, whatever *you* want to do is fine with me." In this way we escape responsibility for the final decision by laying it on *you*. But we really retain control by putting *you* in a situation where *you* always have to play defense. "I can't understand it, the newspaper said it was a very good restaurant," *you* say, chewing

245

on a veal cutlet with the texture and flavor of a wallet. And as any football coach will tell you, you can't score on defense, because the offense
has *control* of the ball. "It's perfectly all right," I say magnanimously,
"I'll make myself a salad if we ever get home."

Another way we obscure our desire for control is in a disingenuous
display of noncontrol. "Let it all hang out," as we used to say, "but
don't violate my space," as we used to say right after that. When somebody with whom I'm working suggests to me that we "just see what
happens," it almost always means what that person *thinks* will happen is
what that person *wants* to happen. And if that person really doesn't
know what will happen, it means that person thinks *I* know what will
happen but they want something *different* to happen, they just don't
know *what*. "It is not enough that you succeed," someone once said,
"your friends must fail." This is certainly true of control. The unvary-
ing rule is that when two or more are gathered together, only one of
them is in control. Democracy doesn't work because all the people are
in control at the same time. Democracy works because each person
takes control of different things, creating a nation of committee chair-
persons.

In most situations, although control can change hands quickly and
subtly, somebody always has it. In the military, impersonating an officer
is not a court-martial offense because the officers want to make sure
nobody but them gets to wear stars, bars, and other martial jewelry. It's
because the officers are worried that the impersonator will take control.
We can't have that. What is boot camp, after all, but an eight-week
course in how to be controlled?

Secretly we admire obvious control freaks because they seem so
much more in control than we are. That's why even though "control
freak" has a negative connotation, there's a lot of envy in it too. It's like
accusing someone of wretched excess. We'd all like to try some excess,
just to see how far we have to go before it gets really wretched. The difference is we vote for obvious control freaks, and we don't vote for the
obviously, wretchedly, excessive. (Usually we find out later that the
control freaks we voted for are also wretchedly excessive, and then we
don't vote for them. Or at least we shouldn't.) Who would want a president of the United States who wasn't a control freak, especially with all
the yobbos presidents historically have around them? ("I am in charge
as of now."—General Alexander Haig, the control freak poster boy of
the 1980s.) Control freaks definitely have their place. It's just unfortunate that their place is so often in the boss's office where we work.

In all of life's endeavors, however, the thing we would most like to
control is our death. I think this desire is a splendid example of inherent

human perversity—trying to control the thing we have the least chance of controlling. But partly it is fear, and not just the natural fear of death.

None of our normal controlling tricks work with death. We can't pretend we don't care how we die, because we are then forced to say, "No, it won't bother me if I suffer excruciating pain for years. Nope, no problem." We also cannot ostensibly pass responsibility for the control of our death along to somebody else, at least not until death is imminent. In a sense Ed Decker gave control of his death to his family and Evergreen Hospice, but he was at the stage where he could do nothing else. If a robust, energetic, healthy Ed had marched into Evergreen twenty years before and told them he was checking in to die, they would have called the police. (Conversely, Coogan Vick never gave control away.) Generally, for those of us thinking about our deaths but without a particular due date to aim for, we can pass along the funeral arrangements and all other postmortem activity to others, but premortem activity is nontransferable. You don't have any other choice. And that makes the only trick left—"let's wait and see what happens"—not a control ploy, but a curse. You're not in control if you're doing what everybody else on earth is doing, and it's scaring the hell out of you.

For centuries people have been trying to avoid that curse. Surrounded by pestilence, war, and plague, the Spanish of the 1400s became especially active in trying to control their deaths. *Ars moriendi,* they called it, the art of dying. Spanish kings staged their own deaths and funerals just to see how things would go. Noble folk would preorder requiem masses from the church to assure that their demise would be properly sanctified. In some cases they didn't have the cash handy to pay for the services, so they paid with land. Because of this practice, the Catholic church owned a third of Spain, as some people had purchased more than three thousand requiem masses each. (Job-security-wise, it was probably a real good time to get your kid organ playing and choir singing lessons.)

Historically there are many cultures where knowing at least the *time* of your death has been considered appropriate knowledge for a person to have. Even now the Tibetan Buddhist high lamas attending His Holiness the Dalai Lama have to ask for his permission to die. Some time ago one of the Dalai Lama's principal advisers, Rato Rinpoche, asked to die, or as he said, "shed his old skin." But the Dalai Lama denied the request, because he needed Rinpoche too much just then. So Rinpoche went back to work. Two years later he asked again, and his request was granted. Rinpoche seated himself in the lotus position and shed his skin. Still in the lotus position, he was cremated nine days later.

In Tokyo I bought a wonderful book of death poems by Zen monks. The story of each poem's creation is included, and for the vast majority of poets the monk awoke in the morning, announced he was going to die, wrote the poem, "and then laid down his pen, and died."

There's no question human beings have at least some limited control over the time of their death. Reports of prisoners of war who literally willed themselves to death are common. It is an axiom in the theater that no actor has ever died on stage. He or she always makes it to the wings. And in 1990 the University of California at San Diego did a study of 2.7 million natural deaths. The findings were published in *Psychosomatic Medicine Journal* (you may get paper cuts from the pages, but nobody will believe you) and showed among other things that Chinese American women were significantly less likely to die of stroke, heart disease, and cancer in the week before the Harvest Moon Festival than the week after, when their death rate increased by more than 30 percent.

A similar study done some years ago reported that Jewish mortality was 31 percent below normal just before Passover and went up by the same percentage immediately afterward. In both the Jewish and Chinese American cases the theory is that people willed themselves to stay alive for a few more days, just as I think Coogan Vick willed herself to stay alive, period.

The U.C. San Diego research also showed that statistically men have a tendency to die right before their birthdays, while women are more likely to die the week after their birthdays than at any other time of the year. A researcher in the field suggests that men use birthdays to assess their business failures and thus dread the event, whereas women use birthdays to assess their family successes. And because the family is around and happy for the birthday celebration, women delay their death until afterwards. But regardless of the reason, in all the cases above the individual was controlling to some small extent one of the factors of his or her death.

There is an obvious way to control almost all the other factors, those elements that so frighten us now. If you take your own life, you have complete control over when, where, and how you die. You might also think you're controlling *why* you die as well, but realistically that question is answered by those who survive you. They may choose to believe the note and/or clues you leave behind, or they may choose to ignore completely what you say and find a different reason that suits their particular needs and assuages their guilt. You can leave a note saying, "My mother drove me to it," but nobody will ever know if your mother finds the note first. "He was such an underachiever," Mom will say, "a dead-end job, filthy habits, and that girlfriend! From hunger! I saw it coming. Funny he didn't leave a note, though." But societally speaking, if you commit suicide, a misinterpretation of your motives is the least of your problems.

Every culture I can find has a general condemnation of suicide. In Western Europe centuries ago it was punished by a forfeiture of the suicide's estate, and indignities to the corpse, like that old favorite, a stake through the heart. Many cultures would not allow a suicide to be buried in consecrated ground. One common location of burial for a suicide was at a crossroads, on the theory that a suicide would produce a malevolent ghost, but the crossroads would so confuse the ghost about which way to go, he or she would just stay in the coffin for eternity.

Among the Chinese, suicide is instant unhappy ghosthood, and there is very little your descendants can do to upgrade you to "ancestor" if you have killed yourself. Upgrading through the proper rituals can be done in accidental deaths like Mr. Wei's, but in China if you do yourself in, you had better be prepared to wander unhappily through the spirit world *forever.*

In Ghana a person who commits suicide is quickly buried without a funeral. In fact, suicide is such a taboo there that Dr. Boiteng, the Kumasi medical examiner, frequently deals with families who are desperately trying to prove their deceased died for some other reason, in some other way. Drinking insecticide with a palm wine chaser is a very common method of suicide in Ghana. A common excuse from the family is that the dead person was enchanted into drinking insecticide by a sorcerer or fetish priest. Dr. Boiteng usually can avoid these explanatory attempts, but sometimes the family insists that the sorcerer be tried for murder. In the interests of justice, Dr. Boiteng then must become the calm man of science who cannot ignore the facts. I've read the same thing happens in Italy, especially in rural villages. Local medical examiners will obligingly list obvious suicides as accidental deaths so that the deceased has not committed a mortal sin in the eyes of the Church.

In most cultures the prohibition against suicide is primarily religious in nature. "Thou shalt not kill," says the Seventh Commandment, not "thou shalt not kill except thou." Only God grants life, and therefore only God can take it away. Although Bob Wilkins points out in *The Bedside Book of Death* that there is no explicit condemnation of suicide in the New Testament. (The many religious persons who wish to debate that contention should contact Bob directly, thank you very much. Bob's in control on that one.)

The difficulty with the orthodox religious view these days is that science has found so many ways to assist God in His life-sustaining work.

And if Doctors Cutler, Rudman, Dean, and their colleagues are correct, we are on the threshold of major breakthroughs in scientifically assisted life prolongation. Everyone I talked to in the life extension field emphasized that what they are trying to do is extend youth, not old age, but at least for now it seems like old age has been the principal benefactor. In many cases life isn't being sustained, breathing is. More than two thousand years ago Seneca wrote, "If [old age] destroys my faculties one by one, if it leaves me not life but breath, I will depart from the putrid or tottering edifice." Many people today feel the same way: "If I'm putrid, pull the plug." And isn't plug pulling a form of either assisted suicide or homicide?

Seventy percent of all deaths in America (and a similar percentage in Britain) are now negotiated in some way. Just what is being negotiated, and with whom? Life and death, obviously, and either with the patient or his or her relatives. The moment a patient and attending physician agree to "do no more," they are in fact doing one of two things, depending on how you look at it. They are either breaking the commandment and killing, or conspiring not to help God scientifically anymore. No matter which action you think they are taking, there is no question that such decisions are being made thousands of times a day, all over the world. The medical establishment condemns assisted suicide principally by citing the Hippocratic oath, which says, "First, do no harm." But as scientifically prolonged but meaningless life continues, many people would like to add an amendment to the rule: "Maybe, do nothing."

As this is being written, Dr. Jack Kevorkian, the Michigan physician who has assisted terminally ill people to take their own lives, is once again charged with murder. This time around the police raided his home in the night, kicked in his door, and found . . . nothing. I don't know Dr. Kevorkian. I certainly wanted to talk to him for this book, but the moment he heard the general subject matter he went to ground and declined. Given that the media delights in calling him "Dr. Death," I could hardly blame him. It seems to me Kevorkian's principal crime is that he's slapped my culture in the face with its own hypocrisy on the subject of assisted death. He's forced us to admit what has been quietly going on in hospitals and convalescent centers for decades and general society for centuries. In the days before giant hospitals and ubiquitous medical care, the great majority of people died in their homes. And especially in the case of the elderly, the country doctor called to the sickbed may have been able to do something to prolong the patient's life, but didn't. The family and physician assumed it was that person's "time to die," and so did the person. Nobody called watching Gramps die quietly in his bed homicide or suicide. They called it life.

So why do almost all cultures condemn suicide as a general and/or religious principle? People better qualified than me have tried to answer that. From a cursory glance at various cultures it is obvious that suicide is a threat to society, as well as an indication of both personal and societal weaknesses. "My God, people don't do such things," Hedda Gabler's husband Tesman says on discovering his wife's body. In a sense we are all Tesmans, making our world sane by making it familiar and orderly, and ignoring those aspects of it that disrupt that order. Suicide disrupts our world far more than simple death, because death is inevitable and suicide is not. It is a clear indication that something is wrong with an individual, and therefore possibly with us all. Recall that hole in the fabric of society that needs to be repaired after any death, to prove that life goes on. It is doubly hard to fill after a suicide. The very nature of the death implies the fabric may be rotten and not worth repairing.

There are also the strong feelings of guilt that suicides inevitably engender in their acquaintances. Many years ago a man named Burt with whom I had once worked killed himself. Six months before, he had moved to a farm a few hundred miles away, and I knew vaguely that his domestic situation was difficult at best. He was being supported by a woman he loathed, forced by her to live in a place where she was the only person he knew. But he was unemployed at the time and there was nothing he thought he could do to change his situation.

Except there was, and he did it. When I heard a few days after the fact that Burt had killed himself, I felt in some small way personally responsible. He had invited me to come visit him on the farm a few times. I told him I would, but I never really had any intention of doing so. The farm was a long way off, I disliked his lady friend almost as much as he did, and Burt and I were certainly not close friends. But those invitations and my polite lies in response were the first things I remembered when he died. He had been crying out for some contact with his world, of which I was a small part. And I had ignored the cries. If only I had visited him, I said to myself, maybe . . .

I was wrong, of course, and not a little egotistical. If only he had experienced Me on the Farm he wouldn't have done what he did? Hardly. Burt's problems were far too complicated to be solved by a few drop-ins from his friends and acquaintances. But the feeling that I could have done something has lingered with me for more than twenty years, as I think it has for all the people he knew who felt they had forsaken him. At his funeral there were a dozen of us who had been invited over and never gone. Individually I was relieved. Frank knew him better than I did; he should have gone. But collectively we all felt lousy, and we should have. Burt would have agreed, but he also would have been

surprised at the many people who mourned his loss. In that one small
thing he was lucky.

•

Syozo Morimoto was not so lucky. He was a Kyoto newspaperman
whose wife died when his two sons were quite young. He was going to
remarry a few years later, but the boys disliked his fiancée and ran away
in protest. A policeman found them and brought them home. The policeman told Mr. Morimoto that if he wanted to do right by his sons,
he wouldn't marry someone they didn't like. He should raise the boys
alone.

For twenty difficult years, that's what he did. He worked very hard,
dedicated his life to his motherless children, and eventually put them
through college. After the oldest son graduated, he ran away again and
did not return. Though his younger brother stayed at home, he wasn't
brimming with gratitude. Compared to Mr. Morimoto's kids, King
Lear's elder tots were a couple of real swell gals.

As Mr. Morimoto remembers that time there is still pain and astonishment in his voice. "My younger son used to say, 'I don't need you. I
don't want to live with you anymore.' He had a girlfriend, and as he
got closer to her, he wanted to live with her instead of living with me. I
dedicated my whole life to my kids, and then my kids left me. I was
alone. I thought, 'I may as well die.' And when I said that to my kids,
they said, 'Oh, that's just bluff, just talk. If you want to die, go kill
yourself.' "

So he did. Or at least he tried. "I've often seen people slit their
wrists in television dramas. I thought that was the way to go. I locked
all the doors and windows of my apartment and closed all the curtains.
I filled the bathtub full of water and got naked into the bath. The room
was completely dark and closed. I took a razor blade and started hack-
ing away at my wrists. But I couldn't get much blood to come out. The
bathwater was getting red, but I wasn't losing consciousness. And as
soon as I cut a vein it would heal up pretty quick."

Mr. Morimoto sliced away at his arms for some time—he doesn't
know how long. He would surely have died in that bathtub except that
he'd forgotten an appointment with a salesman who was coming to his
home. When the salesman arrived and got no answer at the door he convinced the building manager to open the apartment. Syozo Morimoto
was rushed to the hospital, and saved.

"I'd always believed that if one did one's best one would be happy.
If you lived honestly and full of love, honesty and love would come
back to you. I poured all my love and all my life into my children in the
very simple belief that they would one day recognize that, and love me

and live with me and care for me too. So when they walked out on me I felt totally betrayed."

"A lot of Western suicides come out of loneliness, lack of recognition, and a feeling of loss of direction," Carl Becker told me, and he could have been talking about my late friend Burt. Hawaii-born Dr. Becker has been living and working in Japan for more than twenty years. Now he teaches humanities at Kyoto University. One of his particular interests is suicide, but Carl Becker doesn't just sit in his office and study reports. For some time he has been working as a counselor with Japanese people who are either contemplating suicide, or have attempted it.

"Loneliness and lack of recognition may be factors in Japan too," he says, "but there are other factors which are more prominent here that you don't find so much in the West. In Japan suicide isn't like in Christianity, where it's considered a sin. It's neither a sin here, nor is it against the law. It's criminal to assist the suicide, but it's not criminal to suicide.

"Sympathy suicides are common. If a famous movie star suicides, some young people imitate the suicide, dying in the same manner that the movie star did. But maybe the most common reason is failure."

Syozo Morimoto is one of Dr. Becker's clients, and he's a prime example of a failure-motivated suicide. He failed with his children (and faced loneliness and lack of recognition because of it) and therefore sought death.

"Other kinds of failure suicides include failure in exams, failure to get your children into the right school or job, failure in a marriage which would result in a divorce. The Japanese have tremendous concern with honor, with keeping family pride. Even the traditional hara-kiri, which literally means 'cut belly,' was in part a way of showing society that your organs are red, that your blood is pure, unsoiled. [The method says] 'It's not just that I'm dying, but that I'm dying in a way that is painful to me, and I'm willing to undergo that pain to show that I am innocent of the rebuke or disapproval that you are rendering against me.' "

Dr. Becker's reference to hara-kiri again brings up that hoary perception of Japan as Suicide Central to the world. For too many American baby boomers, our first introduction to Asian culture was tales of kamikaze pilots. I seem to remember a period in my preteens when I thought kamikazes were the only troops the Japanese had in the Second World War; certainly I thought that all Japanese pilots were kamikazes eager to die for the emperor.

With my generation thus conditioned it was relatively easy for American government propagandists in the 1960s later to convince a good percentage of the population that the Vietnamese, "being Asians, don't care about death like we do." As I recall, this was first used to dismiss the Buddhist monks who were immolating themselves in protest on Saigon's streets—"It means nothing to them, really"—and eventually to explain why even though we had reports and figures to show that the North Vietnamese were losing every battle and had appalling casualties, they weren't giving up. And though many of the reports and the figures were eventually shown to be bogus and self-serving propaganda, for some Westerners the contention lingers that Asian people are very nonchalant about their deaths.

Nonsense, said both Carl Becker and Syozo Morimoto. Becker quoted Jean-Paul Sartre. "You can tell what somebody believes in by what he's willing to die for." Westerners tend to die for principles, like freedom, democracy, keeping the world safe. The Japanese will die to save face, to preserve honor, to protect their family or to protect the name of the family. Those concerns with honor and face are no longer very dominant in Western culture, if they ever were. Because the people who were most concerned with face never went to America in the first place. They had names and reputations in Europe. Becker says, "Suicide has been a common form of protest here, too. If you weren't able to change a fixed situation, you could register protest by suiciding in a dramatic way"—which certainly explains the Vietnamese monks.

Mr. Morimoto contended that most of what Westerners see as suicide in Japan isn't suicide anyway. "You foreigners tend to think of hara-kiri or kamikaze as suicide, but I would make the distinction between suicide and hara-kiri or kamikaze. What I did was suicide, because I was dying for a selfish reason. I was only thinking of myself. However, in the case of kamikaze, many of my own classmates, people my own age, were in the special forces, the kamikaze forces. And I know how they felt because I talked to them before they took off. Nobody was rejoicing to die in that situation, but they did feel that it was an honor. And they weren't dying for their own sakes. They were dying for the sake of something larger, the honor of the country and the honor of the emperor.

"In the case of slitting your stomach, you don't do that for your own benefit, for your own enjoyment or desire, but for the name and honor of the shogun or the clan. I make a big distinction between people who are taking their lives for others' benefit and those who are taking their lives out of selfish reasons."

Mr. Morimoto touches on an aspect of suicide that it seems to me most people would prefer to ignore. Just as almost every culture on earth condemns individuals for taking their own lives, at the same time almost every culture allows for exceptions to the taboo against suicide. And the dividing line, as Morimoto points out, is whether your death is for the benefit of some aspect of society or for your personal benefit. The former is accepted and considered heroic, while the latter is condemned. Martyrs die for their faith, and the church praises them forever. Soldiers throw themselves on grenades to save their buddies and receive posthumous medals. And the greater number of people who benefit from your voluntary death, the more heroic the death is.

Stated as such, it seems self-serving and hypocritical of societies only to allow those suicides that serve the community interest. And I suppose it is. As a community we seem to be saying, "It's all right to die for us, but forbidden to die for you." But I had a hard time feeling righteous about society's double standard regarding suicide standing on top of Masada.

•

Masada is a thirteen-hundred-foot-high plateau in Israel, sticking up out of the Judean desert near the Dead Sea like a loaf of bread on a baking sheet. The area on top is roughly twenty acres, and has been used as some kind of fortress since at least 100 B.C. (Masada means "fort.") Geographically and historically, Masada is a spellbinding place, but it is the emotional impact of Masada that has attracted Jews and others the world over to come and see for themselves.

In 66 A.D. the Roman garrison at Masada was attacked and defeated by a small army of Jewish Zealots. Four years later, first Jerusalem and then Judea fell to the Romans, which made Masada, one long march away, the last outpost of the Jews.

"It was almost a matter of pride to the Romans that they had to get the Zealots off Masada, because this was the last ember that was still aglow." Eitan Campbell looks out over the ruins of Zealot buildings, a synagogue and school, over the vast Judean desert towards Jerusalem. He talks about the story and the sacrifice that first captured his imagination as an American teenager in New England. He is an assistant curator at Masada now, spending his days in the place of his dreams.

"In 72 A.D. ten thousand troops of the Tenth Roman Legion under Flavius Silva came to Masada to defeat the Zealots. The Romans were thirsty and tired. They should have been back in Rome celebrating their victory over Judea. And because of 960 Zealots, they were stuck out here, laying siege."

Following their usual procedure in such cases, the Romans built eight camps around the base of Masada and waited for the Zealots to surrender from lack of food and water. But they had badly underestimated the resourcefulness and preparedness of their opponents. On top of the rock, the Zealots, led by Eleazar Ben Yair, were well prepared for a siege. They had plenty of food and water stored away from previous raids against the Romans, plus an ingenious system to capture rainwater. Months later Silva realized the siege would not work. Using slave labor, the Romans began building a huge ramp up to the top of Masada.

Campbell: "The Romans were known throughout history for their atrocious acts. It was no secret here. So when they finally came up the ramp, they were ready for a real . . . a real party. But Ben Yair took that party away from them, and took it away in the most shocking way as far as the Romans were concerned."

The night before the Roman legion would obviously reach the top of Masada, Ben Yair called a meeting, probably of just the men, and probably in the synagogue. Eitan Campbell and most historians believe it was Ben Yair himself who made the proposal and convinced the others. They would rob the Romans of their victorious slaughter, and die a free people. All 960 Zealots would die that night by their own hands.

"They decided on ten men to help everyone. They killed the wives and children and the men in groups. And then the ten men between them drew lots to see who would be the last. There's a trick in the religion, you see. Suicide is very forbidden. Under the circumstances though, this was considered a favor done out of love between them all. And so they killed each other, and in fact only the last man committed suicide after he set everything afire. Except one storeroom. This was done to prove that it wasn't because of food and not because of water that they did what they did.

"When the Romans came up the next morning, they were shocked. Dead silence. They called out for war, they called out for battle. Nothing. They couldn't figure it out, and they started to look around. They saw everything going up in flames. And then they found each family, family, family, all together. And they were stunned. I am sure they were stunned. And that's why the Romans didn't mention Masada. It wasn't something they could really go home and say, 'Hey, look what we did!' "

Two Zealot women and five children were found hiding in the water channels. They were able to tell the story of the Zealots to Josephus, the Roman scholar and historian. Were it not for their survival, the story of Masada might never have been known. Even today, there are people who argue that it didn't really happen. They use as their principal evidence the fact that of the supposedly 950 plus bodies on top of that rock, the skeletal remains of fewer than fifty people have ever been found. Where did the bodies go? Eitan Campbell thinks he knows, and eventually he hopes to prove conclusively that Masada happened as Josephus described it. And he thinks one important body has already been found.

"Not up here on top, but on the lower level of the northern palace they found three skeletons; a man, woman, and child. Although the man was a Zealot, he had a very nice breastplate, which was extremely rare. And with a woman and child—this was the composition of Ben Yair's family. Why was his body still here and all the rest disappeared? My theory is that the Romans were a very superstitious lot. When they realized this was Ben Yair, they didn't want any part of this warrior. They said, 'OK, we don't go down to that level anymore. This one we leave alone.' And that's where he stayed until we found him in 1963."

For Jews, and especially the people of Israel, it doesn't really matter anymore whether Masada happened as described or not. The plateau has become a symbol, as Eitan Campbell says, of "the fight for freedom, the stand of the few against the many, and the resolve to take a courageous step and to get through it." Some Israeli military forces come to Masada after their training to take a special vow that "Masada shall not fall again." It's a popular place for bar mitzvahs too, and schoolchildren visit each year by the thousands. I stood on Masada and watched a fifty-year-old accountant from Minneapolis quietly weeping for the memory of families who have been dead for two thousand years. And all this sacred remembrance for people who committed suicide— or, if you accept their fiddling with the law, massive homicide. But they did it for principle, honor, and above all for the ultimate benefit of the community. You only have to stand on Masada for a few minutes and watch the Israeli Air Force training in the skies overhead, which they often do, to realize how that rock and those self-sacrifices continue to inspire that nation. The spirits of the Zealots leap from the earth to the sky.

As with most heroic deaths, however, your perception of Masada depends on your perspective of the world. Two days after I visited Masada it was Easter. I was invited to have dinner with a Christian Arabic family, a travel agent who had been most helpful in setting up Christian and Palestinian things for me to do in Jerusalem and environs.

The meal was excellent, and the man and his wife were fine hosts. But after dinner, sitting on his porch thirty feet from the start of the West Bank, he asked me where I had been besides the places he'd sent me. I mentioned Masada.

"If you've seen Jonestown, you've seen Masada," he said abruptly. At the time I thought it was an appalling comparison. The more than nine hundred followers of Jim Jones who slaughtered themselves with a poisoned soft drink at "Jonestown" in Guyana in 1978 had nothing in common with the Zealots who died at Masada almost exactly nineteen hundred years before. Certainly nobody rational has ever suggested Jones's followers were martyrs dying the heroic death. They were fools following a madman.

In retrospect, however, my host was right in some ways. In both cases, a large group of people seeking religious freedom agreed to the suggestion of their charismatic leader that they kill themselves rather than lose that freedom. And yet Masada is perceived by millions, and certainly not just by Jews, as an inspiring story of faith, courage, and sacrifice. Jonestown, on the other hand, is perceived by everyone as almost inconceivable group insanity. But isn't that what most of the Roman soldiers must have thought when they began looking around the plateau top that had just become theirs?

In fact, after Jonestown many Americans did find it impossible to accept the idea that any one person could convince more than nine hundred other people to commit suicide. Charles Manson talking a few California ne'er-do-well maniacs into committing brutal crimes was one thing, the kind of event easily labeled (and forgotten) as an "isolated incident." But there were just too many people in Jonestown to dismiss their deaths as meaningless. And so the facts of those deaths led to extremely uncomfortable questions about the sanity of us all. I remember America breathing a collective sigh of relief when reports were released indicating there was physical evidence that not all of Jones's followers went voluntarily, just as the nation was similarly relieved at the evidence some of David Koresh's followers had been shot in Waco, Texas. We can believe a mass murder much more easily because it means only one, or two (or two hundred?) of those present were really so easily moved to die.

The Palestinian travel agent was wrong to equate Jonestown and Masada. He was wrong not because of what happened in each place but because of what happened afterwards, and continues to happen. Society accepts the deaths of the Zealots at Masada as a noble sacrifice and the dead themselves as heroes. Society declines to do the same with the dead of Jonestown or Waco, and I doubt very much whether that will change in the next 1900 years. Once again, the justification for suicide isn't up to the individual contemplating the act, but to the society in which he or she lives.

Which brings me back to Jack Kevorkian. The suicides on which he has assisted did not benefit society. They were strictly for the personal benefit of the individual who died, and presumably for that person's family. Therefore, they were not acceptable to society, and Kevorkian was especially unacceptable for being involved in them. But it would be churlish in the extreme to suggest someone suffering from ceaseless pain with no hope of recovery was being "selfish" to end that pain once and for all. I don't think even Mr. Morimoto would do that.

When GI Joe falls on a hand grenade and saves five of his buddies, he's a hero. What if it were just four buddies? Or only two? What if Joe throws himself on a (symbolic) hand grenade with no buddies there at all, and saves himself from further hideous pain? Why does he suddenly become a coward and a posthumous outcast?

What Kevorkian is doing is asking us to expand our societal definition of an acceptable suicide. He almost seems to be trying to create a new classification somewhere between heroic and condemned. By his actions, and his justification of them, he is asking us to include those deaths that benefit solely the individual who commits the act.

It's far from a new idea. In ancient Greece and Rome such suicides were common. Jocasta, Oedipus's mom, hung herself, and Hannibal the Elephant General killed himself rather than surrender to Rome. These were suicides of honor, including not only death with dignity but suicides by warriors escaping their enemies and women protecting their chastity. The Cynics, Epicureans, and Stoics all encouraged suicide in such situations, and even more commonplace events as well. Zeno, the Stoic founder, was so disgusted by stubbing his toe that he limped home and hung himself.

The acceptability of personal, nonheroic suicide rose and fell in succeeding centuries. There are fourteen suicides of varying acceptability in Shakespeare's works (*there's* a trivia question for the know-it-all of your acquaintance—name them.) By the age of Romanticism, suicide practically became fashionable, as young men throughout Europe read Goethe's *Sorrows of Young Werther* and copied the title character's demise.

So suicidal tides do change. Now, in a time when personal freedom and choice is very important in many cultures, it would seem that what Kevorkian suggests is not that extraordinary. And in fact I've noticed with interest that those who oppose him often ignore the basic ethical and moral questions he raises. Instead, they try to prove that the people he's helped actually recanted at the last minute, or were somehow forced to do the procedure against their will. Once again, murder is easier for us to deal with than suicide. Without the facts of each case, I can't possibly argue whether they did or did not sincerely want to die, but certainly they didn't *all* recant. The moral question remains. And as science finds more ways of keeping us breathing instead of living, that question will become ever more important.

•

Those supporting Doctor Kevorkian have a difficult time before them because historically society has a difficult time with suicide, for reasons stated earlier. But change has happened and continues to happen. In fact, it may be happening right now in Japan. In Japanese *karoshi* literally means "death from overwork." And though people have died from working too hard all over the world, perhaps only in

Japan and a few other countries has such a demise been considered a Good Death. The industrial miracle that is postwar Japan is due in no small part to the dedicated people of the country. They work a hundred hours more a year than their American counterparts, rarely taking the vacations they've earned. The result is a nation that has literally risen from the ashes to become a financial behemoth. And because the na-tion—the society—benefited from the hard work, in a sense death from hard work was considered to be as glorious as death in battle. Though karoshi is not precisely suicide because the deceased doesn't desire it, as one Japanese described the phenomenon, "Karoshi is the modern ver-sion of *seppuku*, or hara-kiri. It's considered an honor, the ultimate sacrifice."

That's changing for a number of reasons. The Japanese government has severely restricted the definition of karoshi in what some contend is an effort to avoid paying compensation claims. Nevertheless, the gov-ernment has taken notice of the fact that stress-related illnesses like strokes and heart attacks are the nation's second and third largest killers, after cancer. The government has urged corporations to reduce overtime and even proposed "No Overtime Day" and "No Overtime Week."

Some corporations have responded even without government prod-ding. In 1992 Sony Chairman Akio Morita urged longer vacations and better pay for the Japanese worker, saying it was time for Japan to "reinvent itself to blend with prevailing attitudes and practices." Some of his fellow corporation executives were shocked.

Perhaps the strongest indication that the Good Death attitude towards karoshi is changing is in the courts. The families of dead work-ers are suing employers for driving their loved ones into early graves. No samurai's mother ever filed suit against the shogun for her son's seppuku, but the business equivalent is happening now in Japan. The result is that karoshi might just go from being a socially accepted death to a socially rejected death. Those in Western nations who would seek a similar but opposite change in opinion regarding the suicide of the suf-fering should certainly be encouraged by that.

For a growing number of people, one other thing besides changing societal approval has proven to be a deterrent against karoshi and other forms of suicide in Japan. Carl Becker now uses this phenomenon in his counseling of suicidal people, and his prime success story is Syozo Morimoto. The outside observer might think Mr. Morimoto survived his suicide attempt because a salesman showed up literally in the nick of time. But Mr. Morimoto says he survived because, lying there in his bathtub bleeding, he had a near-death experience. And it was *awful*.

"I drifted down into the tub and I heard sounds like steel pipes crashing together. There were flashes of light like lightning. I felt a strong wind, and lost consciousness. I saw my body slumped in the red water and felt chills, not of the body, but against what I'd done, that I shouldn't have done this, it was a mistake to have killed myself. I had to apologize. Please forgive me! It was like I was crying out in my heart. I watched my body slip underwater, and I felt myself get colder, claustrophobic and suffocated. Now the self I'm feeling with is up above the bathtub even though the real body is underwater. The body I'm looking down with felt like it was flying through the air, through tremendous wind, like a typhoon. And with this wind all sorts of things were flying at me, and by me, and eventually through me. As they shot past I could hear them flying by my ears, as if somebody had thrown a rock or a baseball at me. At first they were just unrecognizable blobs and then gradually they took shapes; birds, chickens, animals, faces, heads. And I looked at my body and it was like my body was glowing, a million fireflies, a million points of light. These weird objects kept flying through me and as they passed through my body it would turn black for an instant and then return to its firefly light. And I got very afraid. And all the time I kept wanting to say, 'Please forgive me. It's a mistake. Forgive me.' Finally I felt myself falling down a deep, dark space, like falling through a well. And then I realized I was wearing something and I became conscious of what I was wearing. I was wearing hospital clothing and I woke up in a hospital bed. My son was standing by the bedside berating me. 'You shouldn't have suicided,' he was saying. 'What got into your head?' "

I thought the presence by his bedside of Mr. Morimoto's egregious lout of a son was an especially nice touch. Mr. Morimoto's life had not changed a bit from bath to bed. He still had wasted twenty years on two kids who deserved to be punted around a parking lot for a few days. He was still alone. He still had a tendency to take bad advice. ("Don't remarry" from the police officer and "Oh, go ahead, kill yourself" from his sons were perhaps two suggestions Mr. Morimoto might have ignored.) Yet because of his near-death experience he would never be suicidal again.

"I'd seen the world at a great distance, like an astronaut might see it. And it looked very small, and the problems I was facing felt very small. At the same time I realized we're not living by our own power, that life and death are not supposed to be man's decision. They're a decision at a much higher level than ours.

"Even today I have a weak heart. Sometimes my heart stops. I average only a fraction of the heartbeats I'm supposed to have. But since this near-death experience, I've worked more than the average man. I do heavy labor. And the reason is not because my heart is strong, but on the contrary, because my spirit is strong."

Like Mr. Morimoto before his near-death experience, the majority of students and even a lot of workers in Japan feel there's nothing after death, according to Carl Becker. So suicide offers a real attraction as the end of all problems. "But what if there is an afterlife?" Becker asks his clients.

"I tell them about near-death experiences of suicide attempters like Mr. Morimoto's which are unpleasant, but which do report continued experience. I can't guarantee a single client who's contemplating suicide is going to have an NDE, much less a pleasant or an unpleasant one. But the very fact that you might continue to feel something after you intend to cut your life short is enough to stop a lot of people from taking the knife or the poison, at least that night."

The use of near-death experiences in suicide prevention is a minor part of the NDE experience. Increasingly over the last few decades, the occurrence of NDEs has captivated the imaginations of millions, as millions of people have had them. In my city and many cities there are NDE support groups where people try to interpret what they've seen and discuss how it changed their lives. There have also been some fascinating recent studies of the near-death experiences of children.

Near-death experiences themselves have been reported for centuries, of course. In 1206 an Essex farmer named Thurkill found himself in a Hieronymus Bosch painting, with nests of piercing snakes among other terrors, and a fiery hallway leading off to hell. Or that's where he assumed it went. Chances are the signage was minimal.

Thurkill and Morimoto—as well as the South Asian Hindu who reported riding to heaven on a "bespangled cow"—are in the minority when it comes to the details of their experience. By far the majority of people who have had NDEs report their lives passing before their eyes, the feeling that they are racing through dark spaces, seeing deceased relatives, and finally coming to a place with a very bright light, a place from which they "return" to earth. The overwhelming feeling during this out-of-body migration is euphoria and peace. In a 1982 Gallup poll of eight million Americans who had NDEs, one-third recalled being in an ecstatic or visionary state.

That was certainly the experience of Takemasa Kimura. He used to be a Kyoto businessman, and I suspect a prime candidate for kiroshi. But in 1983, in the hospital for intestinal surgery, he had a fairly traditional near-death experience. He floated above his body in the hospital bed, saw the white light, and watched his life pass before his eyes.

Towards the end he felt his nurse physically trying to pull him back. She was successful, but a different Mr. Kimura landed in that bed.

"Before the experience, I felt death was the end of everything. But I can no longer believe that. I now think there's going to be something continuing after death, and it's probably going to include a life review where I have to evaluate my own actions, my own life, and I want to be proud of the way I continue to live. Now when it's my time to go, I'm ready to go peacefully."

Mr. Kimura has become an ardent practitioner of Zen Buddhism. He meditates daily for hours, and hasn't looked at a profit-and-loss statement for a decade. In a way he was his own Ghost of Christmas Past, Present, and Future, and has become a peaceful, euphoric Zen Ebenezer.

•

New Zealand Maori Bill Awa actually believes he made it to heaven during his near-death experience. Like Takemasa Kimura, Awa is an older man who was in the hospital at the time. He suddenly found himself standing with two hooded figures who were about to launch a boat across a lake. He pleaded with the figures to let him come along, and they agreed. On the other side Bill saw people cooking food over volcanic steam holes—crayfish, mussels, eels, and other fish.

"When the food was prepared, it was a beautiful spread, a banquet. They gestured for me to eat and I said, 'I'm sorry, I cannot partake of your food, I don't feel like eating.' And then I woke up and saw my wife by my bed."

Intrigued by what he had experienced, Bill Awa asked a Maori minister what it meant.

"He said, 'Boy, do you know what you've done? You've been there and you've come back! And you're lucky! If you had eaten the food that was laid out for you, you wouldn't have come back.' "

Bill's near-death experience doesn't seem to have changed his life much. As an elder of the Maori Ngati Porou people, his life has a powerful spiritual aspect anyway. We talked standing at the foot of the Ngati Porou's sacred burial mountain. It's a place where Bill says he has always felt strongly the *wirra*—the combined spirit—of his people, alive and dead. So a visit to a heavenly clambake wasn't about to turn him around much. He feels calmer about heaven, but he said that's because he's always liked to eat, and now he knows they eat well there.

Which brings up an interesting aspect to some near-death experiences, especially the pleasant ones. People have a tendency to see the things they care about the most, even if they don't realize how much they care. Most people see deceased family members, but the family is traditionally something we care about. But there are lots of exceptions to the bright light/dead family NDE. Timothy Ferris, in a December 1991 article in the *New York Times Magazine* (extracted from his book *The Mind's Sky: Human Intelligence in a Cosmic Context*), tells of an English professor colleague who was on an airliner that suddenly plunged thirty-four thousand feet. During the descent the professor's mind inexplicably filled with lines from Shakespeare's poetry. And I would suspect that the Hindu man on the bespangled cow particularly likes cows, and likes them bespangled.

In that same article, Ferris offers an interesting physiological explanation for near-death experiences. He points out that the traditional NDE doesn't happen only to people who are medically near death. A century ago a Swiss geology professor and alpinist named Albert Heim took a short step off a tall mountain. And in his fall Heim saw a bright white light, and felt euphoric and free of anxiety. He watched his life pass before his eyes. But of course he wasn't near death until he hit the bottom. Intrigued by his experience, Heim interviewed other slightly careless mountain climbers, as well as masons and roofers who had experienced and survived similar falls. He found that they too had had feelings of peace and euphoria, seen similar medleys of their lives, and been entranced by that ubiquitous ten-thousand-watt light.

Ferris concludes, "If . . . the mental transfigurations [experienced] while falling closely resemble modern near-death accounts, then the phenomenon of the near-death experience tells us about trauma, not death. And if it doesn't tell us about death, it doesn't tell us about life after death either."

Physically, in times of stress—like falling or nearly dying—our bodies turn out juices that enable us to increase our awareness and response time and reduce our sensitivity to pain. These are perfectly natural physical defense mechanisms designed to help us survive the situation. Adrenaline and other fancy stuff fairly bubble in the blood and brain, producing, yes, euphoria, through some of the same physiological processes that encourage dopers to take up a heavy evening of cloud counting. And in such a state it could be we see heaven, because our concept of heaven was created centuries ago by people who had near-death experiences. So you can't use visions of heaven in near-death experiences as proof that heaven exists. The argument is circular and recalls H. L. Mencken's line about God creating man in His own image, and man, being a gentleman, returning the favor. The only thing near-death experiences may prove is that in the millennia before Thomas Edison people were still attracted to really good illumination.

Are near-death experiences real glimpses of the life beyond, or the natural result of flooding the body with adrenaline and polypeptides? Carl Becker says that ultimately it doesn't make any difference. Mr. Morimoto is alive today because he believes, and Mr. Kimura is a happier, healthier man because he believes too.

Dr. Becker presents an analogy. "If you walk down Waikiki beach hand in hand with your girlfriend, and you see the sunset and listen to the music, a scientist could evaluate what's going on in your brain, how that's being recorded, the wave length, the sound waves. He could tell you scientifically everything that's happening in your brain. But the more he looks at what your brain is doing, the less he knows about what the experience really means to you as a living human being. So to evaluate an experience as humans, we have to look both at the inputs in the brain, but also at what the person is telling us about what that means to them. And the same is true for near-death experiences. Human beings are looking for meaning. If we don't find meaning in our experience, no matter how chemically important it is to us, we'll forget it. If we find meaning in a coincidence, no matter how chemically irrelevant it is, it can make a big change in our lives. And that's the way it is with the near-death experience, whether it has a chemical basis or not."

Near dying or long falling is not the way many of us would choose to get the message that Mr. Morimoto and Mr. Kimura got: the message that life is too important to waste on trivial matters. Better we should find it out walking on the beach at Waikiki, hand in hand.

CHAPTER FOURTEEN

AFTERWARD: AN AFTERWORD

Two sweet old Unitarian ladies died, and as their souls ascended they came to a signpost hanging in the firmament. The signpost had two arrows, one pointing off to the right and one pointing off to the left. "This Way to Heaven," it said on the arrow pointing right. "This Way to a Discussion of Heaven" it said on the arrow pointing left.

They went left.

When I was fourteen my Sunday school teacher at Ye Olde Unitarian Church, the fretful Squeak Schneider, presented the preceding thigh-slapper as "the only known Unitarian joke." Squeak was not prone to either giving or receiving sarcasm, so I think he meant it. It was a factual statement for him, and probably accurate as well.

After he told the Joke we had that Sunday morning's planned discussion of Unitarian heaven. We learned there isn't one. Or if there is, no Unitarian has ever seen it because no Unitarian has ever gone right. ("Ha ha."—Squeak Schneider.) So true to most of my Liberal Religious Youth training, what we really talked about was everybody else's heaven. Unitarians seem to delight in turning religious subjects and occasions into opportunities for cross-cultural education. On Christmas we usually heard about the birth of Buddha. My grandfather, the Australian political scientist/Methodist, was asked to give the guest sermon at our church one Easter Sunday. He quickly got into the Unitarian swing of things, speaking for an hour without once mentioning Jesus on Easter. Mostly he concentrated on the plight of the indigenous peoples of the South Pacific, who would not be enjoying an Easter dinner that afternoon because of the white man's historic oppression. Although this is certainly a legitimate subject for discussion, at the same time an unaware observer would have concluded from my grandfather's "sermon" that Easter was the time when Unitarian Americans memorialized the death of Prince Kalawalawatu. The congregation found his remarks to be just the stuff.

I digress, digression being one of the few sacred rites of the Unitarian church. I don't remember much about our discussion that Sunday school morning concerning the various available heavens, except that Squeak's joke was the high point. We fourteen-year-olds walked away from class without much reassurance that if we lived a righteous life our reward would be anything other than a box in the ground, just like the guys who lived it up and let the devil take the hindmost. We were apparently supposed to be comforted by the fact that although we didn't get a heaven, we didn't have to spend our lives covering our hindmosts either. In life, Squeak seemed to be saying, honor is on the honor system.

At the time I remember thinking that wasn't the thing to tell hormone-heavy fourteen-year-olds. I personally didn't feel much incentive not to wallow in pride, covetousness, lust, anger, gluttony, envy, and sloth. They're inside me, just itching to get out. Or at least they were when I was fourteen. Those were the days.

Now, thirty years later, I find myself launching into, not heaven, but a discussion of heavens (and hells), literally turning myself into the Unitarian Joke. An acquaintance told me I was actually fortunate in this regard. A Liberal Religious background, he argued, infused as it was with seeing all sides of a question (and discussing them so thoroughly that the question itself gets lost), would enable me to be objective about the religious convictions of others, vis-à-vis the life everlasting. But ignorance has often been mistaken for objectivity, and this may be one of those occasions. I do not embark on this part of the Trip with confidence.

The problem is that there are so many different heavens and hells, so many different ways to attain or avoid them. It used to be easier. But nowadays fluffy white clouds, harpists, and the Old Man with the long beard who looks like Laurence Olivier in *Clash of the Titans*—my concept of heaven in my early years—is a decidedly minority viewpoint, if in fact you could find anybody who could still describe heaven in such a way without giggling. But that's not to say there aren't people who envision spending eternity in a very solid place.

For instance, on Papua New Guinea there's a group of people called the Vanatinai who weren't doing all that well in the early 1940s. Then the United States Marines showed up, busily keeping the South Pacific safe for democracy. The leathernecks brought with them canned food, suitable shelter, Lucky Strikes, and other fancy stuff. And they shared their largess with the local community, as Americans are wont to do.

"Where do these magical things come from?" asked the tribespersons. As a result, for almost fifty years now some of the Vanatinai have believed that heaven is the United States of America. (They've obviously never been in Chicago in January.) The United States is where the souls of their dead go, after they turn white. The United States is from where the Few, the Proud, the Gods will someday return with more Lucky Strikes. If they knew that many of their deities trained at a place called Devil's Island, it would be spiritually devastating for them.

I am not making fun of these people in the least. On the contrary, I admire their pragmatism. Their heaven and its emissaries have done a lot more for them than any demonstrable benefits of the heaven envisioned by a billion other people. The Vanatinai even get postcards from heaven, showing some of its scenic wonders, like the Bridge of the Golden Gate and the Faces of the Old Gods on Mt. Rushmore. How many clergypersons, trying to convince their flock of a blissful afterlife, would give their vestibules for one single certifiable postcard from heaven that they could pass around during vespers? Many.

On the other end of the heaven scale from those who believe it's a real place are the more mystical. (Not the Unitarians. We're mystified, not mystical. Big difference.) I mean people like the Jewish scholar who described heaven as being outside space and time; not a *place* but a *state* of the soul, so that we should speak of *becoming* heaven, not *going* to heaven; a wonderful notion. It was another Jewish scholar who wrote, "Even as fish do not know the element of fire because they exist ever in its opposite, so are the delights of the world of the spirit unknown to this world of flesh." In other words, for those of us waiting here in Fleshworld it is useless to speculate on the nature of heaven. Only time will tell. . . .

In the course of the Trip I asked most of the people I talked to about their beliefs in the afterlife. Bill Groves, the Australian undertaker, wouldn't tell me. "I deal with too many different faiths to commit," he said. Not far away, Michelle the White Lady is eager to get to a fluffy-clouds kind of place and slip on her white wings and flowing white robe. Michelle is basically looking at an all-white wardrobe from now through eternity, because the heaven she envisions looks a lot like the White Ladies, without all the stiffs.

Patiently waiting in Florida to be cryonically frozen so he can join his wife, Joe Cannon doesn't believe in an afterlife at all. "That's one of the reasons I'm going to be frozen," he said. "I'll go with science over superstition any day."

In his last weeks alive, Ed Decker was thinking a lot about his father. Ed wondered what it was going to be like to meet him in heaven. "He died thirty-one years ago, when he was seventeen years younger than I am now," Ed said. "So when we meet is he going to be thirty-one years younger than I am, or seventeen years younger? Or maybe I get to pick what age I want to be in heaven. Let me tell ya, eighty-two ain't it."

Before he died I wish Ed could have met Pastor James Miller. Because Pastor Miller would have told Ed he could be whatever age he wanted to be in heaven, and whatever anything else too. Pastor Miller would have made Ed believe it too, because his own belief is overpowering. It's because of people like him that I'm going on this heaven quest. For those of us still alive, ultimately a discussion of heaven and hell is really a discussion of people and their beliefs. It's not the signpost that's important, it's the two sweet old ladies. And if we Unitarians are anything, we are people people. So what follows is a thoroughly incomprehensive series of encounters with religious leaders and followers who have thought a great deal not only about the life to come, but the life that is.

"Do you want to live again a new life where there is no sin? A new life where there's no damnation? A new life where folks don't talk about you? Can you witness? There's a new life where folks don't criticize you! There's a new life where folks don't wake you up! There's a new life where folks always howdy and never good-bye! Ain't God all right!?"

Sunday morning in Warrenton, Florida, and Pastor James Miller is in the pulpit. Except Pastor Miller hasn't gotten anywhere near the pulpit for ten minutes. He's working the room, up and down the aisles, in and out of the pews, going right into people's faces and hearts asking his two questions over and over again. Can you witness? Ain't God all right? And the parishioners of the First Baptist Church of Warrenton say yes and yes and yes again, as Jesus and Pastor Miller fill their hearts and minds in equal measure. When he's really rolling, Pastor Miller has been known to preach for four hours, and never lose a customer.

On weekdays James Miller is a police officer across the state line in a small Alabama town. He's been doing that for twenty-five years. When he told me his story after the church service, I said, "There can't have been many black police officers in rural Alabama in the 1960s." He smiled and said, "I was the first." There was fire in his eyes when he said it, and pride, and pain, too. Pastor Miller has taken a lot of crap in his life. And besides his ironclad faith and hypnotic speaking ability, that may be his power as a preacher. He knows his people and knows what they've been through because he's been through most of it himself. He knows what kind of heaven they want, one where people howdy, and don't talk about you, and don't wake you up until you're ready. It's his heaven too.

"I'm a poor man," he said to me, quietly, thoughtfully. He seemed like a completely different person from the passionate enchanter I had just seen delivering the gospel. "But I'm an heir and I will inherit all those things my Father has promised. In the South down here, you can tell where a rich person lives because you'll see a paved road heading toward his mansion. Well, I'm going to have a mansion too, but my road is going to be paved with gold. You see, I'm biding my time down here. I'm living just to make it down here in order to get where my wealth really is. Nothing I have ever achieved on earth is going to match what I have done in order to be there with God. I don't want any top spot in heaven, I don't want to preach, I just want to be there. When I open my eyes after I die I'm going to be looking into the face of Jesus and he's going to say, 'Welcome, Brother Miller, you made it.' "

"But Pastor Miller, a lot of religions say that even though there's a heaven, without being sinful you shouldn't put all your eggs in that basket. You should live each day here on earth to the fullest. You shouldn't bide your time."

"Mr. Palmer, put all your eggs in that basket. All of 'em."

Although Pastor Miller is good with his flock on the subject of heaven, he's spectacular on hell. But he has to be. He told me hell is a much harder sell than heaven.

"And just as there is a reality in heaven, hell is also a reality! You hear what I'm saying?" By the time he got to hell in the service, Pastor Miller wasn't saying it anymore, he was singing it, like an operatic recitative, tuneless but musical, rhythmically mesmerizing.

"And hell is not going to be made up of strangers! Can you witness? If you happen to go down there, you will see folks that you recognize! You all hear me today? Maybe you'll even see some of the folks you were sitting beside in church! You'll see unbelieving preachers, preachers that say, 'Don't do as I do, do as I *say* I do!' Those false preachers are not just going to hell! They're going in the front seat!"

His experience tells him people want to believe in heaven's eternal bliss, but not hell's infernal suffering. He thinks the most important task of any minister is to convince his parishioners that if they continue in sin, there is a place for them. And that place is hell.

"Our job is to warn mankind of the second coming of Christ, and to let them know that when Christ comes back, Christ is coming back *angry.*"

In Pastor Miller's basic Baptist afterlife, there's no way your descendants can help you, either. If you open your eyes after you die and you're looking in the devil's face and he says, "Too bad!" you've had it for eternity. No upgrading. Your fate is entirely in your hands.

"Pastor Miller scares me about hell, yes he does." Albert Jackson chuckles, but he means it. Ever since being transferred to the Warrenton area three years ago, Albert and his family have been members of Pastor Miller's congregation. Albert Jackson doesn't look like he scares easily. He's a career Navy man in his mid-forties, the Senior Enlisted Adviser to the Chief of Naval Education and Training in Pensacola. But from his bearing he clearly hasn't been pushing a desk all his life. This is a guy who has walked into and back out of some pretty tough places in his time.

Although he and his family have many different activities, First Baptist of Warrenton—and their faith—seem to be the cornerstones of the Jacksons' lives. Albert is a deacon, and with his daughter a member of the choir. They all go to services on Sundays, Bible study and prayer meeting on Wednesday nights, and spend a lot of time on church-related activities. They are deeply religious people, and yet I was surprised there wasn't a single religious artifact on display in their home—no biblical pictures, no crosses, no parables on plaques.

"What that says is that I have Christ in me," he explains. "And that's where I always carry him. I don't need those things to constantly remind me."

The other thing that surprised me about Albert Jackson was his willingness to doubt the physical existence of heaven and hell. He certainly believes righteousness is rewarded and sin is punished, but as to where and how he doesn't sound as positive as his pastor.

"I haven't figured that one out yet," he says. "I have not come to grips with those realms [of heaven and hell.] The Bible tells me that this earth will be torn asunder and a new earth in heaven will replace it, but I haven't come to the visualization of whether that will be right here or if it will be on a different plane."

Pastor Miller is a man of faith with experience in the world, while his parishioner Albert Jackson is a man of the world with experience in faith. As far as belief in a heaven with gold-paved roads and no wake up calls, that may be the only difference between them. Because theirs isn't a difference of belief, merely the reporting of that belief. James Miller can look at a stranger and describe heaven without pause, without embarrassment, because he's had years of practice and he knows that the slightest doubt from him is an abnegation of his duty to his flock. Albert Jackson knows that to someone who most likely doesn't believe, that solid, mansion-filled heaven and fiery, pitchforky hell probably sound a little silly. So he hedges his conversational bet to keep from sounding a little silly himself. But I don't think for a moment that he doesn't believe every bit as much as James Miller. There's a big solid heaven, and if you maintain a righteous life you are going to be there. Both men take that gloriously for granted.

•

Sheikh Bassam Jarrar: "We have a saying. 'If I had one foot in heaven and the other outside heaven, then I would still not feel secure.' The Muslim will not take anything for granted because the responsibilities are too great. By the same token, he will not despair, because God is merciful. Those who despair are the heretics."

Sheikh Jarrar is a teacher, religious and political leader in his native Palestine. I heard a lot about him before we met. His political activities had apparently made him distasteful to Israeli authorities, so he was not allowed to enter Jerusalem. He did anyway, and we met in a secret location in the city. But even without the melodramatic details of getting together with him, it was clear from the Palestinian Muslims who were helping me that Sheikh Jarrar was a sometimes mysterious force to be reckoned with, a powerful, charismatic leader of his faith and his people. I was expecting a fierce old man in flowing black robes, with black burning eyes set deep in a leathery face; rather like Saleh Al Baroghouty but with a full white beard and many more teeth.

However, the man who walked in the door could have just come off the set of a photo shoot for the Beirut edition of *Gentleman's Quarterly;* immaculate black sweater and slacks, precision grooming all the way. He was in his forties, a strikingly handsome guy who carried himself in a relaxed but still commanding way. When he told me that from early childhood he has been called "the Sheikh"—which in this case means "teacher"—I didn't doubt him for a moment. His eyes, dark but not burning, were relatively friendly. He did at least have a full beard (jet black, well trimmed) and darn fine teeth. He laughed easily and often but could become serious very quickly. I suspect he understood English well, but he chose not to speak it, except once.

"Is it difficult to live a good Islamic life?" I asked.

"In the past difficult," he said, laughing. "Now very easy."

It may have been my Unitarian belief in the power of discussion, but all the time I talked to Sheikh Jarrar I wished Pastor Miller could have been there too. The two men have a lot in common, personally, professionally, and even religiously. Each man has been threatened by societal forces and has not only withstood the conflicts but has risen above them through courage and dedication. Each man knows his business as a religious leader and has acquired a devout following, in no small part through sheer force of personality. And they are both going to much the same heaven by the same route, even though each man would be amazed to meet the other one there. And not just because Pastor Miller is sure he is going, and Sheikh Jarrar says, "Only the damned are sure."

For him all religion is composed of facts that human beings have made into laws. The facts are the same for every faith, which is why some kind of afterlife is a part of all religious belief. But through faulty interpretation and translation into law, the religions became divided. Islam came about to correct the misinterpreted concepts of the prophets. And thus where a conflict still remains, it represents a "defect in the belief" caused by human misinterpretation. These defects are crucial, especially concerning the Day of Judgment. According to Islam, it is very important that all religious views on the Day of Judgment should be the same.

Sheikh Jarrar: "Exactly like Christians, the Muslim believes that after death there is a reckoning. The reckoning can be in punishment or in absolution. The punishment goes to people who have received the Message but have acted in contradiction to it. The absolution is granted to those who also have received the Message and followed its transcripts. And those who have not received the Message are not faced with the reckoning."

"What happens to them?" I asked, being one who has not only not received the message, but doesn't capitalize it.

"Their fate is unknown, except that we know they will not be punished. We don't know if they will be rewarded." I thought he might be talking about Christians, Jews, a Unitarian, Hindus, and so forth, but a Muslim acquaintance back in Seattle said he wasn't. He was referring to people who haven't even had access to the Message, like obscure rain forest tribespeople. My acquaintance explained that Jews don't believe in all the prophets so they're in trouble, Hindus have more than one god so they're not making it, and although Muslims revere Christ as a prophet, most Christians make him a god, which is one god too far. (Nondenominational capitalization has been utilized in the previous sentence.)

That's why I suspect Sheikh Jarrar will be astounded to meet Pastor Miller in heaven. And Pastor Miller will be equally astounded to meet the Sheikh, because he believes that only those who accept Jesus as their sole lord and savior are heaven-bound. Not about to happen to Sheikh Jarrar. Too bad really, because they would have a good time together up there, hanging around Pastor Miller's mansion in the cool of the evening, sipping a couple of frosties, arguing about why you need a gold driveway when there's nothing to buy and everybody else can have a precious metal carport just by asking.

I asked both men why human beings needed the reward of heaven to live righteous lives in the first place. Jewish theologians have written of the concept that human beings automatically know they have to "earn" heaven. It is part of our "divine spark." Possibly, but eternal bliss seems like a pretty good prize for doing something you should do anyway, just as eternal torture seems like a pretty harsh punishment for not following the message, or accidentally being a Buddhist.

Pastor Miller answered with justice and sin. He contended that human beings are inherently sinful creatures and therefore need to understand what's in it for them if they are successfully to overcome their inherently nasty ways. And by so doing and being rewarded for righteousness with heaven, they also vindicate God's justice. Where would the justice be if everybody got in no matter what kind of lives they led?

I don't think Sheikh Jarrar believes we're all naturally sinful. We're just naturally ignorant of the importance of the Message. He would certainly agree with Pastor Miller that human beings need to know where they stand with their creator, and what they might be standing in for eternity.

"A human being in Islam should be living between two poles—hope and fear. As a teacher, when I give a student a test I make it not too easy and not too difficult. If it's too easy it means that the student is not afraid and does not prepare for the test. And when it's too difficult, then the student loses hope and despairs. And the best principle in teaching—my personal view—is when the student is afraid of failure and hopes for success. So with life. If you try to interpret people's attitudes, you'll find they are afraid of one thing [punishment] and hope for something else [absolution.] And that's as it should be. Without the Day of Judgment or the awareness that such a day will come, then people will have no excuse to continue living; no excuse for sacrifice; no excuse to help others. *There would be no meaning to life itself.* My

entire existence is founded in belief in the Day of Judgment. Any religion that does not include it is futile. Religion is not only a belief, it is a
law. And the law would lay the constraints or the guidelines for people
to follow in that religion. Without punishment or absolution, then it's
like civilian laws without punishment. Nobody would abide by them. If
religion does not include the Last Judgment, then people would look
upon it as a philosophy, rather than as a religion."

•

Archbishop Dionysius Behnam Yacoub Jajjarvi isn't waiting for the
Day of Judgment to get his reward. He believes he has a lot of it now.
His life is spent in paradise. Since 1983 Archbishop Jajjarvi has been
the Syriac Orthodox Patriarchal Vicar in the Holy Land and Jordan.
Born in the Iraqi city of Mosul in 1925, he never considered any life
other than the priesthood, entering the seminary at age sixteen. Now
his church, St. Mark's Convent, is in Jerusalem's Old City, literally
around the corner from the Church of the Holy Sepulchre, where Jesus
was entombed.

When I arrived one of his assistants led me upstairs to a reception
area. The assistant came back a few minutes later with coffee in which
you could float nails, and I waited. The archbishop's waiting room
looks like what you might expect if the William Morris Agency in Hollywood were a religious operation and not a talent agency. On the walls
were a dozen pictures of the archbishop with the religiously famous,
dominated by a two-shot with the pope. "My close personal friend,"
the archbishop told me later, and indeed they looked like old friends;
two savvy guys in fancy costumes with similar problems, powers, and
perks.

When the archbishop appeared I was surprised to see he looked a lot
like my wife's Uncle Jack, who was a small-town barber for half a century. But deliberate, soft-spoken Uncle Jack acted more like an archbishop, or what I expected an archbishop to act like. Archbishop Jajjarvi,
on the other hand, was all over the place, bouncing from chair to chair,
telling a few inside pope stories, fetching more coffee himself. He is a
small man with a constant look of pleasant, almost childlike surprise, as
if he'd just heard the family was going to Disneyland for spring break.
The thing I remember most about him was that he was wearing the
standard archbishop-around-the-office robes, but down below he had
on bright red socks. He made you wonder about the pope's socks.

"Would you like the tour?" he asked, more as a statement than a
question. And so we were off at a trot, looking at his plant. For the
archbishop being around the corner from the holiest church in Chris-
tendom is a silver lining with a cloud. His faith is rejuvenated by the

proximity, but his natural promotional sense is bothered by the fact that everybody goes there and nobody but his own Syriac flock comes to St. Mark's. "Holy Sep is nice if you like that sort of thing," he came close to saying a number of times. "But a lot of stuff happened here at St. Mark's too."

Beginning in the basement: "See over there?" he said, pointing to a spot near the wall. "That's where Christ washed the feet of his disciples. Right there. He spent time here. And his mother! Mary was here a lot. Come upstairs!"

Up in his sanctuary, around on the back side of the altar, the archbishop has what he says is the only painting of the Virgin Mary done from life. And though I'm sure there are those who would question the painting's historical authenticity, it very definitely is a life portrait of someone of that era. And a nice face she has, too. She looks like a person you could grow very fond of.

"St. Luke did it—the disciple? He was a painter. He signed the wall over here too. Come." And we were off again.

There were other sights on the tour that didn't mean a whole lot to a lapsed Unitarian. Still, St. Mark's is in microcosm fascinating the same way Jerusalem is fascinating, even for the vaguely religious. All these events you've heard about since childhood actually happened somewhere, and that somewhere is Jerusalem. Like washing the feet. Of course, he had to wash those feet somewhere! Why not the basement of St. Mark's, or whatever it was called back then?

(My favorite Israel-as-historic-site story happened on the way to Masada. I took a cab. Even though it's a long drive down a good highway, everybody told me that was the way to go unless I wanted to spend nine long hours on a tour bus with schoolchildren. On the left as we drove along was the Dead Sea, and on the right there was a long, broken chain of steep, rocky foothills occasionally highlighted by caves of various sizes. The cabdriver was chatty, as most Jerusalem cabdrivers are, and fast, as they are too. But at one point he slowed down from eighty to sixty and pointed to what looked like a small, nondescript cave halfway up the hill. "That's where they found the Dead Sea Scrolls," he said, and sped up again.)

The archbishop and I finally settled back upstairs in his inner office and talked about paradise. He said the office, and the church, are it.

"It's because the kingdom of heaven is spiritual, you see, not necessarily physical or material, but spiritual. After the death, not a special place, a definite place called heaven or a definite place called hell. Maybe a physical place, but above all spiritual. When our Lord was crucified, two thieves were with him, the right thief and the left thief."

(This way to a discussion of thieves.) "And the right thief, finally he said to our Lord, 'Please, remember me in your paradise, remember me in your kingdom.' And the Lord answered, 'Today you will be with me in paradise.' But you see, *the thief was already there, even on the cross!* Where is the paradise? Where is our Lord is paradise, every place. That means in the church itself is paradise because Jesus exists in the church always, continually, spiritually."

"So in a sense, this is paradise?"

"Absolutely. Our God has created man from the beginning, and given him complete freedom to choose, to make goodness or to make badness. The good man is with the Lord and is happy. The bad man is unhappy."

"A person who lives a good life in everything is already partially in paradise, and when he dies, more paradise? And the person who lives a bad life is already in hell, and when he dies hell gets worse?"

"Absolutely."

The archbishop went on to say that a person always knows when he or she is good or not good. As an example he used Adam, who tried to blame Eve for tricking him into eating the apple, but Adam always knew he shouldn't have done it. In heaven as in traffic court, ignorance of the law is no excuse. Humankind likes to make mistakes, said the archbishop, but we always know.

A few days later it was Easter. The archbishop was going to lead services for his followers at his famous neighbor, Holy Sepulchre. Not surprisingly, it's an extremely popular place on Easter Sunday, with what seems like four thousand different Christian denominations wanting to use the immediate area around the sepulchre itself for their observances. So they are scheduled in brief bursts, scheduled tighter than commercials on the Superbowl broadcast. The Syriac Christians had a half hour window in the morning along with three other denominations, the four faiths working all four sides of the sepulchre simultaneously.

The place was a dim, noisy madhouse, the air so thick with incense it looked like there were open fires in there somewhere. I squeezed in to see Archbishop Jajjarvi do his stuff, and though I got no closer than ten feet (or about five thousand people) from him, even from there the transformation in the man was startling. The snappy little guy I knew had turned into an imposing religious figure, dressed all in gold and wearing one of those hats that looks like a small tollbooth. (I couldn't see his socks.) He chanted his ancient chants with fervor while his followers bowed their heads and answered as they had been trained. But even in the midst of this most holy and solemn occasion, he still had that look I originally thought was pleasant surprise. Now I realized it was not surprise, but profound joy.

Archbishop Jajjarvi told me he doesn't fear death because this life cannot offer the eternal happiness he knows the next life will give him. And he is a happy man because he already has a taste of it. He is in heaven, even now.

•

"For the Shin Buddhists, our understanding is that this is hell."

Plump, pleasant Dennis Yoshikawa did not look like a person residing in hell. Born in Denver around forty years ago, he has been a Shin Buddhist priest in Kyoto for many years, originally attracted to the faith—an offshoot of Pure Land Buddhism—as philosophy rather than religion. "But I'm working on it," he said, for now Shin Buddhism is both in his life.

If I understand him correctly, this is hell because:

> A. Human beings suffer in hell.
> B. All human beings are suffering.
> C. All human beings are in hell.

We all suffer because we are ignorant. We are ignorant because we are deluded. What we see and what we think are true are not true, because our ego taints our senses and sense. Our ego so dominates our lives, in fact, that there is no difference between suffering and joy. They are both ego-driven. Therefore they are both deluded perceptions that keep us from the real joy of truth.

"So in Shin Buddhism," Dennis Yoshikawa explained, "our understanding is that to solve the problem of death, one must first solve the problem of life, of living life. If one is able to do that, to live a truly human life, then there's nothing to be feared by the experience of death, because the experience of death is a natural part of life. In traditional Buddhism, your state of mind at the moment of death is important to your existence in the afterlife. But not in Shin Buddhism, because if you know how to live life, then your state of mind is unimportant at any given moment. It's always there."

Achieving the proper Shin Buddhist state of mind both in this life and in preparation for the next doesn't sound as easy as taking Jesus into your heart, for instance. According to Dennis, a much higher percentage of Christians find Jesus than Shin Buddhists who achieve enlightenment. Although the term he uses for enlightenment, *ojo,* could be translated as "born again."

For one thing, Christians get a lot of professional help, people like Pastor Miller who point the way up the right path. In Shin Buddhism, however, everyone is equal before the sect's particular divinity, Amida Buddha. There is no distinction between lay members and clergy. And though the founder of Shin Buddhism, Shinran Shonin, spoke of the religious experience, or *shin-jin* of enlightenment, he spoke of it in the past tense.

"Which means he had achieved it already. So he left in his teachings what was necessary to experience this, but he didn't tell us *how* to go about it. In our faith one doesn't enter a monastery and practice religious austerities in an attempt to have a religious awakening. You must try to have this religious experience within the mundane life that we all live—getting married, raising children, holding a job. That's what makes Shin Buddhism very, very difficult."

That's not all that makes it difficult. Although experiencing shin-jin is life's ultimate goal, you can't be obsessive about it. What's more egomaniacal than obsession? And if you are successful and do experience shin-jin, or more accurately, receive it from Amida Buddha, you don't know it. If it is received, you affect the people around you so strongly that only they can confirm your experience. People who believe they have experienced shin-jin, in other words, only know one thing for certain. They know they *haven't* experienced it. Like Dennis Yoshikawa.

"No, I haven't found it. Because I'm seeking in the first person. First person means evil. If I was completely free, then I would not use the first person. And I wouldn't be talking to you."

It's an interesting conundrum. If you ask a Shin Buddhist if she has received shin-jin from Amida Buddha and she says yes, it really means no, because someone who says yes is wrong. And if she answers no, it means either she's lying—which seems unlikely for a person who has achieved a perfectly truthful life—or she really means yes, in which case she probably wouldn't have answered you in the first place. But then if the answer was really yes no matter what she said, you really wouldn't have had to ask the question in the first place because you would have known. I think Dennis would say the only proper answer to the question is "you tell me," or possibly "don't ask."

Enlightenment in Shin Buddhism is achieved through chanting the Amida Buddha's name, but it must be chanted in precisely the right way, "from the lips, spontaneously," according to Shinran Shonin. Dennis said he's met a few people who have made it, and in the simple recitation of the name you could hear and feel something different.

"According to Shinran, 'one only has to recite it once, but it better be good.' " He laughed. Dennis Yoshikawa is able to joke about his quest for shin-jin, but at the same time he feels a strong sense that time is running out in his own life. But even that sense of time passing means he's still not there.

"Time in Buddhism is not linear. Past, future, and present are all in this one instant. The importance of life is lived from each instant to each instant. So when you ask if I feel like time is running out, I say yes. But if I'm living my life with shin-jin, then time's not a factor at all. And at the moment of death I know enlightenment is assured, because I have already experienced it. That's shin-jin."

"What happens if you die having not experienced it?"

"Then you return."

"You get another shot? That's reassuring."

"No it isn't."

"No?"

"Because it's very difficult to be born a human."

"Ah. If you return as a bluebottle fly, you're not going to make it this time. If you're a really good bluebottle fly, you may eventually come back as another human, and get another shot?"

"Right. But there's no guarantee. So if you have been so fortunate to have been given this shot as a human, don't blow it."

And Dennis Yoshikawa laughed again, I suspect mostly because he knew our conversation was almost over. Near the end I asked him to describe the Pure Land, that heaven where the enlightened go after death, and he turned pale. He said there are some Shin Buddhists who believe it is a real, physical place, and others who, well . . . and then he sort of gave up. Trying to sum up centuries of religious teaching and thought about death and the afterlife for a Unitarian in a few terse phrases was no easier for Dennis Yoshikawa than it had been for Bassam Jarrar.

•

It seemed very easy for Henry Mittwer, however. Like Dennis Yoshikawa, Mittwer is American-born, but has chosen to spend many of his seventy-four years in Japan. He is a Zen Buddhist monk, author of books on flower arranging and the tea ceremony. Watching Henry Mittwer asking neighborhood business people for donations to his temple, or teaching his apprentices the precise and proper details of making and serving tea, he seems to be a person for whom everything is important; a control freak down to his sandals. And he probably is, but within a very limited time frame. And that time frame is *right now.*

"Basically Zen people don't care about life after death. We are completely concerned with right now. We are living right now. And any question you have about life after death, that's up to the people who want to think that way. It's a philosopher's or a scientist's job, not a religious person's concern. It's not that we don't necessarily believe in an afterlife, it's just that it's unimportant."

Zen makes a distinction between moral and religious concerns that is difficult for many people raised in a Western tradition to understand.

We look to religion to provide answers and guidance on moral questions. Morality and religion are inextricably bound together. But not in Zen.

"That's why Zen is not, in a Western sense, a religious practice at all," Henry Mittwer said. "We just practice zazen—meditation—in order to be completely free."

So Zen offers neither the carrot of heaven nor the stick of hell to its followers. Those afterlife options and the moral life choices they require must come from somewhere else. All Zen provides is a method to achieve freedom.

Henry Mittwer spends much of his day meditating. He sits outside on the porch of an ancient temple, before a pond surrounded by green trees. Although busy Kyoto is only a few hundred yards away, where he sits it is quiet, with the only sounds coming from a small waterfall, the birds in the trees, the ducks on the pond. It is one of the most beautiful places I have ever seen. It is, in fact, the heaven I'd hope to glimpse in a near-death experience; a place so simple and yet so powerful that you can't imagine ever being bored there, even for eternity. For me the pond is peace. For Henry Mittwer it is freedom.

"This pond has a special meaning," he said. "The shape of the pond is that of the Chinese character 'heart.' And the big carp swimming in there represent us swimming like mad but going nowhere. Across the pond there's a waterfall. The legend is that if a carp tries hard and swims up the waterfall, then that carp turns into a dragon and can fly away into the sky, completely free. And that's the freedom we are looking for, freedom from death, or birth, or all that. Freedom from the greed, the desires, freedom from all that junk."

"But isn't one person's definition of 'free' a lot different than another's?" I asked him.

"I know people who live in small towns in Wyoming who would think that the perfect 'free' life would be having all the money in your jeans you wanted and a new, hot pickup truck and being able to drink beer every night in town and still be able to get up at dawn and work hard all day. Exactly some of those life things you would classify as junk."

"Sure."

"So would they be free if they had those things?"

"No. They'd be happy." (Free is always happy, but happy isn't always free.) "But once you start facing death here and there, you stop to think, 'Hey, what's going on here? I was happy until yesterday but then my father kicked off, or my new pet died.' Now your cowboy is going to start thinking, 'What's gonna happen to me?' And this is important, death is very important. You keep questioning it until there are no more questions to ask. You come to a blank wall. So instead of looking outside for an answer, you start looking inside. That's why when you see a statue of Buddha the eyes are slit open. That means they're not looking at the outside world, they're looking inside themselves for the answers. We meditate, we open our eyes and look inside, pressing and pressing for the right answers. Then all of a sudden it comes. About twenty-five hundred years ago Siddhartha Buddha had an enlightenment, and that means nothing but complete freedom. Freedom from all that junky stuff. As the Chinese say, when you know the truth in the morning, you may die without regret in the afternoon."

To achieve personal freedom then, the enlightenment that allows us to deal with life's real problems and fears, we have to sacrifice our interest in the more mundane, superficial, Bud Lite kinds of situations that give us temporary happiness but no insight. To know yourself completely may be a case of knowing you're above that sort of thing, above the junk of life. And in Zen, knowing yourself is everything. Henry Mittwer told me of a noted Zen practitioner who says to each foreigner he meets, "Glad to meet you, sir, how are you, sir, and *what* are you, sir?"

Because self-knowledge comes from meditation in Zen, meditation becomes everything as well. The extremely precise tea ceremony, as well as flower arranging, calligraphy, and other activities are supposed to be kinds of meditations as well, so that self-contemplation doesn't have to cease in order to perform the necessary tasks of daily life. But Dennis Yoshikawa contends they also serve another purpose, as kinds of Zen achievement tests, or your ZATs.

"The reason why their religious disciplines and practices are so regimented, so strictly outlined," Dennis said, "is because they are attempts to see what progress is being made in one's religious search. Particularly in some schools of Zen, you have a teacher whose . . . primary role is to tell the disciple whether or not that religious experience he has had is true or false."

•

The Shin Buddhist answer to "Is there a heaven?" can be reduced to "Yes, but good luck getting there." The Zen Buddhist answer to the same question would seem to be "What difference does it make?" The Jewish answer to most afterlife questions appears to be "It depends whom you ask." At least that's what Rabbi Vicki Hollender kept having to say to me.

Those aware of the history of the Jewish faith will know already that anybody named Rabbi Vicki is not exactly Orthodox. "Rabbi Vicki" sounds like a character in a William Hamilton cartoon in the *New*

Yorker. But to think of her in that way is doing the real person a disservice. Fourteen years ago her graduating class from the Jewish Institute of Religion at Hebrew Union College in Cincinnati included more women rabbis than had previously existed in the whole of Jewish history. There were nine of them, and they went off into a no-woman's-land with encouragement from one side and condemnation from the other. Like her people, Rabbi Vicki Hollender has had to be a survivor and a fighter, not necessarily in that order.

Personally she is a thoughtful, soft-spoken woman with a ten-year-old daughter, an apartment full of books about Judaism that range from little text and big pictures to the most serious theological works, and a black cat named Socks.

"I had a wonderful Jewish name for that cat but my daughter insisted on Socks. At least it was before Bill Clinton's cat Socks became famous."

More than almost any other religion, the perception of the afterlife in Judaism depends not only on whom you ask, but when you ask. According to the writings of English rabbi Louis Jacobs, there have been eras in history when most Jews believed strongly in *olam haba*—the world to come. Talmudic rabbis taught that this life is a preparation for the next, and Rabbi Jacobs contends that the Jew in medieval times, like Christians and Muslims, saw his or her life on earth as temporary, with a real home in heaven. There have been Jewish eras and peoples who believed in Judgment Day and resurrection, Ezekiel's vision and the coming of a Messiah, reincarnation, and a kind of hell, although the doctrine of eternal punishment is not big in the faith.

Well, says Rabbi Hollender, that depends on whom you ask, even as to what went on in this Jewish heaven. She says, "One thought was that there was a Gan Eden, this wonderful garden that people would go to. But there are all kinds of theories about what people did once they got there. Some people thought they would get to study the Torah all day. But other people weren't too enthusiastic when they heard that. They thought there was going to be eating and drinking and celebrating." And that latter view would seem to confirm her belief that, unlike both Christianity and Islam, heaven hasn't been used in the Jewish faith as a reward as much as it has been presented as a consolation for suffering on earth. Perhaps the scholarly would see constant study of the Torah as a consolation, but it's not hard to believe others would want some party time too.

Far from being confusing to the modern Jew, Rabbi Hollender thinks her faith's apparent inconsistency regarding what comes next has resulted in a unique smorgasbord of available heavens.

"When I look at Jewish tradition, I see the choices. There are a number of possibilities here. We don't quite know what's going to happen but we have a sense through the ages that something's beyond that door. So we can pick and choose from our history. . . . So, for instance, here is a concept that the soul is immortal but the body stays in the ground, and here is the possibility for reincarnation. We hear the voices of the mystics and the rabbis all echoing in the chorus. It's a rich table to feast from and choose what feels right."

Rabbi Hollender points out that just as Jews through history have perceived different heavens that suited their needs at the time, so modern Jews can pick from those historic perceptions a heaven that suits their personal needs at different times in their lives.

"It gives me the opportunity to know that here is a chorus that my people spoke about and that they're all bequeathed to me. They're there for me to use as my entrance into the next world."

In one way Rabbi Hollender has already taken steps to assure a kind of survival after her death, although that wasn't her motivation for doing it. She has written what's called an "ethical will." Regular wills say who's going to get the beach property and grandma's old ring. Ethical wills, a relatively recent phenomenon, principally in the Jewish community, don't try to pass on goods, but instead values. Vicki Hollender's ethical will for her daughter includes what her mother thought was important in life, what kind of truth she saw and what thoughts and dreams she wishes to give to the generations that succeed her. Rabbi Hollender says it's almost like becoming Solomon, trying to distill what this life is about. And it's a benefit not only to the receiver of the will, but to the person who writes it, rewrites it, and keeps rewriting it as time goes on and her personal values and perceptions change. Like Zen meditation, creating an ethical will forces you to think about *what* you are.

Through the ethical will, parenthood, her work as a rabbi but finally just by being who she is, Vicki Hollender knows that the continuity between generations is assured. We all pass on knowledge to our descendants, just as we all receive knowledge through remembrance of our ancestors. Remembrance is especially important in the Jewish tradition, where so many ancestors have been lost before their time—before they had much of a chance to pass on anything except memories of their courage and spirit.

Remembrance is more than just tradition for Vicki Hollender. She realizes that her own safety and survival in America were merely a matter of some of her ancestors catching the right boat in time. She feels as much of an obligation to them, those that made the boat, and those that didn't, as she feels to her daughter; an obligation not to forget, and not to let her descendants forget either.

"To mark their names and memories in ways that they could not in their own lives. It is a sacred task, to take that which was extinguished, and light it, keep it lit, and pass it on to the next generation to hold that light."

Even a Unitarian can understand that, support it, and try to do it. It's the only afterlife we can be sure of now. My sons may be surrounded by images of death, but they are also surrounded by me. And I don't plan to let them escape.

                                          •

The Trip of a Lifetime is over, and it has ended in immortality. Not bad. The one thing we know for sure about life after death is that even if we don't continue in some physical or conscious state, we are still eternal. Spiritually, intellectually, we will survive as long as someone remembers us, as long as "attention is paid" to who we were.

In our deepest fears of death, social and intellectual (and genetic) immortality may not offer much solace. "What's that to me? I'll be dead!" is a legitimate complaint. But knowing we will live on in any way has been a comfort to human beings since there were human beings, and we should take comfort where we can, especially in the face of death.

In some ways social immortality is easy—for Rabbi Hollender, as easy as an ethical will. And as long as you can convince yourself that you're going to achieve it, you get all the predeath value from it even if you're wrong. With physical immortality there can be some hellishly nasty surprises. Those Spaniards who bought thousands of requiem masses went to their graves thinking they were covered, remembrance and heavenwise. I don't know about heaven, but I do know we remember them. Perhaps being remembered as those nutters who bought all the masses and like fools impoverished themselves just so they'd be remembered was not their intention, but it still worked, didn't it? We remember them, if for nothing other than that. The survival of the intellectual spirit is real and demonstrable *now.*

In the end, one of the joys of taking this Trip of a Lifetime has been the opportunity to contribute to the immortality of the people I've met, if only by including them in this book and telling something of their lives. I've always thought Will Rogers's "I never met a man I didn't like" was indicative of either a liar, a person who didn't get out much, or somebody who was able to extricate himself from most of the world. But the fact is that there's not a person in this book I didn't like. The King of Happiness in Taiwan is not a guy I'd like to spend much time with, and I'd probably rather not know the full story of Jackie McMullen's life, but I still liked them, and all the others.

I was especially impressed by all the strong women, of all ages and backgrounds: Joye Carter, Sara Shay, Coogan, Alexis and Cathy Vick, Mairead Maquire, Jackie Massey, Rabbi Vicki Hollender, Pastor Eddiemae Layne, and even in death, the powerful Marguerite Jackson McClain. If, because of this book, they are known and remembered by strangers I couldn't ask for more. If you have mourned for Marguerite McClain and Ed Decker, rejoiced with the Vicks, gotten angry with the Shays, the Al Baroghoutys, and even the Martins, then thank you. You have made them immortal, by paying attention to their lives.

I'll admit an interest in my own social immortality as well. Whenever it is that I go to my grave I'll be a little bit happier knowing that fifty years later somebody might very well find a copy of this book in a cardboard box and say, "My great-grandfather did this." By then, of course, an actual book will be regarded with the same vague curiosity we regard the dial phone and stereopticon today, but at least it will be something. Up in heaven I'll be one pleased angel.

So listen up, great-grandkids. I'm sorry I couldn't tell you what it's like to die, or what happens after that. But for that third question you want answered, I leave you with this:

The Malagash people of Madagascar answer the question, "Why do we have to die?" with a fable.

> The Creator gave the first woman and the first man a choice. "You may choose between two kinds of death," the Creator said. "Death like the moon, being reborn over and over again. Or death like the tree, which puts forth new seeds before it dies, and then lives on through its progeny."
>
> For the woman and the man it was a difficult choice, but they finally decided to have children, even at the cost of their own eternal lives.

Remember that, kids. Everyone you meet, everyone whose life you affect, is a seed that carries a bit of you into eternity. Act accordingly.

Because they made the right choice.

ACKNOWLEDGMENTS

I have labored in television for a long time, and the problem with television, one of many problems with television actually, is that you never get to thank anyone except on those rare occasions when you get an award. And even then, just as you get to the podium some guy holding a stopwatch is sure to dart out of the shadows and whisper, "Make it fast, Bud, we're running late." So you have to cut your six minutes of prepared thanks down to a tight, bright forty-five seconds of mumbling, invariably leaving out a number of people who then hate you forever.

Conversely, when writing a book the tendency is to thank too many people, so that the thank-you section runs to forty-six pages and wipes out whole forests in Guatemala, as well as boring the whiskers off the readers. I have seen thank-you sections like that in other people's books and often wondered who in God's name reads them besides the author's friends looking for their own names and the author's enemies seeking grounds for a libel action.

However, this is my first book, and I may never write another. When you're on the death beat it tends to make you a bit of a fatalist. There may be a runaway beer truck out there somewhere with my name on it. So my very strong inclination here is to thank everybody who has ever been of help or encouragement to me, starting with Mrs. Nygren in the second grade. And the hell with worrying about who, if anybody, will wade through it.

So that's what I'm going to do. I won't concern myself with creating a thank-you section that makes any sense to anybody but the people thanked herein, and those who think they should be, because none of the others have even read this far.

Thank you, Mrs. Nygren. Thank you Mesdames Arkley, Wakefield, Wallace, and (especially) Hayward as well, plus the Misters Wichterman, Greiner, and Caley. Many of these people, especially the early grade-school ladies, let me sit at my desk and write short stories while the rest of the class droned away over addition and subtraction worksheets. Perhaps these fine teachers feared I would never be much of a mathematician—a fully justified fear, as it turned out—but now with a twelve-dollar pocket calculator I am just as good a mathematician as any of those other kids, and some of them still can't write a simple declarative sentence.

I would also like to thank the assistant librarian of the Mercer Island High School library, who on her own volition removed the school copy of *Catcher in the Rye* in 1964 and burned it. I promised the principal back then I would never tell what I knew of this incident but it has inspired me for almost three decades to write something myself that would also make that stupid, stupid person nervous enough to get out her Zippo. Maybe this is it, and if it isn't, I'll catch her the next time around. If I live. She is already dead, I think, but if you've read the book tacked onto the front of these acknowledgments, you know that doesn't make any difference. Her miserable wandering ghost is still around somewhere, and I hope to affect it before it can affect me.

This sums up twelve years of public school education.

Moving ahead thirty years, I will confess what you probably already realize. One conceit running through this entire book is a lie. And that is the use of the first person singular. *Death: The Trip of a Lifetime* was hardly a solo journey, so a general thanks to those who set me on the path, and those who went along. As you well know, and some of you have rightly pointed out to me on numerous occasions, I could not have done it without you.

Nobody would have wanted me to, in fact, so initial thanks must go to KCTS 9, the public television station in Seattle that originated the *Death* project, created the television series, hired me to work on it, and then hustled the money so there would be something to work with. The

Corporation for Public Broadcasting, the Public Broadcasting Service, and the Pacific Rim Programming Consortium also deserve thanks for paying the money. Thanks as well to the individuals in those places who talked themselves and then their respective institutions into funding a series about death. I should think it was not an easy decision. I know it wasn't an easy sell from the number of businesses and corporations, large and small, who were initially attracted to international exposure through underwriting the series, and then dove under their corporate carpets when they learned what the subject was. Personally I think they were shortsighted to assume Mr. and Mrs. Shopper would stroll past their establishments and say, "No, we don't want to go in there. They think we're going to die someday. I saw it on television." Quite a few movie production companies and distributors refused even to sell us clips from their films because they didn't want to be associated with the subject of death in any way. These same movie companies have churned out dozens of grisly, violent, exploitive films throughout the last fifty years or so, the hypocritical creeps.

The KCTS general staff was extremely helpful and supportive, beginning with CEO Burnie Clark and *Death* boss Elizabeth Brock. One of my unforgettable moments on this project was seeing the expression on Burnie Clark's face the first time he viewed footage of the series. It was the embalming in San Francisco, and as the needle came out through Max's nostril Burnie's face screamed, *"I gotta sell this to the same people who bought Big Bird?"* But all he said was, "This is a rough cut, right?" Thank you, Burnie.

The KCTS *Death Squad* was invaluable. Associate Producer Brenda Louie produced and went on the trips to the East Coast of the United States, Taiwan, Japan, and India, and did a splendid interview with His Holiness the Dalai Lama before I arrived. Simon Griffith did the same production work for Australia and New Zealand before becoming a Science Guy, and Producer Sue McLaughlin took charge of the trips to Britain, California,

Northern Ireland, Israel, and Ghana. (I believe the only place she didn't try the local cuisine was California.) In addition, Assistant Producer Lisa Hardmeyer supervised all the shooting in the Pacific Northwest. It was Lisa who spent the most time with Ed and Anne Decker. She really should have been part of that story, because her sincere compassion for Ed and her friendship with Anne and Nancy were more than just a television producer doing her job. She became for that brief time a welcome member of their family, and had much to do with making Ed's last two weeks as good as they were.

All of the above people did exceptional work in research as well. Until beginning this project I had minimal involvement in Asian cultures and beliefs, only because other interests had taken up my time. Brenda had the unenviable task of first trying to understand some of the complexities of the Tibetan, Chinese, Japanese, and Indian cultures herself, and then trying to explain them to me.

Sue not only researched and produced the trips she took, but was central to creating the television programs and forming the whole approach to the subject. I'll probably have nightmares for years built around the image of Ms. McLaughlin reading something I've written, suddenly looking like an unpleasant aroma has entered the room, and then saying, "I have a few problems with this." But in retrospect she was right as many times as I was—and quite possibly more—and if there is justice in the world she will soon get the opportunity to do the kinds of programs she wants to do. And if so, I hope she gets a producer just like her, heh heh heh.

The Death Squad was enhanced during the two years by many unpaid interns who came and went. Public television stations—and some commercial stations as well—survive by exploiting (that's right, exploiting) young college graduates—usually female—who are willing to work for next to nothing or nothing itself in exchange for experience and perhaps a line in their resumes. They are wonderful to have around, and not just because they do so much of that administrivia us big stars hate to do. They have energy, talent, and best of all, dreams that have not yet been dulled by reality. And if they are lucky those dreams will come true and to hell with reality; or To Reality with Hell, which was an alternate title for Chapter 14. Some of those interns who worked on *Death* I hardly met, some I saw a lot, but they all made worthy contributions. I would particularly mention Jennifer Steele, Rosemary Garner, Shay Salyer, and Jennifer Dahlman, and not only because someday in the near future I expect us big stars will be asking them for a job.

In the course of our travels, we occasionally met people who first sneered at the idea of television, and then sneered at our idea for this television project. Some academics make bizarre proprietary claims regarding death as it is dealt with by various cultures. ("You're going to Tzintzuntzan? But the Mexicans are mine!") They see others as interlopers in their territory, especially anyone without advanced degrees.

My favorite was an anthropologist we ran into in Kumasi. She had done her renowned fieldwork on the Ashanti some thirty years before and had been living on it ever since. Now she had returned in what she hoped would be triumph to show a spotty teenage son "her" Ghana. But her Ghana had changed; the natives no longer threw themselves at her feet, other anthropologists—including my friend Dr. Mato, mentioned below—had come and done better work subsequently, her thirty-year-old mosquito netting was inadequate, and to top it off there was this television crew staying at the same hotel. Additionally, her son had gotten into some bad foofoo and was spending the majority of his time throwing up on her Ghana.

"What is this television series about?" she asked me one afternoon, rather the way you might ask someone if it was their dog leaving the messes on your lawn. And when I told her she snapped, "Death? Death! Don't you think you're trespassing in the domain of the anthropologists?" (Which could come as a big surprise to almost every poet who ever lived.)

"And who is the host of this program?"
"I am."
"No, really, who is the host?"

I saw her later that evening in the hotel restaurant, regaling her child with stories of the old days when she was the intrepid Bwana Anthropologist Ma'am and the research grants weren't *nearly* what they are today. The kid looked like he had to throw up some more. Only this time it wasn't the foofoo.

However, from our experience people like her are in the minority, and there were many scholars who gladly gave of their time and expertise to start the *Death* project going and keep it going.

In the beginning there was the LaConner group, a collection of experts who came to artsy little LaConner, Washington, to sit around a motel conference room table for three days and talk about the Big D. They were Margaret Alexiou of Harvard, Sandra Bertman of the Program of Medical Humanities at the University of Massachusetts Medical Center, David and Dorothy Counts of McMaster University and the University of Waterloo, respectively, Carlos Eire of the University of Virginia, and Myra Bluebond-Langner, then at Rutgers.

They were all splendid, especially in showing us that from the strange and unfamiliar actions of a relatively few people it is possible to see common threads of belief that affect all people. There was a moment when Dr. Alexiou and the Drs. Counts realized that the residents of some rural Greek villages performed almost the same rituals for almost the same reasons as the Kaliai people of Papua New Guinea. I don't know if that realization was a big deal for them, but it was a kick for me. It proved that although *Death* was a huge subject, there was a commonality of human ritual and belief that made the topic at least a bit manageable. Up until that moment I thought I'd be researching and traveling on this baby for twenty-five years and then if I was still alive I'd actually be ready to put some of it down on paper and videotape.

Even so, dozens of people have told me we "didn't go to the right places" or that we *had* to go someplace they knew about where the body in a funeral gets up and dances and the funereal cloth is cedar bark, and so forth. I expect I'll hear more such comments before the runaway beer truck gets me. To all those critics, let me just say you're absolutely right. Two hundred thousand people die every day, on the average, and they all deserve to have the tales of their deaths told.

The experts we had in the field were usually excellent. Dr. Robert Wilkins, the London psychiatrist who appears in the second chapter and wrote *The Bedside Book of Death* (from which I pilfered most of the information about body snatchers) went far beyond the call of death duty to lead us around his city. The sane enthusiasm he and his friend Julian Litten exhibited for spending so much time researching death and dying was and continues to be a comfort whenever people ask what I've been doing and then decline to shake my hand thereafter. And it was a true joy to see Julian's horrified expression when I told him of the White Ladies.

Right before we went to India we called an India expert for travel tips and he said, "The one thing you must know about India is that you should never go there the first time." Right he was, and he could also have been talking about Ghana. Both countries are fascinating places but they can be problematic if you're trying to do some work in a limited amount of time. Our success in Ghana was due in large part to the expertise, assistance, and friendship of the aforementioned Dr. Dan Mato of the University of Calgary. For twenty years Dr. Mato has been going to Ghana to study the funeral practices of the Ashanti people, with particular emphasis on funeral art like adinkra cloth. You can't buy or rent twenty years of experience; it must be given freely, and that is what Dan Mato did, to my unending gratitude.

He was also of great help in restaurants. Everyone who ever complained about a restaurant should go to an eating establishment once with Dan Mato to see how bad it could be. Through no fault of his own, Dr. Mato has never ordered anything that was available that night. In fact,

I think if he went to Bob's House of Asparagus, Bob would be out of asparagus the night Dan showed up. So we quickly learned never to let Dan order first, because he might go for what we wanted and then they'd be out of it. But if, on the other hand, one ordered the fried cod quickly before Dan could, the waiter would invariably say to Dr. Mato, "Your friend just got the last cod." And to prove that this was not exclusively a Ghanaian phenomenon, when Dan visited Seattle some time later we took him to dinner and they were out of the salmon he ordered. Salmon. In Seattle. Where eight of the kids in my third-grade class were salmon.

This has nothing to do with death, of course, unless you consider that Dan Mato has spent his life *never* eating what he really wanted to eat in a restaurant and yet he has never murdered a waiter, chef, or maître d'. I believe such a deep and abiding reverence for life deserves mention.

We usually had caretakers in the field as well, local folk to set things up in advance and then make sure we got there. These people were usually extremely helpful, and when they weren't they were easy to ditch. I would especially thank, first, Kate Abba and Jo Horan in Australia. Ms. Abba told us the historic motto of some white folks who have worked with the aboriginal people of her country: "Befriend them, and then betray them." But through sometimes sheer will she kept us from doing anything completely stupid with the aboriginals.

Our baby-sitter in Japan was the redoubtable Kunio Kadowaki, and Dave Barry is absolutely right, Kunio does say "Ha, ha, ha" when he laughs, just like it's written out in books. Fortunately, Kunio laughs a lot.

In Israel two photographers as different as they could be were of great help. I think Alex Ben Dor has photographed every important news story in the Middle East since the plague of locusts. It became a challenge to us to suggest a place we wanted to go that Alex hadn't shot at least four times. We never did, and that experience was very helpful. He is a fine man, a good shooter, and a splendid host. I especially thank him for inviting me to Passover dinner with his family in Jerusalem. It was the first Passover I had ever attended, and I can't think of a better place or better people with whom to share the experience.

The day we were scheduled to go to the West Bank, Alex was otherwise occupied, so we hired a young Palestinian photographer named Bethina Khoury. It was a tense day, because the Palestinians believe that film crews identifying themselves as Americans are often Israeli spies. So they can be completely unhelpful, or worse. However, Ms. Khoury not only convinced her fellow Palestinians of our integrity but went much farther, including translating my conversations with the Al Baroghouty family as she photographed them, a very difficult thing to do. She also helped me understand the feelings of the Palestinian people, why they cling so desperately to what looks like the worst farmland that side of Death Valley. Having made her acquaintance, I no longer see all Palestinians as Yasir Arafat-ish; not that I ever should have. Now I know at least one of them to be an intelligent, talented, charming young woman who loves her land and her people and is doing what she can to make the world see them as she does.

And as long as I'm thanking photographers, every member of the KCTS photography staff worked on *Death* at one time or another. Although their work did not directly affect this book, their good eyes and ears certainly affected the way I saw the things I saw, so thanks to Tom Speer, Greg Davis, Rob Reed, Mark Pingry, Valery Vozza, Resti Bagcal, Fugate Holt, Merle Carey, Cleve Ticeson, and Peter Rummel. We also had the good luck to work with two of the best shooters in the world, Paul Ree in Australia, and Freddie George in India.

Drew Keller was the chief editor of the television series, and his reactions to people and places were of great help. And I would be remiss in not thanking B. D. Wong, a wonderful actor who brought

the Grim Reaper alive, only to see him killed ("Art hath an enemy called ignorance."—Ben Jonson).

One of the conclusions of this book and the television series is that there *is* one life eternal that can be proven now, before death; the intellectual, social continuity between generations. Woody Allen once said, "I don't want to live forever through my work. I want to live forever because I don't die." I wish him luck, but for now the work survives, and changes forever we who see it. Therefore I think it would be churlish of me not to thank the spirits of those whose work over the years has given me entertainment, inspiration, and whatever insight I have.

Let one serve for all. Shortly before the *Death* project began, Jim Henson died. I didn't know him well at all. When I was doing a Seattle radio talk show in the mid-1970s he was one of the first people I interviewed long distance. In the middle of that interview a woman called in and said her six-year-old daughter would like to talk to Kermit the Frog. I started to get rid of her, because I've always thought you don't ask performers to perform unless you're paying them. But Henson cut me off and said, "I think Kermit's around here somewhere. Hey, Kermit, phone for you!" And way off in the background an unmistakable voice said, "Coming!" I had told Henson the interview would be twenty minutes at most, but for the next hour and a half kids called up and talked to the characters Henson voiced at the time; Kermit, Ernie, Rowlf the Dog. When a child wanted to talk to Bert, I heard Henson's voice very faintly say, "Frank, kid wants Bert," and Frank Oz came on too and described the oatmeal he was having for lunch. It was a gracious, generous thing for both men to do. Years later I spent a half hour with Henson when he was on the road selling one of his movies. I found him to be a splendid man whose love of life and his fellow living creatures was infectious. His death was devastating for me, and still is. During the past two years I have thought of him often, because that sudden absence from the world I knew helped me understand more than any reading or research just how painful even remote deaths can be for those who survive, the overwhelming feelings of frustration and anger that never entirely go away. If it seems odd that the death of a television performer I didn't really know should affect me that way, all I can say is that he was a great artist, and his death was doubly sad because he took his art with him. Ernie died too.

For those of you who are reading this section simply to be polite, I have now reached the list-of-names-big-finish, and therefore you may want to bail out. For those who expected to find their name before now and didn't, this is your last chance.

I interviewed more than two hundred people for *Death,* and talked to many more about the project. There are hundreds of others who provided specific help on this project or have influenced me and my work over the years. Although there isn't space to thank them all, there are some who simply must be mentioned. Most of you know why you are listed here, and if you don't, what difference does it make?

They are Lucy Mohl, Bill Fenster, Kelly Robinson, Penny Foote, Cliff Hillhouse, Maralyn Crosetto, Cliff Lenz, Rod Davis, George Ray, Lena Sharpe, Dr. Joe Appiah-Kusi, Jessica Mitford, David Duvall, Pete Palmer, Laura Dushkes, Cathy Cain, Charlie McAliese, Erika Warmbrunn, Laurence Ballard, Marcia and John Crosetto, Anne Huey, and the guy who said to me, "I'll tell you how you know when you're dead. If you're over forty and you wake up in the morning and nothing hurts, you're dead."

Finally, yes, finally, thanks to Renee Wayne Golden, agent and attorney, for making this book possible and having faith in the ability of a TV guy to write something more than a minute and a half long. Similar thanks for exactly the same reasons to the folk at Harper San Francisco.

Thanks to my parents, Harvard and Gertrude Palmer, for similar faith over a much longer time.

And thanks to my family for many reasons. Imagine what it's been like living with someone who has had to immerse himself in death, how you would come to dread any social situation because somebody might just casually mention funerals, longevity, putrefaction, Ghana, flowers, tombstones, body snatchers, cryonics, or Stephen King novels, and off he'd go like a geyser. That's what they have been through. And now I promise it is over.